KT-446-244

EARLY MUSIC HISTORY 14

EARLY MUSIC HISTORY 14

STUDIES IN MEDIEVAL
AND
EARLY MODERN MUSIC

Edited by

IAIN FENLON
Fellow of King's College, Cambridge

CAMBRIDGE
UNIVERSITY PRESS

Published by the Press Syndicate of the University of Cambridge
The Pitt Building, Trumpington Street, Cambridge CB2 1RP
40 West 20th Street, New York, NY 10011–4211, USA
10 Stamford Road, Oakleigh, Melbourne 3166, Australia

First published 1995

Phototypeset in Baskerville by Wyvern Typesetting Ltd, Bristol
Printed in Great Britain at the University Press, Cambridge

ISSN 0261–1279

ISBN 0 521 558433

SUBSCRIPTIONS The subscription price (excluding VAT) of volume 14, which includes postage, is £50.00 (US $92.00 in USA and Canada) for institutions, £32.00 (US $55.00 in USA and Canada) for individuals ordering direct from the Press and certifying that the annual is for their personal use. Airmail (orders to Cambridge only) £10.00 extra. Copies of the annual for subscribers in the USA and Canada are sent by air to New York to arrive with minimum delay. Orders, which must be accompanied by payment, may be sent to a bookseller, subscription agent or direct to the publishers: Cambridge University Press, The Edinburgh Building, Shaftesbury Road, Cambridge CB2 2RU. Payment may be made by any of the following methods: cheque (payable to Cambridge University Press), UK postal order, bank draft, Post Office Giro (account no. 571 6055 GB Bootle – advise CUP of payment), international money order, UNESCO coupons, or any credit card bearing the Interbank symbol. EU subscribers (outside the UK) who are not registered for VAT should add VAT at their country's rate. VAT registered subscribers should provide their VAT registration number. Japanese prices for institutions (including ASP delivery) are available from Kinokuniya Company Ltd, P.O. Box 55, Chitose, Tokyo 156, Japan. Orders from the USA and Canada should be sent to Cambridge University Press, 40 West 20th Street, New York, NY 10011–4211, USA.

BACK VOLUMES Volumes 1–13 are available from the publisher at £45.00 ($85.00 in USA and Canada).

NOTE Each volume of *Early Music History* is now published in the year in which it is subscribed. Volume 14 is therefore published in 1995. Readers should be aware, however, that some earlier volumes have been subscribed in the year *after* the copyright and publication date given on this imprints page. Thus volume 8, the volume received by 1989 subscribers, is dated 1988 on the imprints page.

CONTENTS

NOTES FOR CONTRIBUTORS

PRESENTATION

Contributors should write in English, or be willing to have their articles translated. All typescripts must be double spaced *throughout*, including footnotes, bibliographies, annotated lists of manuscripts, appendixes, tables and displayed quotations. Margins should be at least 2.5 cm (1″). The 'top' (ribbon) copy of the typescript must be supplied. Scripts submitted for consideration will not normally be returned unless specifically requested.

Artwork for graphs, diagrams and music examples should be, wherever possible, submitted in a form suitable for direct reproduction, bearing in mind the maximum dimensions of the printed version: 17.5×11 cm ($7″ \times 4.5″$). Photographs should be in the form of glossy black and white prints, measuring about 20.3×15.2 cm ($8″ \times 6″$).

All illustrations should be on separate sheets from the text of the article and should be clearly identified with the contributor's name and the figure/example number. Their approximate position in the text should be indicated by a marginal note in the typescript. Captions should be separately typed, double spaced.

Tables should also be supplied on separate sheets, with the title typed above the body of the table.

SPELLING

English spelling, idiom and terminology should be used, e.g. bar (not measure), note (not tone), quaver (not eighth note). Where there is an option, '-ise' endings should be preferred to '-ize'.

PUNCTUATION

English punctuation practice should be followed: (1) single quotation marks, except for 'a "quote" within a quote'; (2) punctuation outside quotation marks, unless a complete sentence is quoted; (3) no comma before 'and' in a series; (4) footnote indicators follow punctuation; (5) square brackets [ ] only for interpolation in quoted matter; (6) no stop after contractions that include the last letter of a word, e.g. Dr, St, edn (but vol. and vols.).

BIBLIOGRAPHICAL REFERENCES

Authors' and editors' forenames should not be given, only initials; where possible, editors should be given for Festschriften, conference proceedings, symposia, etc. In titles, all important words in English should be capitalised; all other languages should follow prose-style capitalisation, except for journal and series titles which should follow English capitalisation. Titles of series should be included, in roman, where relevant. Journal and series volume numbers should be given in arabic, volumes of a set in roman ('vol.' will not be used). Places and dates of publication should be included but not publishers' names. Dissertation titles should be given in roman and enclosed in quotation marks. Page numbers should be preceded by 'p.' or 'pp.' in all contexts. The first citation of a bibliographical reference should include full details; subsequent citations may use the author's surname, short title and relevant page numbers only. *Ibid.* may be used, but not *op. cit.* or *loc. cit.*

ABBREVIATIONS

Abbreviations for manuscript citations, libraries, periodicals, series, etc. should not be used without explanation; after the first full citation an abbreviation may be used throughout text and notes. Standard abbreviations may be used without explanation. In the text, 'Example', 'Figure' and 'bars' should be used (not 'Ex.', 'Fig.', 'bb.'). In references to manuscripts, 'fols.' should be used (not 'ff.') and 'v' (verso) and 'r' (recto) should be typed superscript. The word for 'saint' should be spelled out or abbreviated according to language, e.g. San Andrea, S. Maria, SS. Pietro e Paolo, St Paul, St Agnes, St Denis, Ste Clothilde.

NOTE NAMES

Flats, sharps and naturals should be indicated by the conventional signs, not words. Note names should be roman and capitalised where general, e.g. C major, but should be italic and follow the Helmholtz code where specific ($C_{,}$, C, $Cc c'$ c'' c'''; c' = middle C). A simpler system may be used in discussions of repertories (e.g. chant) where different conventions are followed.

QUOTATIONS

A quotation of no more than 60 words of prose or one line of verse should be continuous within the text and enclosed in single quotation marks. Longer quotations should be displayed and quotation marks should not be used. For quotations from foreign languages, an English translation must be given in addition to the foreign-language original.

NUMBERS

Numbers below 100 should be spelled out, except page, bar, folio numbers etc., sums of money and specific quantities, e.g. 20 ducats, 45 mm. Pairs of numbers should be elided as follows: 190–1, 198–9, 198–201, 212–13. Dates should be given in the following forms: 10 January 1983, the 1980s, sixteenth century (16th century in tables and lists), sixteenth-century polyphony.

CAPITALISATION

Incipits in all languages (motets, songs, etc.), and titles except in English, should be capitalised as in running prose; titles in English should have all important words capitalised, e.g. *The Pavin of Delight*. Most offices should have a lower-case initial except in official titles, e.g. 'the Lord Chancellor entered the cathedral', 'the Bishop of Salford entered the cathedral' (but 'the bishop entered the cathedral'). Names of institutions should have full (not prose-style) capitalisation, e.g. Liceo Musicale.

ITALICS

Titles and incipits of musical works in italic, but not genre titles or sections of the Mass/English Service, e.g. Kyrie, Magnificat. Italics for foreign words should be kept to a minimum; in general they should be used only for unusual words or if a word might be mistaken for English if not italicised. Titles of manuscripts should be roman in quotes, e.g. 'Rules How to Compose'. Names of institutions should be roman.

AUTHORS' CORRECTIONS

It is assumed that typescripts received for publication are in their final form. There may be an opportunity to make minor emendations at the copy-editing stage, but corrections in proof *must* be restricted to printer's and publisher's errors. Any departure from this practice will be at the discretion of the editor and the publisher, and authors may be subject to charge.

Early Music History (1995) *Volume 14*

RUTH I. DEFORD

TEMPO RELATIONSHIPS BETWEEN DUPLE AND TRIPLE TIME IN THE SIXTEENTH CENTURY*

One of the most challenging problems in the performance of sixteenth-century music is the interpretation of tempo relationships between passages of duple and triple time. After *c.* 1520 binary signatures became standard for most pieces, and ternary passages within them were notated as *sesquialtera* or triple proportions.[1] The signs of these proportions ostensibly specify precise tempo relationships between the binary and ternary passages, but in practice they could be interpreted in a variety of ways depending on time, place and musical context, as well as on the notation itself.

The main reason for the ambiguity of proportional signs is that they serve two distinct purposes: first, to notate precise changes of tempo, in which case the music to which they apply may or may not have ternary metrical character, and second, to notate triple metre, regardless of its tempo relationship to a preceding duple metre. Signs of *sesquialtera* are particularly problematic. They could represent not only three notes in the time of two, in accordance with their literal meaning, but also triple,

---

* I thank Alexander Blachly, Bonnie Blackburn, Michele Fromson and Benito Rivera for their helpful comments on this article.
[1] Giovanni Spataro complained about this degeneration of the mensural system in a letter to Giovanni del Lago of 4 January 1529: 'V. E. vede bene che a tempi nostri li signi ordinati da li antiqui sono tenuti in poco pretio et existimatione, et che solo usano questo signo ₵, et de le proportione solo uxano la sesqualtera.' ('You see well that in our times the signs established by the ancients are held in little esteem, and that they use only this sign ₵, and of the proportions, they use only *sesqualtera.*') *A Correspondence of Renaissance Musicians*, ed. B. J. Blackburn, E. E. Lowinsky and C. A. Miller (Oxford, 1991), p. 336. Scholars often point out that signs of imperfect *tempus* could be used when the metre was actually triple, but this convention usually applied only to instrumental music.

duple and indeterminate proportions with the preceding mensuration, as follows:

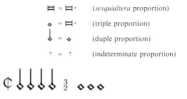

The interpretation of proportions is complicated by ambiguities in the relationship between the two binary signs, C and ₵, to which they relate. The significance of these signs may differ in three distinct and partially independent respects: the unit of time in which the music to which they apply is measured, the *tactus* and the tempo. In principle, pieces in ₵ are measured in breves and pieces in C in semibreves.[2] Measurement in breves means at the minimum that a piece contains a whole number of breve *tempora* and that breve rests are not notated in syncopated positions. It may mean that the breve is a meaningful unit of metrical organisation in audible ways as well. Major cadences may fall exclusively on the downbeats of breve *tempora*, and aspects of the music such as the spacing of voice entries, the metrical placement of repeated passages and the details of rhythmic patterns and text placement may be governed by the breve time unit. The extent of audible metrical organisation on the breve level in ₵ declined throughout the century, but most composers continued to observe the superficial requirements of determining the lengths of pieces and notating rests in the theoretically correct way in ₵.[3]

---

[2] A few theorists of the early part of the century believed that even pieces in C should properly be measured in breves, but they admitted that this principle was not observed in practice. G. M. Lanfranco, *Scintille di musica* (Brescia, 1533; facsimile edn in Bibliotheca Musica Bononiensis, sez. II, 15, with preface by G. Massera (Bologna, 1970)), pt 2, p. 68, complains that many composers fail to observe the binary number of semibreves not only in C, but even in ₵, which is a much worse error. Spataro, in a letter of 30 January 1531 to Pietro Aron, acknowledges that he made an error in putting an odd number of semibreves in a motet in C, but says that the error is unimportant, because the signature calls for a semibreve *tactus*; if the piece had been in ₵, the error would have been serious. *A Correspondence of Renaissance Musicians*, ed. Blackburn, Lowinsky and Miller, pp. 415–16.

[3] There are exceptions, especially in the music of the second half of the century, that demonstrate the declining significance of the breve *tempus* at that time. For example, R. Casimiri, *La polifonia vocale del secolo XVI e la sua trascrizione in figurazione musicale*

The *tactus* (also called *battuta*, *misura*, *ictus*, *compas*, etc.) is the motion of the hand, finger or foot by which time was measured in performance. It consists of two equal strokes, down and up, in both C and ₵. In the traditional view, it corresponds to the time unit in which the music is measured, that is, the semibreve in C (C ↓ ↓) and the breve in ₵ (₵ ◇ ◇). By *c.* 1500, however, pieces in ₵ often had a semibreve *tactus*, and by *c.* 1560 the semibreve had become the normal *tactus* of both signs. The breve *tactus* continued to be used in some places until well into the seventeenth century, however, and a minim *tactus* in C was also a possibility in the last quarter of the century.[4] The choice of *tactus* could depend on the preference of the conductor, local custom, the skill of the singers or the rhythmic character of the specific piece.[5] Theorists who describe two possible *tactus* for one

---

moderna (Rome, 1942), pp. 43–5, n. 94, lists pieces in ₵ by Palestrina that contain odd numbers of semibreves.

[4]   For summaries of sixteenth-century views on *tactus*, see W. Frobenius, 'Tactus' (1971), *Handwörterbuch der musikalischen Terminologie*, ed. H. H. Eggebrecht (Wiesbaden, 1971–), and J. A. Bank, *Tactus, Tempo, and Notation in Mensural Music from the 13th to the 17th Century* (Amsterdam, 1972), pp. 203–49. M. Praetorius, *Syntagma musicum* (Wolfenbüttel, 1614–20; facsimile ed. W. Gurlitt, Documenta Musicologica, ser. 1, nos. 14, 15, 21 (Kassel, 1958–9)), iii, pt 2, ch. 7, p. 49, says that a breve *tactus* is still used in some elegant chapels and schools in his time. According to the table in Bank, *Tactus, Tempo, and Notation*, pp. 226–30, a minim *tactus* not representing augmentation is first mentioned as a possibility for unskilled singers in C. Sebastiani, *Bellum musicale* (Strasburg, 1563), ch. 12, but Sebastiani says only that the *tactus minor* is for unskilled singers, and does not specify the value to which it applies. The earliest evidence for a minim *tactus* in C may therefore be E. Hoffmann, *Musicae practicae praecepta* (Wittenberg, 1572), ch. 10. Earlier references to half-*tactus*, such as that in M. Agricola, *Musica figuralis deudsch* (Wittenberg, 1532), ch. 6, sigs. Giiiᵛ–iiiiʳ, probably apply only to the semibreve in ₵. Agricola defines the half-*tactus* as a semibreve of ₵ or a minim of C, but all his examples of it apply to the semibreve.

[5]   H. Glarean, *Dodecachordon* (Basle, 1547; facsimile edn in Monuments of Music and Music Literature in Facsimile, ser. 2, 65 (New York, 1967)), bk 3, ch. 7, pp. 203–4 (trans. C. A. Miller, Musicological Studies and Documents 6 (n.p., 1965), ii, p. 232), associates the choice of *tactus* with geography, saying that the breve *tactus* is still common in Germany, but that the French prefer the semibreve. He also points out that the semibreve *tactus* is easier for students. A. Ornithoparchus, *Musice active micrologus* (Leipzig, 1517), bk 2, ch. 6, sig. Fiijᵛ (trans. J. Dowland (London, 1609), p. 46; facsimile edns of both in *A Compendium of Musical Practice*, ed. G. Reese and S. Ledbetter (New York, 1973), pp. 56 and 166), similarly associates a semibreve *tactus* in ₵ with the unlearned. L. Zacconi, *Prattica di musica* (Venice, 1592, repr. 1596; facsimile edn in Bibliotheca Musica Bononiensis, sez. II, 1 (Bologna, 1983)), bk 1, ch. 36, fol. 25ʳ, points out the correlation between *tactus* and rhythmic character, saying that even though pieces in ₵ are usually sung with a semibreve *tactus*, they should not have that signature unless a breve *tactus* would also be comfortable for them.

3

sign often give them different names, but the terminology varies from one writer to another.[6]

The tempo relationship between the two signs was controversial in theory and quite variable in practice. The traditional view is that the stroke diminishes the note values by half, so that a given value in ₵ lasts half as long as the same notated value in C and a breve *tactus* in ₵ is the same length as a semibreve *tactus* in C. In practice, however, the tempo proportion between the two signs in independent pieces was usually less than 2:1, so that a breve *tactus* in ₵ was somewhat longer, and a semibreve *tactus* somewhat shorter, than a semibreve *tactus* in C.[7] Since the notated values are generally longer in ₵ than in C, the rate of motion is slower in ₵, even though the *tactus* is faster when it corresponds to the semibreve. The distinction between the two signs became increasingly blurred towards the end of the century as the breve *tactus* and meaningful metrical organisation on the breve level declined.

Ternary proportions of both C and ₵ are notated as *sesquialtera* or, less often, as triple proportion. *Sesquialtera* may be notated in groups of three semibreves or minims, either white or black, and may be introduced by a mensuration sign with the figures $\frac{3}{2}$ or 3, by the figures $\frac{3}{2}$ or 3 with no mensuration sign, or by black notes with no sign or figures. It was often called 'major' or 'of

---

[6] See Bank, *Tactus, Tempo, and Notation*, pp. 226–30, for a summary of the terminology applied to different types of *tactus*.

[7] The meaning of the stroke through the mensuration signs ₵ and Ø is the subject of several recent studies. E. Schroeder, 'The Stroke Comes Full Circle: Ø and ₵ in Writings on Music, ca. 1450–1540', *Musica Disciplina*, 36 (1982), pp. 119–66, maintains that the stroke always meant diminution by half in ₵, but could indicate diminution by a third in Ø until *c.* 1540. A. M. Busse Berger, 'The Myth of *Diminutio per tertiam partem*', *Journal of Musicology*, 8 (1990), pp. 398–426, and *Mensuration and Proportion Signs: Origin and Evolution* (Oxford, 1993), pp. 120–48, concludes that the theory of diminution by a third in Ø was limited to a small number of German theorists and based on a misunderstanding of Johannes de Muris. R. C. Wegman, 'What is "Acceleratio mensurae"?', *Music and Letters*, 73 (1992), pp. 515–24, argues that the stroke in both Ø and ₵ indicated a semibreve *tactus* that was faster by an indeterminate amount than the *tactus* of the undiminished signs. The sign C became rare after *c.* 1520, but was revived in the *note nere* madrigal around 1540 and remained common in madrigals throughout the century. C. Dahlhaus, 'Zur Entstehung des modernen Taktsystems im 17. Jahrhundert', *Archiv für Musikwissenschaft*, 18 (1961), pp. 223–40 (esp. pp. 227–8), and J. Haar, 'The *Note nere* Madrigal', *Journal of the American Musicological Society*, 18 (1965), pp. 22–41 (esp. pp. 22–5), demonstrate that C requires a semibreve *tactus* that is slower than the semibreve of ₵, but not twice as slow, in that context.

tempus' when written in semibreves, 'minor' or 'of prolation' when written in minims and 'hemiolia' when the notes were black. Although the figure 3 (with or without a mensuration sign) was sometimes regarded as a sign of triple proportion, it was not distinguished in practice from $\frac{3}{2}$.[8] The same signs and note values were used for pieces beginning in triple metre or written in triple metre throughout. Theorists disagree about whether the value representing the ternary time unit (the breve in major *sesquialtera* and the semibreve in minor) should be regarded as perfect without a sign specifying perfect mensuration, but in practice it usually was.[9]

In the classic theory of Tinctoris and Gaffurius, proportions are defined as ratios of note values only, but since their realisation in performance depends on their relationship to the *tactus*, many sixteenth-century theorists define them as ratios of note values to each other and to the *tactus*.[10] Nearly all of them agree that

---

[8] The equivalence of the signs 3 and $\frac{3}{2}$ is confirmed not only by their indiscriminate use by sixteenth-century composers (about which numerous theorists complained to no avail), but also by early seventeenth-century sources in which one of them appears in the vocal parts and the other in the basso continuo. For example, several pieces in Lodovico Grossi da Viadana's *Cento concerti ecclesiastici* (Venice, 1602) use the signature $\Phi\frac{3}{2}$ in the vocal part simultaneously with 3 in the continuo as a sign of triple proportion of ₵. In *Decantabat populus Israel*, the barring of the continuo confirms the meaning of the proportion: it is in breves in both ₵ and 3, but the first perfect breve of the proportion is included in the same bar as the preceding semibreve when the proportion begins in the middle of a breve *tempus*, and must therefore have the same value as a semibreve of ₵. Modern edition in Viadana, *Opere*, ser. 1, I, ed. C. Gallico, Monumenti Musicali Mantovani 1 (Kassel, 1964), p. 30.

[9] F. Gaffurius, *Practica musicae* (Milan, 1496; facsimile edn in Monuments of Music and Music Literature in Facsimile, ser. 2, 99 (New York, 1979)), bk 4, ch. 5, sigs. ggiij^v–iiij^v (trans. C. A. Miller, Musicological Studies and Documents 20 (n.p., 1968), pp. 180–1), maintains that a proportion cannot make notes perfect. Giovanni Spataro devoted much of his *Tractato di musica . . . nel quale si tracta de la perfectione da la sesqualtera producta in la musica mensurata exercitate* (Venice, 1531; facsimile edn in Bibliotheca Musica Bononiensis, sez. II, 14, with preface by G. Vecchi (Bologna, 1970)) to refuting the opinion of Gaffurius on this point. Theorists continued to disagree about the matter throughout the century.

[10] For example, S. Heyden, *De arte canendi* (Nuremberg, 1540; facsimile edn in Monuments of Music and Music Literature in Facsimile, ser. 2, 139 (New York, 1969)), bk 2, ch. 5, pp. 86–7 (trans. C. A. Miller, Musicological Studies and Documents 26 (n.p., 1972), p. 83), defines a proportion as 'a measurement in which two different numbers are compared to notes or to notes and *tactus*' ('qua duo diversi numeri, aut Notularum inter se, aut Notularum & Tactuum, conferuntur'). J. Oridryus, *Practicae musicae utriusque praecepta brevia* (Düsseldorf, 1557), ch. 13 (ed. in R. Federhofer-Königs, *Johannes Oridryus und sein Musiktraktat*, Beiträge zur Rheinischen Musikgeschichte 24 (Cologne, 1957), p. 152), and A. Wilphlingseder, *Erotemata musices practicae* (Nuremberg, 1563), bk 2, ch. 11, p. 262, repeat Heyden's definition almost verbatim.

the three notes of *sesquialtera, hemiolia* or *tripla* that form a ternary unit, whether semibreves or minims, are sung to one *tactus* when the proportion appears simultaneously in all voices. This *tactus* is often described as an unequally divided, 'proportionate' *tactus*, with two thirds of its length on the downstroke and one third on the upstroke ($\frac{3}{2}$ ◇ ◇ ◇ or $\frac{3}{2}$ ♩ ♩ ♩),[11] although some theorists insist that it should be equally divided ($\frac{3}{2}$ ◇ ◇ ◇ or $\frac{3}{2}$ ♩ ♩ ♩) in spite of the ternary grouping of the notes that it measures.[12] The tempo proportion between a ternary passage and a preceding binary one depends on the relationship of the length of the proportionate *tactus* to the binary one. Any ambiguity of the *tactus* of the binary mensuration leads necessarily to ambiguities in the interpretation of the proportion.

THE CONFUSION BETWEEN *SESQUIALTERA* AND TRIPLE PROPORTION

Several theorists of the 1520s and 1530s, including Pietro Aron, Stephano Vanneo and Giovanni Maria Lanfranco, explain how *sesquialtera* could relate consistently to both the note values and the *tactus*: when the *tactus* of the binary mensuration is a semibreve (in C and O) *sesquialtera* should apply to the minims, and when it is a breve (in ₵ and Ø) it should apply to the semibreves. In this way, the three notes that form a metrical unit, whether minims or semibreves, are performed on one *tactus* and equated with two notes of the same type in the preceding mensuration. Any other notation or interpretation of the *tactus* creates inconsistencies between the basic sign and the proportion. Aron explains as follows:

[11] The earliest source to use the term *tactus proportionatus* may be N. Wollick, *Enchiridion musices* (Paris, 1509), bk 2, ch. 6 (sig. h vi^v of the 1512 edn). Wollick says that it applies to three semibreves in triple proportion (either in all voices or in one voice in a 3:1 ratio with others) and in *sesquialtera*. According to Frobenius, 'Tactus', p. 8, the first source to describe it unambiguously as an unequally divided *tactus* is Agricola, *Musica figuralis deudsch*, ch. 6.

[12] Sebald Heyden and his followers were the leading proponents of equal *tactus* for all types of mensurations and proportions. See below, note 41.

Some others put this sign in the beginning of their song, O, in which it is understood that each semibreve occupies a beat, and then with little care they bring in a *sesquialtera* proportion with breves and semibreves. In this order and form three results may occur, two contradictory and one difficult for the performer or singer. First, when the beat is on the semibreve and they wish to make *sesquialtera*, they get triple proportion, because one beat, which contained one semibreve before, contains three afterwards. The second contradiction is that if you want to make a *sesquialtera* proportion, you must depart from the first measure, which was one semibreve per beat, and go to the measure which is appropriate to this sign, ₵. This is an error because all proportions refer directly to the preceding sign. The third result, which is difficult to perform, is that you could make a *sesquialtera* proportion in the same figure and form without changing the measure of the sign by having every note syncopated. This proportion would result in every note being doubled, which would be a proper and true *sesquialtera*, but since this method is little used, you should take care that when you wish to form a *sesquialtera* under this sign, O, you make your notes semibreves and minims, and not breves and semibreves. In this manner you will see three minims in a beat against one semibreve, which is *sesquialtera*, and thus you will not fall into the errors we have shown above. Thus every *sesquialtera* formed under the beat of a breve should be shown with breves and semibreves, white or black, but that which is found under the beat of semibreves or minims is shown in the form of semibreves and minims, as is manifest in the sesquialtered semibreve in perfect and imperfect prolation.[13]

[13] 'Sono alcuni altri che inanzi pongono in principio del suo canto il segno seguente O, nel qual segno e diputato ciascuna semibreve passare per una misura, & con poca avertenza adducono la sesqualtera proportione con brevi & semibrevi, nel qual ordine & forma acadono tre effetti, dui contrarii, & uno difficile al pronuntiante over cantore. Per il primo havendo data la misura ne la semibreve, & volendo creare la sesqualtera, ne risulta tripla, perche prima passava per una battuta una semibreve, di poi ne passa tre. Per il secondo effetto contrario aviene, che se pur tu vuoi creare la sesqualtera proportione, a te e dibisogno mutarti da la prima misura quale era una semibreve per battuta, & entrare ne la misura qual si conviene a questo segno ₵ & e errore, per che tutte le proportioni drittamente si riferiscono a lo antecedente segno. Il terzo effetto di difficulta e che ben puoi creare la sesqualtera proportione ne le figure & forma medesima, senza rimuovere la misura del segno in questo modo, faccendo che ciascuna nota sia syncopata, laqual proportione resultera, che tutte le note resteranno dupplicate, per laqual cosa ne sara la giusta & vera sesqualtera, ma perche questo modo poco e usitato, avertirai quando sotto tal segno O tu pensarai formare una sesqualtera, fa le tue note di semibrevi & minime acompagnate, & non di brevi & semibrevi, nel qual processo verranno in battuta tre minime contra una semibreve, quale e sesqualtera, et cosi non incorrerai in tali errori da noi di sopra dimostrati. Per tanto ciascuna sesqualtera formata sotto la battuta di una breve, e di bisogno segnarsi con brevi & semibrevi vacue o piene, ma quella che si ritruova ne la battuta di semibrevi o minime, fa che la sua forma si mostri di semibrevi & minime, cosi a te sia manifesto de la semibreve sesqualterata ne la prolatione perfetta & imperfetta.' P. Aron, *Thoscanello de la musica* (Venice, 1523; rev. edn with

The different notations and interpretations of *sesquialtera* of C or O that Aron describes in this passage may be illustrated as follows:

(1) correct, normal *sesquialtera*: C (or O) ◇ = $\frac{3}{2}$ ♩ ♩ ♩;

(2) incorrect *sesquialtera* interpreted as triple proportion:
C (or O) ◇ = $\frac{3}{2}$ ◇ ◇ ◇ ;

(3) difficult and unusual *sesquialtera* of two *tactus*:
C (or O) ◇ ◇ = $\frac{3}{2}$ ◇ ◇ ◇.

Aron's incorrect *sesquialtera* (no. 2) entails two contradictions. First, if the *tactus* contains one semibreve before the sign and three semibreves after it, the proportion is 3:1, or *tripla*, not *sesquialtera*. The effect is still that of three notes in place of two on each *tactus*, but the notation specifies three semibreves in place of two minims, not three notes in place of two of the same type. Second, a sign indicating a semibreve *tactus* (C or O) is incompatible with a proportion requiring a breve *tactus*. His difficult and unusual *sesquialtera* (no. 3) creates a complex syncopation between the beat and the notes (two *tactus*, or four strokes, corresponding to three equal notes or their equivalent) and creates an effect quite different from that of replacing two notes with three on a single *tactus*.[14] Aron does not specify whether the *tactus* of the proportions is equally or unequally divided, but that issue does not affect his arguments.

Vanneo makes the same point, again complaining about musicians who confuse *sesquialtera* with triple proportion by writ-

Aggiunta published as *Toscanello in musica* (Venice, 1529, 1539 and 1562); facsimile of 1539 edn, ed. G. Frey, Documenta Musicologica, ser. 1, 29 (Kassel, 1970)), bk 2, ch. 33, sig. Giij'; trans. P. Bergquist, Colorado College Music Press Translations 4, 3 vols. (Colorado Springs, 1970), II, pp. 47–8. My translation differs from Bergquist's in that I do not interpret the 'ne' in the expression 'ne sara la giusta & vera sesqualtera' as a negative. The wording of my translations often differs from that of the published translations cited, but my interpretations of the meanings are essentially the same unless otherwise noted.

14   This passage refers specifically to major *sesquialtera* of O, in which the syncopation is more complex than in major *sesquialtera* of C, because the two semibreves of O that are replaced by three in the proportion do not form a complete metrical unit. Aron evidently intends the same reasoning to apply to major *sesquialtera* of C, however, because he uses the sign ¢, not Φ, in his second contradiction, and he states the general rule at the end of the passage in terms of the beat of the preceding mensuration, not the perfect or imperfect character of the *tempus*. The passage is discussed in Berger, *Mensuration and Proportion Signs*, pp. 222–4.

ing it in semibreves when the mensuration to which it relates has a semibreve *tactus*:

> I have observed in addition another not insignificant error arising accidentally from an almost universal manner of writing by musicians, when they place before *sesquialtera* one of these two signs: O C, for they are the same in measure, since the notes under them follow the same measure and individual semibreves are measured by one beat, and then they place breves and semibreves in *sesquialtera* proportion such that three semibreves are contained in and measured by one beat. Nothing is more inappropriate to *sesquialtera* proportion, for this applies rather to triple proportion, as the experienced student will easily confirm.[15]

Lanfranco, like Aron, calls attention to the undesirable syncopation between the *tactus* and the notes that results from a literal interpretation of major *sesquialtera* under signs requiring a semibreve *tactus*:

> To avoid the difficulty of syncopation and to give a comfortable tempo to the notes, and so as not to form another proportion in place of *sesquialtera*, *sesquialtera* under the signs of integral *tempus*, whether perfect or imperfect [O or C], which are placed at the beginning of the song as a foundation for the proportions that follow, should (for those who do not wish to change the measure in the middle – a thing that applies to simple practitioners and is most inappropriate) be made up of semibreves and minims. But if the said signs are cut [Ȼ or ₵] (so that the measure is placed on the breve), the said *sesquialtera* should be made of breves and semibreves.[16]

---

[15] 'Aliud insuper non mediocre vitium universam fere musicorum manum temere sequi animadverti, cum ante sesquialteram ex his duobus alterum praeponant signum O C, idem namque sunt in mensura, sub his enim notulae signis militantes eandem imitantur mensuram, et singulae semibreves uno mensurantur ictu. Deinde ipsi sesqui- altere proportionis breves ac semibreves dedicant notulas, inventes treis semibreves unico ictu contineri ac mensurari, quo nil ineptius est in sesquialtera proportione, id enim potius triplae congruit proportioni, ut solerti exploratori facile constabit.' S. Vanneo, *Recanetum de musica aurea* (Rome, 1533; facsimile edn in Bibliotheca Musica Bononiensis, sez. II, 16, with preface by G. Vecchi (Bologna, 1969)), bk 2, ch. 30, p. 68; ed. and trans. of bk 2, chs. 20–37 (*On Proportions*) by A. Seay, Colorado College Music Press Texts/Translations 2 (Colorado Springs, 1979), pp. 32–3.

[16] 'Per fuggire la difficulta della Sincopa, & per dar tempo commodo alle note: & per non formare un'altra proportione in luogo della Sesqualtera: facciasi la detta Sesqual- tera sotto a i segni del Tempo interi: o perfetti: o imperfetti che siano: proposti nel principio del Canto per fondamento delle proportioni: che seguono (chi non volesse cangiare per la via la misura: cosa che e da prattico semplice: & inconvenientissima) facciasi di Semibrevi: & di Minime. Ma essendo i detti segni traversati (percioche la misura e posta su la Breve) formasi la detta Sesqualtera di Brevi: & di Semibrevi.' *Scintille di musica*, pt 2, p. 73.

The change of measure in the middle of a song to which Lanfranco refers could be understood as a change in either the speed of the *tactus* or the written value to which it refers, but given the context the latter meaning is more likely. The implication is that a *sesquialtera* written in groups of semibreves under an integral sign will either be interpreted literally, creating unwanted syncopations and a tempo that is too slow, or as a triple proportion, in which case the *tactus* will change from the semibreve to the breve in the middle of the piece.

The above quotations make it clear that groups of three notes in *sesquialtera*, whether semibreves or minims, were ordinarily understood to correspond to one *tactus*. As long as the *tactus* is the breve in diminished signs and the semibreve in integral ones and *sesquialtera* of each is notated in the theoretically correct way, the proportion poses no problems. All these authors, however, complain that musicians commonly è wrote major *sesquialtera* in integral signs and expected it to be performed as triple proportion. In his *Lucidario in musica*, Aron warns that a similar problem arises when performers use a semibreve *tactus* in ₵: either a major *sesquialtera* proportion will be misinterpreted as *tripla* or the performers will have to reduce the length of the *tactus* by half to perform it correctly:

For that sign [₵] they give the measure to the semibreve, and they commit this impropriety in order to be able to sing with greater ease. In this way they run into no little error and confusion, because the measure that they give to the semibreve will ruin what the composer intended. If after many notes there is a *sesquialtera*, I would like these people who give the beat to the semibreve to tell me, when they get to this *sesquialtera*, what proportion will it be? Certainly it cannot be said to be *sesquialtera*, but *tripla*. And this happens because they put three semibreves in the beat of the preceding semibreve, which is most wrong. . . . And there are also many who, singing such a sign with one semibreve per beat, having arrived at *sesquialtera*, change the measure to adjust to that of the *sesquialtera*.[17]

[17] 'Per lo qual segno [₵] essi danno la misura sopra la semibreve, & questo inconveniente commettono per poter con piu loro facilita cantare, Et per tal modo incorrono in errore, & in non poca confusione, perche la misura che essi tengono nella semibreve verrà a dannare quello, che dal Compositore è inteso, & immaginato, conciosia cosa che dopo molte note nascera una sesqualtera habitudine, Per laqual cosa io vorrei un poco, che mi dicessero questi tali, che danno la misura sopra una semibreve per battuta, poscia che saranno giunti alla detta sesqualtera, che proportione sara quella? Certo non si puo dire, che essa habbia da essere sesqualtera, ma tripla si bene, Et

Some theorists who support the orthodox view that the *tactus* is the semibreve in integral signs and the breve in diminished ones nevertheless allow *sesquialtera* to be notated in either minims or semibreves under both signs, claiming that the *tactus* of the proportion depends only on its own notation, not on the sign to which it relates. A surprising source of support for this position is Sebald Heyden's *De arte canendi*, a work devoted to a comprehensive explanation of the mensural system in strictly proportional terms based on the principles of Gaffurius, including explanations of how to realise the relations between different signs in performance on the basis of their relationship to a single, uniform *tactus*. Given the premisses of his system, Heyden should logically have allowed *sesquialtera* only in the forms advocated by the theorists quoted above, but his definitions and examples of it do not conform to these principles and are mutually contradictory. He calls *sesquialtera* 'a proportion in which three minims or a semibreve and a minim are sung to one *tactus*', but illustrates it with an example of minor *sesquialtera* of ₵ that must have six minims per *tactus* if the *tactus* of ₵ is the breve.[18] He then defines *hemiolia* as 'exactly the same as *sesquialtera*, for it is called ἡμιόλιος by the Greeks', and comments: 'I do not see any good reason why musicians want to distinguish one from the other, unless it is because blackening of notes alone, without other proportional signs, indicates that three semibreves in *tempus* and three minims in *prolatio* are given to each *tactus*.'[19] In the example that follows, where Heyden changed the original notation to illustrate his point, three black minims of C in the tenor have

---

questo averra perche essi passeranno tre semibrevi sopra la battuta della detta semibreve, La qual cosa è falsissima. . . . Et quanti ce ne sono anchora, che cantando tal segno per una semibreve per battuta giunti alla sesqualtera muteranno misura per accomodarsi a quella della sesqualtera.' P. Aron, *Lucidario in musica* (Venice, 1545; facsimile edn in Monuments of Music and Music Literature in Facsimile, ser. 2, 68 (New York, 1978)), bk 3, ch. 6, fols. 20ʳ⁻ᵛ. The passage is discussed in Berger, *Mensuration and Proportion Signs*, p. 224.

[18] 'Quae est Proportio Sesqualtera? Ea est in qua tres Minimae, aut Semibrevis & Minima uni Tactui accinuntur.' Heyden, *De arte canendi*, bk 2, ch. 5, p. 92; trans. Miller, p. 86.

[19] 'Hemiolia Proportio quae est? Eadem est planè cum Sesqualtera, idem ipsum enim Graecis ἡμιόλιος significat. Cur autem hanc ab illa distinctam voluerint Musici, nihil equidem firmi video. Nisi forte hoc nigror Notularum effecerit, quo solo ea fermè absque aliis signis Proportionalibus in Tempore, tres Semibreves: In Prolatione tres Minimas singulis Tactibus accommodandas significat.' *Ibid.*, p. 94; trans. Miller, p. 87.

11

the same value as three black semibreves of the same mensuration in the bass; thus the bass is in fact in triple proportion, 'a proportion in which a perfect breve or three semibreves fit a *tactus* of one complete semibreve' according to Heyden's own definition[20] (see Example 1).[21] Apparently the tradition of singing a group of three semibreves or minims to a single *tactus* regardless of the mensuration or proportional sign was so strong that even

Example 1. Johannes Ghiselin, 'Cum Sancto Spiritu' from the Gloria of the *Missa Narayge*; S. Heyden, *De arte canendi* (Nuremberg, 1540), bk 2, ch. 5, pp. 94–5, bars 1–4

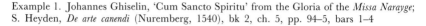

[20] 'Quae est Proportio Tripla? Ea est, in qua Brevis perfecta, aut tres Semibreves, unius integrae Semibrevis Tactui adaptantur.' *Ibid.*, pp. 89–90; trans. Miller, p. 85. In Petrucci, *Missarum Ghiselin* (Venice, 1503), the mensuration signs, beginning with the discantus, are: $\Phi 3$, $\mathbb{C}_2^3$, $\mathbb{C}$ and $\mathbb{C}$; both tenor and bass are notated in black breves and semibreves. Trans. Miller, p. 135.

[21] Modern edition of Heyden's example in *De arte canendi*, trans. Miller, p. 87. The note values and mensuration signs in all my examples are the same as those in the sources, except that ties are used for notes that cross barlines. Barring is editorial unless otherwise noted.

Glarean, *Dodecachordon*, bk 3, ch. 11, p. 218 (trans. Miller, II, p. 291), quoted this example and commented that the composer 'has made *sesquialtera* and *tripla* equal under these signs, Φ and O, which is understandable at any rate. However, because he has combined these two with the trochaic metre, and this in a twofold designation, namely, with the formula of *prolatio* in the tenor and of *tempus* in the bass, so we can indeed say that this perchance has been created through the freedom of a composer.' ('In quo Sesquialteram Triplamque aequavit his signis Φ & O. Quod utique intelligitur. Verum quod eas ambas Trochaicae rationi adplicuerit, Idque duplici pernotatione, videlicet Prolationis formula in Tenore, Temporis autem in Basi, id vero est quod licentia factum Symphonetae forte dicere possemus.') *Ibid.*, p. 215; trans. Miller, p. 239. The same example, with Heyden's alteration of the original notation, was also quoted by Oridryus, *Practicae musicae utriusque praecepta brevia*, ch. 13 (ed. Federhofer-Königs, p. 155), and Wilphlingseder, *Erotemata*, bk 2, ch. 11, pp. 288–9.

Heyden's imposingly logical and consistent system could not overcome it.

If the semibreve is regarded as the normal or exclusive *tactus* of both C and ¢, major *sesquialtera* must be understood as triple proportion under both signs unless the *tactus* of the proportion differs in tempo from that of the preceding sign.[22] It remained common practice to notate ternary proportions as major *sesquialtera* in ¢ and minor *sesquialtera* in C even when the *tactus* of both was the semibreve, partly because of tradition and partly because minor *sesquialtera* implied pairing of perfect semibreves in ¢ by analogy with the pairing of imperfect semibreves preceding the proportion. The perfect breves of major *sesquialtera* were not paired even if they had the same value as a semibreve of ¢.

Adrian Petit Coclico, who says that the semibreve is the common *tactus* of all signs in his time, describes the various species of ternary proportions as follows: '*Tripla, sesquialtera* and *hemiolia* of *tempus* and prolation are much in use among musicians, and they all have the same meaning and measure, although they are not all notated the same way, as may be seen in the following examples and table'[23] (see Example 2).[24] In his classification of types of measure, Coclico describes the one used for these proportions as a single type: '*tripla, sesquialtera* or *hemiolia* of *tempus* and prolation, [which] moves in three semibreves or minims ◇ ◇ ◇ 𝅗𝅥 𝅗𝅥 𝅗𝅥',[25]

[22] A. Planchart, 'Tempo and Proportions', *Performance Practice: Music before 1600*, ed. H. M. Brown and S. Sadie, The Norton/Grove Handbooks in Music (New York, 1989), p. 140, and Berger, *Mensuration and Proportion Signs*, p. 224, mention the confusion between triple and *sesquialtera* proportions in sixteenth-century notation. Berger speculates, no doubt correctly, that the source of the confusion was the ambiguity of the *tactus* of ¢.

[23] 'Tripla, Sesquialtera, Hemiola temporis & prolationis maxime in usu sunt apud Musicos, & idem de his est iudicium & eadem mensura, non tamen eodem modo pinguntur, ut patebit in exemplis sequentibus et tabula.' A. P. Coclico, *Compendium musices* (Nuremberg, 1552; facsimile, ed. M. Bukofzer, Documenta Musicologica, ser. 1, 9 (Kassel, 1954)), pt 2, 'De prolationibus usitatis', sig. Gij^r; trans. A. Seay, Colorado College Music Press Translations 5 (Colorado Springs, 1973), p. 18.

[24] Modern edition in Coclico, *Compendium*, trans. Seay, Ex. 41. Seay transcribes the tenor mensuration sign as Ⓞ$^3_2$. It is unclear in the source, but must be either ¢$^3_2$ or C$^3_2$, because it is labelled 'prolatio imperfect[a], sive sesquialtera' and Coclico (sig. Fiij^v) defines prolation as perfect or imperfect on the basis of the quality of the *tempus*. The line through the sign is faint and may or may not be intentional. The clef sign in the tenor is between the mensuration sign and the $^3_2$. Seay transcribes the original clef of the bass incorrectly as f4.

[25] 'Quinta est tripla, & sesquialtera aut Hemiola temporis & prolationis, ac in tres

Example 2. A. P. Coclico, *Compendium musices* (Nuremberg, 1552), pt 2, 'De prolationibus usitatis', sigs. Gij[v]–iij[r], bars 1–5

Gallus Dressler distinguishes between *hemiolia* in a single voice, which must be interpreted literally (although with the rhythms dotted, to conform to the binary mensuration of the other voices), and *hemiolia* in all voices, in which three black semibreves are sung to one proportionate *tactus*[26] (see Example 3). Since Dressler regards the semibreve as the normal *tactus* of ₵, the black breve–semibreve combination in the example takes one *tactus* when the coloration is in all voices, but two when it is in a single voice. Other theorists also discuss the possibility, implied by Dressler's example, of interpreting major *hemiolia* as triple proportion. Nicolaus Listenius and Johannes Oridryus say that coloration in all

semibreves, vel minimas agit ◇ ◇ ◇ ♩ ♩ ♩.' *Ibid.*, 'De tactu et mensura, diminutionis & augmentationis', sig. Hiij[r]; trans. Seay, p. 19.

26 'Ad Sesqualteram Proportionem etiam Hemiola referatur, quae quando in una voce notatur ut Sesqualtera, quando simul in omnibus vocibus occurit, ad tactum proportionatum canitur.' G. Dressler, *Musicae practicae elementa* (Magdeburg, 1571), pt 3, ch. [7] ('caput ultimum'), sig. N3[v]. Dressler may have taken this idea from Agricola, who describes the difference between coloration in all voices and coloration in a single voice as follows: 'And thus whenever all voices have three black semibreves at the same time, as in *tripla*, they are sung to the proportionate *tactus*, as the following example shows. But when the blackening of imperfect notes is not found simultaneously in all voices, the black notes must be sung in the manner demonstrated above for *sesquialtera*.' ('Und so werden alzeit/ wens alle stymmen zugleich haben drey schwartze Semibre. wie inn der Tripla/ auff den Proportien Tact gesungen/ wie das volgent Exem. ausweist. Wo aber die schwertzung der unvolkomen Noten/ nicht in allen stymmen zugleich erfunden/ so müssen die selbigen schwartzen Noten nach ausweisung/ wie oben von der Sesquialtera berürt/ gesungen werden.') *Musica figuralis deudsch*, ch. 12, sigs. N[v]–Nii[v].

14

Example 3. G. Dressler, *Musicae practicae elementa* (Magdeburg, 1571), pt 3, ch. [7] ('caput ultimum'), sigs. N3ᵛ–N5ᵛ, bars 1–13

parts represents triple proportion or *hemiolia*,[27] and Gregor Faber and Friedrich Beurhaus call coloration an internal sign of triple proportion.[28]

Andreas Raselius defines binary measure as 'when all notes retain their essential value, or when one semibreve or two minims

---

[27] N. Listenius, *Musica* (Wittenberg, 1537; facsimile of Nuremberg, 1549 edn, ed. G. Schünemann, Veröffentlichungen der Musik-Bibliothek Paul Hirsch 8 (Berlin, 1927)), pt 2, ch. 12, sig. e8; trans. A. Seay, Colorado College Music Press Translations 6 (Colorado Springs, 1975), p. 42. Oridryus, *Practicae musicae utriusque praecepta brevia*, ch. 13; ed. Federhofer-Königs, pp. 154–5. Oridryus illustrates this point with Heyden's example (Example 1 above) in which three black minims in the tenor are equated with three black semibreves in the bass. Neither voice has a mensuration sign in Oridryus's version of the example.

[28] G. Faber, *Musices practicae erotematum libri II* (Basle, 1553), bk 2, ch. 13, p. 227. F. Beurhaus, *Erotematum musicae libri duo* (Nuremberg, 1580; facsimile, ed. W. Thoene, Beiträge zur Rheinischen Musikgeschichte 47 (Cologne, 1961)), bk 1, ch. 13, p. 65.

come in one unit of time' and ternary measure as 'three semi-breves or three minims sung in one *tactus*, commonly called *tripla*'.[29] The signs of binary measure are C, ₵ and C2; those of ternary measure are O_2^3, 3, C3 and black notes with or without signs. Ternary measure may be written in groups of semibreves or minims, and according to the accompanying diagram each three-note group is equivalent to a semibreve of the binary signs regardless of the sign, colour or note values (see Figure 1).

There is abundant evidence in practical as well as theoretical sources that major *sesquialtera* was often understood in relation to the semibreve rather than the breve *tactus* of ₵. Most of it is found in intabulations, but other types of renotations and occasional instances of proportions simultaneous with binary signs provide further support for this interpretation.

Examples 4a–c illustrate three versions of the anonymous chanson *Je demeure seule*, all published by Pierre Attaingnant: the vocal original, an intabulation for voice and lute, and an intabulation for solo keyboard.[30] In the original the proportion is notated in

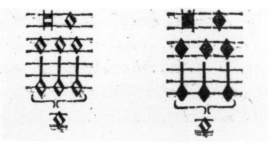

Figure 1   A. Raselius, *Hexachordum* (Nuremberg, 1589), ch. 5, sig. E3ᵛ (reproduced by permission of the Musikabteilung, Bayerische Staatsbibliothek, Munich)

---

[29]   'Quae est [dimensio] binaria? Cum essentialem omnes notulae valorem retinent: seu cum semibrevis una, vel duae minimae in unam dimensionem veniunt. . . . Quae est mensura ternaria? Cum tres semibreves vel tres minimae uno tactu canuntur: & hac vulgo vocatur tripla.' A. Raselius, *Hexachordum* (Nuremberg, 1589), ch. 5, sig. E3ᵛ.

[30]   Modern edition of the original and the keyboard intabulation in *Pierre Attaingnant Transcriptions of Chansons for Keyboard*, ed. A. Seay, Corpus Mensurabilis Musicae 20 (n.p., 1961), pp. 150–1. Facsimile of the keyboard intabulation in *Chansons und Tänze*, ed. E. Bernoulli (Munich, 1914), pp. 12–13. Modern edition of the voice and lute intabulation in *Chansons au luth et airs de cours français du xviᵉ siècle*, ed. A. Mairy, G. Thibault and L. de la Laurencie, Publications de la Société Française de Musicologie (Paris, 1934), pp. 24–6. The barlines in Examples 4b and 4c are in the sources. The tie in the voice part of Example 4b at bars 4–5 is editorial.

Example 4a. Anon., *Je demeure seule*, bars 15–21; P. Attaingnant, *Quarante et deux chansons musicales a troys parties* (Paris, 1529; RISM 1529⁴), fol. 4ʳ

groups of semibreves under the sign 3; in the lute intabulation the vocal part retains its original notation, but the values in the lute part are reduced by half under the same sign; and in the keyboard intabulation there is no change of signature and the rhythms of the proportion (which are written as dotted to adapt them to the binary sign) are interpreted with the equivalent of three semibreves of the original in the time of one.[31] Attaingnant

---

[31] All of the values are halved in the keyboard intabulation. The barring of the duple sections of the voice and lute intabulation differs from that of the vocal and keyboard versions because the intabulator omitted a semibreve of transitional material between the two statements of the opening section. The barring of the ternary passage does not follow the metrical groupings, which begin at the figure 3 and contain a semibreve plus minim (or three minims) each. The following errors have been corrected in the transcription of Example 4b, but not in the tablature notation: bar 15, note 1, lower note of the lute part is *d*, not *f*; bar 16, note 2 of the voice part is missing; bar 20, the first two rhythmic signs in the lute part are semiminims, not minims. The 'copie exacte de l'original' in the edition of this piece in *Chansons au luth*, p. 26, omits the *c* in bar 20, note 1, and includes an *f* with the *c'* in bar 17, note 3, that seems to

Example 4b. Anon., *Je demeure seule*, bars 15–20; Attaingnant, *Tres breve et familiere introduction pour entendre & apprendre par soy mesmes a jouer toutes chansons reduictes en la tabulature du lutz* (Paris, 1529), fols. xxxii^v–xxxiii^r.

published another lute intabulation of the same piece in which the values are reduced by half under the sign 3 in the proportion, as in the arrangement for voice and lute.[32]

Many manuscripts and prints of German organ tablature similarly halved the values of notes written in major *sesquialtera*. Since most of them were not solo keyboard arrangements, which might arguably have different aesthetic premisses from their vocal models, but literal transcriptions for organists accompanying

have been erased in the source. The transcription of the piece *ibid.*, pp. 24–5, emends it much more drastically than I have.

[32] Attaingnant, *Tres breve et familiere introduction pour entendre & apprendre par soy mesmes a jouer toutes chansons reduictes en la tabulature du lutz* (Paris, 1529), fols. xxxi^v–xxxii^r. Modern edition in *Preludes, Chansons and Dances for Lute Published by Pierre Attaingnant, Paris (1529–1530)*, ed. D. Heartz (Neuilly-sur-Seine, 1964), p. 27.

Example 4c. Anon., *Je demeure seule*, bars 15–19; Attaingnant, *Vingt et six chansons musicales reduictes en la tabulature des orgues espinettes manicordions & telz semblables instrumentz musicaulx* (Paris, 1531; RISM 1531[8]), fols. lxxxvi[v]–lxxxvii[r]

choirs, they represent a contemporary interpretation of the meaning of the original notation.[33] A comparison of Figure 2, part of an intabulation of Wert's motet *Transeunte Domino* by Johannes Rühling, with Example 5 illustrates this principle.[34]

Because of the custom of notating proportions as major *sesquialtera* in ₵ and minor *sesquialtera* in C, the note values in proportions were occasionally changed when the binary sign was changed. Examples 6a–b illustrate a ternary passage from Giovanni de Macque's madrigal *Son'acqua viva* that was notated as major *sesquialtera* in the first edition, where it is signed ₵, and in minor *sesquialtera* in a later edition, where it is signed C. The note values under the binary signs are the same in both versions.[35]

[33] A survey of twenty sources of German keyboard tablature from *c.* 1580 to *c.* 1620 indicates that this procedure was used in about two thirds of them. The repertory in these sources consists mostly of motets from *c.* 1560 to *c.* 1600, nearly all originally in ₵ with proportions notated as major *sesquialtera* or *hemiolia*. See C. Johnson, *Vocal Compositions in German Organ Tablatures, 1550–1650: A Catalogue and Commentary* (New York, 1989), and H. M. Brown, *Instrumental Music Printed Before 1600: A Bibliography* (Cambridge, MA, 1965), for information on these sources. I am grateful to Professor Johnson for making his microfilms of them available to me.

[34] Modern edition of Wert's motet in his *Opera omnia*, ed. C. MacClintock and M. Bernstein, Corpus Mensurabilis Musicae 24 (n.p., 1961–77), xi, pp. 42–50. In the tablature notation, the vertical stroke represents a semibreve, the stroke with one flag a minim and the stroke with two flags a semiminim.

[35] This example is discussed in W. R. Shindle, 'The Madrigals of Giovanni de Macque' (Ph.D. dissertation, University of Indiana, 1971), i, pp. 89–91. I am grateful to Professor Shindle for making his microfilms of both editions of this piece available to me. The fourth note of the canto, bar 4, is *f♯'* in the source of Example 6b. The

Figure 2   Giaches de Wert, *Transeunte Domino, secunda pars*, bars 39–53; J. Rühling, *Tabulaturbuch* (Leipzig, 1583), fols. 43ᵛ–44ʳ (reproduced by permission of the Musikabteilung, Bayerische Staatsbibliothek, Munich)

A bit of 'eye music' in Marenzio's madrigal *Dolorosi martir* (see Example 7) illustrates a similar principle.[36] The piece is in ₵, and the word 'notte' ('night') is set in black notes to illustrate its meaning. Because of the signature, Marenzio chose a breve and a semibreve, rather than a semibreve and a minim, for the black notes, but they are set against a rest in the bass that makes it clear that they are equivalent to a white semibreve, not a white breve.

Two books of organ tablatures by Jakob Paix, published in 1583 and 1589,[37] demonstrate that a literal interpretation of major *sesquialtera* was still recognised as possible for music of the mid-century, although triple proportion was normally assumed

text underlay in the alto, bars 4–5, is incorrect in the source of Example 6b and has been emended by comparison with Example 6a.

36   Modern edition in Marenzio, *Sämtliche Werke*, ed. A. Einstein, Publikationen älterer Musik 4.1, 6 (Leipzig, 1929–31; repr. Hildesheim, 1967), ı, pp. 16–18.

37   *Ein Schön Nutz unnd Gebreüchlich Orgel Tablaturbuch* (Laugingen, 1583) and *Thesaurus motetarum* (Strasburg, 1589).

Tempo relationships between duple and triple time

Example 5. Giaches de Wert, *Transeunte Domino, secunda pars*, bars 39–53; Wert, *Motectorum quinque vocum, liber primus* (Venice, 1566), p. 13

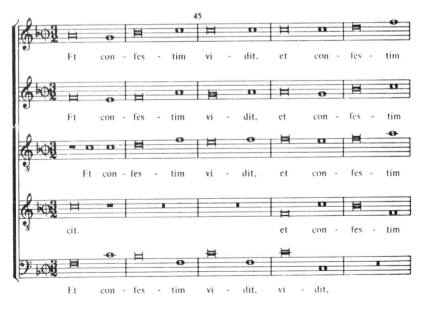

Example 5 (*cont.*)

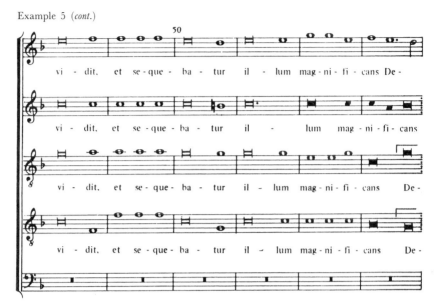

Example 6a. Giovanni de Macque, *Son'acqua viva, prima parte,* bars 4–8; *Sonetti novi di Fabio Petrozzi Romano* (Rome, 1609; RISM 1609[17]), p. 10

Example 6b. Macque, *Son'acqua viva*, *prima parte*, bars 4–9; Macque, *Il sesto libro de madrigali a cinque voci* (Venice, 1613), p. 18

Example 7. Luca Marenzio, *Dolorosi martir*, bars 18–22; Marenzio, *Il primo libro de madrigali a cinque voci* (Venice, 1580), p. 9

in the absence of clear indications to the contrary. Paix normally reduced the values of passages in major *sesquialtera* by half, as in Example 5, but in Rore's motet *Fratres scitote* he adopted an unusual notation to make it clear that a true *sesquialtera*, or the closest practical approximation to it, was intended (see Example 8 and Figure 3).[38] The passage in question has two series of black breves separated by a semibreve rest in a context where the coloration must be only an indication of tempo, since the rhythm has no ternary character. The literal meaning is three black breves in the time of two breves of the preceding ₵, a rhythm corresponding to the difficult syncopation described by Aron, but in relation to a breve *tactus* of ₵ rather than a semibreve *tactus* of C. Paix transcribed all but one of the black breves as dotted semibreves with no proportional sign (thus representing them as three quarters, instead of two thirds, of a white breve) and labelled the passage 'sesquialtera proportio'. This interpretation must have been suggested by the practice of performing a black breve as three quarters of a white breve when it was followed by a black semibreve in a binary context (i.e. ◼ ◆ = ◇. ♪).[39] The omission of the dot from the semibreve before the rest must be an error, since the passage has only thirty-one minims without it. Assuming this is the case, the length of the passage is eight breves, in contrast to seven in the original. This is the closest approximation to the original rhythm that can feasibly be performed with a semibreve *tactus*. (If three equal notes on two *tactus* are a difficult syncopation, three on

---

[38] Modern edition of Rore's motet in his *Opera omnia*, ed. B. Meier, Corpus Mensurabilis Musicae 14 (n.p., 1959–77), VI, pp. 164–8.

[39] The prevalence of the concept that three quarters of a white breve was one of the basic values of the black breve, rather than a variant of two thirds of a white breve, may be seen in Vincente Lusitano's incorrect etymology of the term 'emiolus'. He says that the term means 'one and a half' and is applied to black notes because they are worth one and a half of the next smaller value in a binary context. ('Ma nel numero binario, le figure maggiori nere perdeno la quarta parte, & chiamasi numero emiolus, perche la tal figura maggiore tiene tutta & mezza della minore che gli è aggiunta.') *Introdutione facilissima et novissima di canto fermo, figurato, contraponto semplice, et inconcerto* (Rome, 1553; facsimile edn in Libreria Musicale Italiana Musurgiana 7 (Lucca, 1989)), sig. C ('Della battuta'). The term actually refers to one and a half notes taking the same amount of time as one note before the proportion, so that the value of each note is reduced to two thirds. The dotted rhythm in which the larger value is three quarters of its white equivalent is a variant of the original meaning.

Tempo relationships between duple and triple time

Example 8. Cipriano de Rore, *Fratres scitote*, bars 65–76; Paris, Bibliothèque Nationale, Rés. Vmn MS 851, pp. 63–5

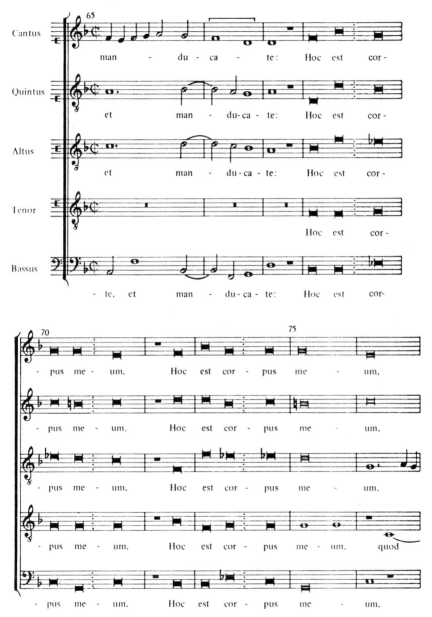

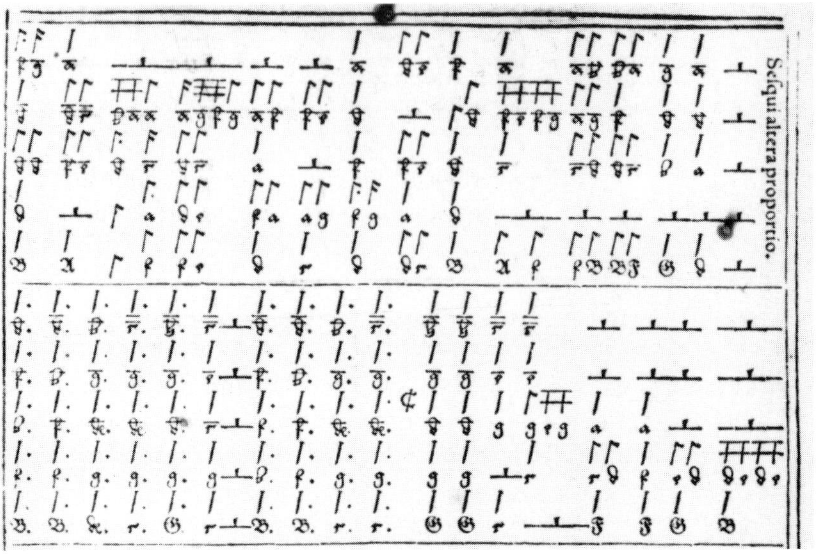

Figure 3 Cipriano de Rore, *Fratres scitote*, bars 60–78; J. Paix, *Thesaurus motetarum* (Strasburg, 1589), fol. 28ʳ (reproduced by permission of the Musikabteilung, Bayerische Staatsbibliothek, Munich)

four *tactus*, or eight strokes, are a practical impossibility.) The transcription is a clear demonstration of the difficulty of representing a true *sesquialtera* of ₵ without ambiguity, and therefore of the extent to which proportions had become subordinate to the semibreve *tactus*, by this time.

OTHER INTERPRETATIONS OF *SESQUIALTERA* AND TRIPLE PROPORTIONS

The evidence discussed so far suggests that proportions notated with signs of major *sesquialtera* could be performed either as written, with three semibreves equivalent to two of the preceding sign, or twice as fast, with three semibreves equivalent to one, and that the latter option became increasingly common throughout the century. Although this account satisfactorily explains many examples, it is almost certainly not complete. There is also evidence that ternary proportions were not always strictly proportional to the binary mensurations preceding them, and

26

that when they were, the proportion was sometimes duple, rather than *sesquialtera* or triple.

The hypothesis that there was a choice of only two tempos, one twice as fast as the other, for proportions notated as major *sesquialtera* in ¢ entails logical problems that should cast doubt on its validity even if there were no concrete evidence to contradict it. First, the *tactus* of ¢ could be chosen by the conductor on the basis of various factors unrelated to the proportions in a piece. It does not seem reasonable that the tempo of the proportions should differ by a factor of two on the basis of this choice. Second, if both ¢ and C are conducted in semibreves and the semibreve of ¢ is faster than that of C, and if the *tactus* of all proportions equals a semibreve of the preceding sign, then proportions notated in semibreves in ¢ will be faster than proportions notated in minims in C. This interpretation contradicts the principle that larger written values normally represent longer units of time except when different signs are combined simultaneously. Furthermore, the rhythms and textures of proportions of ¢ are often more complex than those of C and seem to require a slower tempo, not a faster one. Third, there is a great variety of rhythmic styles associated with both of the binary signs and their various proportions, and there is no consistent correlation between the styles of binary and ternary passages within pieces. If the tempos of both binary and ternary passages are determined at least partly by their own character, they cannot always be strictly proportional to each other. Ternary passages do not fall neatly into two categories, one suggesting a *sesquialtera* relationship to ¢ and the other a triple relationship, but often seem to require a tempo somewhere between these extremes.

Some of the best evidence for the practice of performing proportions at a tempo independent of that of the preceding binary mensuration comes from theorists who complain about the practice, insisting that the *tactus* should remain constant throughout a piece. Heyden is especially clear about this:

Through this carelessness of changing the *tactus* the relationship and nature of all proportions having mutually dissimilar signs are confused and defective. Indeed, even now we make our burden all the heavier as the need to invent different kinds of *tactus* has become less. For when we see many kinds of *tactus* invented simply to change the tempo of a composition frequently, making it now slower, now faster, and now very fast, then I ask, what are we to make of those novelty-seekers' understanding of proportions, augmentations and diminutions? From the art itself it is absolutely certain that they wanted to show through various kinds of *tactus* the same thing that early composers had indicated more correctly and artistically either by a diminution of signs or by proportions.[40]

Heyden rejects the possibility of a proportionate *tactus* with unequal subdivision, even though it would not contradict his theory of strict proportionality between signs if it were the same length as the equal *tactus*.[41] His objection to the proportionate *tactus* may have been largely theoretical, since he insists that things cannot properly be called proportional unless they are referred to the same unit of measure, but he undoubtedly also recognised the practical difficulty of keeping a time unit exactly consistent while changing its subdivision. Furthermore, even if the tempo proportion is executed precisely, the subdivision of the *tactus* affects the way a ternary passage is perceived. An equal *tactus* stresses its three-against-two relation to the fundamental

---

[40] 'Per eam enim temeritatem variorum Tactuum, omnis ratio & natura Proportionum, quàm diversa signa inter sese habent, confusa, ac omnino deformata est. Quod quidem etiam nunc tanto aegrius ferimus, quanto minus opus fuerat plures, ac eas diversas Tactuum species excogitare. Cum enim tam multiplices Tactuum species ob hoc tantum excogitatas videamus, ut motum cantus subinde mutarent, nunc tardiorem, nunc concitatiorem, nunc properantissimum faciendo. Quaeso ergo, quid nam illos novatores, de Proportionibus, Augmentationibus, ac Diminutionibus intellexisse credamus? Certum utique est, ex arte ipsa, quod illi per diversas species Tactus praestare voluerunt, idem veteres per integritatem, aut diminutionem Signorum, aut Proportiones, multo & rectius, & artificiosius praestitisse.' Heyden, *De arte canendi*, Dedication, sig. A3ʳ; trans. Miller, p. 20. The wording implies that Heyden is objecting to changes of tempo within a piece, not to different tempos for different pieces. These tempo changes coincide with changes of signs and types of *tactus*, and must therefore include non-proportional interpretations of proportion signs.

[41] C. Dahlhaus, 'Zur Theorie des Tactus im 16. Jahrhundert', *Archiv für Musikwissenschaft*, 17 (1960), pp. 22–39 (p. 32), claims that since Heyden used the term *tactus proportionatus* he did not reject the concept. Dahlhaus uses this argument to support his claim that the three kinds of *tactus* to which Heyden objects (*De arte canendi*, bk 1, ch. 5, p. 41; trans. Miller, p. 53) are not the major, minor and proportionate *tactus* described by other theorists, but three different speeds of *tactus*. In fact, however, Heyden says explicitly that the *tactus* is always equally divided (bk 1, ch. 5, p. 40; trans. Miller, p. 53). In the dedication (sig. A3ᵛ; trans. Miller, p. 20), he says that proportions cannot be sung properly with different types of *tactus*, and in bk 2, ch. 7, pp. 110–17 (trans. Miller, pp. 97–100), he offers various proofs that integral, diminished and proportionate signs are all sung to the same *tactus*, implying that these are the three types of measure that others associate with different types of *tactus*. Dahlhaus's reasoning is therefore not convincing.

binary measure, while an unequal *tactus* sounds like an independent metre that relates to the binary one only at the points of transition. Lodovico Zacconi devotes much of the third book of his *Prattica di musica* to this point, insisting that the effect of proportions conducted with equal *tactus* is completely different from that of proportions conducted with unequal *tactus*. Because these two types of measure are so different, Zacconi believes they should not even be called by the same names. He regards the term 'proportion' as proper only to triple metre with unequal *tactus* (which, ironically, is probably not mathematically proportional to duple in his system) and uses the terms *tripla*, *sesquialtera* and *hemiolia* for ternary measures governed by equal *tactus*. The latter types may be called 'proportions' only if they are qualified as 'proportions of unequal figures', in contrast to true proportions, which are 'of unequal *tactus* and [unequal] figures'.[42] Since Heyden's concern is with proportional relationships and not with metrical character, it is not surprising that he favours the type of *tactus* that emphasises the relationship of ternary passages to binary ones, rather than the one conforming to their own metre.

Most theorists who allow three types of *tactus*, two equally and one unequally divided, say nothing about how the tempo of the unequal *tactus* relates to either of the equal ones. This omission is especially striking when there is a choice of *tactus* in ¢ but no explanation of which one is the standard of reference for the proportions. The implication seems to be that the proportionate *tactus* is an independent entity not necessarily dependent on either of them.[43] There are many different opinions about what the two types of equal *tactus* are called, how they relate to the signs C and ¢, and what is the proper tempo proportion between them, but the same ambiguity in their relationship to unequal *tactus* applies in all cases.

---

[42] Zacconi, *Prattica di musica*, bk 3, chs. 8–9, fols. 136ᵛ–138ᵛ; chs. 23–5, fols. 148ᵛ–149ᵛ; and chs. 31–4, fols. 151ᵛ–152ᵛ.

[43] Bank, *Tactus, Tempo, and Notation*, p. 230, says that 'the tactus proportionatus is always explicitly stated to be an independent tactus having a duration of its own, which really does not fit in very well with the theory of the one tactus'. I have not found such explicit descriptions of the independence of the *tactus proportionatus* from the binary *tactus*, but the failure of theorists to mention the issue seems to imply this conclusion.

A few theorists acknowledge the existence of ternary passages that are not proportional to the preceding mensuration without condemning them. Glarean defines a measure with three semibreves per *tactus* as follows:

Moreover, also in these signs O3, C3, our times have used the diminution of the *tactus* very freely, in that three semibreves would be counted in one *tactus*, indeed an admirable and majestic *tactus*. The ordinary singers now improperly call this *tripla*, although it is comparable to no single note, as the triple ratio demands, but moves along with equal value in the four voices. I prefer to call it trochaic, although it often has the iambus in endings, and also to call it a tribrach, which is common to both these metric feet. ... Some omit the sign and blacken all notes, others also blacken the notes and apply the sign, and many falsely consider this *hemiolia*, while *hemiolia* is really *sesquialtera*. Therefore, this diminution has undoubtedly acquired the name *tripla* because it has three semibreves in one mensuration, namely, in one *tactus*. Some signify this merely by the placement of the number 3, and they are justly reproved by Franchinus. Some draw a circle above the 3 in this way $_3^O$, indicating that it is the ratio of *tempus perfectum*, but diminished by the speed of the *tactus*, because, according to their statement, the number added to the circle indicates the diminution. Some also draw a semicircle with a 3, as C3, in *sesquialtera* ratio whenever it occurs in minims, and they are to be reproved no less than those who are accustomed to indicate *tripla* by the 3 only.[44]

Some indicate the trochaic ratio by a plain 3, others by this sign ₵3. Josquin uses mostly the complete circle, to which he subjoins a 3, and we shall sometimes follow this ratio. Furthermore, many cannot distinguish between, much less determine, *tripla*, *hemiolia* and the trochaic form. Although *tripla* is double in ratio of speed to *hemiolia*, yet the

---

[44] 'Caeterum in his quoque signis O3 C3 nostra aetas tactus diminutionem nimis licenter usurpavit, ut treis semibreveis uno tactu, magnifico quidem illo, & augustiore numerentur: Vulgus cantorum nunc triplam improprie vocat, quippe quae ad nullas unas notulas comparationem habeat, ut poscit tripla Ratio, sed in quatuor vocibus aequo valore incedit. Eam ego Trochaicam dicere malim, quanque Iambum saepe in conclusionibus habet, & Tribrachyn, ut duobus his pedibus communem. ... Sunt qui absque signo omnes denigrant notulas, quidam etiam denigrant cum signo, multi Hemioliam falso putant, cum Hemiolia vere sit sesquialtera. Triplae nomen ea diminutio inde haud dubie obtinuit, quod treis una mensura, hoc est uno tactu habeat semibreveis. Quidam hanc unico duntaxat ternarij Charactere praeposito innuunt, qui à Franchino recte reprehenduntur. Quidam super ternario circulum pingunt hoc modo $_3^O$ significantes temporis perfecti rationem esse, sed tactus celeritate imminutam, quod numerus, ut aiunt, circulo additus diminutionem significet. Quidam etiam in sesquialtera ratione, quoties ea in minimis obvenit, semicirculum cum ternario C3 pingunt, qui non minus reprehendendi sunt, quam qui triplam uno ternario pingere consuevere.' Glarean, *Dodecachordon*, bk 3, ch. 8, p. 206; trans. Miller, II, pp. 234–5.

trochaic mensuration is very much different from *tripla* and *hemiolia* both by another mensuration as well as by another formula of singing.[45]

The defining features of Glarean's 'trochaic ratio' are as follows: (1) It applies to ternary rhythms found in all voices simultaneously. Glarean's examples of true proportions, all taken from other theorists, apply exclusively to relationships between simultaneous contrasting signs.[46] (2) The three semibreves that form a metrical unit are sung to one *tactus*. The last sentence of the above quotation might imply that this *tactus* is unequal, in contrast to the equal *tactus* appropriate to true proportions, although Glarean does not say so explicitly. (3) The *tactus* is not strictly proportional to any note value of the preceding binary mensuration. (4) In practice, there is no consistent notational distinction between the trochaic ratio and true proportions. Glarean believes that proportions should be shown with ratios of two numbers, while the single number 3 with a mensuration sign is an acceptable sign of trochaic ratio, but he admits that others do not observe this distinction. He accepts coloration as a sign of either trochaic ratio or *sesquialtera*.[47]

Listenius defines *hemiolia* as black notes in all parts and says that it is faster than triple proportion on account of the colour and often associated with simple counterpoint.[48] Nevertheless, his examples of it, which have no mensuration sign, are complex enough to suggest that he regards three black semibreves as faster than a white breve, not faster than a white semibreve (see Example 9; there are no white notes in the example on which to base the comparison, but the amount of time allotted to a white semibreve of ¢ or C at a normal tempo would be short for three black semi-

---

[45] 'Alij Trochaicam rationem simplici ternario indicant. Alij hoc signo ¢3. Iodocus ferme circulo integro, cui subijcit ternarium, quam rationem, & nos aliquando sequimur. Caeterum Triplam. Hemioliam, ac Trochaicam formam multi distinguere, imò discernere nequeunt. Cum Tripla ad Hemioliam, in celeritatis ratione sit dupla. At Trochaicae, & alia mensura, & alia canendi formula, longe à Tripla atque ab Hemiolia distincta.' *Ibid.*, ch. 11, p. 214; trans. Miller, II, p. 239.

[46] *Ibid.*, pp. 216–19 and 229–38; trans. Miller, II, pp. 244–6 and 300–2.

[47] *Ibid.*, pp. 206 and 215; trans. Miller, II, pp. 234 and 246.

[48] 'Hemiola, est quando Notae denigratae aequaliter in omnibus cantilenae partibus procedunt. Et quidem citius quam in Tripla proportione, idque ob colorem. Habet enim color plus agilitatis, quam albedo, quae in his Triplam proportionem, suo signo praefixo, efficit. Nonnunquam Hemiola simplicem contrapunctum refert, quod saltem admonendum duxi.' Listenius, *Musica*, pt 2, ch. 12, sig. f'; trans. Seay, p. 43.

Example 9. N. Listenius, *Musica* (Nuremberg, 1549), pt 2, ch. 12, sig. f^v

breves of the example).[49] In any case, the qualitative wording of his tempo description ('citius quam in Tripla proportione') clearly indicates a relationship that is neither *tripla* nor *sesquialtera*. Several other theorists, including Friedrich Beurhaus,[50] Adam Gumpelzhaimer,[51] Ambrosius Wilphlingseder[52] and Thomas Morley,[53]

[49] Modern edition of the example in Listenius, *Musica*, trans. Seay, p. 44. In the editions of 1543, 1548 and 1549, bar 3, note 2 of the discantus is a dotted minim, not a dotted semibreve. My correction of the bar is different from Seay's. The example, which is identical in the above three editions, contains several instances of unorthodox part-writing and dissonance treatment. I have not examined earlier editions, which might have a more correct version of it.

[50] 'Hemiolia similis est Tripla vel sesquialtera, nisi quod celerius & subtilius canatur.' Beurhaus, *Erotematum*, bk 1, ch. 13, p. 67.

[51] 'Quid est Hemiolia proportio? Eadem planè est cum Tripla, nisi quod ea, propter nigredinem, plus agilitatis habeat, quam albedo. Was ist Hemiolia? Hemiolia ist gleich der Triplae proportioni/ allein das sie umb schwertze willen mehr behendigkeit hat in der Mensur/ dann die Tripla.' A. Gumpelzhaimer, *Compendium musicae*, 6th edn (Augsburg, 1616), ch. 9, fol. 16^r. (The first edition was published in 1591.)

[52] 'Quid est Hemiolia Proportio? Eadem plane est cùm Sesquialtera, nisi quòd ea, propter nigredinem, plus agilitatis habet, quam albedo. Nonnunquam etiam simplicem contrapunctum refert.' Wilphlingseder, *Erotemata*, bk 2, ch. 11, p. 287.

[53] 'Heere is likewise another ensample wherein *Tripla* is in all the parts together, which if you pricke al in blacke notes, will make that proportion which the musitions falslie termed *Hemiolia*, when in deed it is nothing else but a round *Tripla*. For *Hemiola* doth signifie that which the *Latines* tearme Sesquipla or sesquialtra: but the good

also suggest that proportions notated in black notes may be faster by an unspecified amount than proportions notated in white notes.

Vicentino may imply that ternary passages need not be strictly proportional to binary ones when they are found in all parts by denying the validity of their classification as 'proportions of inequality'. He says that a proportion in which the semibreves are in ternary groups in all voices, improperly called *sesquialtera*, should be called a 'proportion of equality', since the measurement of the notes is the same in all parts. (This distinction echoes the one made by Glarean in the passage quoted above.) Anticipating the objection that the three semibreves are compared to the two previously constituting one *tactus*, he says:

If anyone wants to salvage this proportion by saying that the beat is in relation to the breve, and that this breve is heard in the measure, and to prove with this reason that the proportion is properly called *sesquialtera*, it can be answered that it is necessary to hear two against three in singing, and not beat two against three.[54]

Vicentino may not even agree with those who say that the *tactus* of the proportion relates to the breve, but if he does, the wording ('và alla ragione di breve') does not necessarily mean that it has the same length as the preceding breve. Zacconi, for example, insists that ternary proportions of ₵ should be notated in groups of semibreves so that the perfect breve of the proportion will 'correspond to' the imperfect breve of ₵, as in Example 6a above,

---

Munks finding it to go somwhat rounder then common tripla, gave it that name of *Hemiolia* for lacke of another.' T. Morley, *A Plaine and Easie Introduction to Practicall Musicke* (London, 1597; facsimile edn Westmead, Farnborough, Hants, 1971), pt 1, p. 30; ed. R. A. Harman (London, 1952; 2nd edn, 1963), p. 52. 'If more blacke semibriefes or briefes bee togither, then is there some proportion, & most commonly either *tripla* or *hemiolia*, which is nothing but a rounde common *tripla* or *sesquialtera*.' *Ibid.*, annotations to p. 9, v. 18; ed. Harman, p. 115. (The word 'round' means 'fast' in these contexts.) H. Hell, 'Zu Rhythmus und Notierung des "Vi ricorda" in Claudio Monteverdis *Orfeo*', *Analecta Musicologica*, 15 (1975), pp. 87–157 (p. 123), calls Morley an isolated and relatively early witness for a faster tempo for coloured notes, but Morley probably took the idea from Listenius and Beurhaus, both of whom he cites as authorities at the end of his book.

[54] 'E se alcuno volesse salvare detta proportione, & dire che la battuta và alla ragione di breve, et che in la misura s'intende essa breve, & con tal ragione provare che detta proportione è ben detta sesqualtera; si risponderà che è necessario sentire cantare due contra tre, & non battere due contra tre.' N. Vicentino, *L'antica musica ridotta alla moderna prattica* (Rome, 1555; facsimile, ed. E. E. Lowinsky, Documenta Musicologica, ser. 1, 17 (Kassel, 1959)), bk 4, ch. 31, fols. 87ᵛ–88ʳ.

but the correspondence to which he refers is purely notational; the proportion would have the same meaning if the binary sign were C and the proportion were written in half-values, as in Example 6b.[55] Orazio Tigrini repeats Vicentino's definition of ternary rhythms in all voices as 'proportions of equality' without any reference to arguments for regarding them as proportional to the preceding mensuration, implying that such a relationship is of no importance to him.[56]

Joachim Burmeister recommends that both binary and ternary mensurations be taken at moderate tempos, more slowly if they have many short values than if they do not. There is no suggestion that they are proportional to one another: 'Care must be taken that equal measure be neither too slow nor too fast if the song does not have many coloured notes; but if it is made up of coloured notes, a noticeably slower tempo is required. Similarly, unequal measures should also be sung moderately.'[57] He cites other theorists (Glarean, Hoffmann, Heinrich Faber, Zanger and

[55] 'Spesse volte i Compositori si obligano volontariamente senza esser astretti da nisciuno; perche nel comporre delle cantilene loro si servano nel principio come ho detto de i segni della Breve, & cosi dovendovi introdurre una Proportione si trovano esser astretti d'introdurvi la maggiore per far che i segni delle oppositioni circa la quantità delle figure si corispondino, & non fare ch'esse oppositioni sieno contrarie.' Zacconi, *Prattica di musica*, bk 3, ch. 57, fol. 173ᵛ. Zacconi recommends (*ibid.*) that a composer who prefers to notate proportions in groups of semibreves in C, thinking the rhythm will be easier to read that way, should change the initial sign to ₵. Thus it is clear that a proportion notated in semibreves in ₵ has the same relationship to the preceding music as a proportion notated in minims in C, as in Examples 6a–b above.

[56] O. Tigrini, *Il compendio della musica* (Venice, 1588; facsimile edn in Monuments of Music and Music Literature in Facsimile, ser. 2, 25 (New York, 1966)), bk 4, ch. 22, p. 130. Adriano Banchieri uses the term *proportioni d'equalità*, but defines the tempos of these proportions in the traditional way, in his *Cartella musicale* (Venice, 1614), documents 4–7, pp. 29–32. The distinction between proportions of equality and proportions of inequality is also found in Wollick, *Enchiridion musices*, bk 5, ch. 6 (sig. h viᵛ of the 1512 edn), where the two types are said to be performed to the same proportionate *tactus*.

[57] 'Cura est & diligentia adhibenda, ut Isodimeris mensura, cantum plurimis coloratis notis non scatentem, non nimis protracta, nec quoque nimium properans demetiatur: Contextum verò coloratarum notarum protractione evidenti. Sic & Anisodimereos mensura mediocritatem teneat.' J. Burmeister, *Musica autoschediastike* (Rostock, 1601), accessio 3, sectio 2, sig. Aa4ʳ. On Burmeister's theories of mensuration and *tactus*, see M. Ruhnke, *Joachim Burmeister: Ein Beitrag zur Musiklehre um 1600*, Schriften des Landesinstituts für Musikforschung Kiel 5 (Kassel, 1955), pp. 76–84. Bank, *Tactus, Tempo, and Notation*, p. 247, cites this passage as evidence that ternary passages had lost most of their proportional character by *c.* 1600, but non-proportional tempo relationships must have existed throughout the sixteenth century, with or without the approval of theorists.

Heyden) who object to the term 'proportionate *tactus*' (*mensura proportionata*), but accepts it himself because the two strokes of the *tactus* are proportional to each other in a 2:1 ratio, not because the notes following the proportion sign are proportional to those preceding it.[58]

Michael Praetorius supports the idea that proportions notated in semibreves, which apply to ₵, should generally be slower than proportions notated in minims, which apply to C. Having said that the 'modern Italians' define *sesquialtera* as three semibreves in the time of two in ₵ or three minims in the time of two in C,[59] he comments that many people interchange the various proportional signs indiscriminately. Some, he says, recommend abolishing *sesquialtera* and *hemiolia* altogether and using only one sign of *tripla* for all such proportions, but he believes two signs should be retained for traditional proportions: *tripla*, written in semibreves with the sign $\frac{3}{1}$ or 3, for motets and concertos, and *sesquialtera*, written in minims with the sign $\frac{3}{2}$, for madrigals, galliards, courantes, voltas and other songs requiring a fast *tactus*. To these types he adds a third, which he calls *sextupla* or *trochaico diminuto*, for pieces requiring a new type of very fast *tactus*.[60] The semibreve *tactus* of motets, which are associated with the sign ₵, is faster than the semibreve *tactus* of madrigals and other pieces in C, although the notes move more slowly in ₵ because the

---

[58] 'Those [who call the unequal *tactus* "proportionate"] do not do so wrongly in my opinion, because there is a fixed proportion between the parts of the *tactus*, descent and ascent; they are in duple ratio with each other.' ('Quod illos meo judicio non injuria fecisse puto. Est enim inter Tactus partes depressionem & elevationem certa proportio. Habent enim ad se invicem ut analogia dupla.') *Ibid.*, sigs. Aa^v–Aa2^r.

[59] Praetorius, *Syntagma musicum*, III, pt 2, ch. 7, p. 52. Praetorius is probably referring to Adriano Banchieri's *Cartella musicale*, document 5, pp. 29–30. According to P. Aldrich, *Rhythm in Seventeenth-Century Italian Monody* (New York, 1966), pp. 30–5, Antonio Brunelli (*Regole utilissime per li scolari* (Florence, 1606)) likewise advocates a literal interpretation of all types of *sesquialtera* and *hemiolia* proportions.

[60] 'Ac licet quidam in ea sint opinione, etiam Sesquialteram & in Hemiola Notulas denigratas abolendas esse, cùm & hae & si quae aliae hujus generis sint, per unicam Triplam exprimi possint: Tamen incommodè fieri haud dixero, commodioris si distinctionis ergò in gratiam Canentium certis relinquantur Cantionum generibus: Tripla nempe in Motetis & Concertis; Sesquialtera verò in Madrigalibus, praesertim autem in Galliardis, Courrantis, Voltis & aliis id generis Cantionibus, in quibus celeriori Tactu necessariò opus est, retineatur: Propterea, quod pleraeque harum Cantionum tam celerem Tactum requirant, ut pro novitate rei, mihi de novis nominibus, non eum in modum antehac usurpatis, cogitandum fuerit, atque adeò voce Sextupla vel Tactu Trochaico diminuto rem exprimere conatus sim.' Praetorius, *Syntagma musicum*, III, pt 2, ch. 7, p. 53.

written values are longer.[61] Since the binary sign with the faster *tactus* corresponds to proportions with the slower *tactus*, the *tactus* of the proportion must differ from that of the preceding sign in at least one of these types, and probably in both.[62]

The variety of notations and styles in Lassus's *Sacrae cantiones quinque vocum* (Nuremberg, 1562) and the different interpretations of them in contemporary intabulations illustrate the difficulty of interpreting proportions simply as *sesquialtera* or *tripla* without intermediate alternatives. Three pieces in the book have *sesquialtera* or *hemiolia* passages simultaneously in all voices: *Clare sancto-*

---

[61] Praetorius says that madrigals and other pieces in C, which have many semiminims and fusas, move faster, while motets, which are signed ¢ and have many breves and semibreves, move more slowly. The semibreve *tactus* must be faster in ¢ than in C to mediate between the extremes of the note values, so that the slow tempo will not become tedious and the fast will not run away out of control, like the horses of the sun in the hands of Phaethon. ('Jetztiger zeit aber werden diese beyde Signa meistentheils also observiret, dass das C fürnemlich in Madrigalien, das ¢ aber in Motetten gebraucht wird. Quia Madrigalia & aliae Cantiones, quae sub signo C, Semiminimis & Fusis abundant, celeriori progrediuntur motu; Motectae autem, quae sub signo ¢ Brevibus & Semibrevibus abundant, tardiori: Ideo hic celeriori, illic tardiori opus est Tactu, quò medium inter duo extrema servetur, ne tardior Progressus auditorum auribus pariat fastidium, aut celerior in Praecipitium ducat, veluti Solis equi Phaetontem abripuerunt, ubi currus nullas audivit habenas.') *Ibid.*, p. 50. He admits, however, that tempo cannot be chosen on the basis of the sign alone, but must also take account of the text and the character of the music. ('Es kan aber ein jeder den Sachen selbsten nachdencken, und ex consideratione Textus & Harmoniae observiren, wo ein langsamer oder geschwinder Tact gehalten werden müsse.') *Ibid.*, p. 51.

[62] Praetorius's views on tempo have been interpreted in various ways. H.-O. Hiekel, 'Der Madrigal- und Motettentypus in der Mensurallehre des Michael Praetorius', *Archiv für Musikwissenschaft*, 19–20 (1962–3), pp. 40–55, maintains that Praetorius regards the breve of ¢ as equal to the semibreve of C and the semibreves of *tripla* in ¢ as equal to the minims of *sesquialtera* in C. C. Dahlhaus, 'Zur Taktlehre des Michael Praetorius', *Die Musikforschung*, 17 (1964), pp. 162–9, and P. Brainard, 'Zur Deutung der Diminution in der Tactuslehre des Michael Praetorius', *ibid.*, pp. 169–74, demonstrate why Hiekel's interpretation cannot be correct. Dahlhaus suggests (p. 168) that Praetorius may have intended the perfect breve of *tripla* to correspond to the semibreve of C, and the perfect semibreve of *sesquialtera* to the semibreve of ¢, even though this explanation contradicts Praetorius's earlier statements about the signs typical of motets and madrigals. In 'Zur Entstehung des modernen Taktsystems', pp. 232–3, Dahlhaus proposes a different explanation: *tripla* of ¢ relates to the breve *tactus*, and *sesquialtera* of C to the semibreve *tactus*. Neither of these explanations is convincing. Praetorius's description agrees with standard notational practice, and his view that the semibreve is the normal *tactus* of both C and ¢ is clear. Dahlhaus's doubts result from his assumption that the *tactus* of a proportion must be the same as that of the preceding sign, but what Praetorius says is exactly the opposite: the tempos of proportions, like those of binary signs, must be determined by the character of their music, and this will generally result in a slower tempo for proportions of ¢ than for proportions of C. Praetorius is a late witness, but the music to which he refers in this chapter is mostly from the late sixteenth century and his comments make sense in relation to that repertory.

rum has both minor *hemiolia* in a simple style and major *sesquialtera* that is much more complex; *Surgens Jesus* has major *hemiolia* in a style similar to the minor *hemiolia* of *Clare sanctorum*; and *Non vos me elegistis* has major *hemiolia* in an intermediate style (see Examples 10a–d).[63] The musical context clearly implies that the minor *hemiolia* in Example 10a should be interpreted literally. The contrast between this passage and the major *sesquialtera* in the same piece (Example 10b) suggests that Lassus also intended a literal meaning for the latter notation. In that case, it would seem logical to apply a literal interpretation to the major *hemiolia* in the same book (Examples 10c and d) as well, even though the passages with that notation differ greatly in complexity, and Example 10c is the type of coloured passage often described as triple proportion by theorists.[64] If this was the composer's intention, however, his contemporaries apparently did not understand it. All these proportions are notated as minor *sesquialtera* in most intabulations.[65] Since they cannot all be that fast, the intabulators must have intended the more complex ones to be slower than the tablature notation indicates, but not as slow as major *sesquialtera*, for which they could have retained the original notation.

---

[63] Modern editions in Lassus, *Sämtliche Werke*, ed. F. X. Haberl and A. Sandberger (Leipzig, 1894–1926), v, pp. 144–50 (*Clare sanctorum*), 60–3 (*Surgens Jesus*) and 141–3 (*Non vos me elegistis*). The source has the word 'laudes' in place of 'laudem' in the lower four voices of Example 10b. The proportional sign in Example 10b is 3, rather than $\mathsf{C}\frac{3}{2}$, in Le Roy and Ballard's 1571 edition of the book. In the modern edition, the rhythm of Example 10a, bar 17, bass, notes 3–4, is transcribed incorrectly as semibreve–minim.

[64] In *Non vos me elegistis*, there is a white breve simultaneous with three black semibreves in the penultimate measure of the proportion (not shown in Example 10d). This might be taken as evidence that three black semibreves are equivalent to a white breve before the proportion, but if the tempo of the proportion is different from that of the preceding section, the white breve could be understood to relate only to the tempo in effect at that point.

[65] All three motets are notated this way in the manuscript Regensburg, Fürstliche Thurn- und Taxissche Hofbibliothek, F. K. Musik no. 22. The same notation is found in *Non vos me elegistis* in J. Rühling, *Tabulaturbuch* (Leipzig, 1583), and Bernhard Schmid (the father), *Zwey Bücher: Einer Neuen Kunstlichen Tabulatur* (Strasburg, 1577; RISM 1577[12]), and in *Surgens Jesus* in Paix, *Ein Schön Nutz unnd Gebreüchlich Orgel Tablaturbuch*, Rühling, *Tabulaturbuch*, and Regensburg, Fürstliche Thurn- und Taxissche Hofbibliothek, F. K. Musik no. 24. The proportion in *Surgens Jesus* is notated as major *sesquialtera* in Braunschweig, Stadtarchiv, MS G II 7:60; Munich, Bayerische Staatsbibliothek, Mus. MS 1640; and Passau, Staatliche Bibliothek, MS 115. See Johnson, *Vocal Compositions*, and Brown, *Instrumental Music*, for catalogues of these sources.

Example 10a. Orlando di Lassus, *Clare sanctorum, secunda pars*, bars 11–18; Lassus, *Sacrae cantiones quinque vocum* (Nuremberg, 1562), p. 22

Example 10b. Lassus, *Clare sanctorum, secunda pars*, bars 45–59; Lassus, *Sacrae cantiones quinque vocum*, p. 22

There is one tempo relationship between the binary signs and their ternary proportions that preserves the identity of a time unit between them and solves some of the problems discussed above: the semibreve or minim of the proportion may be equated, respectively, with the minim or semiminim of the preceding

Ruth I. DeFord

Example 10b (*cont.*)

40

Tempo relationships between duple and triple time

Example 10c. Lassus, *Surgens Jesus*, bars 44–50; Lassus, *Sacrae cantiones quinque vocum*, p. 20

Example 10d. Lassus, *Non vos me elegistis*, bars 43–52; Lassus, *Sacrae cantiones quinque vocum*, p. 16

mensuration, creating a duple proportion between the ternary
sign and the binary one:

The *tactus* of major *sesquialtera* of ₵ is then one and a half times
as long as a semibreve (or three quarters as long as a breve) of
₵, and the *tactus* of minor *sesquialtera* of C is three quarters as
long as a semibreve of C. This relationship equates the principal
motor unit (most often the minim in ₵ and the semiminim in
C) of the binary mensuration with that of the proportion and
makes the lengths of their respective *tactus* unequal. The advantages of this option are that it allows a tempo between the
extremes of *sesquialtera* and *tripla* for ternary passages and that it
agrees with Praetorius's view that the semibreve *tactus* of ₵ is
faster than that of C, but the *tactus* of its proportions is slower.
If, for example, the semibreve of ₵ is two thirds as long as the
semibreve of C, the perfect breve *tactus* of its proportions is one
and a third times as long as the perfect semibreve *tactus* of
proportions of C. Translated into arbitrary metronome marks,
the relationship is as follows:

₵	◊ = 90	C	◊ = 60
	♩ = 180		♩ = 240
₵ 3/2	◊ = 180	C 3/2	♩ = 240
	☐· = 60		◊· = 80

Most scholars have assumed that this type of relationship is
typical of modern metres, in contrast to sixteenth-century proportional relations, and that it rarely existed before *c.* 1600 at
the earliest.[66] It may, however, have been known much earlier.

Theoretical support for this position is weak. Agricola seems
to describe a relationship of this type, but his wording is ambiguous and does not agree with what he says elsewhere in his
treatise:

Just as the two numbers 3 and 2 are in *sesquialtera* proportion, the
proportionate *tactus* is measured in the same way when it is taken

---

[66] Dahlhaus, 'Zur Entstehung des modernen Taktsystems', p. 223, characterises the
difference between modern metres and Renaissance mensurations in this way.

slowly in relation to the whole *tactus* or fast in relation to the half-*tactus*. For example, the half-*tactus* in this sign ¢ contains two minims, but the proportionate *tactus* always contains three minims. Therefore the proportionate *tactus* is taken as much as one minim slower than the other two. And since it is measured in the manner of *sesquialtera* in relation to the other *tactus* and contains them one and a half times in itself, it can properly be called sesquialterate or proportionate *tactus* (as the musicians write). Also it is not used everywhere, but only in perfect prolation, as mentioned in chapter 4, or in triple proportion and *hemiolia* when they are found in all voices at the same time, and so a semibreve is sung in the same measure as a minim otherwise is.[67]

This passage appears to say that each of the semibreves in a proportion of ¢ will equal a minim of ₵, and the proportionate *tactus* (three semibreves) will therefore be one and a half times as long as the semibreve *tactus* (which Agricola calls 'half-*tactus*') of ₵.[68]

There are a few references in sixteenth-century treatises to coloration as a sign of duple proportion, but their significance

---

[67] 'Gleich wie sich die beide Ciffern 3 und 2 in Proportione sesquial. zu hauff haben/ also wird der Proporcien Tact wenn er langsam/ gegen dem gantzen/ odder gegen dem halben/ so er risch geschlagen wird/ geachtet·und abgemessen/ als ein Exempel. Der halbe Tact in diesem zeichen ¢ begreifft solcher ♩ ♩ ii. aber der Proporcien Tact alzeit der ♩ ♩ ♩ iii. Darumb wird der Proporcien Tact/ soviel als eine Minima ♩ langsamer dann die andern beide gefüret/ Und dieweil er nach der art der sesquialtern/ gegen den andern Tacten geschatzt/ und sie anderthalb mal in ihm beschleust/ mag er billich sesquialteratus odder Proportionatus Tactus (wie die Musici schreiben) genant werden. Auch braucht man ihn nicht überal/ sondern allein in Prolatione perfecta/ wie im 4. Cap. berürt/ odder in Proportione Tripla/ Hemiola/ wenn sie alle stymmen zu gleich haben/ und so wird alzeit eine Semibre. nach der masse/ wie sonst eine Minima gesungen.' Agricola, *Musica figuralis deudsch*, ch. 6, sig. Gv{r}.

[68] Berger, *Mensuration and Proportion Signs*, pp. 107–8, suggests that Agricola meant to say that the proportionate *tactus* is a minim faster, not a minim slower, than the other two *tactus*, but the passage makes sense and is internally consistent if the expression 'nach der art der sesquialtern/ gegen den andern Tacten geschatzt' is understood to mean that the 3:2 proportion applies to the lengths of the *tactus*, not to the note values. Thus in a triple or *hemiolia* proportion of ₵, the *tactus* will include three semibreves, each equivalent to a minim of ¢, and will be 50% longer than the semibreve half-*tactus* of ¢. Berger transcribes the mensuration sign in this passage as ₵, rather than ¢.
   The problem with Agricola's testimony is not so much in the ambiguity of this passage as in the contradictions between different descriptions of the proportionate *tactus* in the same treatise. For example, in the passage immediately preceding this one (sig. Giiii{v}), he says that a semibreve in the proportionate *tactus* is almost as fast as, rather than equal to, a minim of ¢ ('fast so risch/ als sonst eine Minima im halben Tact ¢'). A. Mendel, 'Some Ambiguities of the Mensural System', *Studies in Music History: Essays for Oliver Strunk*, ed. H. Powers (Princeton, 1968), pp. 137–60 (pp. 140–8), discusses additional contradictions among Agricola's statements about the tempo of the proportionate *tactus*.

is unclear. Ornithoparchus says: 'Most commonly the *Colour* doth cause a Duple proportion in the imperfect figures, (as *Franchinus* saith *lib. 2* cap. II.) which *Henry Isaack* in a certaine *Alleluia* of the Apostles, did thus both wittily, and truely dispose.'[69] The reference to Gaffurius is probably to book 2, chapter 4, of the *Practica musicae*, where blackening is described as reducing the length of minims and smaller values by half,[70] but Ornithoparchus's example has a bass in which longs and breves are diminished by half through blackening (see Example 11).[71] Heyden, perhaps following Ornithoparchus, says that 'if many notes are blackened the blackening rather frequently causes a *hemiolia* proportion, and sometimes *proportio dupla*'.[72] He promises further discussion and examples at a later point, but never again

Example 11. A. Ornithoparchus, *Musice active micrologus* (Leipzig, 1517), bk 2, ch. 12, sig. Giijᵛ; trans. J. Dowland (London, 1609), p. 57

[69] Ornithoparchus, *Musice active micrologus*, bk 2, ch. 11, sig. Giijᵛ; trans. Dowland, p. 57; *A Compendium of Musical Practice*, pp. 67 and 177.

[70] Gaffurius says nothing about coloration as duple proportion in bk 2, ch. 2, of the *Practica musicae*, but in bk 2, ch. 4, sig. aaiiijʳ (trans. Miller, p. 76), he refers to Tinctoris's definition of black minims (called 'semiminims' by others) as 'minims in duple proportion'. Tinctoris discusses the terminology in *Proportionale musices*, ch. 5, in *Opera theoretica*, ed. A. Seay, Corpus Scriptorum de Musica 22 (n.p., 1975–8), IIA, pp. 16–17; trans. A. Seay, Colorado College Music Press Translations 10 (Colorado Springs, 1979), p. 7. This usage may have been the source of later claims that coloration can indicate duple proportion.

[71] Modern edition in *A Compendium of Musical Practice*, pp. 67 and 177. M. Picker, *Henricus Isaac: A Guide to Research* (New York, 1991), p. 172, is unable to identify the example in the surviving works of Isaac.

[72] 'Si vero plures Notulae denigratae fuerint, tum frequentius Proportionem Hemioliam, nonnumquam Duplam nigredo efficit, quod utrumque suis exemplis infra constabit.' Heyden, *De arte canendi*, bk 2, ch. 1, p. 62; trans. Miller, p. 69.

mentions the possibility. The theorists mentioned above who claim that *hemiolia* proportions are faster than proportions notated in white notes might have been thinking of them as duple, rather than *sesquialtera*, although they do not say so specifically.

Practical sources prove without doubt that this relationship did exist, at least for proportions notated in black minims in relation to C; in this case, the black minim of the proportion is equated with a semiminim of white notation, to which it is identical in appearance. This interpretation was apparently most common in villanellas, which were often not measured in regular semibreve units at all (the lengths of sections or whole pieces could be an odd number of minims, and cadences could fall on any minim). Proportions based on the semibreve make little sense without a regular semibreve measure in the piece. Francesco Mazzoni's villanella *Di donne non vorrei* illustrates this relationship: in bar 9 a rest with the value of a black minim is notated as a semiminim rest, and in bar 13 a white minim in the upper two voices is equated with a black semibreve in the bass (see Example 12).[73]

There is no such concrete evidence for the interpretation of other ternary signs as duple proportion, but there are pieces in which the musical context implies that such an interpretation would be appropriate. In Ingegneri's motet *Super flumina Babilonis*, a proportion begins in the middle of a phrase (with the words 'de canticis Syon') in choir I, and the same phrase is then imitated by choir II entirely within the proportion (see Example 13).[74] A duple interpretation of this proportion is the only one

[73] Hell, 'Zu Rhythmus und Notierung', pp. 97–105, uses similar arguments to demonstrate (convincingly, in my opinion) that the same proportion exists between the ritornello of 'Vi ricorda, o boschi ombrosi' and the preceding C in Monteverdi's *Orfeo*. He traces the origin of the relationship to certain canzonettas and dances of the later sixteenth century (*ibid.*, pp. 105–23). F.-J. Machatius, 'Über mensurale und spielmännische Reduktion', *Die Musikforschung*, 8 (1955), pp. 139–51, calls this proportion 'spielmännische Reduktion' ('players' diminution'), in contrast to 'mensurale Reduktion' (diminution in which the *tactus* remains constant), because he believes that it originated in the kinds of dances and simple songs performed by popular instrumentalists. C. Dahlhaus, 'Die Tactus- und Proportionenlehre des 15. bis 17. Jahrhunderts', *Hören, Messen und Rechnen in der frühen Neuzeit*, ed. F. Zaminer, Geschichte der Musiktheorie 6 (Darmstadt, 1987), pp. 335–61 (p. 343), citing the passage from Agricola quoted above (n. 67), asserts that this interpretation of *sesquialtera* was not limited to pieces of popular character, but coexisted in all genres with interpretations in which the *tactus* remains constant.

[74] I am grateful to Michele Fromson for making her microfilm of this piece available

Example 12. Francesco Mazzoni, *Di donne non vorrei*, bars 6–14; Mazzoni, *Il primo libro delle canzoni alla napolitana a tre voci* (Venice, 1569; RISM 1569[29]), p. 2

that preserves the uniformity of tempo in the first phrase and makes the two phrases identical to each other. This meaning could not have been expressed by simply writing the phrase in half-values without changing the binary sign, because the first three bars of the proportion would have taken nine minims, the cadences would have fallen on the fourth and second minims of the breve *tempus*, and the following phrase (bar 70) would have begun on the second minim of the *tempus*.

If proportional signs could be interpreted in so many different ways in the sixteenth century, is there any reliable way to determine their meaning in specific pieces? It may be that closer investigation will reveal greater consistency in particular repertories than for the century as a whole, although most

to me. The rhythm of cantus 1 in bar 67 is semibreve–breve in the source. I have emended it to breve–semibreve by comparison with cantus 2, bar 69.

Example 13. Marc'Antonio Ingegneri, *Super flumina Babilonis*, bars 60–75; Ingegneri, *Liber sacrarum cantionum* (Venice, 1589), p. 16

writers of the period who attempted to find such patterns concluded that they did not exist. The only other alternative is to evaluate each case on its own merits. If a literal reading of any sign or an interpretation of major *sesquialtera* as triple proportion seems appropriate, it should probably be preferred to other alternatives that are less widely documented. Proportion signs are especially likely to be only indications of tempo, and therefore to require a literal interpretation, when the music to which they apply does not have ternary metrical character, as in Example 8. If a strictly proportional tempo seems too slow or too fast, a slightly different one that is close enough to preserve a feeling of proportionality may work

Example 13 (*cont.*)

well.[75] If none of these options produces a musically satisfactory result, the possibility of a duple or indeterminate relationship may also be considered.[76]

[75] I am grateful to Alexander Blachly for suggesting this possibility to me. His recordings of Lassus's *Cantate Domino* and Wert's *O sacrum convivium* with the Pomerium Musices on *The Flemish Masters: Netherlanders in Italy in the 16th Century*, I, Classic Masters CMCD-1007 are excellent examples of how it can work in practice. In the former the proportion is notated as minor *hemiolia*, with three black minims corresponding to a white semibreve in the same phrase (as in Example 10a), and in the latter it is notated as major *sesquialtera* under the sign Φ^3_2 (as in Example 5). In the performances of both, one third of the *tactus* of the proportion (a black minim or a white semibreve, respectively) is almost as slow as a minim of ¢, but the perceived relationship is between the complete *tactus* of the proportions and the semibreve of ¢, not between the smaller values.

[76] In a review of the performance of Taverner's *Western Wynde* mass by The Sixteen,

Example 13 (*cont.*)

Chronological considerations must also play a role. A breve *tactus*, and thus a literal reading of major *sesquialtera* of ¢, is more likely earlier in the century and was probably quite rare after *c.* 1560.[77] The proliferation of rhythmic styles and the decline

directed by Harry Christophers, on Hyperion CDA 66507 (recorded in 1991), *Early Music*, 21 (1993), p. 138, David Mateer points out that the triple-time sections are performed in duple proportion to the duple-time sections (a semibreve of triple equals a minim of duple), and that this solution works well in practice despite its lack of theoretical support.

[77] R. Bowers, 'Some Reflection upon Notation and Proportions in Monteverdi's Mass and Vespers of 1610', *Music and Letters*, 73 (1992), pp. 347–98, claims that all the proportions in Monteverdi's 1610 Vespers, including passages of major *sesquialtera* (in relation to C in the vocal part and ¢ in the basso continuo) in two sections of the Magnificat *a7*, should be interpreted literally. He cites several theorists, some of whose views he interprets in questionable ways, to support this opinion and calls those

in the distinction between ₵ and C in the last three or four decades of the century suggest that duple and indeterminate relationships became more common at that time. In many cases, differing interpretations of the same piece may have equal claim to historical authenticity. Different performers undoubtedly understood the same piece in different ways, and it is possible that composers did not always have a single interpretation in mind when they wrote proportion signs.

The search for reliable formulas to solve the problem of tempo relationships between different mensuration and proportion signs is nothing new. It occupied many of the best thinkers about music in the fifteenth and sixteenth centuries and has been a challenge to modern scholars for well over a century, but no consensus has ever been reached on the issues involved. Musical reality was too complex and diverse to be reducible to such formulas, and no amount of classifying or theorising about symbols can eliminate the need for musical judgment in interpreting them.

Hunter College and Graduate Center of the
City University of New York

who suggest other possibilities 'committed polemicists' (p. 370, n. 48). Considering the common complaints of strict theorists about practitioners (composers as well as singers) who do not follow their precepts, however, the term 'polemicists' might better apply to them than to their more liberal colleagues. Bowers's interpretations of minor *sesquialtera* and triple proportion are plausible, but his interpretation of major *sesquialtera* (pp. 377–9) is not. The *tactus* of the sections in which the proportion occurs is clearly the semibreve, since the proportion sometimes begins in the middle of a breve *tempus* (a fact obscured by the irregular barring of the binary passages in Bowers's Example 21, p. 379), and the tradition of interpreting *sesquialtera* in relation to the *tactus* was nearly a century old by that time.

Early Music History (1995) Volume 14

JAMES GRIER

ROGER DE CHABANNES (d. 1025), CANTOR OF ST MARTIAL, LIMOGES*

We know only two things with certainty about the life of Roger de Chabannes. He was a monk at the abbey of St Martial in Limoges by the year 1010, at which time he served as the teacher of his nephew, Adémar de Chabannes.[1] And when he died, on 26 April 1025, he held the position of the abbey's cantor.[2] Both pieces of information come to us from Adémar, monk at St Cybard in Angoulême, historian, homilist and tempestuous pol-

* A shorter version of this article was delivered at the Annual Meeting of the American Musicological Society in Montreal, 7 November 1993. I thank Margot E. Fassler for her thoughtful response. This study is part of a project to edit the complete works of Adémar de Chabannes for the Corpus Christianorum Continuatio Mediaeualis, directed by Richard Landes of Boston University. I am grateful to the Principal's Development Fund and the Advisory Research Committee, both of Queen's University, Kingston, Ontario; the Social Sciences and Humanities Research Council of Canada; and the A. Whitney Griswold Faculty Research Grant and the John F. Enders Research Assistance Grant, both of Yale University, for a series of grants that funded research trips to Paris and Limoges during the period 1989–94. For permission to reproduce photographs of materials in their collections, I thank Mme Véronique Notin of the Musée Municipal de l'Évêché, Limoges, M. Robert Chanaud of the Archives Départementales de la Haute-Vienne, Limoges, and M. François Avril of the Salle des Manuscrits, Bibliothèque Nationale, Paris. I am also very grateful to M. Avril and Mme Contamine of the Section Latine, Institut de Recherche et d'Histoire des Textes, for their many kindnesses.

[1] Adémar de Chabannes, *Chronicon*, 3.46, ed. J. Chavanon, *Chronique*, Collection de Textes pour Servir à l'Étude de l'Histoire (Paris, 1897), p. 168; and J. Lair, *Études critiques sur divers textes des Xe et XIe siècles*, ii, *Historia d'Adémar de Chabannes* (Paris, 1899), p. 190. The date is given in the next paragraph, *Chronicon*, 3.47, ed. Chavanon, p. 169; and Lair, *Historia*, p. 191. The three recensions of this work do not agree in all particulars: see Lair, *Historia*, esp. pp. 92–104, 236–7, 277–84, who also prints in parallel columns all versions of 3.16–66 (pp. 104–235) and 3.66–70 (pp. 237–45). Elsewhere, Adémar calls Roger 'meus magister': [Adémar de Chabannes], *Commemoratio abbatum lemouicensium basilice S. Marcialis apostoli*, ed. H. Duplès-Agier, *Chroniques de Saint-Martial de Limoges* (Paris, 1874), p. 8. Both texts will be newly edited in Adémar's Complete Works, to appear in the series Corpus Christianorum Continuatio Mediaeualis.

[2] Roger as cantor: Adémar, *Chronicon*, 3.61, ed. Chavanon, pp. 186–7; Lair, *Historia*, pp. 226–7. Death date: [Adémar], *Commemoratio abbatum*, ed. Duplès-Agier, p. 8.

emicist in the campaign to win recognition for St Martial as an apostle.[3] Other evidence, which also may well originate from Adémar, attests to Roger's death date and office. A large tombstone, which appears to be the lid of a sarcophagus and which today reposes in the Musée Municipal de l'Évêché in Limoges, bears the inscription: 'VI. KL. MAI. REQVIEVIT ROTGERIVS CANTOR' (see Figure 1).[4] The abbey's first necrology, in Paris, Bibliothèque Nationale, fonds latin, MS (hereafter Pa) 5257 (fols. 44^v–69^r), bears the entry 'Rotgerius Le[mouicensis]', added on fol. 52^v beside the date 26 April.[5] Jean-Loup Lemaître concludes from the agreement in death date that both items refer to Roger de Chabannes, and suggests that Adémar may have

[3] On Adémar's biography, see L. Saltet, 'Une discussion sur Saint Martial entre un Lombard et un Limousin en 1029', *Bulletin de Littérature Ecclésiastique*, 26 (1925), pp. 161–86, 279–302; 'Une prétendue lettre de Jean XIX sur Saint Martial fabriquée par Adémar de Chabannes', *ibid.*, 27 (1926), pp. 117–39; 'Les faux d'Adémar de Chabannes: Prétendues décisions sur Saint Martial au concile de Bourges du 1er novembre 1031', *ibid.*, 27 (1926), pp. 145–60; and 'Un cas de mythomanie historique bien documenté: Adémar de Chabannes (988–1034)', *ibid.*, 32 (1931), pp. 149–65; and R. Landes, 'The Making of a Medieval Historian: Ademar of Chabannes and Aquitaine at the Turn of the Millenium' (Ph.D. dissertation, Princeton University, 1984). For further bibliography, see J. Grier, '*Ecce sanctum quem Deus elegit Marcialem apostolum*: Adémar de Chabannes and the Tropes for the Feast of Saint Martial', *Beyond the Moon: Festschrift Luther Dittmer*, ed. B. Gillingham and P. Merkley, Wissenschaftliche Abhandlungen 53 (Ottawa, 1990), p. 28, n. 2.

[4] Limoges, Musée Municipal, Inv. Arc. L. 155; see M. Marcheix and J. Perrier, *Guide du Musée Municipal: Collection Archéologique* (Limoges, 1969), no. 245, p. 111. Its discovery is announced in [M.] Ardant, 'Médailles et monnaies trouvées à Saint-Martial de Limoges', *Mémoires de la Société Royale des Antiquaires de France*, 14 (1838), pp. 165–6. See also Ardant, 'Note sur le tombeau du chantre Roger, retiré des fouilles de l'église de St-Martial, à Limoges', *Bulletin de la Société Royale d'Agriculture, Sciences et Arts de Limoges*, 18 (1840), pp. 30–2; [J. R. A.] Texier, *Manuel d'épigraphie suivi du recueil des inscriptions du Limousin* (Poitiers, 1851), no. 53, pp. 113–15; E. Castaigne, 'Dissertation sur le lieu de naissance et sur la famille du chroniqueur Adémar, moine de l'Abbaye de Saint-Cybard d'Angoulême, faussement surnommé de Chabanais, né vers 988 et mort vers 1030', *Bulletin de la Société Archéologique et Historique de la Charente*, 4 (1850), pp. 83–4 and n. 8; R. Favreau, J. Michaud and E.-R. Labande, *Corpus des inscriptions de la France médiévale*, ii, *Limousin: Corrèze, Creuse, Haute-Vienne* (Poitiers, 1978), HV 51, pp. 153–4 and pl. XXVII, figs. 54–5; and J.-L. Lemaître, *Mourir à Saint-Martial: La commémoration des morts et les obituaires à Saint-Martial de Limoges du XIe au XIIIe siècle* (Paris, 1989), pp. 335–6, 478–9.

[5] Pa 5257 dates from the late eleventh century, after the Cluniac takeover of St Martial in 1063; see J.-L. Lemaître, *Répertoire des documents nécrologiques français*, 2 vols., Recueil des Historiens de la France, Obituaires 7 (Paris, 1980), ii, no. 2764, p. 1140; *idem*, *Mourir à Saint-Martial*, pp. 119–20, 233–40, 293–300; and *Synopse der cluniacensischen Necrologien*, ed. J. Wollasch, 2 vols., Münstersche Mittelalter-Schriften 39 (Munich, 1982), i, p. 41. For the entry, see *Synopse*, ed. Wollasch, ii, p. 232; Lemaître, *Mourir à Saint-Martial*, p. 478 and n. 15 (p. 493), gives, incorrectly, fol. 53^r.

Figure 1   The tombstone of Roger de Chabannes (Limoges, Musée Municipal de l'Évêché, Inv. Arc. L. 155)

been responsible for the erection of the tombstone.[6] Finally, a marginal note in the Easter tables in Pa 5239 (fol. 19[r]), beside the year 1025, reads: 'obierunt Vgo abbas Rotgerius cantor'.[7] Adémar could be the ultimate source for all this evidence: besides Lemaître's conjecture about the tombstone, the entries in Pa 5239 and 5257 may descend from Adémar's account of Roger's death in the *Commemoratio abbatum*.

The name Roger also appears in Pa 1138, part of an eleventh-century proser, at the bottom of fol. 50[r].[8] Hans Spanke and Richard Crocker both claim that this note refers to Roger de Chabannes.[9] Jacques Chailley points out, however, that this manuscript contains two prosae that recognise the apostolic status of Martial, *Alma cohors* and *Laudum da falanx*.[10] They are written

---

[6] Lemaîte, *Mourir à Saint-Martial*, pp. 478–9, where he further notes that the entry does not recur in the two later necrologies found in Pa 5243 (late eleventh century; fols. 93–136) and Pa 5245 (late twelfth century; fols. 136–63). Both, however, record the name Rotcherius, which could simply be a variant spelling, for this date (Pa 5243, fol. 107[r]; Pa 5245, fol. 145[v]); on the former, see *Synopse*, ed. Wollasch, II, p. 232. Adémar also erected a funerary plaque for St Martial: Limoges, Musée Municipal, Inv. Arc. L. 37; see Marcheix and Perrier, *Guide du Musée Municipal: Collection Archéologique*, no. 136, p. 63. See also Favreau *et al.*, *Corpus des inscriptions*, II, *Limousin*, HV 52, pp. 154–6 and pl. XXVIII, figs. 56–7; and Lemaître, *Mourir à Saint-Martial*, p. 491.

[7] Some of the marginal notations in Pa 5239 were written by Adémar; see D. Gaborit-Chopin, *La décoration des manuscrits à Saint-Martial de Limoges et en Limousin du IXe au XIIe siècle*, Mémoires et Documents Publiés par la Société de l'École des Chartes 17 (Paris and Geneva, 1969), p. 204; and Landes, 'The Making of a Medieval Historian', pp. 128–35. That concerning Roger is not in his hand.

[8] This manuscript, together with Pa 1338, fols. 1–143, constitutes a single proser. For a reconstruction of the original manuscript, see *Analecta hymnica* (hereafter *AH*), 55 vols., ed. G. M. Dreves, C. Blume and H. M. Bannister (Leipzig, 1886–1922), VII, pp. 6–8; R. L. Crocker, 'The Repertoire of Proses at Saint Martial de Limoges (Tenth and Eleventh Centuries)', 2 vols. (Ph.D. dissertation, Yale University, 1957), I, pp. 127–50; J. Chailley, 'Les anciens tropaires et séquentiaires de l'école de Saint-Martial de Limoges (Xe–XIe s.)', *Études Grégoriennes*, 2 (1957), pp. 179–80; *idem*, *L'école musicale de Saint Martial de Limoges jusqu'à la fin du XIe siècle* (Paris, 1960), pp. 96–8; and H. Husmann, *Tropen- und Sequenzenhandschriften*, Répertoire International des Sources Musicales B V[1] (Munich, 1964), pp. 136–7. I tentatively transcribe the note as 'Rotgerius in hoc peccator'; L. Delisle's transcription, 'Les manuscrits de Saint-Martial de Limoges: Réimpression textuelle du Catalogue publié en 1730', *Bulletin de la Société Archéologique et Historique du Limousin* (hereafter *BSAHL*), 43 (1895), p. 11, 'Rotgerius miser peccator', is palaeographically impossible.

[9] H. Spanke, 'St. Martial-Studien: Ein Beitrag zur frühromanischen Metrik', *Zeitschrift für Französische Sprache und Literatur*, 54 (1931), p. 286; Crocker, 'The Repertoire of Proses' I, p. 127, and II, p. 126; and *idem*, 'The Repertory of Proses at Saint Martial de Limoges', *Journal of the American Musicological Society*, 11 (1958), p. 153. Lair, *Historia*, p. 226, n. 1, tentatively identified this Roger as Roger de Chabannes.

[10] Pa 1338, fols. 130[v]–132[v], 132[v]–134[v], respectively; Chailley, *L'école*, p. 97 and n. 2. Both are older melodies that Adémar may have adopted for the feast of St Martial.

in the manuscript's first hand, among a series of prosulae. Elsewhere in the manuscript, a third apostolic prosa, *Arce polorum*, also appears in the principal hand in a similar context.[11] The monks at St Martial did not officially endorse the apostolic status of Martial until after 18 November 1028, which then becomes a *terminus ante quem non* for the date of Pa 1138/1338. Consequently, the Roger mentioned in Pa 1138 cannot be Roger de Chabannes, who had, of course, died before the compilation of Pa 1138/1338. Moreover, evidence that emerges from the music manuscripts created at St Martial during his lifetime shows that the liturgy for Martial's feast prior to A D 1028 was rigorously episcopal in its orientation. The Roger of Pa 1138, therefore, is a younger monk who may have been a musician or even cantor in the generation after Roger de Chabannes.

A tantalising new piece of evidence may establish Roger's presence in the abbey in the last decade of the tenth century. A charter from the abbey, which records a land transaction dated 25 August 992, is signed 'Rotgerius scripsit' (see Figure 2).[12] Full prosopographical data for the abbey is lacking, but from the necrology in Pa 5257 it would appear that the name Rotgerius was by no means rare at St Martial in the eleventh century. Wollasch's index gives no fewer than seventy-eight monks of this name.[13] Some of these are designated as Cluniac monks, and a few appear among the *peregrini*, but a comparison with the other necrologies printed by Wollasch demonstrates that Rotgerius is much more common at St Martial than elsewhere.[14]

They both appear in his hand as untexted sequences in Pa 909, fols. 121^v–122^r, 116^{r-v}, and Pa 1121, fols. 65^r, 62^v–63^r, respectively. See also Crocker, 'The Repertoire of Proses', I, pp. 203, 204, 264, 267, and II, pp. 14, 48. Editions of the texts: *Alma cohors*, *AH*, VII, no. 218, p. 238 (see also *AH*, LIII, no. 244a, pp. 392–3); *Laudum da falanx*, *AH*, VII, no. 160, pp. 175–7.

[11] Pa 1338, fols. 5^v–8^v; see Crocker, 'The Repertoire of Proses', I, p. 130. This may have been composed by Adémar: it appears in his hand as a prosa and as an untexted sequence in Pa 909, fols. 198^r–199^v and 118^r, respectively. Edition of text: *AH*, VII, no. 168, pp. 185–6.

[12] Limoges, Archives Départementales de la Haute-Vienne, MS 3 H 89 (24). Text published in *Chartes, chroniques et mémoriaux, pour servir à l'histoire de la Marche et du Limousin*, ed. A. Leroux and A. Bosvieux (Tulle, 1886), no. 4, p. 10.

[13] *Synopse*, ed. Wollasch, I, p. 199b.

[14] *Ibid.*, pp. 199b–200a. After the two necrologies from St Martial, Pa 5257 and 5243, that with the next highest incidence of the name is from Marcigny-sur-Loire (Paris, Bibliothèque Nationale, nouvelles acquisitions latines, MS 348), with twenty-seven occurrences of the name.

Figure 2 Limoges, cliché et document Archives Départementales de la Haute-Vienne, MS 3 H 89 (24)

Moreover, a second charter, dated March 1016, shows that at least one other monk of the same name lived at St Martial during the lifetime of Roger de Chabannes.[15] Among the witnesses is one Rotgerius Berget. His name occurs after that of the abbot Iosfredus, whose name, in turn, follows those of the lay donors. The surname Berget may have been used to distinguish this monk from Roger the cantor. With the available evidence, therefore, we cannot make more than a tentative identification of Roger de Chabannes as the scribe of the 992 charter. Nevertheless, the likelihood of his having performed this task is great. Susan Rankin observes that another musician, Notker Balbulus of the abbey of St Gall, wrote similar charters for his house, and Margot E. Fassler, in a seminal article, shows that those who rose to the rank of cantor were among the best educated monks in the community.[16]

If I am right in naming Roger de Chabannes as the scribe of the 992 charter, that identification carries two important ramifications. First, Roger was present at St Martial by 992 at the latest, eighteen years before our previous earliest date. Moreover, it is unlikely that the preparation of this document would have been entrusted to someone who had recently arrived, and so we can speculate that he had already been a monk there for some years by the time the charter was written. Second, it may be possible to identify the Roger who inscribed the charter as the scribe of one or more of the music manuscripts preserved from the abbey.

This is the limit of our factual knowledge about Roger. What follows is a hypothesis built on three types of evidence. First, Adémar reports additional details about his family that allow us to infer more of Roger's biography. Second, Adémar's own accomplishments as a musician attest, indirectly at least, the abilities of his teacher. Finally, the pattern of surviving music manuscripts from St Martial demonstrates that the first decades

---

[15] Limoges, Archives Départementales de la Haute-Vienne, MS 3 H 89 (19) (text published in *Chartes, chroniques et mémoriaux*, ed. Leroux and Bosvieux, no. 5, p. 11).

[16] S. Rankin, ' "Ego itaque Notker scripsi" ', *Revue Bénédictine*, 101 (1991), pp. 268–98; and Margot E. Fassler, 'The Office of the Cantor in Early Western Monastic Rules and Customaries: A Preliminary Investigation', *Early Music History*, 5 (1985), pp. 29–51.

of the eleventh century witnessed a complete reorganisation of the liturgical music used at the abbey, a reorganisation in which Roger participated as a senior member of the musical hierarchy at St Martial, if he did not, in fact, supervise it himself.

Adémar gives us a reasonably full picture of his genealogy back into the tenth century.[17] His mother's family formed part of the aristocratic military élite in the region around Angoulême, which sought close ties with the ecclesiastic hierarchy.[18] For his mother, Hildegarde, married Raymond de Chabannes, whose family was well established in ecclesiastic circles in Limoges. Two of Raymond's great uncles occupied important positions in the diocese of Limoges during the tenth century: Aimo and Turpin were, respectively, abbot of St Martial and bishop of Limoges.[19] In Raymond's own generation, his two older brothers served as senior officials at St Martial. Adalbert, presumably the eldest, was deacon from the time of Abbot Guigo (who reigned 974–91) until his death on 21 April 1007.[20] The middle brother, of course, is our cantor, Roger de Chabannes (see Figure 3).

[17] Castaigne, 'Dissertation', pp. 81–3 and genealogical table following p. 96; and Lair, *Historia*, pp. 273–6. For other genealogical details, see L. Levillain, 'Adémar de Chabannes, généalogiste', *Bulletins de la Société des Antiquaires de l'Ouest*, ser. 3, 10 (1934–5), pp. 254–63.

[18] Adémar, *Chronicon*, 3.45, ed. Chavanon, pp. 167–8; Lair, *Historia*, pp. 187–8. He characterises two of his maternal uncles, Abbo and Raymond, as 'strenuissimos duces, corpore robustos, animo bellicosos' ('most vigorous leaders, their bodies as strong as oak trees, and warlike in spirit').

[19] [Adémar], *Commemoratio abbatum*, ed. Duplès-Agier, pp. 3–4. On Aimo, see C. de Lasteyrie, *L'abbaye de Saint-Martial de Limoges: Étude historique, économique et archéologique précédée de recherches nouvelles sur la vie du saint* (Paris, 1901), pp. 62–3. On Turpin, see J. Becquet, 'Les évêques de Limoges aux Xe, XIe et XIIe siècles', *BSAHL*, 104 (1977), pp. 75–82. These are the only ancestors named by Adémar; for other genealogical speculations on his family, see J. Nadaud, *Nobiliaire du diocèse et de la généralité de Limoges*, 2nd edn (Limoges, 1882; repr. Paris, 1974), pp. 44–7; and M. Aubrun, *L'ancien diocèse de Limoges des origines au milieu du XIe siècle*, Publications de l'Institut d'Études du Massif Central 21 (Clermont-Ferrand, 1981), p. 134 and n. 1.

[20] [Adémar], *Commemoratio abbatum*, ed. Duplès-Agier, pp. 4–6; and the necrologies in Pa 5257 (fol. 52ᵛ), Pa 5243 (fol. 106ᵛ) and Pa 5245 (fol. 145ʳ); on the first two, see *Synopse*, ed. Wollasch, ii, p. 222. Codex Pa 1969 bears the colophon 'ADALBERTVS DECANVS ME FIERI IVSSIT' (fol. 162ᵛ); see L. Delisle, *Le cabinet des manuscrits de la Bibliothèque Impériale*, 4 vols., Histoire Générale de Paris (Paris, 1868–81; repr. Amsterdam, 1969, and New York, 1974), i, p. 388; C. Samaran and R. Marichal, *Catalogue des manuscrits en écriture latine portant des indications de date, de lieu ou de copiste*, ii, *Bibliothèque Nationale, fonds latin (nos 1 à 8.000)* (Paris, 1962), p. 99; Les Bénédictins du Bouveret, *Colophons de manuscrits occidentaux des origines au XVIe siècle*, 6 vols., Spicilegii Friburgensis Subsidia 2–7 (Fribourg, 1965–82), i, no. 102, p. 13; and Landes, 'The Making of a Medieval Historian', pp. 135–7.

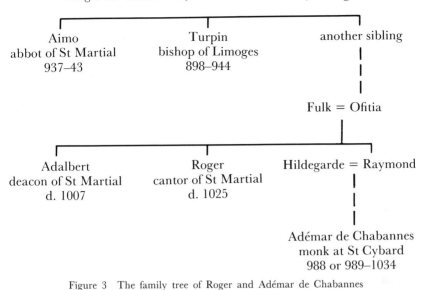

Figure 3   The family tree of Roger and Adémar de Chabannes

This family biography allows us to speculate on Roger's age and the trajectory of his career. For the former, we must calculate backwards from Adémar's statements about his own age, from which we can infer the age of his father, Raymond, and so make an educated guess at Roger's birth date. In 1029, Adémar calls himself a quadragenarian.[21] Now, he could not have been much more than forty years of age because his parents had just made the trip from Chabannes to Limoges, a journey of some thirty kilometres (Adémar states they had come 'de longinquo') and not likely to be undertaken by anyone much over sixty.[22] Scholars usually accept 988 or 989 as Adémar's birth date, and so Raymond must have been born between 965 and 970. These dates, in turn, serve as a *terminus post quem non* for his older brother, Roger, who, therefore, was probably born between 960 and 965. In view of his family's involvement in the church hierarchy and the positions he and his brother Adalbert eventually attained, it

[21]   Adémar de Chabannes, *Epistola de apostolatu sancti Martialis*, ed. J.-P. Migne, *Patrologiae cursus completus: Series latina* (hereafter *PL*), 221 vols. (Paris, 1844–64), cxli, col. 89. A new edition of this letter is forthcoming in Corpus Christianorum Continuatio Mediaeualis. On these calculations, see Landes, 'The Making of a Medieval Historian', pp. 108–15.
[22]   Adémar, *Epistola de apostolatu*, *PL*, cxli, col. 94.

is most likely that Roger entered St Martial as an oblate before he reached his teenage years, no later than 975. His nephew Adémar, for example, states that he had lived at St Cybard since his 'tenderest youth' ('ab ipsa tenerrima pueritia').[23]

This highly speculative biography of Roger helps to explain his career at St Martial. Fassler establishes that the office of cantor was among the most important in the medieval monastery, with broad responsibilities for the celebration of the liturgy and the creation and maintenance of liturgical books.[24] For Roger to have risen to a position of such authority, he must have been a respected and able musician, learned in liturgical practices and a competent scribe. These qualities are compatible with the epithets Adémar bestows on him: 'famous', 'shining in wisdom' and, finally, 'most famous' ('inclitus', 'sapientia fulgidus' and 'clarissimus').[25] It seems reasonable to conclude that both his pedagogical responsibilities in 1010 and his eventual elevation to cantor were attained through long and distinguished service in the monastery.

We do not know when he became cantor, but his appointment most probably occurred after the completion of his nephew's studies at St Martial (i.e. sometime after 1010), because Adémar does not identify him as cantor in that context. This account is consistent with my tentative identification of Roger as the scribe of the 992 charter. At that time he would have been approximately thirty years of age, a monk with about twenty years' seniority who would have spent a significant amount of time in the scriptorium and would therefore have been a suitable person to record a land transaction.

Adémar himself was an accomplished musician, and at least some of the credit for his competence may be attributed to his teacher, Roger.[26] Three music manuscripts with notation in

---

[23] *Ibid.*, col. 89.

[24] Fassler, 'The Office of the Cantor'. She notes, pp. 43–51, that by the mid-eleventh century the offices of cantor and armarius (librarian) seem to have been combined at Cluny. They were still separate at St Martial in the early part of the century, however: Adémar identifies Roger and Aldebert as cantor and armarius, respectively: *Chronicon*, 3.61, ed. Chavanon, p. 187; Lair, *Historia*, pp. 226–7.

[25] Adémar, *Chronicon*, 3.46, 61, ed. Chavanon, pp. 168, 186; Lair, *Historia*, pp. 190, 226; *Commemoratio abbatum*, ed. Duplès-Agier, p. 8.

[26] On Adémar's musical activities, see L. Delisle, 'Notice sur les manuscrits originaux d'Adémar de Chabannes', *Notices et extraits des manuscrits de la Bibliothèque Nationale et*

Adémar's hand survive. The endleaves at the back of Pa 1978 consist of a bifolium with both music and text in Adémar's hand (fols. 102^r–103^v).[27] The bifolium contains portions of an Office for St Cybard (the patron of his home abbey in Angoulême), and of what seems to be an Office for the octave of St Martial. Codices Pa 1121 and 909 are among the celebrated group of Aquitanian troper-prosers. These manuscripts are organised in *libelli* in which pieces of the same liturgical classifications are grouped together.[28] Pa 1121 contains a complete sequentiary (i.e. a *libellus* of untexted and partially texted sequences, called *sequentiae* in Aquitaine) for the full liturgical year written in Adémar's hand (fols. 58^r–72^v).[29] Adémar signed the *libellus* in three places (fols. 58^r, 60^r and 72^v), identifying himself in the last entry as the music scribe of the sequentiary; the limited text of the *libellus* is in his hand as well.[30]

Our principal source for Adémar's musical activities is Pa 909. Scholars have recognised his hand in several additions to the

autres bibliothèques, xxxv (Paris, 1896), pp. 350–3; P. Hooreman, 'Saint-Martial de Limoges au temps de l'Abbé Odolric (1025–1040): Essai sur une pièce oubliée du répertoire limousin', *Revue Belge de Musicologie*, 3 (1949), pp. 5–36; J. A. Emerson, 'Two Newly Identified Offices for Saints Valeria and Austriclinianus by Adémar de Chabannes (MS Paris, Bibl. Nat., Latin 909, fols. 79–85^v)', *Speculum*, 40 (1965), pp. 31–46; M. Huglo, 'Codicologie et musicologie', *Miscellanea codicologica F. Masai dicata MCMLXXIX*, 2 vols., ed. P. Cockshaw, M.-C. Garand and P. Jodogne, Publications de Scriptorium 8 (Ghent, 1979), i, pp. 76–81; Grier, '*Ecce sanctum*', pp. 28–74; and *idem*, 'Editing Adémar de Chabannes' Liturgy for the Feast of Saint Martial', *Music Discourse from Classical to Early Modern Times: Editing and Translating Texts*, ed. M. R. Maniates, Conference on Editorial Problems 26 (New York, 1993), pp. 17–43.

27 Identified by Delisle, 'Notice', pp. 350–2; see also Lair, *Historia*, p. 281.
28 Crocker, 'The Repertoire of Proses', i, pp. 190–5, 246–58; Chailley, 'Les anciens tropaires', pp. 169–71, 174–7; *idem*, *L'école*, pp. 81–3, 88–92; Husmann, *Tropen- und Sequenzenhandschriften*, pp. 118–19, 130–1; and P. Evans, *The Early Trope Repertory of Saint Martial de Limoges*, Princeton Studies in Music 2 (Princeton, 1970), pp. 48–9. On the *libellus* structure of this type of manuscript in general, see M. Huglo, 'Les libelli de tropes et les premiers tropaires-prosaires', *Pax et sapientia: Studies in Text and Music of Liturgical Tropes and Sequences in Memory of Gordon Anderson*, ed. R. Jacobsson, Acta Universitatis Stockholmiensis, Studia Latina Stockholmiensia 29 (Stockholm, 1986), pp. 13–22; and *idem*, *Les livres de chant liturgique*, Typologie des Sources du Moyen Age Occidental 52 (Turnhout, 1988), pp. 64–75.
29 Identified by Delisle, 'Notice', pp. 352–3.
30 The signatures have been printed in full many times, first by Delisle, *Le cabinet des manuscrits*, i, pp. 388–9; and more recently in Huglo, 'Codicologie et musicologie', p. 79 (where two errors have entered the text of the colophon on fol. 72^v: in the first line, Huglo prints 'dogmata' for 'dogmate', and in the last line, 'actus' for 'actis').

codex, all of which concern the apostolic liturgy for St Martial.[31] The earliest layer of the book, however, seems to have originated in the scriptorium of St Martial as a commission for the neighbouring house of St Martin in Limoges. This deduction follows from a comparison of the contents of Pa 909 with those of Pa 1120 and 1121, two large troper-prosers produced at St Martial for its own use in the first decades of the eleventh century.[32] Codex Pa 1121, of course, is that to which Adémar later added a sequentiary, as noted above. The repertory in the original layer of Pa 909 exhibits great similarities with both these manuscripts.[33] The troped Mass for the feast of St Martin, however, is greatly expanded in Pa 909 over that found in its two models, and so attests the book's intended use at St Martin, as Chailley suggests.[34]

New evidence firmly places this original layer of Pa 909 in the scriptorium at St Martial, and that is the identification of Adémar de Chabannes as the music scribe in significant portions of the first phase of the book's production (see Table 1).[35] This identification also provides a more specific date for the execution of the codex, and indicates Adémar's status in the abbey's scriptorium on his arrival there in 1028. Adémar seems to have witnessed some of the events surrounding the death of Count William of Angoulême on 6 April 1028, and so he arrived at St Martial sometime between then and the dedication of the new abbatial basilica on 18 November, an event he also witnessed.[36]

[31] First noted unequivocally by Hooreman, 'Saint-Martial de Limoges', pp. 16–30. See also Emerson, 'Two Newly Identified Offices', pp. 33–5; Grier, '*Ecce sanctum*', pp. 35–40; and *idem*, 'Editing Adémar de Chabannes' Liturgy', pp. 18–23.

[32] Crocker, 'The Repertoire of Proses', I, pp. 176–209; Chailley, 'Les anciens tropaires', pp. 167–71; *idem*, *L'école*, pp. 80–3; and Husmann, *Tropen- und Sequenzenhandschriften*, pp. 128–31. Pa 1121 descends from Pa 1120: see Evans, *The Early Trope Repertory*, pp. 47–8; and A. E. Planchart, 'The Transmission of Medieval Chant', *Music in Medieval and Early Modern Europe: Patronage, Sources and Texts*, ed. I. Fenlon (Cambridge, 1981), pp. 353–60.

[33] Grier, '*Ecce sanctum*', pp. 54–69.

[34] Troped Mass for the feast of St Martin: Pa 909, fols. 54^v–57^r; Pa 1120, fols. 62^r–64^r; Pa 1121, fols. 41$^{r–v}$. Chailley, 'Les anciens tropaires', p. 174; and *L'école*, pp. 88–92; see also Grier, '*Ecce sanctum*', pp. 68–9. Cf. Husmann, *Tropen- und Sequenzenhandschriften*, pp. 118–19, who, in view of the added apostolic liturgy for Martial, ascribes the original layer also to the use of St Martial.

[35] Gunilla Iversen, Richard Landes and I collaborated on the identification.

[36] Adémar gives a detailed report of Count William's death in *Chronicon*, 3.66–8, ed. Chavanon, pp. 190–4; Lair, *Historia*, pp. 235–44. Our best sources for the dedication are Adémar's sermons, which survive in autograph in Pa 2469, fols. 89^r–97^r, numbered

Table 1 *Portions of Pa 909 in which the music only was copied by Adémar de Chabannes*

Folios	Inventory
9^r–40^v, 49^r–59^r	Proper tropes
86^r–109^v	Ordinary tropes
126^r–140^r	Tracts
140^r–149^v	Benedictions, litany, antiphons, miscellaneous items for Easter
150^r–165^v	Processional antiphons
166^r–167^r	Alleluias
168^v–173^v	Antiphons for Easter
174^r–197^v	Alleluias
246^r–251^r	Processional antiphons
251^r–257^v	Tonary
258^r–269^v	Antiphons

Therefore, work on Pa 909 began after April 1028. The fact that the copying of so elaborate a manuscript should be entrusted to Adémar suggests that members of the scriptorium at St Martial had a great deal of respect for his competence as a musician and scribe.

After 18 November 1028, the monks at St Martial hatched a plot to have their patron recognised as an apostle. Adémar was either an early recruit or himself the ringleader. In any event, he soon took on a leading role, compiling a new apostolic liturgy to celebrate Martial's elevation in status. To accommodate his creation, he appropriated Pa 909, now in an advanced but incomplete state.[37] He made several additions to the codex, in all of which he wrote both text and music (see Table 2). Most of these additions concern the new apostolic liturgy for the feast of St Martial directly, or embellish his cult indirectly by supplying materials for the feasts of his companions Valery, Austriclinian

38–46 in Delisle's inventory: 'Notice', pp. 282–3. Editions: excerpts from nos. 38, 39, 44, and all of 46, E. Sackur, *Die Cluniacenser in ihrer kirchlichen und allgemeingeschichtlichen Wirksamkeit bis zur Mitte des elften Jahrhunderts*, 2 vols. (Halle, 1892–4), II, pp. 479–87; no. 44, Lasteyrie, *L'abbaye de Saint-Martial*, pièce justificative 5, pp. 422–6; and no. 45, *Sermo III*, *PL*, CXLI, cols. 120–4. A complete edition of the sermons is forthcoming in Corpus Christianorum Continuatio Mediaeualis.

[37] Chailley, 'Les anciens tropaires', p. 175; *idem*, *L'école*, p. 89; Gaborit-Chopin, *La décoration*, p. 183; Evans, *The Early Trope Repertory*, pp. 32–3; Grier, 'Ecce sanctum', p. 35; and *idem*, 'Editing Adémar de Chabannes' Liturgy', pp. 19–22.

Table 2   *Adémar de Chabannes's additions to Pa 909*

Folios	Inventory
41^r–48^v	Proper tropes (fols. 42^r–46^v: troped Mass for St Martial)
59^r–61^v	Proper tropes
61^v–62^r	Alleluias for St Martial
62^v–77^v	Office and miscellaneous liturgical items for St Martial
79^r–85^v	Offices for Sts Valery and Austriclinian
110^r–125^v	Sequentiae (fols. 118^r–119^v: sequentiae for St Martial)
177^v–178^r	Alleluias for St Martial
198^r	Sequentia
198^r–201^v	Prosae for St Martial
202^r–205^r	Versus de Sancto Marciale LXXta IIo
205^{r-v}	Sequentia
251^r	Processional antiphon for St Martial
254^r–257^v	Tonary: additions by Adémar

and Justinian. On 3 August 1029, the monks of St Martial inaugurated the new apostolic liturgy. Unfortunately, it met with disaster. A Lombard monk, Benedict of Chiusa, appeared just as the procession before Mass was starting, and denounced the liturgy as a heresy and an insult to God. His charges swayed the crowd and, more important, Bishop Jordan of Limoges and Abbot Odolric of St Martial. The next day Adémar, in disgrace, beat a hasty retreat to St Cybard, where he spent the rest of his life concocting evidence to establish the apostolic status of Martial.[38]

Political reverses aside, these three manuscripts illustrate Adémar's achievements as a musician. His scribal output evinces a thorough and sophisticated knowledge of contemporary musical notation.[39] He consistently uses the *custos* at the end of each line,

---

[38] Adémar, *Epistola de apostolatu*, *PL*, cxli, cols. 89–112; for commentary, see Saltet, 'Une discussion'. The proceedings of the Council at Limoges in 1031, ed. P. Labbe and G. Cossart, *Sacrosancta concilia*, 16 vols. (Paris, 1671–2), ix, cols. 869–910; and ed. G. Mansi, *Sacrorum conciliorum noua et amplissima collectio*, 31 vols. (Florence and Venice, 1759–98), xix, cols. 507–48. These proceedings include a large interpolation that is an invention of Adémar's; see Saltet, 'Les faux', pp. 145–6 and n. 6; and 'Un cas de mythomanie', pp. 152–7. The Council's proceedings will be newly edited in Corpus Christianorum Continuatio Mediaeualis. For an example of some of the evidence that Adémar invented, see R. Landes, 'A Libellus from St. Martial of Limoges Written in the Time of Ademar of Chabannes (989–1034): "Un faux à retardement" ', *Scriptorium*, 37 (1983), pp. 178–204.

[39] Facsimiles of manuscript pages in his hand are printed in Delisle, 'Notice', pl. VI, between pp. 240 and 241 (Pa 1978, fol. 102^v; music and text in Adémar's hand); *Introitus-tropen*, i, *Das Repertoire der südfranzösischen Tropare des 10. und 11. Jahrhunderts*,

sometimes in the form of the letter 'e' (designating 'equaliter'), to indicate the relationship between the last note of a line and the following note. Other *litterae significatiuae* confirm large jumps in the melody that are accurately heighted.[40] He also places roman numerals at the beginning of most pieces that include a verse sung to a tone (e.g. responsories for Matins and antiphons) to indicate the modal assignment of the melody and therefore which tone is to be sung for the verse.[41] Here he follows the practice found in Pa 1085, an antiphoner written at St Martial before the dedication of 18 November 1028, and to which we shall return presently. All these features were relatively recent developments in musical notation, and they show that Adémar was at least current in his knowledge of the maturing technology.

Several of the pieces in the apostolic liturgy for St Martial are either unica or survive in no earlier source. In view of Adémar's close personal involvement with the campaign around Martial's apostolicity, it is quite likely that some or all of these items were

ed. G. Weiss, Monumenta Monodica Medii Aeui 3 (Kassel, Basle, Tours and London, 1970), pl. VI, p. XXXIV (Pa 909, fol. 36ᵛ; music only in Adémar's hand); *Corpus troporum* (hereafter *CT*), iv, *Tropes de l'Agnus Dei*, ed. G. Iversen, Acta Universitatis Stockholmiensis, Studia Latina Stockholmiensia 26 (Stockholm, 1980), pl. XV, p. 319 (Pa 909, fol. 108ᵛ; music only in Adémar's hand); and Grier, 'Editing Adémar de Chabannes' Liturgy', pls. I and II, between pp. 24 and 25 (Pa 909, fols. 42ʳ, 70ᵛ; music and text in Adémar's hand).

[40] On *litterae significatiuae* in general, see P. Wagner, *Einführung in die gregorianischen Melodien: Ein Handbuch der Choralwissenschaft*, ii, *Neumenkunde: Paläographie des liturgischen Gesanges*, 2nd edn (Leipzig, 1912), pp. 233–51; R. van Doren, *Étude sur l'influence de l'abbaye de Saint Gall (VIIIe au XIe siècle)*, Académie Royale de Belgique, Classe des Beaux-Arts, Mémoires, no. 2, fasc. 3 (Brussels, 1925; also published as Université de Louvain, Recueil de Travaux Publiés par les Membres des Conférences d'Histoire et de Philologie, ser. 2, 6 (Louvain, 1925)), pp. 94–118; R.-J. Hesbert, 'L'interprétation de l' "equaliter" dans les manuscrits sangalliens', *Revue Grégorienne*, 18 (1933), pp. 161–73; J. Smits van Waesberghe, *Muziekgeschiedenis der Middeleeuwen*, ii, *Verklaring der Letterteekens (litterae significatiuae) in het gregoriaansche Neumenschrift van Sint Gallen: Een Onderzoek naar de historische Waarde van den zoogenaamden Notker-Brief en naar den Oorsprong en de Beteekenis der Letterteekens in St. Gallen*, Nederlandsche Muziekhistorische en Muziekpaedagogische Studiën A (Tilburg, 1939–42); and J. Froger, 'L'épître de Notker sur les "lettres significatives": Édition critique', *Études Grégoriennes*, 5 (1962), pp. 23–71. On *litterae significatiuae* in Aquitanian notation, see R. L. Crocker, *The Early Medieval Sequence* (Berkeley, Los Angeles and London, 1977), pp. 21–2 and pl. III, p. 455. On Adémar's use of the *custos*, see M. Huglo, 'La tradition musicale aquitaine: Répertoire et notation', *Liturgie et musique (IXe–XIVe s.)*, Cahiers de Fanjeaux 17 (Toulouse, 1982), pp. 260–1.

[41] Visible in Delisle, 'Notice', pl. VI, between pp. 240 and 241 (Pa 1978, fol. 102ᵛ). See M. Huglo, *Les tonaires: Inventaire, analyse, comparaison*, Publications de la Société Française de Musicologie, ser. 3, 2 (Paris, 1971), pp. 110–11.

composed by him.[42] This circumstantial evidence finds support from a series of erasures in some of these pieces that reveals Adémar in the process of making compositional revisions as he was writing his fair copy.[43] Furthermore, John A. Emerson notes that the texts of items in the Offices for Sts Valery and Austriclinian are drawn from Adémar's sermons on the lives of these saints, and so he probably composed the music to which the texts were set.[44] Adémar emerges as a composer whose style is perhaps not the most distinctive, but who is intimately familiar with the prevalent musical practices of his time.[45]

To be sure, the history of music is filled with individuals whose achievements outstripped those of their teachers, and Adémar certainly had ample opportunity, between his studies with Roger around 1010 and the time he wrote Pa 1978, 909 and 1121, to broaden his musical expertise significantly. Nevertheless, the level of competence that Adémar exhibits strongly suggests that he received a thorough training in the fundamentals of music from his master, as Adémar calls him, Roger de Chabannes.

Evidence for Roger's own musical activities at St Martial comes from the extant music manuscripts written for use in the abbey during the first decades of the eleventh century, just the period when Roger would have reached the zenith of his professional musical activities. Two manuscripts, in particular, attest a significant codification of the abbey's liturgical music at that time. They are Pa 1085 and 1120, which, between them, transmit virtually all the music necessary for the performance of the Divine Office and Mass, respectively. It is my hypothesis that these codices were produced under the supervision of Roger, as cantor, and represent a major project undertaken by him soon after the assumption of his duties in that office.

An examination of the earlier music manuscripts from St Martial reveals why such a codification was necessary. Three liturgical music manuscripts that predate Pa 1085 and 1120 survive from St Martial. The first is Pa 1240, the tenth-century troper-proser

---

[42] Hooreman, 'Saint-Martial de Limoges', pp. 16–30.
[43] Grier, '*Ecce sanctum*', pp. 47–50.
[44] Emerson, 'Two Newly Identified Offices', pp. 40–6.
[45] For an analysis of an introit trope composed by Adémar, see Grier, '*Ecce sanctum*', pp. 50–4.

compiled at St Martial under the influence of northern French repertories and notational practices.[46] This codex also contains a brief antiphoner and an added liturgical miscellany that are important for our evaluation of the later manuscripts from St Martial.[47] Two schools of thought exist on the date of the codex. Most scholars place the main body of the first part of this codex (fols. 1–78) in the third or fourth decade of the century on the basis of the acclamations in *Christus uincit* (fol. 65[r]).[48] Others, beginning a century ago with Léopold Delisle and Léon Gautier, suggest a date of the late tenth century on palaeographical grounds.[49] The problem seems far from being solved, but if the later date is correct, it is significant for the biography of Roger de Chabannes, because he would thereby become a witness to the production of the earliest extant music manuscript from St Martial.

[46]   P. Evans, 'Northern French Elements in an Early Aquitanian Troper', *Speculum musicae artis: Festgabe für Heinrich Husmann zum 60. Geburtstag am 16. Dezember 1968*, ed. H. Becker and R. Gerlach (Munich, 1970), pp. 103–10; see also A. E. Planchart, *The Repertory of Tropes at Winchester*, 2 vols. (Princeton, 1977), I, pp. 178, 201–6.

[47]   J. A. Emerson, 'Neglected Aspects of the Oldest Full Troper (Paris, Bibliothèque Nationale, lat. 1240)', *Recherches nouvelles sur les tropes liturgiques*, ed. W. Arlt and G. Björkvall, Acta Universitatis Stockholmiensis, Studia Latina Stockholmiensia 36 (Stockholm, 1993), pp. 206–17.

[48]   Originally the date 933–6 was tentatively posited in *Le codex 903 de la Bibliothèque Nationale de Paris (XIe siècle), Graduel de Saint-Yrieix*, Paléographie Musicale (hereafter PalMus) 13 (Tournay, 1925–30), p. 123, where the possibility that Pope John X (914–28) could be meant by the acclamations is ignored and a false date for the accession of John XI, who reigned 931–6, is given; see Chailley, *L'école*, pp. 78–9, who accepts this date. Crocker, 'The Repertoire of Proses', I, pp. 49–50, gives 923–34, on the basis of a false date for the death of Abbot Stephen of St Martial, who died in 937 (Lemaître, *Mourir à Saint-Martial*, p. 149). Samaran and Marichal, *Catalogue des manuscrits . . . portant des indications de date*, II, p. 61, date the manuscript 931–4, using a false date for the death of Turpin, bishop of Limoges, who died in 944. Planchart, *The Repertory of Tropes at Winchester*, II, p. 348, gives 923–36, correct except that the book could not have been written during the reigns of Popes Leo VI and Stephen VIII (928–31). The correct dates, then, are 923–8 (delimited by the accession of King Raoul of France in 923 and the death of John X in 928) or 931–6 (delimited by the reign of John XI). See also Emerson, 'Neglected Aspects', pp. 193–217, esp. pp. 199 and 204–8.

[49]   Delisle, *Le cabinet des manuscrits*, III, pp. 271–2; L. Gautier, *Histoire de la poésie liturgique au moyen âge: Les tropes* (Paris, 1886), p. 122; and Husmann, *Tropen- und Sequenzenhandschriften*, pp. 137–8. At a conference in October 1985, Jean Vezin and François Avril expressed their agreement with this position; reported in *CT*, VII, *Tropes de l'Ordinaire de la Messe: Tropes du Sanctus*, ed. G. Iversen, Acta Universitatis Stockholmiensis, Studia Latina Stockholmiensia 34 (Stockholm, 1990), p. 55 and n. 47 (p. 59). See also R. Landes, 'L'accession des Capétiens: Une reconsidération selon les sources aquitaines', *Religion et culture autour de l'an mil: Royaume capétien et Lotharingie*, ed. D. Iogna-Prat and J.-C. Picard (Paris, 1990), p. 159.

The other two manuscripts survive in fragmentary form. Pa 1834 preserves, as its endleaves, two bifolia from a troper (fols. 1–2, 151–2).[50] They contain complete troped Masses for Ascension, Pentecost (much of which is illegible on fol. 1^r) and John the Baptist, as well as portions of the Masses for the Dedication and St Peter. By comparing the Ascension Mass in Pa 1240 (fols. 34^v–35^r), 1834 (fols. 151^v, 2^{r-v}) and 1120 (fols. 34^r–36^v), Alejandro Planchart was able to show that Pa 1834 represents an intermediate stage, between Pa 1240 and 1120.[51]

The series of tropes in Pa 1240 is incorporated into Pa 1834 and expanded, possibly under the influence of Pa 1118 or a manuscript like it. The scribe of Pa 1120 then altered, and apparently corrected, the order of tropes. Codex Pa 1834 gives *Quem creditis* at the end of the introit tropes with the rubric 'isti sunt trophi primi' (fol. 2^r; see Figure 4), acknowledging its misplacement.[52] The scribe of Pa 1120 heeded the rubric and placed the trope at the head of the series (fols. 34^{r-v}; see Figure 5). This scribe also altered the position of *Celsa potestas*, which is noted by a cue in Pa 1834 immediately after the misplaced *Quem creditis* (see Figure 4), and then given complete, without music and copied in a different hand, after the offertory and communion tropes for the feast (fol. 2^v).[53] Again, the scribe of Pa 1120 incorporated *Celsa potestas* into the main series of introit tropes for Ascension, still without music (fol. 35^v), and then added a further trope that does not occur in Pa 1834, *Hodie rex glorie*, also without music (fols. 35^v–36^r).[54] These circumstances affirm the chronological sequence of the three tropers.

[50] J. A. Emerson, 'Fragments of a Troper from Saint Martial de Limoges', *Scriptorium*, 16 (1962), pp. 369–72.

[51] Planchart, 'The Transmission of Medieval Chant', pp. 357–60; Emerson, 'Fragments of a Troper', p. 371, also notes the connection with Pa 1120.

[52] Editions of the text: *AH*, XLIX, no. 4, p. 10; and *CT*, III, *Tropes du propre de la messe*, pt 2, *Cycle de Pâques*, ed. G. Björkvall, G. Iversen and R. Jonsson, Acta Universitatis Stockholmiensis, Studia Latina Stockholmiensia 25 (Stockholm, 1982), p. 173. Editions of the music: *Introitus-tropen*, I, ed. Weiss, no. 303, pp. 317–19; and Evans, *The Early Repertory*, no. 100, p. 188. On it location in Pa 1834 and 1120, see Emerson, 'Fragments of a Troper', p. 371; Planchart, 'The Transmission of Medieval Chant', pp. 359–60; and *CT*, III, ed. Björkvall *et al.*, pp. 269–71.

[53] Edition of the text: *CT*, III, ed. Björkvall *et al.*, pp. 65, 188, 203 (individual elements). Edition of the music: *Introitus-tropen*, I, ed. Weiss, no. 298, pp. 311–12.

[54] Emerson, 'Fragments of a Troper', p. 371, and Planchart, 'The Transmission of Medieval Chant', p. 359 and n. 31, mistakenly state that *Celsa potestas* occurs in Pa 1120 after the offertory and communion tropes, and Planchart omits *Hodie rex glorie* from his table for Pa 1120; cf. *CT*, III, ed. Björkvall *et al.*, pp. 270–1.

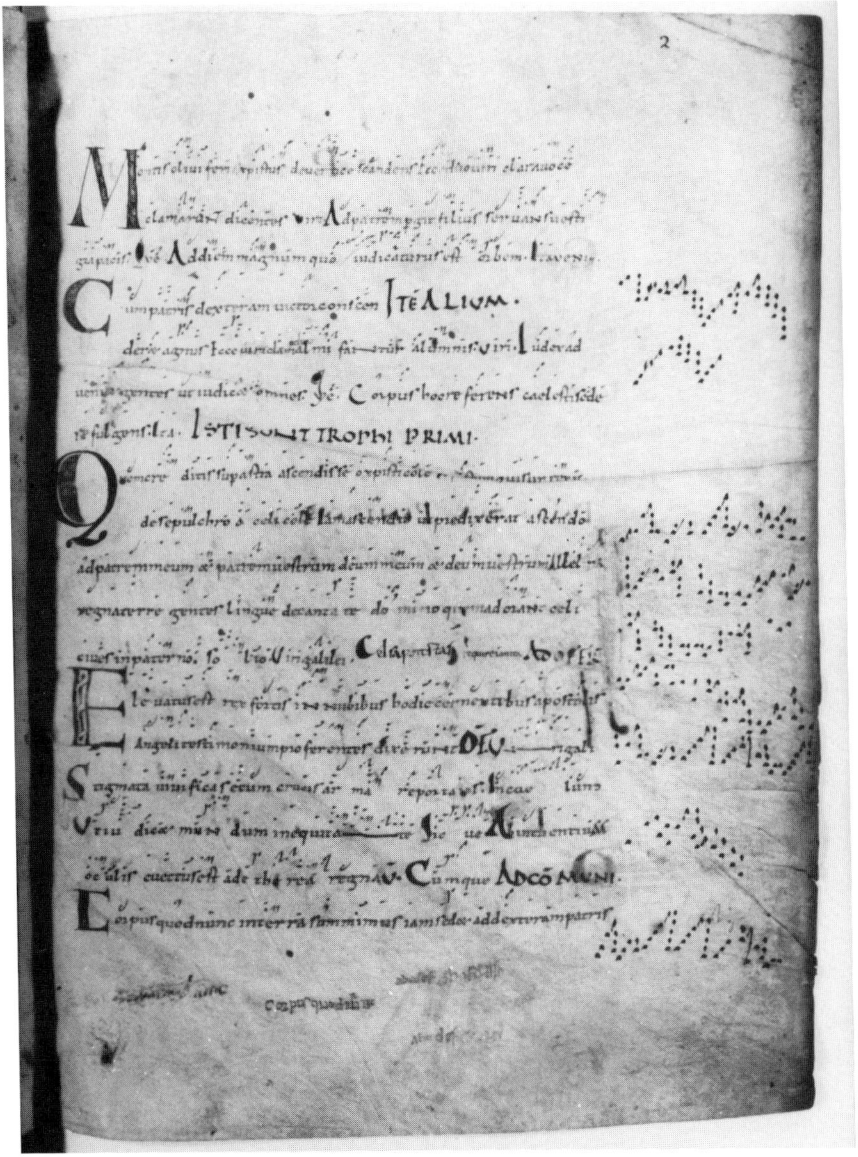

Figure 4   Pa 1834, fol. 2ʳ, feast of Ascension

Although Pa 1834 seems to have been envisaged as an elaborate manuscript, with decorated initials on fols. 2ᵛ, 151ᵛ and 152ᵛ (at the beginning of the Masses for Pentecost, Ascension and St Peter, respectively), it shows marked signs of incompletion. Folio

71

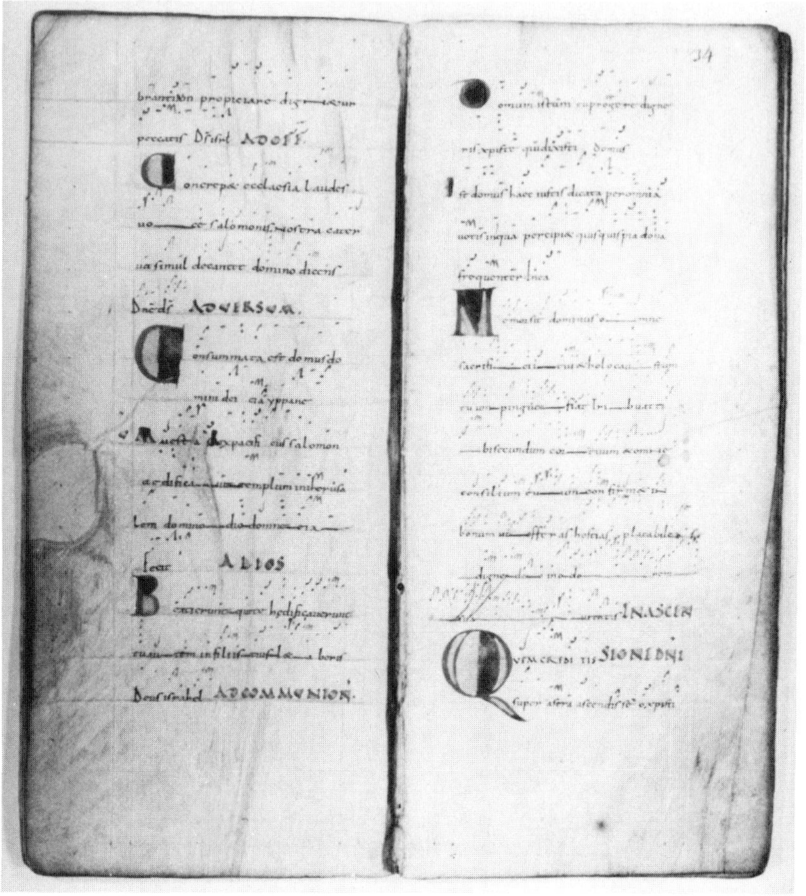

Figure 5   Pa 1120, fols. 33ᵛ–34ʳ, opening of the feast of Ascension

151ʳ, which Emerson considered to be erased, in fact shows no trace of erasure.[55] Much of the bottom right corner of fol. 1 is torn away, with some loss of text on the verso. The Mass for John the Baptist, which begins at this point on fol. 1ᵛ, may also have opened with a decorated initial, which was subsequently removed. The text on the recto, however, stops short of the damaged portion, as if the writing took place after the accident.

---

[55] Emerson, 'Fragments of a Troper', pp. 370–1.

Similar imperfections also appear in the third early manuscript from St Martial, which survives as a palimpsest in the last gathering of Pa 1085. As noted above, the main text of this codex is a list of sung items for the Divine Office, and I attribute its compilation to Roger de Chabannes. Its last gathering (fols. 105–10), however, contains key evidence for the state of liturgical manuscripts at St Martial prior to the compilation of it and Pa 1120, and for the dating of both codices.[56] It is written on a palimpsest, most of which is erased so efficiently that the lower text cannot be read, even with the help of ultraviolet light. The bottom margin was left unerased, however, and enough text is legible there to identify several processional antiphons (see Figure 6).[57] Two other texts remain to be recognised, and the difficulty is compounded by the fact that the lower margin contains only a word or two at the beginning or end of the lines of text. When the palimpsest was created, the parchment was rotated through ninety degrees, so that the lower text runs perpendicular to the upper text, and a portion of the top and left of the original bifolia was trimmed so that they would match the size of the other bifolia in the codex (see Figure 7).

As Figure 7 shows, nearly the whole of the first folios of the original bifolia is missing, leaving only the beginning of text lines on the rectos and the end on the versos. All the text on the second folios was erased. Nevertheless, we can estimate the original size of the bifolia simply by doubling the dimensions of those second folios. Some text, perhaps two lines, has been lost at the top, together with the top margin, and so the height of the original pieces of parchment and the writing frame can only be estimated. The two central bifolia, fols. 106/9 and 107/8, are laid so that the top of the original bifolia now forms the right edge of each bifolium when open. The outer bifolium, fols. 105/10, is laid the other way, with the original top becoming the left edge of the bifolium when open. This bifolium is trimmed in the same way as the other two. Table 3 shows the concordance between the folios as they are currently disposed in Pa 1085 and their original

---

[56]   I thank Professor Virginia Brown for examining the codex with me and confirming some of the codicological details.

[57]   J. A. Emerson, 'Sources, MS, §II, Western Plainchant', *The New Grove Dictionary of Music and Musicians*, ed. Stanley Sadie, 20 vols. (London, 1980), xvii, p. 612.

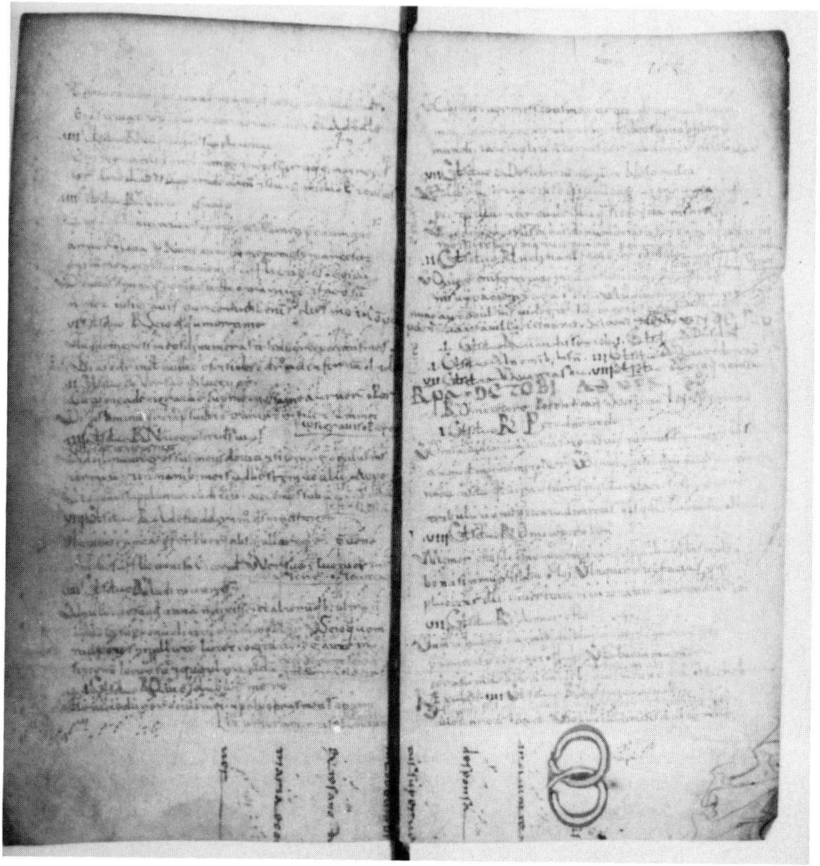

Figure 6   Pa 1085, fols. 107^v–108^r (= fol. B^r), palimpsest

arrangement. Because the lower text runs across the bottom margin of each bifolium, as Figure 6 shows, every page of the lower text occupies two surfaces of the current manuscript.

Like Pa 1834, this manuscript was originally conceived on a lavish scale. Portions of decorated initials survive on fols. X^r and B^r; a less elaborate initial begins the piece on fol. B^r (visible in Figures 6 and 8); some of the text on fol. A^r is written in square capitals; and parts of the text on fols. B^v, A^r and X^v are in rustic capitals. Nevertheless, there are signs that the manuscript was never completed as planned. Several items lack musical notation, even though ample space is available (fols. X^v and A^{r-v}), and

The original bifolia

The bifolia in Pa 1085

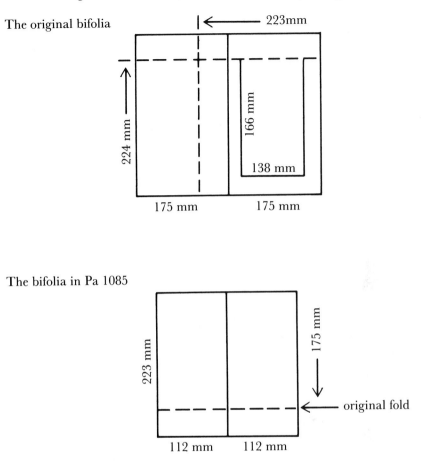

Figure 7   The palimpsest in Pa 1085, fols. 105–10

Table 3   *Concordance of folios in Pa 1085 with original manuscript*

Pa 1085 (bottom margin)	Original manuscript
fols. 109^r and 106^v	fol. A^r
fols. 109^v and 106^r	fol. A^v
fols. 108^r and 107^v	fol. B^r
fols. 108^v and 107^r	fol. B^v
fols. 105^r and 110^v	fol. X^r
fols. 105^v and 110^r	fol. X^v

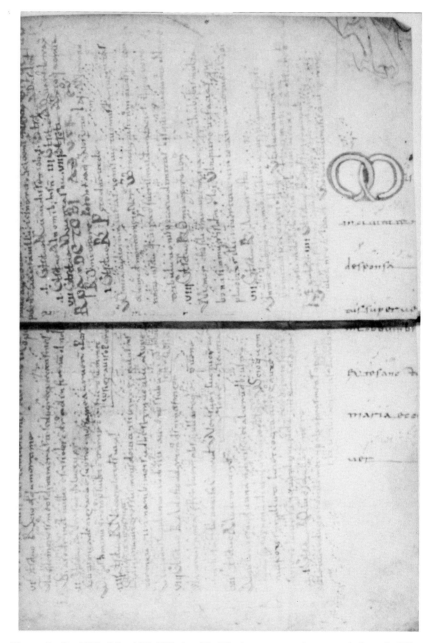

Figure 8 Pa 1085, fols. 107ᵛ–108ʳ (= fol. Bʳ), bottom margin, rotated through 90°, processional antiphon for Advent

the marks of erasure on the complete folios (i.e. those forming the upper three-quarters of the current bifolia) appear, for the most part, along the rules used for the literary text; therefore these folios probably wanted music when they were taken over for the production of Pa 1085. Moreover, the final line on fol. A[r] repeats the text from the previous line, 'paries filium', in what appears to be a *probatio pennae*.

The manuscript was probably never bound before its use as a palimpsest. A pair of binding holes exists in each bifolium, 78 and 67 mm (fols. A and X) and 79 and 68 mm (fol. B) from the original bottom of the parchment. The lower hole in fols. A and B and both holes in fol. X show no signs of wear whatsoever. Furthermore, there is no matching pair of holes at the top of the parchment. It is possible that they were lost when the parchment was trimmed. If, however, the pairs were symmetrical, the trimming removed at least 78 mm of parchment from the top of the bifolium; the original size of each leaf, then, would have been 175×300 (or more) mm. Because relatively little text is missing at the top of each folio, and because the top margin in these manuscripts tends to be narrower than the bottom, I believe that less than 78 mm is missing from the top of the parchment. In that case, the top pair of binding holes was not symmetrical with the lower pair.

How typical is this asymmetry in manuscripts from this scriptorium? The answer does not come easily. The chief problem lies in the fact that the current condition of the manuscripts from St Martial in no way represents their medieval state. To the best of my knowledge, no medieval binding from the abbey survives. Even if one did, it would not necessarily preserve the original condition of the manuscript because the librarians at St Martial, particularly during the thirteenth century, it would seem, conducted an industrious binding campaign, gathering up manuscripts of similar size (and occasionally similar subject-matter) into codices, as the designation 'in uno' or 'in uolumine uno' in the abbey's medieval catalogues attests.[58] Furthermore, the

---

[58] Four of the medieval catalogues have been printed twice: Delisle, *Le cabinet des manuscrits*, II, pp. 493–504; and *Chroniques*, ed. Duplès-Agier, pp. 323–55. For further bibliography and a discussion of the binding programme, see J. Grier, 'Some Codico-

manuscripts were apparently in a sorry state when they arrived at the then Bibliothèque du Roi in 1730, after their purchase from the monks at St Martial, and they were rebound at that time.[59] Consequently, existing binding holes may come from medieval bindings subsequent to the original binding, or from the eighteenth-century binding.

Although it is therefore impossible to make specific statements about the nature of binding in the scriptorium at St Martial during the early eleventh century, it is possible to place the evidence from the palimpsest in Pa 1085 in a more general context. The usual type of binding for a codex from this period uses a single string that runs through a series of holes at the fold of the gathering.[60] At each hole it exits and loops around a cord that lies across the back of all the gatherings. The holes in each gathering, therefore, need not be equidistant or symmetrical (although they often are), but they absolutely must be in the same position to loop around the cord, to which, ultimately, all the gatherings are attached.

Clearly, this description does not accord with the existing binding holes in the palimpsest. Even if another pair of binding holes did, at one time, exist at the top of the parchment, there would still be accommodation for only two cords (one 75 mm from the bottom, the other perhaps 40 mm from the top) in a codex that originally was approximately 275 mm tall. By way of comparison, the eighteenth-century binding of Pa 1085 uses five

logical Observations on the Aquitanian Versaria', *Musica Disciplina*, 44 (1990), pp. 8–16.

[59] On the sale, see Delisle, 'Les manuscrits', pp. 13–33; and S. Balayé, *La Bibliothèque Nationale des origines à 1800*, Histoire des Idées et Critique Littéraire 262 (Geneva, 1988), p. 206. For further bibliography, see Grier, 'Some Codicological Observations', p. 8, n. 4. Codex Pa 9373 contains much of the correspondence concerning the purchase; on the condition of the manuscripts upon their arrival, see esp. the unsigned letter dated 15 September 1730, Pa 9373, pp. 113–14; also the memorandum dated 5 September 1730, *ibid.*, pp. 109–10; and the memorandum of the Abbé Jourdain of 25 April 1732, pp. 207–8 (the latter is printed in Delisle, 'Les manuscrits', pp. 26–31). See also Crocker, 'The Repertoire of Proses', I, pp. 25–31.

[60] J. Vezin, *Évolution des techniques de la reliure médiévale*, Notes sur les Techniques du Livre Ancien, Introduction à la Conservation 2 (Paris, 1973), pp. 4–10, esp. figs. 2 and 4; *idem*, 'La reliure occidentale au moyen âge', *La reliure médiévale: Trois conférences d'initiation*, 2nd edn (Paris, 1981), pp. 38–41 and fig. 18, p. 44, figs. 24–5; and L. Gilissen, *La reliure occidentale antérieure à 1400*, Bibliologia: Elementa ad Librorum Studia Pertinentia 1 (Turnhout, 1983), pp. 13–18. I am grateful to Illo Humphrey for these references.

cords on a codex 223 mm in height. One would therefore expect to find several binding holes spaced out along the original fold in the current bottom margin of the palimpsest. In their absence, I conclude that the manuscript was never prepared for a permanent binding.

The disposition of the binding holes and the wear exhibited in the holes on fols. A and B show that the gathering was temporarily bound, probably with a piece of string, during its compilation while awaiting a permanent binding. The condition of fol. X, which exhibits no wear at its binding holes, indicates that it did not even reach the stage of temporary binding before it was commandeered for the last gathering of Pa 1085, and so further demonstrates the incomplete state of the original manuscript.

The texts on fols. A^{r-v} and B^r belong to the processional antiphons for Advent Sunday: *Venite omnes*, *Ecce carissimi dies* and *Missus est angelus* (see Figures 6 and 8).[61] These three antiphons, in this order, form the Advent procession in both Pa 1120 (fols. 154^r–155^r) and Pa 1121 (fols. 138^r–139^r).[62] *Missus est angelus* also appears in the miscellany of liturgical items at the end of the musical portion of Pa 1240 (fol. 89^r).[63] Folios A and B, therefore, probably constituted the beginning of a *libellus* of processional antiphons. The constitution of the gathering creates a difficulty with this interpretation, however (see Figure 9). Folio A^r is a flesh surface. Most gatherings produced in the scriptorium at St Martial present a hair surface on the outside as first recto and

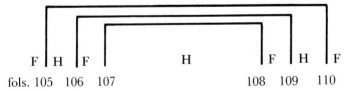

Figure 9   The constitution of the gathering Pa 1085, fols. 105–10

---

[61]   Texts edited in C. D. Roederer, 'Eleventh-Century Aquitanian Chant: Studies Relating to a Local Repertory of Processional Antiphons', 2 vols. (Ph.D. dissertation, Yale University, 1971), II, pp. 165, 109, 134, respectively.

[62]   *Ibid.*, p. 12.

[63]   Emerson, 'Neglected Aspects', p. 214.

last verso.[64] Folio A^r, then, would not normally be the first of a gathering. It is possible, however, that a decorated version of the word 'Venite', the first word of the first processional antiphon, was intended to appear on the verso facing fol. A^r, or perhaps an elaborate rubric introducing the *libellus*. In that case, the first recto would be left blank as a cover. Such an arrangement is found in some Aquitanian manuscripts, but not in any produced at St Martial, to the best of my knowledge.[65]

The fragments of text on fols. B^v and X^v have so far escaped identification. The former is written throughout in rustic capitals, with musical notation entered above.

> T NOMINE
> CIT SVM
> ONOREM
> MENTA
> NC COM
> MVSICAEAR
> LI

These fragments do not correspond to any of the Aquitanian processional antiphons for either Advent or Christmas.[66] Most of the text on fol. X^v is in minuscule, but without musical notation, except above the cues to the responds and above 'Stantes'.

> criste sic dicitur
> age uera fide ipse
> R[esponsorium] et enim
> risti iacob
> IHERVSALEM
> R[esponsorium] Exion
> Stantes

These fragments would appear to belong to responsories, probably for Matins, to judge from the rubrics, but the incipit 'Exion' is not recorded by Hesbert in volume IV of *Corpus antiphonalium Officii*.

---

[64] Grier, 'Some Codicological Observations', pp. 16–17.
[65] Grier, '*Ecce sanctum*', p. 72, and 'Some Codicological Observations', p. 17.
[66] Roederer, 'Eleventh-Century Aquitanian Chant', II, pp. 12–13.

This manuscript, then, was intended to be an elaborate *libellus* of processional antiphons, whose production was aborted during the entry of the musical notation. Its incomplete state is comparable to that of Pa 1834, as mentioned above, and other similarities link these two sets of fragments. Although the text hands differ (minims in Pa 1834, for example, are thicker at the top), they resemble each other closely (see Figures 4 and 8 on pp. 71 and 76, respectively). The musical notation, however, could well have come from the same hand. Neume shapes are very similar, with the exception of the quilisma, whose minim is also slightly thicker at the top in Pa 1834. I conclude that these fragments are closely associated. The dimensions of the parchment show that they do not belong to the same manuscript. Although the writing frame could have been the same size (Pa 1834, 190×137 mm; Pa 1085, 166 (with approximately two lines missing at the top)×138 mm), the folios in Pa 1834 are much wider (206 mm to 175 in Pa 1085). The key difference, however, is the distance between the rules (Pa 1834, 11 mm; Pa 1085, 15 mm).

These fragments, then, constitute what remains of two independent *libelli*, produced about the same time, possibly written by the same music scribe, one of processional antiphons, one of Proper tropes for the Mass. Although both were left incomplete, they represent a significant revision of their respective repertories: Pa 1834 exhibits a greatly expanded repertory of Proper tropes over that found in Pa 1240, its only precedent, and the only source of processional antiphons from St Martial earlier than the palimpsest in Pa 1085 is also the miscellany in Pa 1240. On the basis of its decorated initials, Gaborit-Chopin dates Pa 1834 to the early eleventh century, and, by association, I would assign the fragments in Pa 1085 to the same date.[67] Codex Pa 1834 clearly predates Pa 1120, as Planchart shows (see the discussion above), and so I suggest that the palimpsest in Pa 1085, written at about the same time as Pa 1834, also predates it. At the very least it predates the main body of Pa 1085, in the course of whose production the incomplete *libellus* of processional antiphons was destroyed, and I propose below that Pa 1085 and 1120 were compiled at roughly the same time.

[67] Gaborit-Chopin, *La décoration*, pp. 65, 190.

These circumstances are important for our understanding of Pa 1120 and the main body of Pa 1085. Gaborit-Chopin's date for Pa 1834 provides a *terminus ante quem non* for Pa 1120 and, by association, Pa 1085: both codices must now be dated to the eleventh, not the tenth century as some scholars suggest.[68] Moreover, their production took place, in all probability, some years after the fragments in Pa 1834 and 1085 were abandoned; otherwise the scriptorium would have devoted its resources to the completion of these two manuscripts, which had already consumed some effort, instead of embarking on new projects. Furthermore, these fragments show the scriptorium somewhat in disarray, only able to provide, for the celebration of the liturgy, the obsolete Pa 1240 and the incomplete *libelli* of Proper tropes and processional antiphons.

It is on the basis of this evidence, therefore, that I advance the hypothesis proposed above. Faced with the failure to complete the fragments in Pa 1834 and 1085, the musical community undertook the compilation of Pa 1085 and 1120 to record the liturgical music for Office and Mass. I suggest that they are the products of a newly appointed cantor, who either was charged with the responsibility by the abbot or took it upon himself as a way of putting his mark on the office. I propose that that new cantor was Roger de Chabannes.

Moreover, it is possible that Roger himself wrote the main body of Pa 1085. This suggestion depends on the tentative identification, proposed above, that Roger de Chabannes was the scribe of the 992 charter. The hand of this charter (see Figure 2) bears a strong resemblance to that of Pa 1085 (see Figures 6, 8 and 10). In particular, the form of the letter 'f', with its long descender, is striking. Each document, however, uses a 'g' with a slightly different lower loop; that in the charter of 992 is more closed, that in Pa 1085 more open. The state of the evidence, once again, prevents more than a tentative identification of Roger as the scribe of Pa 1085.

This codex is not well known to the scholarly world, even though it is one of the earliest extant monastic sources for Office

---

[68] Pa 1085: Emerson, 'Neglected Aspects', p. 207. Pa 1120: Chailley, 'Les anciens tropaires', pp. 167–9, and *L'école*, pp. 80–1.

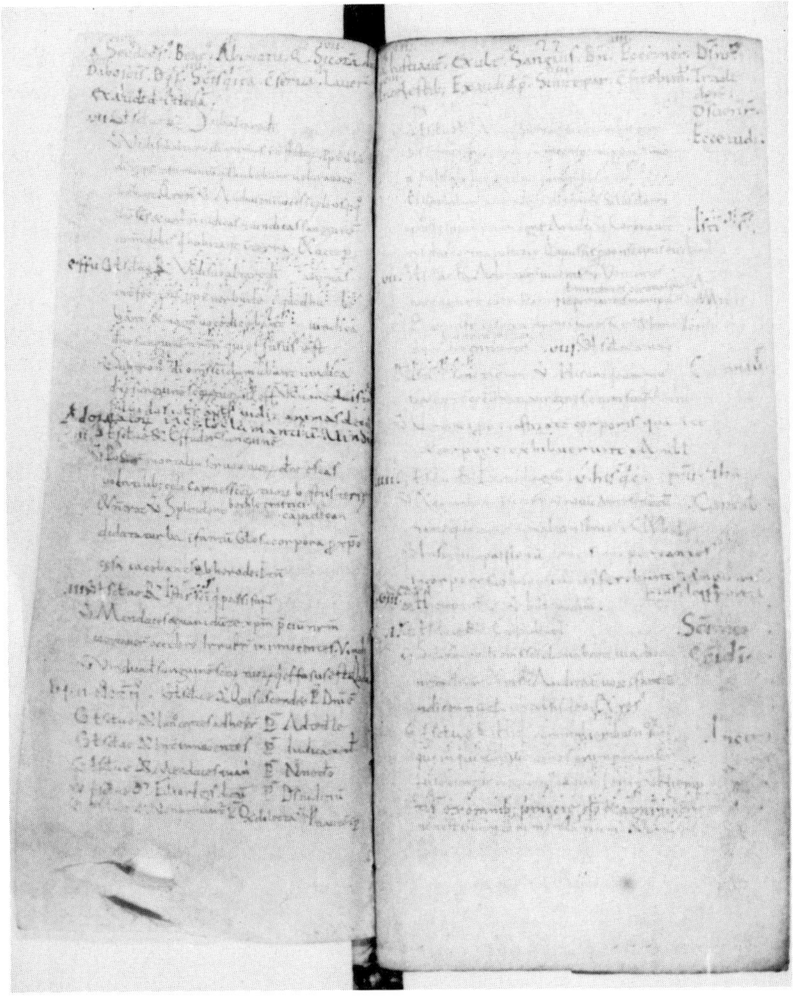

Figure 10   Pa 1085, fols. 21ᵛ–22ʳ, feast of Holy Innocents (28 December)

chants.[69] (The brief antiphoner in Pa 1240, fols. 66ʳ–78ᵛ, predates
Pa 1085, of course.) A firm *terminus post quem non* is provided by
the absence of the dedication of 18 November, the one witnessed
by Adémar, which took place in 1028. The dedication feasts that

[69]   The only monastic chant books for the Office of comparable age cited by D. Hiley,
Western Plainchant: A Handbook (Oxford, 1993), pp. 304–5, are the Hartker Antiphoner
(St Gall, Stiftsbibliothek (hereafter SG), MSS 390–1; facsimile edn in *Antiphonale
Officii monastici écrit par le B. Hartker: No 390–391 de la Bibliothèque de Saint-Gall*, PalMus,

are present fall on 2 May ('Dedicatio basilice quam dedicauit in honore sancti Petri beatissimus Martialis in Lemouicas ciuitate', fols. 65^r–66^r) and 13 October ('Dedicatio ecclesie sancti Saluatoris in monasterio beatissimi Martialis fondatum in Lemouice ciuitatis', fols. 91^v–93^v). These agree with the dedication feasts present in the kalendar of Pa 1240 (fols. 11^r–16^r), the tenth-century troper from St Martial. In fact the list of feasts in Pa 1085 offers only one significant difference from the kalendar of Pa 1240, and that is the presence of the feast of Mary Magdalene (22 July, fol. 78^v). The addition of this feast suggests that Pa 1085 postdates Pa 1240. Danielle Gaborit-Chopin, moreover, dates it to the beginning of the eleventh century on the basis of two drawings, a date consistent with evidence presented here.[70]

The Office of Mary Magdalene, although unremarkable in content, is the earliest on record for this saint. Matins contains a single nocturn (with only three responsories), and most items are borrowed from either the Common of Virgins or the Assumption (see Table 4).[71] Nevertheless, no other source that can be safely dated before Pa 1085 transmits an Office for this feast. Victor Saxer notes that the liturgy for Mary Magdalene began to appear in manuscripts during the eleventh century, but he does not demonstrate that either of his earliest sources (from Orléans and Reims), although both eleventh-century books, dates from the first quarter of the century.[72] This evidence for the veneration of Magdalene at St Martial early in the century affects the interpretation of the twelfth-century

ser. 2, 1 (Solesmes, 1900)) and the Mont-Renaud manuscript (private collection (hereafter MR); facsimile edn in *Le manuscrit du Mont-Renaud: Xe siècle graduel et antiphonaire de Noyon*, PalMus 16 (Solesmes, 1955)); on these manuscripts, see U. Franca, *Le antifone bibliche dopo Pentecoste*, Studia Anselmiana 73, Analecta Liturgica 4 (Rome, 1977), pp. 38–55; and G. M. Beyssac, 'Le graduel-antiphonaire de Mont-Renaud', *Revue de Musicologie*, 39 (1957), pp. 131–50. See also the list of Office manuscripts in R.-J. Hesbert, *Corpus antiphonalium Officii* (hereafter *CAO*), 6 vols., Rerum Ecclesiasticarum Documenta, Series Maior, Fontes 7–12 (Rome, 1963–79), v, pp. 5–18. Codex Pa 17436, the ninth-century manuscript from the abbey of St Corneille in Compiègne, follows the secular or Roman cursus; see Hesbert, *CAO*, i, pp. XVII–XIX; and Franca, *Le antifone bibliche*, pp. 29–37.
70   Gaborit-Chopin, *La décoration*, pp. 68, 184–5.
71   Hesbert, *CAO*, iii and iv, contain the full texts of the Office chants.
72   V. Saxer, *Le culte de Marie Madeleine en occident des origines à la fin du moyen âge*, 2 vols., Cahiers d'Archéologie et d'Histoire 3 (Auxerre and Paris, 1959), i, pp. 153–82, esp. pp. 159–60, 169–70.

Table 4 *The Office of Mary Magdalene in Pa 1085*

Incipit	CAO, III–IV
VESPERS	
A In diebus illis mulier	3224
MATINS	
SVPER VENITE Regem uirginum	1150
FIRST NOCTURN	
A Nominabitur quod fecit	——
R̶ Diffusa est gratia	6446
V̶ Contempsisti enim	
R̶ Veni electa mea	7826
V̶ Audi filia	
R̶ Ista est speciosa	6994
V̶ Ista est quae ascendit	
LAUDS	
A Veni sponsa	5328
A Haec est uirgo sapiens quam	3007
A Veniente	5332
A Benedico te	1703
A Prudentes	4404
R̶ Specie tua	7679
V̶ Intende	
V̶ Inuenta bona	
IN EVANGELIVM A Mulier quae erat	3822
A Optimam partem	4167
A Maria autem unxit	3696bis/3699

lyric repertory of *uersus* that circulated in Aquitaine. Elsewhere, I note the presence in this repertory of songs about Mary Magdalene, including one that begins 'Nouum festum celebremus', and conclude that St Martial was not a likely place of origin for the repertory because of the lack of evidence for her cult.[73] This observation needs reconsideration in view of the testimony presented in Pa 1085.

Although Pa 1085 presents a complete set of Offices for the liturgical year, and within each Office the full complement of sung items, the items themselves are abbreviated. In the usual format, each sung item is represented by its incipit. In addition, a roman numeral, signifying the modal classification of the melody, precedes all items that include a verse or psalm to be sung to a tone (i.e. every invitatory, antiphon and Matins responsory).

---

[73] Grier, 'Some Codicological Observations', pp. 52–6.

As Michel Huglo notes, these numbers were added sometime after the original compilation of the codex.[74] Adémar's use of such modal numbers in Pa 1978 and 909, however, suggests that they were entered into Pa 1085 not long after its completion.

A cue to the lesser doxology ('Gloria patri') appears, where appropriate, between the modal number and the incipit (see Figure 10). Here the practice of Pa 1085 directly contradicts the Rule of St Benedict, and presents the first of several pieces of evidence that indicate the idiosyncratic nature of the liturgy it records. St Benedict stipulates that the doxology is to be sung as part of the last responsory of each nocturn.[75] But, as Figure 10 illustrates, Pa 1085 calls for the doxology at the end of each responsory, in keeping with what Carolingian liturgists understood to be Roman, as opposed to Frankish, practice.[76] The presence of Pa 1085 in a Benedictine house makes this discrepancy with the Rule of St Benedict all the more noteworthy. Moreover, the cue to the doxology ('Gloria seculorum amen') suggests that the entire text, including the section beginning 'sicut erat', was to be sung. Both Amalarius and the twelfth-century *ordo* for Guido of Castille indicate that the doxology after a responsory

[74] Huglo, *Les tonaires*, p. 111.

[75] Benedict of Nursia, *Regula*, 9.6, 11.2, ed. A. de Vogüé and J. Neufville, *La règle de Saint Benoît*, 7 vols., Sources Chrétiennes 181–6 (Paris, 1971–7), II, pp. 510, 514.

[76] *Ordo romanus XVI*, 15, ed. M. Andrieu, *Les Ordines romani du haut moyen âge*, 5 vols., Spicilegium Sacrum Lovaniense, Études et Documents 11, 23, 24, 28, 29 (Louvain, 1931–61), III, pp. 148–9, and n. 15 (Hiley, *Western Plainchant*, p. 74, incorrectly identifies this text as *Ordo romanus VI*); Amalarius of Metz, *Liber de ordine antiphonarii*, 18.6–7, ed. J.-M. Hanssens, *Amalarii episcopi opera liturgica omnia*, 3 vols., Studi e Testi 138–40 (Vatican City, 1948–50), III, p. 55; and Walafrid Strabo, *Libellus de exordiis et incrementis quarundam in obseruationibus ecclesiasticis rerum*, 26, ed. A. Boretius and V. Krause, *Monumenta Germaniae historica* (hereafter *MGH*), *Legum*, ser. 2, *Capitularia regum Francorum*, II (Hanover, 1897), p. 507. The unanimity of these sources allows us to dismiss Pierre Salmon's assertion that Amalarius was referring only to the last responsory of each nocturn, in accord with St Benedict: Salmon, *L'office divin au moyen âge: Histoire de la formation du bréviaire du IXe au XVIe siècle*, Lex Orandi 43 (Paris, 1967), p. 34. See also the twelfth-century *ordo* written for Cardinal Guido of Castille before he became Pope Celestine II (and therefore before September 1143), published as *Ordo romanus XI*, 3, *PL*, LXXVIII, cols. 1026–7 (not edited by Andrieu; see *Les Ordines romani*, I, pp. 309–11). For commentary, see Wagner, *Einführung*, I, *Ursprung und Entwicklung der liturgischen Gesangsformen bis zum Ausgange des Mittelalters*, 3rd edn (Leipzig, 1911), pp. 133–7; H. Hucke, 'Das Responsorium', *Gattungen der Musik in Einzeldarstellungen: Gedenkschrift Leo Schrade*, ed. W. Arlt, E. Lichtenhahn and H. Oesch (Berne and Munich, 1973), pp. 160–2; and R. L. Crocker, 'Liturgical Materials of Roman Chant', *New Oxford History of Music*, II, *The Early Middle Ages to 1300*, 2nd edn, ed. Crocker and Hiley (Oxford and New York, 1990), pp. 126–8.

ends with the words 'spiritui sancto'.[77] Finally, no *repetendum* is indicated after the doxology, and from this absence I infer that the entire respond is to be performed after it, again consistent with Amalarius's description of Roman custom.[78]

Musical notation appears infrequently above the incipits. The texts most often written out in full are the verses for Matins responsories. Figure 10 shows the typical arrangement. It presents a portion of the Office for Holy Innocents (28 December): the responsories for the first nocturn of Matins, all of the second nocturn and the beginning of the third nocturn. At the top of fol. 21ᵛ, for example, the first responsory is represented by its incipit, 'Sub altare Dei'. The verse *Vidi sub altare* then follows, written in full, with a cue to the *repetendum*, 'Quare non', the second verse, *Audiui enim uoces*, again in full, and a final cue for the *repetendum*, 'Et acceperunt'. Here, subsequent cues to the *repetendum* indicate a progressive shortening of the respond after each verse, which Amalarius characterises as a Frankish practice.[79] The antiphons and psalms of the second nocturn, in contrast to the way the responsories are presented, are identified by incipit only.

Also present in Figure 10 are two responsories and the beginning of a third that carries over to fol. 22ᵛ, all given complete. Table 5 gives the full list of responsories for this feast. In all, four of the responsories are presented complete, and, to judge from Hesbert's tables, they knew a much more restricted circulation than the other eight, whose responds are represented by incipit only; these latter occur in all six of the manuscripts Hesbert presents as witnesses of the monastic cursus of the Office.[80] In contrast, three of the four responsories given complete

77 Amalarius, *Liber de ordine antiphonarii*, 18.6, ed. Hanssens, III, p. 55; and *Ordo romanus* XI, 3, *PL*, LXXVIII, col. 1027. See also Wagner, *Einführung*, I, p. 136; W. Apel, *Gregorian Chant* (Bloomington and London, 1958), p. 182; A. Hughes, *Medieval Manuscripts for Mass and Office: A Guide to their Organization and Terminology* (Toronto, 1982), pp. 29, 301; and Hiley, *Western Plainchant*, p. 70.

78 Amalarius, *Liber de ordine antiphonarii*, 18.6, ed. Hanssens, III, p. 55; and *Ordo romanus* XI, 3, *PL*, LXXVIII, cols. 1026–7.

79 Amalarius, *Prologus de ordine antiphonarii*, 12, and *Liber de ordine antiphonarii*, 18.6–8, ed. Hanssens, I, p. 362, and III, p. 55, respectively. But *Ordo romanus* XI, 3, *PL*, LXXVIII, cols. 1026–7, shows that the *repetendum* after each verse is shortened, as in the Frankish practice, but that the final *repetendum*, after the lesser doxology, is complete.

80 Pa 17296 (Hesbert's MS D) places *Cantabant* in Lauds; see Hesbert, *CAO*, II, no. 22, where the contents of all six manuscripts are listed synoptically for this feast.

Table 5 *Responsories for the Office of Holy Innocents in Pa 1085*

Folios	Incipit	*CAO*, IV	Text	Music
	FIRST NOCTURN			
21ᵛ	℟ Sub altare Dei	7713	incipit	no
	℣ Vidi sub altare		complete	no
	℣ Audiui enim uoces		complete	no
21ᵛ	℟ Vidi sub altare	7879/7880	complete	yes
	℣ Sub trono Dei		complete	yes
	℣ Euangelius fulgidus		complete	yes
21ᵛ	℟ Effuderunt sanguinem	6624	incipit	no
	℣ Posuerunt mortalia		complete	no
	℣ Splendent Bethleemitici		complete	no
21ᵛ	℟ Isti sunt sancti qui passi sunt	7022	incipit	partial
	℣ Mendaces et uani		complete	no
	℣ Vindica Domine		complete	no
	SECOND NOCTURN			
22ʳ	℟ Vidi turbam magnam	7881	complete	yes
	℣ Et clamabunt		complete	partial
	℣ Coronauit eos		complete	no
22ʳ	℟ Adorauerunt uiuentem	6050	incipit	no
	℣ Venientes autem		complete	no
	℣ Et ceciderunt		complete	no
22ʳ	℟ Isti sunt sancti qui non	7021	incipit	partial
	℣ Hi sunt qui		complete	no
	℣ Virginei propter castitatem		complete	no
22ʳ	℟ Ecce uidi Agnum	6617	incipit	no
	℣ Et cantabant quasi		complete	no
	℣ Insignum passionum		complete	no
	THIRD NOCTURN			
22ʳ	℟ Cantabant	6266	incipit	no
	℣ Sub trono Dei		complete	no
	℣ Audita est uox		complete	no
22ʳ⁻ᵛ	℟ Hi sunt qui	6816	complete	yes
	℣ Hi empti sunt		complete	yes
	℣ O quam gloriosum est		complete	no
22ᵛ	℟ Hi empti sunt	6812	complete	yes
	℣ Et nemo poterat		complete	yes
	℣ Hi sunt qui		complete	no
22ᵛ	℟ Centum xliiii milia	6273	incipit	no
	℣ Hi empti sunt		complete	no
	℣ Corporeae integritatis		complete	no

appear each in only one of Hesbert's monastic witnesses.[81] The fourth responsory, *Vidi sub altare*, is found in two of the manuscripts edited by Hesbert, each time varying slightly.[82] Table 6 shows the two varying forms, along with the version in Pa 1085, which combines elements of both, and the biblical source of the passage. All four responsories occur in the eleventh- or early twelfth-century Aquitanian antiphoner Toledo, Biblioteca Capitular (hereafter Tol), MS 44.1.[83] Most of this feast is missing from Tol 44.2, but the last responsory of Matins is *Hi empti sunt*.[84]

Furthermore, the scribe of Pa 1085 has entered the music for these four items, including that for the verses. The latter are formulaic and determined by the modal classification of the respond melody, just like the psalm tones in antiphonal psalmody;

Table 6 *The responsory* Vidi sub altare

Rv 6.9–10	F, *CAO*, iv, no. 7879	L, *CAO*, iv, no. 7880	Pa 1085, fol. 21ᵛ
9 uidi subtus altare animas interfectorum propter uerbum dei, et propter testimonium quod habebant, 10 et clamabant uoce magna dicentes: Vsquequo domine (sanctus et uerus), non iudicas, et non uindicas sanguinem nostrum de iis qui habitant in terra?	Vidi sub altare dei animas interfectorum propter dei, et propter testimonium quod habebant; et clara uoce dicebant: Vindica, domine, sanguinem nostrum qui effusus est.	Vidi sub altare dei animas interfectorum propter uerbum dei quod habebant; et uoce magna clamabant: Vindica, domine, sanguinem sanctorum tuorum qui effusus est.	Vidi sub altare dei animas interfectorum propter uerbum dei quod habebant; et magna uoce dicebant: Vindica, domine, sanguinem nostrum qui effusus est.

81   *Vidi turbam magnam* in Benevento, Biblioteca Capitolare, MS V-21 (Hesbert's MS L); *Hi sunt qui* in Zurich, Zentralbibliothek, MS Rh. 28 (R); and *Hi empti sunt* in London, British Library, Additional MS 30850 (S).

82   Hesbert, *CAO*, iv, no. 7879 in Pa 12584 (Hesbert's MS F); and *CAO*, iv, no. 7880 in L.

83   I am very grateful to Professor Ruth Steiner, Director of CANTUS, for supplying me with the inventory of this codex.

84   CANTUS, *An Aquitanian Antiphoner: Toledo, Biblioteca Capitular, 44.2*, Wissenschaftliche Abhandlungen 55, 1 (Ottawa, 1992), p. 9.

the responsorial tones, however, are more elaborate.[85] They constitute the most extensive repertory in the body of Office chant
that is sung entirely by soloists. (Aside from the incipits of the
choral items, the soloists also sing the verses of the invitatory;
these are not written out in Pa 1085.) With the subsequent
addition of the modal numbers this music became redundant,
and it is clear that whoever added the numbers was especially
concerned to assure the modal classification of these melodies.
Therefore, there seem to be two classes of items for which a
complete text, with or without neumation, was included in Pa
1085: first, those sung by the soloists; and second, those in more
restricted circulation, and so probably less well known.

Its manner of presentation resembles that of SG 359, the
tenth-century Mass book from St Gall.[86] Here only graduals,
alleluias and tracts are written out in full, with complete neumation; all other items are represented by incipits, some with
music. Again, the pieces presented in complete form are those
of most interest to the soloists, who sang the tracts and the
verses of the graduals and alleluias. To be sure, both SG 359
and Pa 1085 include music that was sung chorally, namely the
choral responds of graduals and alleluias (in the former) and of
Matins responsories (in the latter). Nevertheless, in both codices,
the pieces that are indicated by their incipits only are those in
which a solo singer would have no responsibilities beyond starting
the choir by intoning the first few words. And so both SG 359
and Pa 1085 could well have served as the reference book during
those sessions when the cantor and weekly cantor planned the
week's liturgy, writing down the incipits of the sung items and
choosing the monks who were to sing or begin them.[87]

---

[85] *Antiphonale sarisburiense*, ed. W. H. Frere (London, 1901–24; repr. Farnborough, 1966),
pp. 3–5; Wagner, *Einführung*, III, *Gregorianische Formenlehre: Eine choralische Stilkunde*
(Leipzig, 1921), pp. 188–216; P. M. Ferretti, *Estetica gregoriana: Trattato delle forme
musicali del canto gregoriano*, I (Rome, 1935), pp. 265–83; Apel, *Gregorian Chant*, pp.
234–41; and Hiley, *Western Plainchant*, pp. 65–6.

[86] Reproduced in facsimile in *Cantatorium (IXe siècle): No 359 de la Bibliothèque de Saint-Gall*,
PalMus, ser. 2, 2 (Tournai, 1924; repr. Berne, 1968).

[87] See, for example, the tenth-century customary from Einsiedeln, *Consuetudines einsidlenses*,
ed. B. Albers, Consuetudines monasticae 5 (Monte Cassino, 1912), pp. 77–80; and
the eleventh-century customary of Cluny, *Liber tramitis aeui Odilonis abbatis*, 2.26, ed.
P. Dinter, Corpus Consuetudinum Monasticarum 10 (Siegburg, 1980), p. 238. See
also Fassler, 'The Office of the Cantor', pp. 39–51. Emerson, 'Neglected Aspects', p.
207, reaches the same conclusion about Pa 1085.

Codex Pa 1085 represents a systematic attempt to record the texts of the Divine Office as celebrated at St Martial in the first decades of the eleventh century. Moreover, the only precedent for it from the abbey is the very brief antiphoner in Pa 1240 (fols. 66^r–78^v). For most Offices, this contains items for Lauds only.[88] In view of the comparable age of Office books from other institutions, Pa 1085 might be a product of the first efforts at St Martial to preserve a complete record of the Office, and I consider this the most likely explanation for its compilation. A second possibility arises, however, from two misfortunes suffered by the abbey in the tenth century. In 953 and again shortly after the beginning of Guigo's reign as abbot in 974, fire swept the monastery.[89] Both Adémar and Bernard Itier, the abbey's librarian in the early thirteenth century, particularly note that the second fire destroyed books. Hence, it is possible that Pa 1085 was compiled to replace a book lost in one of these fires.

Whatever the origins of Pa 1085, the repertory and usage it records show some unique characteristics when compared with other Office manuscripts of the same age. We have already noted its distinctive treatment of the lesser doxology with Matins responsories, among which other unusual features occur. Although all the responsories for its Office of Holy Innocents appear in at least one of the six monastic manuscripts edited by Hesbert, and eight of the responsories occur in all six, none of the six presents exactly the same list as Pa 1085. The distinction sharpens when we broaden our sample by considering the responsories for the four Sundays of Advent, for which Hesbert assembled the data from some 800 medieval and early Renaissance Office manuscripts.[90] Table 7 gives the complete list of responsories for Advent in Pa 1085.[91] The sequence of

---

88   Emerson, 'Neglected Aspects', pp. 206–8.
89   [Adémar], *Commemoratio abbatum*, ed. Duplès-Agier, pp. 4–5; Bernard Itier, *Chronicon*, ed. Duplès-Agier, *Chroniques*, pp. 42–3.
90   Hesbert, *CAO*, v, pp. 5–18, lists the manuscripts consulted. Hesbert did not consider Pa 1085.
91   In Table 7, numbers in parentheses give the numerical codes Hesbert assigned to the Advent responsories; see Hesbert, *CAO*, v, pp. 32–3. An asterisk denotes a verse unique to Pa 1085. For the biblical sources, cf. the identifications in P. Alfonzo, *I responsori biblici dell'Ufficio Romano*, Lateranum, new ser., year 2, no. 1 (Rome, 1936), pp. 136–58.

Table 7 *Responsories in Pa 1085 for the four Sundays of Advent*

Folios	Incipit	Source	CAO, IV (V)
	FIRST SUNDAY OF ADVENT:		
	FIRST NOCTURN		
3ᵛ–4ʳ	℟ Aspiciens a longe	——	6129 (11)
	℣ Quique terrigene	Ps 48.3	
	℣ Qui regis Israel	Ps 79.2	
	℣ Excita Domine	Ps 79.3	
4ʳ	℟ Aspiciebam	Dn 7.13–14	6128 (12)
	℣ Ecce dominator	Is 40.10	
	℣ Potestas eius	Dn 7.14	
4ʳ	℟ Missus est	Lk 1.26–7, 29–32	7170 (13)
	℣ Aue Maria gratia	Lk 1.28	
4ʳ	℟ Aue Maria	Lk 1.28, 35	6157 (14)
	℣ Quomodo in me	Lk 1.34–5	
	SECOND NOCTURN		
4ʳ	℟ Saluatorem	Phil 3.20–1	7562 (15)
	℣ Preoccupemus	Ps 94.2	
	℣ Sobrie et iuste	Ti 2.12–13	
4ʳ	℟ Audite uerbum	Jer 31.10, Is 62.11	6149 (16)
	℣ A solis ortu	Ps 106.3	
	℣ Adnunciate	Jer 4.5	
4ᵛ	℟ Ecce uirgo	Is 7.14, 9.6	6620 (17)
	℣ Super solium Dauid	Is 9.7	
	℣ Tollite portas	Ps 23.7	
4ᵛ	℟ Obsecro Domine	Ex 4.13, 3.7–8	7305 (18)
	℣ Ecce Domine	Ex 4.10, 13	
	*℣ Deus qui sedes	Ps 9.5	
	℣ Qui regis Israel	Ps 79.2	
	THIRD NOCTURN		
4ᵛ	℟ Laetentur caeli	Is 49.13	7068 (19)
	℣ Orietur in diebus	Ps 71.7	
	℣ Tunc exultabunt	Ps 95.12–13	
4ᵛ	℟ Alieni non transibunt	Jl 3.17–18	6066 (62)
	℣ Ecce ego ueniam dicit Dominus et sanabo	Hos 14.5	
	*℣ Non transibit per eam	Is 35.8, Wis 7.25	
4ᵛ–5ʳ	℟ Montes Israel	Ez 36.8	7177 (60)
	℣ Rorate caeli	Is 45.8	
	*℣ Frondete et date	Sir 39.19	
5ʳ	℟ Confortamini	Is 35.3–4	6321 (61)
	*℣ Gressus rectos facite	Heb 12.13, Jb 4.4	
	℣ Ciuitas Hierusalem	Tb 5.26	
5ʳ	℟ Ecce dies ueniunt	Jer 33.14–16	6583 (63)
	℣ In diebus illis	Jer 33.16	
	*℣ Veniet qui eripiat	Rom 11.26	

Table 7   (*cont.*)

Folios	Incipit	Source	*CAO*, IV (V)
	SECOND SUNDAY OF ADVENT: FIRST NOCTURN		
6ʳ	℟ Hierusalem cito	Mi 4.8–9	7031 (21)
	℣ Ego enim Dominus Deus	Is 41.13–14	
	℣ Quare dicis Iacob	Is 40.27	
	℣ Popule meus Israel	Is 41.8, 43.5	
	*℣ Gaude et laetare Syon	Am 4.12	
	℣ Israel si me audieris	Ps 80.9–11	
6ʳ	℟ Ecce Dominus ueniet	Zec 14.5–6, 8–9	6586 (22)
	℣ A solis ortu	Ps 106.3	
	℣ Ecce cum uirtute	2 Chr 17.5, Jude 25	
6ʳ	℟ Hierusalem surge	Bar 5.5, 4.36	7034 (23)
	℣ Leua in circuitu	Is 49.18/60.4, Nm 27.12	
	*℣ Dilataberis ad orientem	Gn 82.14	
6ʳ	℟ Ciuitas Hierusalem	——	6290 (24)
	℣ Ecce dominator Dominus	Is 40.10	
	SECOND NOCTURN		
6ʳ⁻ᵛ	℟ Ecce ueniet Dominus protector	Is 43.14, Rv 14.14	6613 (25)
	℣ Et dominabitur a mari	Ps 71.8	
	*℣ Veniet in nubibus caeli	Mt 24.30/Mk 13.26	
6ᵛ	℟ Sicut mater	Is 66.13–14	7660 (26)
	℣ Dabo in Syon	Is 46.13	
	*℣ Ecce ueniet Dominus quem	Mal 3.1	
6ᵛ	℟ Hierusalem plantabis	Jer 31.5–7	7033 (27)
	℣ Exulta satis	Zec 9.9	
	℣ Sion noli timere	Jn 12.15	
6ᵛ	℟ Egredietur dominus de Samaria	——	6639 (28)
	℣ Et preparabitur in misericordia	Is 16.5	
	*℣ Preparabitur solium iustitiae	Is 16.5, Mal 3.3	
	THIRD NOCTURN		
6ᵛ	℟ Rex noster	——	7547 (29)
	℣ Ecce Agnus Dei	Jn 1.29	
	℣ Super ipsum continebunt	Is 52.15, 11.10	
6ᵛ–7ʳ	℟ Ecce ab [A]ustro	Hb 3.3	6570 (73)
	℣ Aspiciam uos et crescere	Lv 26.9	
	*℣ Ecce uenio cito	Rv 22.12	
7ʳ	℟ Festina ne	Ps 39.18	6728 (92)
	℣ Veni Domine et noli tardare	Hb 2.3	
	*℣ Tuam Domine excita potentiam	Ps 79.3	
7ʳ	℟ Paratus esto	Am 4.12–13	7351 (94)
	℣ De radice Iesse	Is 11.1	
	*℣ Ecce ueniet cum uirtute magna	Is 40.10, 1 Cor 4.5	

Table 7   (cont.)

Folios	Incipit	Source	CAO, IV (v)
	THIRD SUNDAY OF ADVENT: FIRST NOCTURN		
9ᵛ	℟ Ecce apparebit	Rv 14.14, Dt 33.2, Rv 19.16	6578 (31)
	℣ Apparebit in finem	Hb 2.3	
	℣ Dominus de Syna ueniet	Dt 33.2, Is 63.1	
9ᵛ	℟ Bethleem ciuitas	Mi 5.2, 4–5	6254 (32)
	℣ Deus a Libano ueniet	Hb 3.3	
	℣ Loquetur pacem gentibus	Zec 9.10	
9ᵛ	℟ Qui uenturus	Heb 10.37	7485 (33)
	℣ Ex Syon species	Ps 49.2–3	
9ᵛ–10ʳ	℟ Suscipe uerbum	——	7744 (34)
	℣ Paries quidem filium	Is 7.14/Mt 1.21/ Lk 1.31	
	*℣ Salue semper Sancta Virgo	——	
	SECOND NOCTURN		
10ʳ	℟ Aegipte noli	——	6056 (35)
	*℣ Gaude et letare Iacob	——	
	℣ Ecce ueniet Dominus exercituum	Is 3.1	
10ʳ	℟ Prope est ut ueniat	Is 14.1	7438 (36)
	℣ Qui uenturus est	Heb 10.37	
	℣ Reuertere uirgo	Jer 31.21	
10ʳ	℟ Descendet Dominus	Ps 71.6–7	6408 (37)
	℣ Et adorabunt eum	Ps 71.11	
	*℣ Et conflabunt gladios suos	Is 2.4	
10ʳ	℟ Veni Domine et noli	Hb 2.3	7824 (38)
	℣ Excita Domine	Ps 79.3	
	*℣ Miserere templi sanctificationis tuae	Sir 36.15	
	THIRD NOCTURN		
10ʳ⁻ᵛ	℟ Ecce radix Iesse	Is 11.10	6606 (39)
	℣ Dabit illi Dominus Deus	Lk 1.32	
	℣ Radix Iesse qui exsurget	Rom 15.12	
10ᵛ	℟ Docebit nos Dominus	Is 2.3	6481 (70)
	℣ Venite ascendamus	Is 2.3	
	℣ Domus Iacob uenite	Is 2.5	
10ᵛ	℟ Egredietur uirga	Is 11.1, 5	6641 (81)
	℣ Et requiescet super eum	Is 11.2	
	*℣ Egressus eius erit	Mi 5.2, Is 52.15	
10ᵛ	℟ Ecce ueniet Dominus princeps	——	6612 (71)
	℣ Veni Domine et noli tardare	Hb 2.3	
	*℣ Propterea expectat Dominus	Is 30.18	

Table 7   (*cont.*)

Folios	Incipit	Source	*CAO*, ɪv (v)
	FOURTH SUNDAY OF ADVENT: **FIRST NOCTURN**		
11ᵛ	℟ Canite tubam in Syon	Jer 4.5, Is 62.11	6265 (41)
	℣ Adnunciate illut in finibus	Jer 31.10	
	*℣ Properate et clamate	Jos 6.10	
11ᵛ	℟ Octaua decima die	Is 19.20, Ex 23.20, Dt 31.7/ Jgs 2.1	7309bis/ 7886 (42)
	℣ Inuocabitis me et ibitis	Jer 29.12	
	℣ Ego sum Dominus Deus uester	Ex 20.2/Lv 19.36/25.38/Dt 5.6	
11ᵛ	℟ Non auferetur	Gn 49.10	7224 (43)
	℣ Pulcriores sunt oculi eius	Gn 49.12	
11ᵛ	℟ Me oportet	Jn 3.30, 1.27	7137 (44)
	℣ Hoc est testimonium	Jn 1.15	
	℣ Ego quidem baptizaui uos	Mk 1.8	
	SECOND NOCTURN		
11ᵛ	℟ Ecce iam uenit	Gal 4.4–5	6596bis/ 6596 (45)
	℣ Prope est ut ueniat	Is 14.1	
	℣ Propter nimiam karitatem	Eph 2.4, Rom 8.3	
11ᵛ–12ʳ	℟ Virgo Israel	Jer 31.21–2	7903 (46)
	℣ In karitate perpetua	Jer 31.3	
	*℣ Gaude et letare filia	Zec 2.10	
12ʳ	℟ Iuraui dicit Dominus	Is 54.9–10	7045 (47)
	℣ Iuxta est salus	Is 56.1	
	*℣ Non transibunt per Hierusalem	Jl 3.17–18	
12ʳ	℟ Non discedimus	Ps 79.19–20	7227 (48)
	℣ Domine Deus uirtutum	Ps 79.20	
	℣ Memento nostri Domine	Ps 105.4	
	*℣ Intuere et respice	Lam 5.1, Mk 9.21	
	THIRD NOCTURN		
12ʳ	℟ Intuemini	Heb 7.4	6983 (49)
	℣ Et dominabitur a mari	Ps 71.8	
	℣ Precursor pro nobis	Heb 6.20	
12ʳ	℟ Modo ueniet	Mal 3.1, Is 7.14	7172 (53)
	℣ Orietur in diebus	Ps 71.7	
	*℣ Appropinquabit enim salus	Rom 11.11	
12ʳ⁻ᵛ	℟ Adnunciatum est	——	6103 (93)
	*℣ Suscepit infirma nostri corporis	——	
	*℣ Missus ab arce patris	——	
12ᵛ	℟ Nascetur nobis	Is 9.6–7	7195 (91)
	*℣ Adueniet nobis angelus	——	
	℣ In ipso benedicentur omnes	Ps 71.17	

responsories for the second, third and fourth Sundays in Pa 1085 matches none of the monastic manuscripts consulted by Hesbert.[92] The first twelve responsories for the first Sunday (Pa 1085 includes five responsories in the third nocturn for a total of thirteen) agree with Hesbert's group G, consisting of nine manuscripts, all a century or more younger than Pa 1085, and all but one of which are Cistercian in origin.[93] I consider this agreement to be inconsequential.

More important is the accord between Pa 1085 and what Hesbert defines as the Roman or secular cursus. A substantial core of secular Office manuscripts agree in the identity and order of the nine responsories for each of the Sundays of Advent.[94] Pa 1085 retains these pieces, in order, as the first nine responsories for each feast. This arrangement is by no means unique among monastic manuscripts, as Hesbert's tables show, and its presence in Pa 1085, one of the earliest sources of the monastic Office, further substantiates Hesbert's assertion that the monastic cursus derives from the secular Office.[95] The parallel between the repertory of Pa 1085 and the secular cursus does not persist throughout, however. In the Office of Holy Innocents, for example, agreement in the identity of the responsories does not bind the six secular manuscripts edited by Hesbert, in the first place, and, in the second place, Pa 1085 differs from all of them: its second and fifth responsories, *Vidi sub altare* and *Vidi turbam magnam*, respectively, occur in none of the six.[96] These differences illustrate the independence that individual monastic institutions exercised in shaping their liturgies in this period.

The independence of Pa 1085 further emerges from a consideration of its treatment of verses for the Matins responsories. As Tables 5 and 7 show, Pa 1085 regularly lists two or more verses

---

[92] Complete lists of responsories for each of the three Sundays are given in Hesbert, *CAO*, v, pp. 62–8, 86–92, 108–14, respectively. Monastic manuscripts bear sigla starting from 601. Hesbert analyses the groups of monastic manuscripts for these three feasts in *CAO*, v, pp. 84–5, 106–7, 129–30, respectively.

[93] List of responsories, *ibid.*, v, pp. 35–41; groupings of monastic manuscripts, *ibid.*, v, pp. 60–1.

[94] *Ibid.*, v, pp. 27–31. For the manuscripts that agree on each of the Sundays in Advent, see *ibid.*, v, pp. 57–9, 82–5, 104–7, 128–9, respectively.

[95] *Ibid.*, v, pp. 28–31, 233–58.

[96] *Ibid.*, i, no. 22, presents synoptically the contents of all six secular manuscripts for this feast.

for each responsory: every item for Holy Innocents includes two (Table 5), and forty-four of the forty-nine responsories sung on the four Sundays of Advent incorporate two or more verses (Table 7). Three of the Advent pieces list three verses, and one, *Hierusalem cito* for the second Sunday, gives no fewer than five verses. The sheer quantity of verses in the responsories of Pa 1085 far outstrips that of any other known Office manuscript readily available for consultation. Of the 800 manuscripts surveyed by Hesbert, only MR, containing thirty-one Advent responsories with multiple verses, comes close to the prolixity of Pa 1085.[97]

Peter Wagner suggested that multiple verses were exceptional only in older manuscripts, and more common in younger sources.[98] His first observation, however, is based on SG 390–1, a source which Hesbert finds unusual in that it follows the secular form of Matins in giving nine responsories for most feasts instead of the monastic form with twelve.[99] The arrangement of verses, then, may also accord more closely with secular than with monastic usage. Certainly, Amalarius regards the use of one verse to be the norm in secular Matins. In the prologue to his commentary on the antiphoner he suggests that, when two or three verses are supplied for a responsory that is to be sung two or three times in the week, a different verse is used on each occasion.[100] If this were the case, however, there would be no need to mark a different point of departure for the *repetendum* after each verse, usually effecting a progressive shortening of the respond, as the example cited above from *Sub altare Dei*, the first responsory for Holy Innocents, shows.

The number and arrangement of the responsorial verses in Pa 1085 suggest that they served to increase the solemnity of the most important feasts at St Martial (just the reason that Amalarius attributes to his Roman informant – 'propter honorem magnae festivitatis' – but subsequently dismisses in favour of the expla-

---

[97] *Ibid.*, VI, pp. 2–3; Hesbert gives the complete listing of verses for the Advent responsories in all 800 sources, *ibid.*, VI, pp. 56–78.
[98] Wagner, *Einführung*, I, pp. 137–8. See also Hucke, 'Das Responsorium', pp. 159–60; and Hiley, *Western Plainchant*, p. 70.
[99] Hesbert, *CAO*, II, pp. VI–IX.
[100] Amalarius, *Liber de ordine antiphonarii*, Prologue 1–2, ed. Hanssens, III, p. 13.

nation advanced above). For example, when Adémar de Chabannes adapted the existing episcopal liturgy for the abbey's patron
to create an apostolic version, he doubled the number of verses
for each responsory to two.[101] And, in a later version of the
apostolic liturgy, he contemplated using as many as four verses
for each responsory.[102] Other Offices compiled by Adémar show
that, in his mind, the quantity of responsorial verses indicated
the importance of the feast. St Cybard, the patron of Adémar's
home abbey in Angoulême, and Sts Valery and Austriclinian,
companions of St Martial, all held inferior stations to the newly
elevated apostle Martial, and the responsories in their Offices
are supplied with one verse each, with the exception of the
twelfth responsory in Valery's office, which is furnished with two
verses.[103]

Beyond sheer quantity, however, the verses in Pa 1085 exhibit
the manuscript's independence in another way: the number of
Advent verses that are apparently unica. Of the ninety-nine
verses listed for the season in Pa 1085, twenty-seven are unknown
in the 800 manuscripts consulted by Hesbert.[104] These verses are
marked with an asterisk in Table 7. In contrast, the source with
the greatest number of unique verses in Hesbert's survey, a
thirteenth-century breviary from San Rufo, contains only five
verses that are otherwise unattested.[105] Neither MR nor SG 390–
1, on the other hand, contains any unica among its verses for
Advent. Again, Pa 1085 stands out as the witness of a singular
liturgical practice.

How singular? Do the unique verses represent a regional or
even institutional practice, or do they belong to a broader tradition that does not survive in sources elsewhere? An examination
of the verses' literary structure suggests that the unica in Pa
1085 belong to the same milieu as the more widely disseminated
texts. The verses fall into three categories: quotations from scripture, non-scriptural texts and texts that paraphrase or combine

---

[101] Episcopal liturgy, Pa 1085, fols. 76ᵛ–77ʳ; apostolic, Pa 909, fols. 62ᵛ–74ᵛ.
[102] Pa 1978, fols. 103ʳ⁻ᵛ.
[103] Cybard, Pa 1978, fols. 102ʳ⁻ᵛ (see Delisle, 'Notice', pp. 351–2); Valery and Austriclinian, Pa 909, fols. 78ʳ–81ᵛ and 81ᵛ–85ᵛ, respectively (see Emerson, 'Two Newly Identified Offices', pp. 43–6).
[104] Hesbert, *CAO*, vi, pp. 7–55, gives the complete list of verses.
[105] Hesbert's source 534; see *ibid.*, v, p. 17.

several passages from scripture.[106] The first two categories need not long detain us. Although none of the verses in Pa 1085 that are attested elsewhere is non-scriptural, several of the Advent responds are, most notable among which is the first, *Aspiciens a longe*. Non-biblical texts occur frequently in the responsories throughout the liturgical year, especially in the feasts of the sanctorale, which often use the saints' *uitae*, but also in some temporale feasts, such as Christmas.[107]

The last category, texts that use scriptural sources in paraphrase and combination, is of greater significance.[108] The verse *Ecce cum uirtute* provides a good example of the technique. Sung as part of the responsory *Ecce Dominus ueniet*, in the first nocturn of the second Sunday of Advent, it is found in nearly 500 of Hesbert's sources.[109] Table 8 gives the version in Pa 1085 together with its biblical sources. The verse combines passages from the extremes of the Bible (one of the Judaeo-Hebrew historical books and a New Testament epistle) with a commonplace exhortation to create a new text suitable for the liturgical season. A similar adaptation occurs in the verse *Propter nimiam karitatem* (℟ *Ecce iam uenit*, fourth Sunday of Advent, second nocturn), which is also widely known.[110] The responds in Pa 1085, all of which were widely circulated, exhibit the same technique of composition in several instances. Perhaps the most extreme example is *Ecce*

Table 8   *The verse* Ecce cum uirtute

Biblical sources		Pa 1085, fol. 6ʳ
2 Chr 17.5	Confirmauitque Dominus regnum in manu eius,	Ecce cum uirtute ueniet, et regnum in manu eius
Jude 25	imperium et potestas ante omne saeculum.	et potestas et imperium.

---

[106] The scriptural origins of the texts are indicated in Table 7 above. A dash denotes a non-scriptural text.

[107] For an example from the sanctorale, see R. Steiner, 'The Music for a Cluny Office of Saint Benedict', *Monasticism and the Arts*, ed. T. G. Verdon and J. Dally (Syracuse, 1984), pp. 81–113. On Matins for Christmas, see Crocker, 'Liturgical Materials of Roman Chant', pp. 125–6.

[108] On responsorial texts, see Alfonzo, *I responsori biblici*, esp. pp. 30–47.

[109] Hesbert, *CAO*, vi, pp. 20–1.

[110] *Ibid.*, vi, pp. 33–4.

Table 9   *The responsory* Ecce apparebit

Biblical sources		CAO, IV, no. 6578
Rv 14.14	Et uidi et ecce nubem candidam:	Ecce apparebit dominus super nubem candidam,
Dt 33.2	et cum eo sanctorum millia.	et cum eo sanctorum millia,
Rv 19.16	Et habet in uestimento et in femore suo scriptum: Rex regum et Dominus dominantium.	et habens in vestimento et in femore suo scriptum: Rex regum, et Dominus dominantium.

apparebit, the first responsory on the third Sunday of Advent (see Table 9).[111] Pio Alfonzo, who worked primarily on the Hartker Antiphoner, SG 390–1, felt that respond texts of this type were infrequent.[112] Several of the unique verses in Pa 1085 follow the same pattern. One example is *Gressus rectos facite*, from the responsory *Confortamini*, in the third nocturn of the first Sunday of Advent (see Table 10). Here passages from one of the didactic books of the Old Testament and a Pauline epistle are combined, with slight modifications to retain the sense.

Two conclusions result from these observations. First, the unique verses in Pa 1085 agree in literary style with the better-known Advent verses. But do they represent the original work of monks at St Martial, like Roger de Chabannes, who adopted for new compositions the techniques they observed in the central tradition? Or did these unique verses originally form part of that mainstream tradition that has otherwise perished? The second

Table 10   *The verse* Gressus rectos facite

Biblical sources		Pa 1085, fol. 5r
Heb 12.13	et gressus rectos facite pedibus uestris	Gressus rectos facite pedibus uestris
Jb 4.4	Vacilantes confirmauerunt sermones tui,	et vacillantes confirment sermones uestri.

[111] It occurs in all but eighteen of Hesbert's sources: *ibid.*, VI, p. 25. Table 9 gives the text of *CAO* because Pa 1085 provides the incipit only.

[112] Alfonzo, *I responsori biblici*, pp. 37–8.

conclusion helps to answer these questions, and that is that this technique of composition very closely resembles that observed by Kenneth Levy in certain offertories whose texts derive from scriptural books other than the psalter.[113] The creators of these texts adapted scriptural language with the purpose of providing literary material suitable for musical setting. Levy further hypothesises that this type of offertory might have originated in the Gallican liturgy. With this suggestion in mind, it is striking to note that the two widely circulated Advent verses that evince this technique, *Ecce cum uirtute* and *Propter nimiam karitatem*, occur in Pa 1085 and MR, two early west-Frankish sources, but not in SG 390–1, an early east-Frankish witness, which also, according to Alfonzo, rarely uses responds of this type.[114] Even more striking is the juxtaposition of this apparently Gallican technique of composition with the Roman characteristics seen elsewhere in Pa 1085.[115] It is possible, then, that the usage which this codex attests is a unique blend of Gallican and Roman practices.

The abundance of multiple verses in Pa 1085 permits a speculation on the history of responsorial singing in the western liturgy. Many scholars state that, in its earliest form, the responsory consisted of an entire psalm, sung by a soloist, with a choral refrain repeated after each verse, and that the use of a single verse in the Carolingian liturgy constitutes an abbreviation of the original practice.[116] This reconstruction is based upon the

---

[113] K. Levy, 'Toledo, Rome and the Legacy of Gaul', *Early Music History*, 4 (1984), pp. 49–99. See also Wagner, *Einführung*, I, pp. 322–43; P. Pietschmann, 'Die nicht dem Psalter entnommenen Messgesangstücke auf ihre Textgestalt untersucht', *Jahrbuch für Liturgiewissenschaft*, 12 (1932), pp. 87–144, esp. pp. 114–30; and Hucke, 'Die Texte der Offertorien', *Speculum musicae artis*, ed. Becker and Gerlach, pp. 193–203.

[114] Hesbert, *CAO*, VI, pp. 20–1, 33–4. The sigla for SG 390–1 and MR are 500 and 728, respectively; see *CAO*, V, pp. 11, 16. Alfonzo, *I responsori biblici*, pp. 37–9.

[115] On the presence of Gallican items in Aquitanian manuscripts, esp. Pa 776, see A. Gastoué, 'Le chant gallican', *Revue du Chant Grégorien*, 41 (1937), pp. 132–3 (this article consists of a series of contributions to *Revue du Chant Grégorien*, 41–3 (1937–9); repr. separately Grenoble, 1939); M. Huglo, 'Les *preces* des graduels aquitains empruntées à la liturgie hispanique', *Hispania Sacra*, 8 (1955), pp. 361–83; and O. Cullin, 'Une pièce gallicane conservée par la liturgie de Gaillac: L'offertoire Salvator Mundi pour les défunts', *Liturgie et musique*, pp. 287–96.

[116] Wagner, *Einführung*, I, p. 133; Apel, *Gregorian Chant*, pp. 180–5; Hughes, *Medieval Manuscripts*, pp. 26–30 and fig. 2.2, p. 33. On the eastern origin of solo psalmody, see J. Dyer, 'Monastic Psalmody of the Middle Ages', *Revue Bénédictine*, 99 (1989), pp. 41–74; and on its introduction to the West, P. Jeffery, 'The Introduction of Psalmody into the Roman Mass by Pope Celestine I (422–432): Reinterpreting a Passage in the *Liber Pontificalis*', *Archiv für Liturgiewissenschaft*, 26 (1984), pp. 147–65.

vaguely worded descriptions of liturgical singing in patristic writings.[117] St Augustine offers the most specific comments about responsorial singing in two passages, couched in nearly identical words, from his commentary on the psalms, which indicate that the entire psalm was sung in his time.[118] Frankish evidence from the sixth century suggests that the style of performance known to Augustine persisted into that period. Gregory of Tours, when discussing a late sixth-century Frankish context, refers to the *psalmus responsorius*, without defining or describing it.[119] A Gallican source from the sixth century, Pa 11947, the Psalter of St Germain, contains the mark R beside individual verses, which is taken to indicate the choral refrain in a responsorial setting of a complete psalm.[120]

Isidore of Seville, writing around A D 600, describes the responsory as an ancient practice, but does not mention the use of multiple verses or indicate that the responsorial texts are drawn from the psalter.[121] His description, then, contradicts neither Augustine nor Amalarius. Pierre Batiffol understood the texts of the tenth-century responsories to represent a composite state, perhaps originating in the seventh century, despite the presence of readings from an early form of the Latin Bible, predating the translations of St Jerome.[122] This evidence led him to express

---

[117] Most of the pertinent texts are collected and translated in *Music in Early Christian Literature*, ed. J. McKinnon, Cambridge Readings in the Literature of Music (Cambridge, 1987); see esp. passages from Tertullian (McKinnon, no. 78, p. 44), Athanasius (no. 102, p. 54), Basil the Great (no. 139, pp. 68–9), John Chrysostom (nos. 178, 184, pp. 84, 86, respectively), Eusebius of Caesarea (no. 208, p. 98), Sozomen (no. 221, p. 103), Egeria (no. 253, p. 117), Ambrose (nos. 276, 289, pp. 126–7, 130, respectively), Augustine (nos. 364, 374, pp. 159, 162, respectively) and Gennadius (no. 398, p. 170). See also H. Leeb, *Die Psalmodie bei Ambrosius*, Wiener Beiträge zur Theologie 18 (Vienna, 1967), pp. 17–18, 31, 53–80; and Hucke, 'Das Responsorium', pp. 150–5.

[118] Augustine of Hippo, *Enarrationes in Psalmos*, ad 46.1, 119.1, ed. E. Dekkers and J. Fraipont, 3 vols., Corpus Christianorum Series Latina 38–40 (Turnhout, 1956), I, p. 529, III, p. 1776.

[119] Gregory of Tours, *Historia Francorum*, 8.3, ed. B. Krusch and W. Levison, *MGH*, *Scriptores rerum merouingicarum*, I, pt 1, 2nd edn (Hanover, 1937–51), pp. 372–3.

[120] Gastoué, 'Le chant gallican', *Revue du Chant Grégorien*, 41 (1937), pp. 104–5; and M. Huglo, 'Le répons-graduel de la messe: Évolution de la forme, permanence de la fonction', *Schweizer Jahrbuch für Musikwissenschaft*, new ser., 2 (1982), pp. 53–73.

[121] Isidore of Seville, *De ecclesiasticis officiis*, 1.8, ed. C. M. Lawson, Corpus Christianorum Series Latina 113 (Turnhout, 1989), p. 8; see also *Etymologiae*, 6.19.8, ed. W. M. Lindsay, 2 vols., Scriptorum Classicorum Bibliotheca Oxoniensis (Oxford, 1911), without pagination.

[122] P. Batiffol, 'L'origine du *Liber responsalis* de l'église romaine', *Revue des Questions*

grave reservations about the historical connection between the *psalmus responsorius* of late antiquity and the Carolingian responsory.[123] If such an association did exist, the multiple verses in Pa 1085 should betray at least some vestiges of the practice.

The bulk of evidence from the Advent verses in Pa 1085 weighs against accepting this link. First, there is the question of the texts, of both responds and verses, that either are non-scriptural or consist of adaptations of scriptural passages, as illustrated above. Second, many of the texts that are quotations from the Bible come from books other than the psalter. In both these cases, it is difficult to imagine a complete psalm as the historical antecedent.[124] In the second instance, though, the possibility remains that a chapter, or part of one, substituted for a psalm, a point that receives further discussion below. Moreover, the verses, no matter what their origin, exercise a certain amount of mobility. *A solis ortu*, for example, drawn from Psalm 106.3, appears in Pa 1085 with two responsories during the Advent season, and, among the sources surveyed by Hesbert, with a total of twenty-two different responsories, including the two in Pa 1085.[125] In fact, the whole question of the verses' variability speaks strongly against the historical connection with the fourth-century *psalmus responsorius*.[126]

Other evidence presents equally strong arguments. In many cases, respond and verses are drawn from different books of the Bible. The responsory *Saluatorem exspectamus*, for example, occurs in virtually all the manuscripts consulted by Hesbert, and it exhibits considerable stability in the tradition.[127] Hesbert encoun-

Historiques, 55 (1894), pp. 220–8. On the early state of the texts, see *ibid.*, pp. 223–4, citing correspondence from a M. Berger (Samuel Berger, according to Alfonzo); G. M[orin], 'Les témoins de la tradition grégorienne', *Revue Bénédictine*, 7 (1890), p. 321 (also published as part of *idem*, *Les véritables origines du chant grégorien* (Abbaye de Maredsous, 1890; 3rd edn, 1912)); and Alfonzo, *I responsori biblici*, pp. 46–7.

[123] P. Batiffol, *Histoire du bréviaire romain*, 3rd edn, Bibliothèque d'Histoire Religieuse (Paris, 1911), pp. 121–2. See also Hucke, 'Das Responsorium', pp. 157–9.

[124] Crocker, 'Liturgical Materials of Roman Chant', pp. 136–7.

[125] Pa 1085 (see Table 7 above): R *Audite uerbum* (first Sunday of Advent, second nocturn) and R *Ecce Dominus ueniet* (second Sunday of Advent, first nocturn). Hesbert, *CAO*, VI, pp. 7–55.

[126] Hesbert, *CAO*, VI, pp. 1–282, considers this issue with the aim of attempting to establish an 'archetypal' list of verses for the Advent responsories. See also Alfonzo, *I responsori biblici*, pp. 42–5.

[127] Hesbert, *CAO*, VI, pp. 15–16. In Pa 1085 it falls in the second nocturn of the first Sunday of Advent; see Table 7 above.

tered a total of three different verses with it, but the overwhelming majority of sources (751 out of the 756 manuscripts that include it) present one or both of the two verses that occur in Pa 1085. (Five manuscripts, including MR, give both verses.) Furthermore, all three texts (the respond and the two verses) are exact quotations of scripture. But they occur in three different books of the Bible: two Pauline epistles and the psalter. Again, it is difficult to reconcile this item with Augustine's description of responsorial psalmody.

The responsories give the impression, in general, that they are the result of a careful and deliberate selection and combination of texts that are appropriate to the season. *Saluatorem exspectamus* serves as a typical example.[128]

℟ Salvatorem exspectamus Dominum Jesum Christum, qui reformavit corpus humilitatis nostrae, configuratum corpori claritatis suae. (Phil 3.20–1)
℣ Preoccupemus faciem eius in confessione, et in psalmis iubilemus ei, (Ps 94.2)
℟ Qui reformavit corpus humilitatis nostrae, configuratum corpori claritatis suae.
℣ Sobrie et iuste et pie uiuamus in hoc seculo expectantes beatam spem et aduentum glorie magni dei, (Ti 2.12–13)
℟ Qui reformavit corpus humilitatis nostrae, configuratum corpori claritatis suae.
℣ Gloria patri, et filio et spiritui sancto. sicut erat in principio, et nunc, et semper, et in saecula saeculorum, amen.
℟ Salvatorem exspectamus Dominum Jesum Christum, qui reformavit corpus humilitatis nostrae, configuratum corpori claritatis suae.

℟ We await the saviour, the Lord Jesus Christ, who reformed the body of our humility, configured according to the body of his clarity.
℣ Let us come before his face in confession, and let us rejoice in psalms for him,
℟ Who reformed the body of our humility, configured according to the body of his clarity.
℣ Let us live soberly, justly and piously in this age, awaiting the blessed hope and coming of the glory of the great God,
℟ Who reformed the body of our humility, configured according to the body of his clarity.

---

[128] The respond is taken from Hesbert, *CAO*, IV, no. 7562, because Pa 1085 gives only the incipit. The verses are taken from Pa 1085, fol. 4ʳ, as are the cues for the *repetenda*.

℣ Glory be to the Father, the Son and the Holy Ghost. As it was in the beginning, so it shall be now and always, for ever and ever, amen. ℟ We await the saviour, the Lord Jesus Christ, who reformed the body of our humility, configured according to the body of his clarity.

Preoccupemus, the verse from Psalm 94, does not specifically mention the theme of Christ's Advent, although it does exhort the rejoicing that will accompany that event. The two Pauline texts, however, are centrally concerned with the anticipation of the season, and the verse neatly echoes the respond with the key word 'expecto' ('I await'). The whole forms a satisfying literary unit. Moreover, the *repetenda* create logical grammatical units, a matter of some importance to Amalarius.[129] It is to preserve grammatical sense, therefore, that the *repetenda* after both verses are the same, instead of the second repeat's being shortened, because no suitable place to begin the second *repetendum* is available.

The accumulated evidence suggests that, at some time after the late antique period, and possibly not before the seventh century, liturgical responsories were introduced that differed significantly in textual form from the fourth-century *psalmus responsorius*. One example from the Advent responsories in Pa 1085, however, might preserve a trace of the earlier practice. *Docebit nos Dominus* is assigned to the last nocturn of the third Sunday of Advent, where it is presented with two verses, *Venite ascendamus* and *Domus Iacob uenite* (see Table 7 above). The respond was widely circulated, appearing in over 700 of the manuscripts in Hesbert's survey, and both verses in Pa 1085 are attested, although only fourteen manuscripts present *Domus Iacob*.[130] No manuscript known to Hesbert, however, preserves the form of the responsory found in Pa 1085: seven manuscripts give two verses, but all join *Venite ascendamus* with *Ex Sion species*, a verse taken from Psalm 49.2–3.

Aside from its uniqueness, the arrangement in Pa 1085 is also noteworthy for the fact that it combines three texts all taken from the same scriptural passage, Isaiah 2. The first five verses

---

[129] Amalarius, *Prologus de ordine antiphonarii*, 12–13, and *Liber de ordine antiphonarii*, 18.6–8, ed. Hanssens, I, pp. 362–3, and III, p. 55, respectively. See also Crocker, 'Liturgical Materials of Roman Chant', pp. 126–7.

[130] Hesbert, *CAO*, VI, p. 47.

of this chapter describe the new home of God, perched on a mountain top, to which all nations will come for judgment. By analogy, the coming of this new home can be associated with the Advent of Christ, and so the passage can be made to suit the Advent season. Pa 1085 uses verses 3 and 5 for its version of *Docebit*, and verse 4 occurs in one of the unique responsorial verses in Pa 1085, with the responsory *Descendet Dominus* in the second nocturn of the same Sunday (see Table 7 above). It is not beyond the realm of possibility that somewhere in the prehistory of *Docebit* lies a responsorial form similar to that which Augustine describes, which used the first five verses of Isaiah 2. The non-psalmodic nature of the text makes the connection with Augustine's account all the more noteworthy.

Nevertheless, the isolation of *Docebit* in Pa 1085 lessens the weight of its testimony. No other source preserves precisely this combination of texts, and no other Advent responsory in Pa 1085 duplicates the selection of multiple texts from the same passage of scripture. Where two texts share origins, either the responsory uses a single verse (e.g. ℟ *Missus est*, first Sunday of Advent, first nocturn, where Luke 1 is the source of both respond and verse), or it combines two excerpts from the same passage with texts from other sources (e.g. ℟ *Aspiciens a longe*, first Sunday of Advent, first nocturn, which combines two verses from Psalm 79 with a third verse from Psalm 48 and a non-scriptural respond). These examples indicate that, when two or more texts derive from the same scriptural source, their combination is more likely to be the result of compositional planning than the abbreviation of an earlier, fuller responsorial form.

Codex Pa 1085, therefore, preserves a repertory of responsories that is remarkable on a number of counts. Several of the pieces exhibit a compositional technique (namely the combination and adaptation of passages from different books of scripture) that some scholars, principally Kenneth Levy, would associate with the Gallican liturgy. It shares this feature with MR (but not SG 390–1), as it does, too, an abundance of multiple verses in the Offices of important feasts, like the Sundays of Advent and Holy Innocents. This connection, together with Amalarius's apparent unfamiliarity with the practice, and the nearly total absence of such multiple verses in SG 390–1, suggests two hypotheses. First, the usage may be monastic in origin: both MR and Pa 1085 come from Benedictine houses, and Amalarius seems more conversant with the secular liturgy; SG 390–1, though monastic, reflects secular usage in other ways (e.g. by giving nine responsories for many feasts). And, second, it could also reflect an older, Gallican practice, dating back to pre-Carolingian times.

Finally, its treatment of the doxology is unique: it calls for the longer form of the text, which usually occurs in antiphonal psalmody, and for which there is no parallel among readily available Office manuscripts; it requires the doxology to be sung after every responsory, in the Roman custom; and it seems to indicate that the entire respond be sung after the doxology, again in keeping with Roman, as opposed to Frankish, usage. The preference for Roman customs is indeed strange in a house that claimed its origins in a donation of the Frankish emperor Louis the Pious.[131] Whatever the origins of this *mélange* of practice, it is clear that Pa 1085 reflects a highly idiosyncratic liturgy in comparison with other monastic sources of comparable age. The liturgical independence of St Martial became one of the first victims after the purchase and forcible takeover of the abbey by the monks of Cluny in 1062–3.[132] Subsequent books for the Office, namely Pa 743 (an eleventh-century breviary) and Pa 1088 (a

---

[131] See the diploma copied into Pa 5², fol. 221ᵛ; printed in L. Guibert, *Documents, analyses de pièces, extraits & notes relatifs à l'histoire municipale des deux villes de Limoges*, ɪ, Société des Archives Historiques du Limousin, ser. 1, Archives Anciennes 7 (Limoges, 1897), no. 123, pp. 111–12; and Lasteyrie, *L'abbaye de Saint-Martial*, pièce justificative 2, pp. 420–1. See also Adémar, *Chronicon*, 3.16, ed. Chavanon, p. 131; Lair, *Historia*, p. 105; and Sermon 22 of Adémar de Chabannes, Pa 2469, fol. 68ᵛ (Lasteyrie, *L'abbaye de Saint-Martial*, p. 45, n. 2 also cites a sermon on fol. 78ᵛ, but neither Sermon 25 nor 26, both of which appear on this page, refers to the abbey's imperial patron). On the falsehood of this claim, see Lasteyrie, *L'abbaye de Saint-Martial*, pp. 41–50.

[132] The chief narrative source is a note in Pa 11019, pp. 165–9; printed in J.-B. Champeval, ed., 'Chroniques de Saint-Martial de Limoges, Supplément', *BSAHL*, 42 (1894), no. XV, pp. 322–4; and Lasteyrie, *L'abbaye de Saint-Martial*, pièce justificative 7, pp. 427–9. Another copy occurs in Limoges, Archives Départementales de la Haute-Vienne, MS 3 H 6 (3). See also Peter Damian, *De gallica Petri Damiani profectione et eius ultramontano itinere*, 14–15, ed. G. Schwartz and A. Hofmeister, *MGH, Scriptorum*, xxx, pt 2 (Leipzig, 1934), pp. 1043–4; and Geoffrey of Vigeois, *Chronica*, 14, ed. P. Labbe, *Noua bibliotheca manuscriptorum librorum*, ɪɪ, *Rerum aquitanarum, praesertim bituricensium, uberrima collectio* (Paris, 1657), pp. 287–8. For commentary, see Lasteyrie, *L'abbaye de Saint-Martial*, pp. 83–6, and A. Sohn, *Der Abbatiat Ademars von Saint-Martial de Limoges (1063–1114): Ein Beitrag zur Geschichte des cluniacensischen Klösterverbandes*, Beiträge zur Geschichte des Alten Mönchtums und des Benediktinertums 37 (Münster Westfalen, 1989), pp. 46–78.

thirteenth- or fourteenth-century antiphoner) both exhibit a completely uniform Cluniac liturgy.[133]

What can we deduce about the working methods of Roger de Chabannes, if he, in fact, compiled Pa 1085? The main purpose of the codex is to preserve a comprehensive list of the sung items of the Divine Office for the entire liturgical year. Along the way, several features that indicate a unique liturgical usage were recorded, but I would be reluctant to ascribe a great deal of independence to Roger. The unique responsorial verses, for example, may be traces of an older way of singing the responsories, rather than original compositions at St Martial. The Office for Mary Magdalene could constitute an original contribution of Roger. The feast was introduced at St Martial during his lifetime, and the Office in Pa 1085 is the earliest known version. Roger's main goal, therefore, in compiling Pa 1085 was to preserve and record the existing Office liturgy at St Martial rather than to innovate.

Codex Pa 1120, the second manuscript that may have been compiled during Roger's tenure as cantor, is too well known from the literature to require a detailed account here.[134] Two aspects of its makeup pertain to my hypothesis. First, it is the earliest of the troper-prosers in use at St Martial to be organised in *libelli* according to liturgical classification (see Table 11).

Table 11   *The* libellus *structure of Pa 1120*

Folios	Inventory
1^r–66^v	Proper tropes
67^r–102^v	Ordinary tropes (fols. 103^r–105^v, later additions)
106^r–153^v	Prosae
154^r–183^v	Processional antiphons
184^r–213^v	Offertories
213^v–220^v	Antiphons and later additions

[133] Hesbert's sigla for Pa 743 and 1088 are 781 and 784, respectively; see *CAO*, v, p. 13. For their concurrence with the Cluniac sources, see *ibid.*, v, pp. 407–44, esp. pp. 411, 424–5, 429–33, 443.

[134] Crocker, 'The Repertoire of Proses', i, pp. 176–89; Chailley, 'Les anciens tropaires', pp. 165–6; *idem*, *L'école*, pp. 80–1; Husmann, *Tropen- und Sequenzenhandschriften*, pp. 128–9; Evans, *The Early Trope Repertory*, pp. 47–8; and Planchart, 'The Transmission of Medieval Chant', pp. 353–61.

Earlier sources do not present the same uniformity of appearance or organisation. Pa 1240, the tenth-century troper-proser from St Martial, collects Proper tropes into one series ordered by the liturgical kalendar, but it contains no Ordinary tropes, and its prosae, split into two groups on either side of the troper, are only loosely organised according to the kalendar.[135] Pa 1120 represents a significant departure from this mode of presentation, and becomes the standard for the production of liturgical books at St Martial through the rest of the eleventh century, as attested by Pa 1121, 909 and 1119. Moreover, like Pa 1085, 1120 is a soloist's book. All the items to which individual *libelli* are dedicated contain extensive passages to be sung by soloists. Choral passages, in the *libelli* of Proper and Ordinary tropes, and offertories are indicated by incipit only, usually with neumation. It functioned, like Pa 1085 and SG 359, as a reference guide for the cantor, with which he could plan the Mass liturgy.

The second matter of concern is the internal organisation of the items for individual feasts. By comparing the Masses in the fragmentary troper preserved in Pa 1834 with the corresponding portions of Pa 1120, it is possible to assess the procedures and preferences of the latter's scribe. In the Ascension Mass, for example, he not only took some care in managing the order of the material but also exercised his own initiative in expanding the Mass through the addition of *Hodie rex glorie*, as discussed above. This last trope is otherwise unknown in Aquitaine, although it was widely circulated in Italy.[136] The absence of music in Pa 1120 suggests that it was imported from Italy, and at least one of the Italian sources predates the Aquitanian manuscript.[137] Pa 1120 combines it with another element, *Quem euntem*, to form a single-element introductory trope, like *Quem*

---

[135] Crocker, 'The Repertoire of Proses', I, pp. 43–55, II, pp. 91–7; *idem*, 'The Repertory of Proses', pp. 154–7; Chailley, 'Les anciens tropaires', pp. 167–9; *idem*, *L'école*, pp. 78–80; and Husmann, *Tropen- und Sequenzenhandschriften*, pp. 137–9.

[136] *CT*, III, ed. Björkvall *et al.*, pp. 114, 174 (individual elements) and 270–1 (location in the sources); see also *Introitus-tropen*, I, ed. Weiss, Appendix, no. 37, pp. 447–8.

[137] Rome, Biblioteca Apostolica Vaticana, MS Vaticanus latinus 4770. See Les Moines de Solesmes, *Le graduel romain: Édition critique*, II, *Les sources* (Solesmes, 1957), p. 124; and P. Salmon, *Les manuscrits liturgiques latins de la Bibliothèque Vaticane*, II, *Sacramentaires épistoliers évangéliaires graduels missels*, Studi e Testi 253 (Vatican City, 1969), no. 401, p. 156.

creditis, and thereby duplicate the latter's function. In contrast, several Italian sources use the elements to introduce different phrases of the introit.

This manuscript contains several tropes, besides *Hodie rex glorie*, whose texts are given without music. In most cases, although their circulation was restricted within Aquitaine, they were known elsewhere, sometimes quite widely. For example, *O quam glorifico*, sung with the introit *Gaudeamus omnes* for All Saints, appears in Pa 1120 (fol. 62^r) and 909 (fols. 53^v–54^r) without music, and with music in sources from England, northern France and Germany.[138] It would seem that the scribe of Pa 1120 collected these tropes for the sake of completeness, or even curiosity, rather than utility. He may never have intended, therefore, to sing *Hodie rex glorie*, but he copied it to keep a record of other tropes for this introit.

An investigation of the other Masses that Pa 1834 and 1120 share reveals further initiatives on the part of the latter's scribe. In two cases, he restored pieces that Pa 1240 includes in the Mass for John the Baptist, which are omitted from Pa 1834. *Sancte Johannes* appears as a trope *ante sequentiam* in Pa 1240 (fol. 35^v), with music for only the first few words. The rubric in Pa 1120 (fols. 40^v–41^r), 'ALIOS', suggests, however, that the scribe understood it as an introit trope; nevertheless, no cue to an introit phrase follows, and the trope lacks music altogether.[139] Pa 1240 gives only one trope element, *Ipse prebibit ante*, for the communion (fol. 35^v), which then functions as an introduction, like *Quem creditis* in the introit for Ascension. The scribe of Pa 1120 adds it after the trope *Praescius hic* (fol. 41^v), which it shares with Pa 1834 (fol. 152^v). The cue that follows *Ipse prebibit ante*, to the beginning of the communion chant, shows that it is used here in the same way as in Pa 1240. Again, music is lacking, this time from both Pa 1240 and 1120, and the inclusion of both tropes, *Sancte Iohannes* and *Ipse prebibit ante*, seems to be motivated by a desire to retain pieces in Pa 1240 even if they cannot be used in the liturgy.

---

[138] See *AH*, xlix, no. 185, pp. 91–2; *Introitus-tropen*, i, ed. Weiss, Appendix, no. 3, p. 444; and Planchart, *The Repertory of Tropes at Winchester*, ii, no. 80, p. 102.

[139] Edition of text: *AH*, xlix, no. 511, p. 269, where its presence in Pa 1120 is not noted.

The confusion over the rubric for *Sancte Iohannes* recurs with another trope *ante sequentiam*, this time in the Mass for Pentecost. *Hodie repleuit* appears, without music, at the end of the introit tropes (fols. 37^v–38^r), and before the Greek version of the lesser doxology. Like *Sancte Iohannes*, it is introduced by the rubric 'ALIVM', which again suggests that the scribe of Pa 1120 considered it to be an introit trope. It is furnished with a cue, however, unlike *Sancte Iohannes*, and that cue is 'alleluia', which could refer to two places in the Pentecost introit (the immediately preceding trope element, *Angelicis modulis*, has the same cue, introducing the final phrase of the introit), or to a sequence. The latter interpretation is endorsed by Pa 1121 (fol. 24^r) and 1119 (fol. 46^r).[140] If *Hodie repleuit* is to be taken as an introit trope in Pa 1120, it is redundant because of the preceding trope element, *Angelicis modulis*: and if it is a trope *ante sequentiam*, it is out of place, as it should follow, rather than precede, the Greek doxology, as it does in Pa 1121. In either case, the scribe of Pa 1120 exhibits unfamiliarity with the piece and its function, a conclusion that is reinforced by its lack of music.

The Mass for the Dedication contains two pieces that are equipped with music and unknown to Pa 1834. In each case, however, the scribe of Pa 1120 does not integrate the items into the liturgy in a way that is consistent with usage at St Martial, or, in the case of the second piece, elsewhere in Aquitaine. *Beati erunt qui* occurs at the end of the offertory tropes (fol. 33^v), where it is given a cue to the text *Deus Israel*, which marks the beginning of the second section of the offertory chant. It could, therefore, function as an introductory trope to the repeat of the offertory following the second verse, which is abbreviated to use only the second half of the chant. Such a practice is not usual at St Martial, however, where offertories were sung complete for each

---

[140] Evans, *The Early Trope Repertory*, no. 115, p. 196; and *CT*, ɪɪ, *Prosules de la messe*, pt 1, *Tropes de l'alleluia*, ed. O. Marcusson, Acta Universitatis Stockholmiensis, Studia Latina Stockholmiensia 22 (Stockholm, 1976), no. 68.1, p. 133, where its presence in Pa 1120 is unacknowledged. See also *CT*, ɪɪɪ, ed. Björkvall *et al.*, pp. 273–6, where it is not listed among the introit tropes in Pa 1120. *Hodie repleuit* is one of the very few pieces without music in Pa 1120 that is entered in Pa 1121, whose scribe usually omits such items; see Evans, *The Early Trope Repertory*, pp. 47–8, and Planchart, 'The Transmission of Medieval Chant', pp. 354–5. Pa 1121, but not Pa 1119, transmits music for this trope.

repeat.[141] Again, the scribe of Pa 1120 seems to be uncertain as to the exact function of the trope. The scribe of Pa 1121 rectified the difficulty by combining *Beati erunt qui* with another trope element, *Depromit haec templi*, to form a two-element trope for the repeat of the chant either between the verses or after the second verse (fol. 21^r).[142]

Finally, the Mass for the Dedication closes with a long piece that is not identified by rubric, nor cued to any host chant: *Memor sit Dominus* (fol. 34^r). This piece, identified by Amédée Gastoué as Gallican, occurs as a processional antiphon in two Aquitanian graduals, both later in date than Pa 1120. Pa 776 includes it as part of the Pentecost procession (fol. 93^v), and Pa 903 uses it for the Common of a Bishop (fol. 141^v).[143] Neither liturgical indication is consonant with its position in Pa 1120, where, presumably, it functions as part of the recessional after the Dedication Mass. Nothing in the text marks it as Proper for one of these feasts to the exclusion of the others. Hence, the scribe of Pa 1120 exhibits some unfamiliarity with the liturgical disposition of both *Beati qui erunt* and *Memor sit Dominus*, such that it is safe to exclude him as the composer of these two items.

As in the case of Pa 1085, the main purpose of Pa 1120 seems to be one of consolidation rather than innovation. No piece found in it but not in Pa 1834 can be established as the original contribution of its compiler. This conclusion cannot stand as definitive because it is impossible to compare Pa 1120 with Pa 1834 for most of the liturgical year, and it is certainly feasible that some pieces that fall in that portion of the year that Pa 1834 does not include might have been composed by Roger de Chabannes, or whoever compiled Pa 1120. Nevertheless, the extant portions of Pa 1834 provide a large enough sample to suggest that Pa 1120 does not contain a large number of original compositions, if any at all. Moreover, the scribe of Pa 1120 exhibits more than a little confusion over the liturgical assignment

---

[141] See Grier, '*Ecce sanctum*', pp. 39–40, for the arrangement of tropes and host chant in the offertory from the apostolic Mass for the feast of St Martial.

[142] Evans, *The Early Trope Repertory*, no. 96, p. 186. The same arrangement also occurs in Pa 1119, fols. 39^v–40^r, whereas Pa 909, fols. 33^v–34^r, follows the disposition of Pa 1120.

[143] Gastoué, 'Le chant gallican', *Revue du Chant Grégorien*, 42 (1938), pp. 59–60; and Roederer, 'Eleventh-Century Aquitanian Chant', I, p. 159, II, p. 133.

of pieces for which Pa 1834 does not give clear guidance, as in the Masses for the Dedication and Pentecost. He does, however, exhibit an interest in collecting all available tropes, irrespective of the feasibility of their performance at St Martial. A collector and compiler, the scribe of Pa 1120 preserved and recorded the existing Mass liturgy as celebrated at St Martial in the early decades of the eleventh century, without, apparently, making any original contributions.

What do Pa 1085 and 1120 reveal about musical practices at St Martial during Roger's tenure as cantor? Neither codex exhibits original contributions in notational techniques. Already in Pa 1834 and the fragmentary processional in Pa 1085, the main elements of Aquitanian notation are present (see Figures 4 and 8; all examples cited below occur in the former).[144] Most notes are represented by individual puncta. Two forms of the uirga occur; both are used to indicate the end of an ascending line above a particular syllable of text (line 1, above the first syllable of 'oliuiferi'), or to denote the end of the melisma for a syllable when the line is ascending (line 1, above the third syllable of 'oliuiferi'). Descending puncta that are grouped over a single syllable are aligned vertically (line 2, above the second syllable of 'seruans').

Another neume that indicates the grouping of notes over text is the oriscus; shaped like the letter 'm', it represents a note of the same pitch as that immediately preceding with no change of syllable (line 1, above the first syllable of 'oliuiferi'). The notation employs two ligatures: the cliuis and the pes stratus. The former denotes two descending pitches and consists of a uirga ligated to a punctum (line 1, above the first syllable of 'Christus'); the latter looks like a hastily written letter 'u' and indicates two

---

[144] No comprehensive survey of Aquitanian notation exists. See J. Lapeyre, 'La notation aquitaine et les origines de la notation musical d'après les anciens manuscrits d'Albi', *Tribune Saint-Gervais*, 13 (1907), pp. 193–8, 226–36, 255–62, 275–86; *Le codex 903 de la Bibliothèque Nationale de Paris*, pp. 54–211; G. M. Suñol, *Introduction à la paléographie musicale grégorienne*, Paléographie Grégorienne 708 (Paris, Tournai and Rome, 1935), pp. 164–72, 260–81; S. Corbin, *Die Neumen*, Paläographie der Musik, ser. 1, iii, *Die einstimmige Musik des Mittelalters* (Cologne, 1977), pp. 94–100; Crocker, *The Early Medieval Sequence*, pp. 15–26; Huglo, 'La tradition musicale aquitaine', pp. 253–68; and J. Mas, 'La tradition musicale en Septimanie: Répertoire et tradition musicale', *Liturgie et musique*, pp. 280–5.

notes of the same pitch sung for the same syllable (line 3, twice above 'quo'). Three neumes represent liquescence, the epiphonus (ascending; line 2, above 'Ad'), the cephalicus (descending; line 5, above 'ad') and the quilisma (ascending with the first note liquescent; line 3, above the first syllable of 'iudicaturus').

The chief characteristic that distinguishes Aquitanian notation from the other regional dialects is missing in both fragmentary manuscripts, however, and that is the use of heighting above the literary text to show accurate intervallic relationships between pitches. Heighting does indicate relative ascending and descending motion, but notes of the same pitch are not consistently heighted, nor are equivalent intervals indicated by the same distance between notes. For example, the opening of *Quem creditis* appears in Pa 909 (fols. 34^{r-v}, where the music is written in Adémar's hand, AD 1028) as shown in Example 1.[145] The first note in Pa 1834 (Figure 4, line 8) stands far too close to the second note to represent a leap of a fifth, as Pa 909 reads. The second note, which signifies d', is not aligned with later notes that ought to denote the same pitch.

The same problems beset Pa 1085 and 1120 (see Figures 6 and 10 for the former, and Figures 5 and 11 for the latter). Figure 5 shows the opening of *Quem creditis* in Pa 1120, where again the notes that represent d' are not consistently heighted. If anything, even greater difficulties are encountered in Pa 1085, but these stem from the fact that the format of the manuscript was not designed with musical notation in mind. The rules for the text stand between 6 and 9 mm apart; in contrast the two tropers, Pa 1834 and 1120, are ruled at 11 mm, and the palimpsest in Pa 1085 at 15 mm. Consequently, the music scribe of Pa 1085 did not have adequate room to provide accurate heighting

Example 1. *Quem creditis*, Pa 909, fol. 34^r

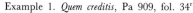

Quem   cre- - - - - - - di- - tis

---

[145] See the editions in Evans, *The Early Trope Repertory*, no. 100, p. 188; and *Introitus-tropen*, I, ed. Weiss, no. 303, pp. 317–19.

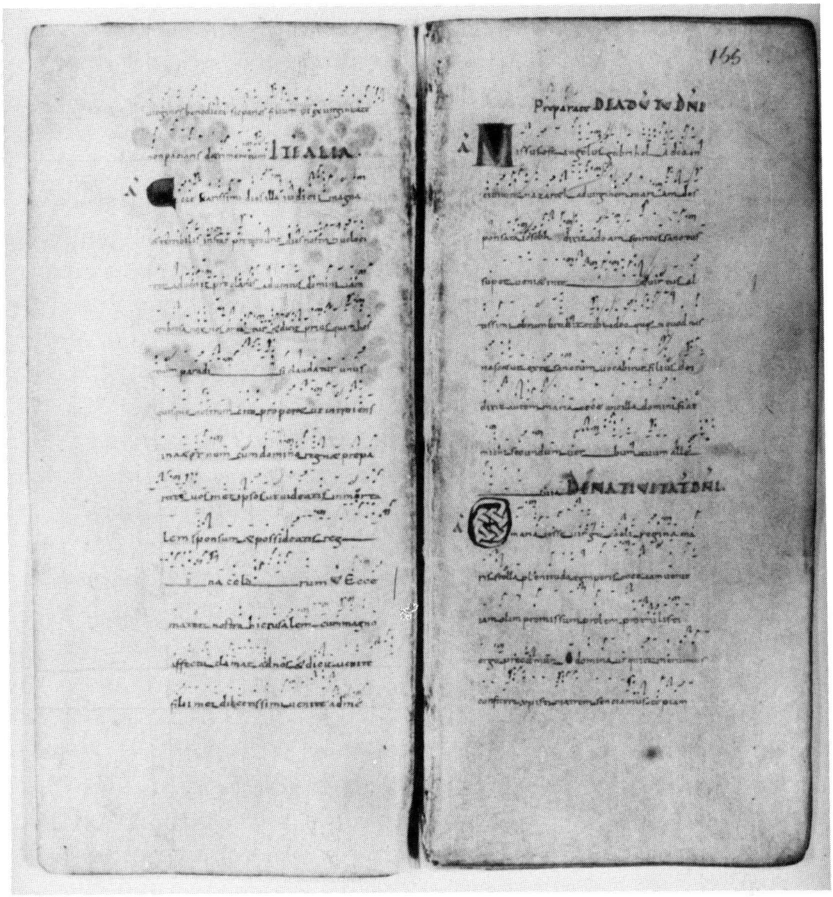

Figure 11 Pa 1120, fols. 154ᵛ–155ʳ, processional antiphons for Advent

even if he had so desired. Figures 5 and 11 reveal another problem with the musical notation in Pa 1120, and that is the horizontal crowding of music. Here, insufficient space separates words and syllables set to melismata. The music is compressed horizontally, and lines of division mark the music of individual syllables.

Both Pa 1085 and 1120 exhibit an early state of notation, representing no development of the techniques visible in the predecessors of Pa 1120. Only in the next generation, with the production of Pa 1121 and 909, did the notation come to provide reliable intervallic information through consistent heighting and use of the *custos*.[146] In fact the inscription of the melodies appears to hold by no means the highest priority in either Pa 1085 or Pa 1120. Their primary purpose is to record the complete cursus of sung items for the Mass and Office, including the full text of material sung by the soloists. In that form they could serve as a guide for the cantor, as discussed above. And that condition might explain the apparent casualness of the notation. The cantor and his solo singers presumably knew the melodies from memory. Where notation occurs (throughout Pa 1120, for example), it functions as a mnemonic aid. This series of manuscripts, then, attests an important stage in the development and use of musical notation at St Martial. First introduced in Pa 1240, the notation of the fragments in Pa 1834 and 1085, the main body of Pa 1085 and Pa 1120 depends heavily on the oral tradition. With Pa 1121 and 909, Aquitanian notation first exhibits accurate visual information regarding intervals, but the melodies contained in those codices still cannot be sung without prior knowledge (see Table 12).

Because of the uncertainty of its notation, it is difficult to assess the melodies preserved in Pa 1120, and thus ascertain the presence of unique variants. A sample of the Proper tropes, however, shows that the scribe of Pa 1120 did assert his individuality in one aspect of the tradition, and that is in the treatment of liquescence. In many cases, this codex disagrees with the other Aquitanian tropers, either in supplying or suppressing liquescence. Moreover, the literary text has no apparent effect on where Pa 1120 differs: diphthongs and multiple consonants, both within a word and in final position, receive equal treatment. Example 2, from the trope *Plebs deuota* from the Mass for the feast of St Martial, shows one instance where a liquescent is lacking in Pa 1120 above a word that ends with two consonants, in disagreement with the rest of the Aquitanian tradition.[147] In a few cases, Pa 1121 alone among the Aquitanian tropers agrees with Pa 1120 in its treatment of liquescence, thus confirming the relation-

---

[146] On Pa 1121, see Evans, *The Early Trope Repertory*, pp. 48, 121–5.
[147] See the editions in Evans, *The Early Trope Repertory*, no. 140, p. 210; and *Introitus-tropen*, I, ed. Weiss, no. 75, pp. 93–4.

Table 12 *Music manuscripts in use at St Martial, Limoges*
c. *990–1030*

Date	Codices	Contents	Notation	Remarks
c. AD 990	Pa 1240	Mass	Northern French	
c. AD 1000	Pa 1834 Pa 1085 palimpsest	Proper tropes Processional antiphons	Aquitanian, imprecise heighting	incomplete
AD 1010–25	Pa 1120 Pa 1085	Mass Office	Aquitanian, imprecise heighting	Roger de Chabannes
AD 1025–8	Pa 1121	Mass	Aquitanian, precise heighting	successor of Roger de Chabannes
April 1028– August 1029	Pa 909	Mass	Aquitanian, precise heighting	commission for St Martin, appropriated for apostolic liturgy by Adémar de Chabannes

ship between these two codices discussed above. The significance of these variants is obscure. They could have arisen from idiosyncratic scribal usage, or they might represent a distinctive performance practice. Only a detailed palaeographical investigation of the textual contexts in which liquescents occur in Aquitanian sources will reveal how the conventions found in Pa 1120 fit into the larger tradition.

Finally, both Pa 1085 and 1120 exhibit a rigorously episcopal liturgy for the abbey's patron. The rubric for his feast in the former reads: 'Natale sancti ac beatissimi patroni nostri domini Martialis praesuli[s] Lemouicensis' (fol. 76ᵛ). 'Praesul' here means 'bishop', of course.[148] The troped Mass in Pa 1120 (fols. 46ʳ–51ᵛ) does not open with so specific a rubric, but the host Proper chants come from the Common of Saints for a confessor-bishop. Some were subsequently erased by Roger's nephew, Adémar, and replaced with his newly composed chants for the

[148] See Grier, '*Ecce sanctum*', pp. 62–4.

Example 2. *Plebs deuota*

apostolic liturgy.[149] Exactly the same treatment is accorded the troped Mass in Pa 1121 (fols. 28^r–32^r), which is closely related to Pa 1120, as mentioned above.[150] Moreover, the earliest layer of Pa 909 probably contained the episcopal Mass for St Martial,

[149] *Ibid.*, pp. 61–2. See also Chailley, 'Les anciens tropaires', p. 167; and *L'école*, p. 81.
[150] Huglo, 'Codicologie et musicologie', pp. 79–80; and Grier, '*Ecce sanctum*', pp. 61–2.

as otherwise there would have been no reason for Adémar to replace it with the apostolic Mass (fols. 42^r–46^v).[151] Therefore, up to and including the production of the first layer of Pa 909 in the second half of AD 1028, there is no hint whatsoever that the apostolic cult of St Martial had made any penetration into the group of monks who worked in the scriptorium, those responsible for the execution of liturgical books. It is perhaps the supreme irony that the work of Roger de Chabannes, who meticulously compiled the liturgy of his abbey in Pa 1085 and 1120, preserving and codifying, but apparently not innovating, was utterly overturned by his star pupil, his nephew Adémar, in an attempt to promulgate the manifestly fraudulent apostolic cult of St Martial.

Yale University

See also Chailley, 'Les anciens tropaires', p. 169, *idem*, *L'école*, p. 82; and Gaborit-Chopin, *La décoration*, pp. 71, 75, 186–7.

[151] Grier, '*Ecce sanctum*', pp. 35–69.

Early Music History (1995) Volume 14

CRISTLE COLLINS JUDD

READING ARON READING PETRUCCI: THE MUSIC EXAMPLES OF THE *TRATTATO DELLA NATURA ET COGNITIONE DI TUTTI GLI TUONI* (1525)*

For Harold Powers

It has often been noted that Pietro Aron's *Trattato della natura et cognitione di tutti gli tuoni* (1525)[1] links traditional eight-mode theory with polyphony by naming actual compositions and asserting the modal categories to which they belonged. The significance of Aron's connection of mode and polyphony has been the subject of a wide variety of historical and theoretical interpretation: in particular, Leeman Perkins based a study of modality in the masses of Josquin on the *Trattato*, while Peter Bergquist argued that Aron's classifications were essentially irrelevant for polyphony.[2] The most recent interpretation of Aron's text appeared

* A preliminary version of this article, entitled ' "Come manifestamente si comprende"?: The Music Examples of Pietro Aron's *Trattato della natura et cognitione di tutti gli tuoni* (1525)', was read as a sixty-fifth birthday offering at a celebration for Harold Powers in Princeton (April 1994). Subsequent versions were read at the Conference on Medieval and Renaissance Music, Glasgow (July 1994) and at Cornell University (September 1994). For helpful comments and criticisms, I am grateful to Gary Tomlinson, Margaret Bent, Bonnie J. Blackburn and David Fallows. Richard Sherr graciously shared his microfilms of four music prints discussed in this article.

[1] Facsimile edn (Bologna, 1970); chs. 1–7 are translated in O. Strunk, *Source Readings in Music History* (New York, 1950), pp. 205–18. The translations in this article follow Strunk unless otherwise indicated. The most comprehensive overview of Aron's theoretical writings remains E. P. Bergquist, 'The Theoretical Writings of Pietro Aaron' (Ph.D. dissertation, Columbia University, 1964). For biographical information and speculation on the two spellings of Aron's surname, see *A Correspondence of Renaissance Musicians*, ed. B. J. Blackburn, E. E. Lowinsky and C. A. Miller (Oxford, 1991), pp. 74–100.

[2] L. Perkins, 'Mode and Structure in the Masses of Josquin', *Journal of the American Musicological Society*, 26 (1973), pp. 189–239; P. Bergquist, 'Mode and Polyphony around 1500', *Music Forum*, 1 (1967), pp. 99–161.

in an article by Harold Powers provocatively entitled 'Is Mode Real?'[3] There, Powers proposed understanding Aron literally and deduced Aron's methods of modal categorisation from a close reading relying solely on the internal evidence of the treatise.[4] The present article complements Powers's by proposing a fundamentally contextual or 'external' view – reading Aron as a reader of Petrucci, so to speak.[5] This entails examining Aron's citations in the larger context of the specific printed repertory from which he drew them and considering the implications of his 'appropriation' of that repertory. Viewing the *Trattato* from this vantagepoint not only raises issues of how we read theorists, but also confronts fundamental assumptions of how music prints were used in the first quarter of the sixteenth century, suggesting a complex picture of the significance of print culture for different communities of musical readers.[6] This approach also highlights issues of orality, literacy and visuality in relation to music prints, perhaps by their very nature the most difficult exemplars of all to understand in the context of print culture. These areas have been explored extensively for non-musical printing,[7] but only minimally with reference to the early years of music printing, where the focus of studies has been primarily technical and demographic.[8]

[3] H. Powers, 'Is Mode Real?': Pietro Aron, the Octenary System, and Polyphony', *Basler Jahrbuch für historische Musikpraxis*, 16 (1992), pp. 9–52.

[4] For summaries of Aron's means of modal categorisation, see Powers, 'Is Mode Real?', and C. C. Judd, 'Modal Types and *Ut, Re, Mi* Tonalities: Tonal Coherence in Sacred Vocal Polyphony from about 1500', *Journal of the American Musicological Society*, 45 (1992), pp. 428–67 (p. 430).

[5] For an overview of 'internal' versus 'external' reading and the significance of appropriation of texts, see R. Chartier, 'Texts, Printing, Readings', *The New Cultural History*, ed. L. Hunt (Berkeley, 1989), pp. 154–75 (pp. 156–8 and *passim*).

[6] On interpretative communities, see R. Chartier, *The Order of Books: Readers, Authors, and Libraries in Europe between the Fourteenth and Eighteenth Centuries*, trans. L. Cochrane (Stanford, 1994), pp. 1–23.

[7] See, for example, W. Ong, *Orality and Literacy: The Technologizing of the Word* (London and New York, 1982), pp. 156–79. With specific reference to 'print culture', see *The Culture of Print: Power and the Uses of Print in Early Modern Europe*, ed. R. Chartier, trans. L. Cochrane (Princeton, 1989), pp. 1–10 and *passim*.

[8] See, for example, S. Boorman, 'Petrucci at Fossombrone: A Study of Early Music Printing, with Special Reference to the *Motetti de la corona*' (Ph.D. dissertation, University of London, 1976). As I will show below, music prints in partbook format have erroneously been assumed to stand outside the domain of 'silent reading', supposedly demanding aural realisation.

I will begin by exploring the meeting-point of Aron's theoretical tradition and contemporary practice through his citations, offering observations about his working methods and appropriation of Petrucci's repertory. I will then use Aron's citations of works ending on A as a means of exploring in detail the multi-levelled interplay of Aron's text with the musical sources he used to substantiate it. Examining Aron's employment of Petrucci prints not only illuminates aspects of the *Trattato*, it also offers a window through which to view the multiple uses to which music prints might be put and suggests an incipient relationship between a theorist and his readers defined by the 'authority' of printed music collections.

One can construct a remarkably complete picture of how Aron went about choosing his examples, observing what he 'left out' as well as what he cited. He refers to polyphonic composition in two treatises: the *Trattato* and the 1529 *Aggiunta* to the *Tos-canello*.[9] The opening chapters of the *Trattato* cite examples of polyphony ascribed to modal categories; the *Aggiunta* cites examples in that other notoriously 'difficult' area of theory: *musica ficta*.[10] Reconstructing Aron's collection of printed sources is a relatively straightforward task. In the *Toscanello* supplement he refers specifically to Petrucci's *Odhecaton*.[11] That he also used the first three of Petrucci's *Motetti de la corona* anthologies is made equally certain by his citation of placement on a page (that is,

[9]   *Thoscanello de la musica* (Venice, 1523); rev. edn with *Aggiunta* published as *Toscanello in musica* (Venice, 1529, 1539 and 1562); facsimile of 1539 edn, ed. G. Frey, Documenta Musicologica, ser. 1, 29 (Kassel, 1970); trans. P. Bergquist, Colorado Springs Music Press Translations 4, 3 vols. (Colorado Springs, 1970).

[10]   Margaret Bent recently completed a close reading of the *Aggiunta* examples ('Accidentals, Counterpoint, and Notation in Aaron's *Aggiunta* to the *Toscanello*', *Journal of Musicology*, 12 (1994), pp. 306–44) analogous to Powers's reading of the *Trattato* examples ('Is Mode Real?'); I am grateful to Professor Bent for making available a typescript of that article before its publication. Bent notes the difficulty that Aron encounters in describing accidentals and comments on his convoluted language. It is only at these moments (discussion of mode and accidentals), when the gulf between the theory Aron articulates and polyphonic practice is greatest, that he refers to specific polyphonic compositions.

[11]   'And note that all the songs and composers mentioned here, one by one, are found in a book called *One Hundred Songs Printed in Order* [i.e. *Odhecaton A*]. I have taken some trouble so that you may more easily reach the goal of this understanding' (*Toscanello*, trans. Bergquist, iii, p. 19).

Table 1 *Aron's citations (*Trattato, *chapters 4–7) and their sources*

Chapter 4

Modes 1 and 2 *D sol re*
  Motetti de la corona II, 7   Jacotin, *Rogamus te Virgo Maria* (mode 1)

  Motetti de la corona II, 8   A. Caen, *Judica me Deus* (mode 1)
  Motetti de la corona II, 16   Mouton, *Congregati sunt* (mode 1)
  Motetti de la corona I, 11   Mouton, *Beata Dei genitrix* (mode 2)
  [*Motetti a5*, 1]   Regis, *Clangat plebs flores* (mode 1)

Mode 1 *D la sol re* with flat signature
  Motetti de la corona II, 3   A. Caen, *Nomine qui Domini*
  Canti B, 43   *Pour quoy fut fuie cette emprise*

Mode 1 *G sol re ut* with flat signature
  [*Missarum liber* II, 1]   Josquin, *Missa Ave maris stella*
  [*Missarum liber* II, 6]   Josquin, *Missa D'ung aultre amer*
  Motetti de la corona I, 8   Févin, *Nobilis progenie*
  Motetti de la corona I, 21   Févin, *Vulnerasti cor meum*

Mode 2 *G sol re ut* with flat signature
  Canti B, 2   Compère, *Virgo celesti*
  ?   Hayne, *D'ung aultre amer*
  [*Odhecaton*, 20]   Hayne, *De tous biens playne*
  Canti B, 7   Pierre de la Rue, *Ce n'est pas*
  Canti B, 24   Orto, *D'ung aultre amer*

Modes 1 and 2 *A la mi re*
  Odhecaton, 64   Josquin, *La plus des plus* (mode 1)
  Odhecaton, 51   Compère, *Si mieulx* (mode 2)

Mode 1 *D la sol re* with flat signature
  (see Spataro correspondence)   Busnoys, *Pourtant si mon*
  (see Crawford)[a]   Constanzo Festa, *Gaude Virgo*
  Canti B, 1   Josquin, *L'homme armé*
  Odhecaton, 30   Japart, *Hélas qu'il est à mon gré*

Mode 1 *D la sol re* (no signature)
  Canti B, 28   Pierre de la Rue, *Fors seulement*
  Canti B, 50   Brumel, *Je déspite tous*
  Motetti de la corona I, 1   Mouton, *Gaude Barbara*

Mode 2 *D la sol re*
  [*Missarum liber* II, 2]   Josquin, *Missa Hercules dux Ferrariae*

Chapter 5

Mode 3 *E la mi*
  Motetti de la corona II, 6   Jacotin, *Michael archangele*
  Odhecaton, 63   Okeghem, *Malheur me bat*
  Motetti de la corona II, 2   Jacotin, *Interveniat pro rege nostro*

Mode 3 *G sol re ut*
  Odhecaton, 4   *Nunca fué pena mayor*

Table 1   (*cont.*)

Mode 3 *A la mi re*
 Motetti de la corona III, 7   Josquin, *Miserere mei Deus*
 [*Motetti de la corona* I, 4?]   Eustachio(?), *Laetatus sum*
 Motetti de la corona II, 11   Benedic anima mea Dominum

Mode 4 *A la mi re*
 Motetti C, 34   *O Maria rogamus te*

Chapter 6

Mode 5 *F fa ut*
 Motetti de la corona III, 6   Josquin, *Stabat mater dolorosa*
 Motetti de la corona III, 10   Josquin, *Alma redemptoris*
 Odhecaton, 13   Caron, *Hélas que pourra devenir*
 [*Antico*]   Mouton, *Quaeramus cum pastoribus*
 Motetti de la corona II, 12   Mouton, *Illuminare illuminare Jerusalem*
 [*Missae* I]   Pierre de la Rue, Sanctus and
             Agnus, *Missa de Beata Virgine*

Mode 6 *F fa ut*
 Odhecaton, 5   Stokhem, *Brunette*
 Odhecaton, 41   Compère, *Vostre bergeronette*
 Odhecaton, 42   Busnoys, *Je ne demande*
 Odhecaton, 48   Agricola, *Allez regretz*
 Odhecaton, 93   Hayne, *A l'audience*
 Motetti de la corona I, 13   Févin, *Sancta Trinitas unus Deus*
 Motetti de la corona I, 20   Févin, *Tempus meum est ut revertar ad
             eum*
 Motetti de la corona I, 22   Mouton, *Celeste beneficium*
 Motetti de la corona I, 23   Févin, *Egregie Christi*

Modes 5 and 6 *B fa mi* with flat signature
 Canti B, 48   Hayne, *La regretée* (mode 5)
 [*Antico*]   Josquin, *O admirabile commercium*
             (mode 6)

Mode 5 *C sol fa ut*
 Canti B, 40   Obrecht, *Si sumpsero*

Chapter 7

Mode 8 *C fa ut*
 Canti B, 12   Orto, *Mon mari m'a diffamée*
 Canti B, 27   *E la la la*

Mode 7 *G sol re ut*
 ?   Mouton, *Missa Ut sol*
 [*Missae* I]   Pierre de la Rue, Gloria from *Missa
             de Beata Virgine*
 (see Spataro correspondence) Zanetto (Giovanni del Lago), *Multi
             sunt vocati*
 Motetti de la corona I, 18   Hylaere, *Ascendens Christus in altum*

Table 1   *(cont.)*

Mode 8 *G sol re ut*	
Odhecaton, 56	Agricola, *Si dedero*
Odhecaton, 72	*C'est possible qui l'homme peut*
Odhecaton, 78	Josquin, *O venus bant*
Odhecaton, 89	*Disant adieu madame*
Canti B, 11	*Je suis amie*
Canti B, 18	*Myn morghem ghaf*
Canti B, 21	Ninot, *Hélas hélas*
Canti B, 29	Compère, *E d'en revenez vous*
Motetti C, 7	*Beata Dei genitrix*
Mode 7 *C sol fa ut*	
Odhecaton, 59	Compère, *Mes pensées*
Odhecaton, 66	*Madame hélas*
Canti B, 19	Josquin, *Comment peult*
Motetti C, 40	*Mittit ad Virginem*
Odhecaton, 2	*Je cuide si ce temps*
Mode 8 *C sol fa ut*	
Odhecaton, 29	*Ne l'oserai je dire*

Note: Titles and attributions in this Table follow the forms of Aron's citations.
^a David Crawford speculates that the *Gaude Virgo* found in Casale Monferrato, Archivio Capitolare, MS D (F) is the composition to which Aron refers. D. Crawford, *Sixteenth Century Choirbooks in the Archivio Capitolare at Casale Monferrato* (Rome, 1975), p. 70.

by voice, stave and text: e.g. 'In the motet, *Ave nobilissima*, in the second contrabass at the end of the second line over the words, "ab omnibus malis et fraudibus" . . .').[12] Another Petrucci print, *Motetti C*, is named in the *Trattato*,[13] and his other undeniable source is Petrucci's second anthology in the *Odhecaton* series, *Canti B*.[14] Probably, but not as certainly, Petrucci's second volume of masses by Josquin should be included in the list.[15] Together, as Table 1 illustrates, these sources account for almost

[12] *Ibid.*, p. 17.
[13] Had Aron not explicitly cited *Motetti C* one might have questioned his access to this source, since he cites only three motets from this collection, far fewer than from any of the other prints he uses in the *Trattato* and *Aggiunta*.
[14] Although Aron never explicitly names *Canti B*, the order of his selections as well as composer indications suggests this as one of his primary sources.
[15] Three masses which appear in this print are cited, but there is no way of positing this as Aron's source with absolute certainty; several works from the first volume of Josquin's masses printed by Petrucci are cited more specifically in the *Aggiunta*, which offers circumstantial evidence that Aron probably had access to both volumes.

all the works Aron cites by name in chapters 4–7 of the *Trattato*.[16] Thus, the bulk of the citations come from seven Petrucci prints first published between 1501 and 1519: *Odhecaton A*, *Canti B*, *Motetti C*, Josquin's *Missarum liber II* and *Motetti de la corona I*, *II* and *III*. The fuller tabulations included in the Appendix to this article give an overview of these Petrucci prints, noting information about their content and indicating those works Aron cited in the *Trattato* and in the *Aggiunta* to the *Toscanello*. Interestingly, although the same primary sources are used for both, the overlap of citations between the two is minimal.

Table 1 gives Aron's citations with his modal ascriptions in order of their appearance in chapters 4–7 of the *Trattato*. The choice and order of Aron's citations reveal his working method and reflect an unprecedented relationship between a theorist and his sources of examples. Aron accepts Petrucci's authority as arbiter of repertory and simultaneously attempts to bolster his own credibility by instantiating his writing with references to printed sources, available in multiple copies with fixed notation. Chapter 4 begins systematically: the first citations – *Motetti de la corona II*, nos. 7, 8 and 16 – are the only motets from that print that fit this modal category and they are cited in order of printed occurrence. Aron supplies examples for every possible termination and signature in this chapter. This is the only chapter to cite examples from the Josquin masses, although examples from this volume could have been adduced for other modes. More examples are given in this chapter than in any other, and Aron draws from the widest variety of sources here.[17] The examples of chapter 5 are slightly more circum-

---

16 Strunk, *Source Readings*, pp. 205–6, lists sources for most of Aron's citations, but makes no distinction between those sources which Aron undeniably used and those which may or may not have been available to him. Table 1 encloses uncertain sources in square brackets, along with additional references to manuscript sources or lost works. Strunk's list is alphabetical, obscuring many of the relationships observed below and, with the exception of the *Odhecaton*, does not indicate the placement of examples within source prints. Bergquist, 'The Theoretical Writings', also follows Strunk's list. Citations for five works for which Strunk cited no source are given here, along with minor corrections to his list.

17 Three of the works cited in this chapter are unknown in any printed source, but one – Busnoys's *Pourtant si mon* – is mentioned in the so-called Spataro correspondence (*A Correspondence of Renaissance Musicians*, ed. Blackburn, Lowinsky and Miller, pp. 350 and 832), and may have been known to Aron through those circles. Similarly, *Multi sunt vocati* (cited in ch. 7) was mentioned by Aron in a letter to Del Lago (*ibid.*, p. 707) and was frequently cited in the correspondence.

scribed and less systematic. Aron gives no examples for one termination he describes (an A final with flat signature), although he
could have cited the tenors of two of the Josquin motets at the
opening of *Motetti de la corona III*, his presumed source for *Miserere
mei Deus*.[18] Especially revealing is Aron's description of the villan-
cico *Nunca fué* as terminating irregularly on G. As Bergquist noted,
Aron has misinterpreted the form of the piece, which ends regularly
on E.[19] This error is symptomatic of Aron's visual orientation,
which takes the last note of the tenor parts in the *Odhecaton* as the
end of the piece, notwithstanding notational conventions which
would seem to indicate otherwise.[20]

Reading Aron through his citations suggests that his process
changed as he continued. Expediency takes over in chapters 6
and 7, where one can imagine Aron thumbing through his prints
searching for examples, completing the appropriation of the repertory for his pedagogical purposes. For example, as Table 1 shows,
the first five citations in the list of mode 6 works all come from
the *Odhecaton* and follow the order of the print; the next four,
taken in order from *Motetti de la corona I*, include all the motets
from that print in this modal category.[21] Similarly, in chapter 7,
the listing of mode 8 works with finals on G moves in order
from the *Odhecaton* to *Canti B* and finally to *Motetti C*. Aron
follows the same sources in the same order for mode 7 ending
on C: *Odhecaton*, *Canti B*, *Motetti C*. Most telling, perhaps, is the
final mode 7 (or first mode 8) chanson, *Je cuide si ce temps*.
As Powers pointed out, the grammatical construction of Aron's
description is ambiguous: he could be describing *Je cuide si ce*

---

[18]   The two motets are *Huc me sydereo* and *Ave nobilissima* which share the same mode 4
tenor with A final and flat signature. However, Aron need not have consulted *Motetti
de la corona III* in the writing of this chapter. The tenor of *Miserere mei Deus*, with its
ascending and descending 'miserere' ostinato, is precisely the sort of tenor that Aron
might have recalled, rather than looked at, for his modal classification.

[19]   Bergquist, 'The Theoretical Writings', p. 286.

[20]   Rather than suggesting a kind of musical incompetence, Aron's 'misreading' may
simply be indicative of the way in which the repertory of the *Odhecaton*, already
retrospective at the time of its initial publication in 1501, was understood twenty-five
years later. In the *Aggiunta* Aron distinguishes between the 'moderns', represented
by the *Motetti de la corona* repertory, and the 'ancients' represented in the *Odhecaton*
(*Toscanello*, trans. Bergquist, III, p. 19).

[21]   Unlike in ch. 4, and to a slightly lesser degree ch. 5, Aron is no longer concerned
here to instantiate every possible termination; see, most notably, his treatment of
endings on *A la mi re*.

temps as either mode 7 or mode 8.[22] Strunk read it as mode 8;[23] Powers argued that Aron must be including it in his mode 7 list on the basis of the 'modal' features of the tenor. Indeed, an addendum seems likely; one may conjecture that Aron had turned back to the start of the *Odhecaton* to begin his listing anew for mode 8 only to discover his omission of a mode 7 chanson.

Aron makes no explicit distinction of genre in his citations between motet, mass and chanson, and he appears to make no concerted effort to represent each genre in each classification. This is particularly true for masses. After the citations from Josquin's *Missarum liber II* in chapter 4, Aron need not have had access to any other mass prints or manuscripts. He cites Pierre de la Rue's *De Beata Virgine* mass twice,[24] but any *De Beata Virgine* mass would have fallen into these modal categories because of the plainchants on which such masses were customarily based. Similarly, the (now unknown) Mouton *Missa Ut sol* might well have received its mode 7 classification from its presumed solmisation basis.[25] Twenty-six works are cited in chapter 4 (modes 1 and 2); eight in chapter 5 (modes 3 and 4); eighteen in chapter 6 (modes 5 and 6); and twenty-one in chapter 7 (modes 7 and 8). Aron's citations are more evenly distributed across the modal spectrum than the actual repertory from which he drew them: approximately half the works in the Petrucci prints from which

---

[22] Powers, 'Is Mode Real?', p. 39. 'Onde gli presenti canti cioe Mes pensies di Compere, Madame Helas, Cenent peult di Josquino, et Mittit ad virginem no altrimenti che del settimo son chiamati, et Je vide sece tamps, &t Loserai dire del tuono ottavo et non settimo come la sua forma et continuo processo ti dimostrano &c.'

[23] 'Thus "Mes pensées" by Compère, "Madame hélas" and "Comment peut" by Josquin, and "Mittit ad virginem" can be assigned only to the seventh tone. But "Je cuide si ce temps" and "Ne l'oserai je dire" will be of the eighth tone and not of the seventh, as their form and extended downward procedure will show you' (Strunk, *Source Readings*, p. 218).

[24] The Sanctus and Agnus Dei are cited as examples of mode 5 on *F fa ut*; the Gloria is cited for mode 7 on *G sol re ut*.

[25] It is notable that two of these mass citations, as well as the reference to Del Lago's *Multi sunt vocati*, also outside the Petrucci repertory, occur among the citations for mode 7 on *G sol re ut* where Aron relies, at most, on a single Petrucci exemplar. Indeed, even that work, Hylaere's *Ascendens Christus in altum*, may have been 'remembered' or been taken from some other (manuscript) source, since Aron makes no other citations from the *Motetti de la corona* anthologies in this chapter. This suggests the possibility that he was no longer referring to those partbooks (although he certainly had them four years later when he prepared the *Aggiunta* to the *Toscanello*). The relatively few citations for mode 7 on G also suggest a dearth of settings that would qualify for that mode in the repertory he had to hand.

he worked would fall into his mode 1 and 2 category, with G finals in *cantus mollis* by far the most common, as the tables in the Appendix demonstrate. Indeed, this 'abundance' of examples may well be responsible for what appears to be a more thorough approach in chapter 4. His citations generally minimise any tonal distinctions between the motet and chanson repertories. Only three of 147 chansons in *Odhecaton* and *Canti B* finish on E in the tenor, while the proportion of such endings in the motet collections (thirteen of 109) is higher:[26] Aron cites one chanson and two motets with terminations on E. Motets that would be described as mode 5 or 6 are more frequent than chansons, but Aron cites them in near equal numbers (nine motets, eight chansons and one mass). And while mode 7 and 8 categories are more frequent among chansons than motets, the repertory at hand represents nothing like the lop-sided proportion of Aron's selection (fifteen from the chanson collections to three from a motet print), which reflects more the particular sources he used for this chapter (*Odhecaton*, *Canti B* and *Motetti C*) than the larger array of sources he had to hand.[27] In other words, Aron is making no attempt to 'represent' the repertory; instead he is appropriating its contents for his own purposes.

Sixteenth-century theoretical discussions of mode which followed Aron's *Trattato*, as well as those in the modern musicological literature, suggest that Aron's assignments of works terminating on *A la mi re* and *C sol fa ut* are among his most problematic. A modern conception which posits 'modality' as a system akin to 'tonality' would argue that most of the compositions Aron cites for these terminations do not function as 'A-final' or 'C-final' works.[28] And the role of 'regular' as opposed to 'irregular' termin-

---

[26] Two other motets in which the tenor extends cadences on E to a termination on B might also be added to this group: Jacotin's *Interveniat pro rege nostro* and Carpentras's *Cantate Domino*. See the discussion of *Interveniat pro rege nostro* below. I have maintained the generic distinctions suggested by the prints in the discussion which follows; thus, the seven works with Latin incipits in *Odhecaton* and *Canti B* have been counted among the 'chansons' as a reflection of the print titles.

[27] It is striking that Aron refers only to the earliest of his Petrucci prints in this chapter; he may well have viewed the three anthologies which first appeared between the years 1501 and 1504 as a related series since his citations also reflect the order of publication.

[28] See, for example, Bergquist's discussion of *Se mieulx* in 'The Theoretical Writings'.

ations in eight-mode theory mediated by Aron's invocation of psalm-tone pseudo-finals as an explanation for endings on A and C was vitiated by the theorising of Glareanus and others. While Powers illustrated brilliantly the internal theoretical consistency and logic which led to Aron's categorisations,[29] an external reading of the interplay of Aron's citations and Petrucci's prints sheds further light on these 'problematic' assignments. This reading suggests not only the way in which the Petrucci repertory may have influenced the realisation of Aron's theorising, but also offers a tantalising glimpse into generic and tonal associations suggested by these citations. As an example, I will focus on the two subsets of his classifications which cite instances of terminations on *A la mi re*. The first set is the pair of chansons he cites in chapter 4 on modes 1 and 2:

Alcuni altri tenori finiranno in A la mi re. bisogna considerare et examinare se el processo suo e conveniente et rationale a tal terminatione, perche essendo fini irregularmente terminata al primo et secondo tuono et non procedendo colla sua forma propria potrebbe facilmente non essere di quel tuono, dato che sia fine irregulare et termine del suo seculorum overo differenza, questo e, che el terzo et quarto tuono ha simil luogo quanto alla differenza come seguitando intenderai. Si che per questa ragione trovandosi adunque la sua conveniente forma, saran chiamati del primo tuono come La plus de plus di Iosquino, el quale per el discorso degli diapenti et sua ascensione e primo tuono, Et del secondo Si mieulx di Loiset compere come manifestamente si comprende. (Aron, ch. 4)

Some other tenors terminate at *A la mi re*. It is necessary to consider and examine whether their *processo* is appropriate and reasonable for that ending, because if [a tenor] ends irregularly terminated for modes 1 and 2 and does not proceed with its proper form, it could easily not belong to the former [mode 1], even though *A la mi re* is [both] an irregular final and a termination for its psalm tone. That is because modes 3 and 4 have the same place for the psalm-tone difference, as you will understand later on. If then in this way of reasoning you find its form appropriate, it will be called mode 1, like *La plus des plus* of Josquin, which from the course of its species of the fifth and its ascent is mode 1. And *Se mieulx* of Loyset Compère is mode 2, as is manifestly to be understood. (Powers, 'Is Mode Real?', p. 32)

---

[29] Powers, 'Is Mode Real?', hastened to point out that the assignments are more revealing of Aron's theorising than representative of the music.

Aron here first raises the possibility of 'irregular endings' and allows that a tenor ending on *A la mi re* may signal mode 1, 2, 3 or 4 depending on its *processo*.[30] He then cites two examples: Josquin's *La plus des plus*, which he assigns straightforwardly to mode 1 on account of its species of the fifth and its 'ascent'; and Compère's *Se mieulx*, which he assigns to mode 2 'come manifestamente si comprende'. A facsimile of the tenor of *Se mieulx* from the *Odhecaton* is given in Figure 1. As Powers pointed out, by any of the criteria Aron outlined for his modal assignments – psalm-tone pseudo-final, species and *processo* – the assignment of this tenor to mode 2 is incomprehensible, in stark contrast to the ease with which Aron's assignment of *La plus des plus* is understood.[31] Powers argued that *A la mi re* must be understood as an instance of confinality, noting that Aron never explicitly invoked confinality as an argument of modal governance of a tenor by an irregular termination;[32] I suggested elsewhere that Aron set himself the task of categorising the tenor and that a process of elimination of his possibilities for tenors ending on A left mode 2 by default.[33] Neither explanation sits

Figure 1   Compère, *Se mieulx* (*Odhecaton*, no. 51, fol. 56ᵛ), tenor

---

[30]   See Powers, 'Is Mode Real?', pp. 30–1, on Aron's use of the term *processo*.

[31]   *Ibid.*, pp. 32–4.

[32]   *Ibid.*, p. 34; however, on confinality, see the discussion of *Benedic anima mea* and *Interveniat pro rege nostro* below.

[33]   C. C. Judd, 'Aspects of Tonal Coherence in the Motets of Josquin' (Ph.D. dissertation, King's College London, 1993, UMI 9501876), pp. 42–4.

easily with Aron's assertion that his classification of *Se mieulx*
to mode 2 is 'manifestly to be understood'. In light of my
observations about how Aron 'read' the Petrucci prints, I can
now offer another, contextual view on the issue. *Se mieulx* is the
first example (no. 51) from the *Odhecaton* with an ending on A
and no signature (see Appendix, Table A1), and its inclusion
may simply represent the comprehensiveness characteristic of
chapter 4 which falls by the wayside in succeeding chapters as
Aron begins to cite possible termination points without adducing
examples. *La plus des plus* (no. 64) is the next work with an A
termination. He has only three other possibilities in the *Odhecaton*: Agricola's *Crions nouel* (no. 75), Stokem's *Ha! traitre amours*
(no. 86) and the anonymous *Puisque de vous* (no. 91); *Canti B*
offers only the two settings of *J'ay pris amours* (nos. 3 and 30).
Aron would have assigned all these other chansons – *Se mieulx*
is the sole exception – to mode 1, primarily because of prominent
la–re descending fifths which conclude the tenor, exactly as in
La plus des plus. Beyond Aron's sample group of prints, there
does exist a complex of chansons which share certain tonal and
textual features with *Se mieulx*,[34] but there was nothing comparable in the repertory in front of Aron in the *Odhecaton* and *Canti
B*. The chansons which end on A, and indeed the motets ending
on A which I will discuss below, would all be described by
Aron by means of their species and *processo* in relatively straightforward terms as ending on a psalm-tone pseudo-final;[35] *Se mieulx*
does obviously stand apart in that respect. Although Aron's
'come manifestamente si comprende' may still strike us as 'optimistic', his assignment seems less incomprehensible when one
looks through these prints as he apparently did, noting the
importance he attached to the *Odhecaton*, the placement of *Se
mieulx* in that print, and the placement of this citation in the
most 'comprehensive' chapter of the *Trattato*.

Aron's comments on the mode 3 and 4 works ending on A
follow in the next chapter:

---

[34] E.g. Compère's *Se pis ne vient*. I am grateful to Mary Kathleen Morgan for bringing
this relationship to my attention.
[35] On Aron's use of psalm-tone pseudo-finals, see Powers, 'Is Mode Real?', p. 35, and
Judd, 'Aspects of Tonal Coherence', p. 46.

Alcuni altri anchora in A la mi re del terzo troverai, negli quali essendo in essi el processo conforme saranno giudicati di esso terzo tuono come Miserere mei deus di Iosquino. Letatus sum di Eustacio et Benedic anima mea dominum dove la prima parte finisce nel suo confinale, la seconda nel finale, et la terza nella differenza, et molti altri cosi si troveranno, Ma se saranno con el segno del B molle. Dico che questi maggiormente si chiameranno del terzo tuono data che nel principio o mezzo non siano proceduti con el debito et conveniente modo, perche chiaramente si vede la regolar sua compositione di mi mi et mi la, la qual si genera da detto A la mi re, ad E la mi acuto, congiunto el superiore Diatessaron quale e mi la, benche di questi pochi se ritruovino per la incommodita dello ascenso suo, excettuando se non fussino a voce simili overo mutate, gli quali saranno giudicati del terzo o quarto tuono quanto alle spetie et discensioni, et non per cagione della differenza ne processo, Per tanto si conclude che tal canti piu tosto saranno chiamati del quarto tuono per la discendente continuatione, come O maria rogamus te nel libro de motetti c et molti altri con questo modo facilmente potrai intendere. (Aron, ch. 5)

You will also find certain other compositions ending on *A la mi re*; when these observe the appropriate *processo* they will be assigned to the third mode. For example, *Miserere mei Deus* by Josquin, *Laetatus sum* by Eustachio, and *Benedic anima mea Dominum* in which the first part ends on the confinal, the second on the final, and the third on the difference, etc. But when they have a flat signature, they are in my opinion to be assigned to the third mode the more readily, even though at the beginning and in their course they fail to proceed in the due and appropriate way, for it is evident that the regular structure of the mode – namely, *mi–mi* and *mi–la* arising from the interval *A la mi re* to high *E la mi*, to which is added the upper diatessaron *mi–la* – will prevail. But because of the inconvenience of their upward range, few such pieces will be found, unless written for equal voices or *voce mutate*. Compositions of this sort are to be assigned to the third or fourth mode in view of their species and downward range, not because of their difference or *processo*. Thus it may be inferred that, in view of their extended downward range, they will in preference be assigned to the fourth mode. For example, *O Maria rogamus te* in the *Motetti C* and many others which you will readily recognise on the same principle.
(after Strunk, *Source Readings*, p. 215)

134

Three points should be highlighted in summary: (1) Aron argues that compositions ending on *A la mi re* which observe the appropriate *processo* belong to the third mode and cites three examples (Josquin's *Miserere*, Eustachio's(?) *Laetatus sum*[36] and *Benedic anima mea Dominum*); (2) he discusses the addition of a flat signature which transforms the species of fifth and fourth to those proper to mode 3, that is, *mi–mi* and *mi–la*; and (3) he discusses assignments to mode 4 based on extended downward range, for which he cites *Rogamus te/O Maria* from *Motetti C*.

The three instances of mode 3 terminating on A are all psalm motets – *Miserere mei Deus* (Psalm 50 with refrain), *Benedic anima mea Dominum* (Psalm 102) and *Laetatus sum* (Psalm 121): each sets a complete psalm text and all invoke a psalm tone to some degree. These motets share the same cleffing and ranges and each concludes on E in the penultimate *pars* and A in the final *pars*. Aron describes this explicitly for *Benedic anima mea Dominum*: the first part ends on the confinal (B); the second on the final (E); and the third on the difference (in the context of this citation, presumably A). The conclusion of each *pars* of the motet is given in Examples 1a–c. The endings of the *prima* and *secunda partes* do indeed follow Aron's description, although the conclusion of the tenor of the *tertia pars* on C♯ seems unexpected in the context in which this citation is made. Aron may be using what he describes elsewhere as an extended final cadence where one part (tenor or cantus) sustains the final.[37] The two cadences given earlier in chapter 5 are reproduced in Example 2; Aron might accept by

---

[36] Strunk, *Source Readings*, p. 205, misidentifies this work, citing *Motetti de la corona* II. There is no known *Laetatus sum* attributed to Eustachio; the only setting of *Laetatus sum* in the Petrucci prints consulted by Aron is attributed to Andreas de Silva, and fits the tonal profile of the motets he discusses here. The attribution to Eustachio (de Monteregalis) belongs properly with the third motet cited in this list, *Benedic anima mea Dominum*. For the purposes of the following discussion I will refer to the setting of *Laetatus sum* by Andreas de Silva, while acknowledging that Aron may have been referring to another setting of this text.

[37] 'And if sometimes, as has become the custom, the composer prolongs his work, amusing himself with additional progressions, you will, in my opinion, need to consider whether the final, as altered by the composer, is suited to and in keeping or out of keeping with his composition, for if reason guide him in what is suited to the tone he will at least see to it that some one part (namely, the tenor or cantus) sustains the final, while the others proceed as required by the tone, regular or irregular, with pleasing and appropriate progressions like those shown below, or in some more varied manner according to his pleasure and disposition' (Strunk, *Source Readings*, p. 212).

Example 1. Eustachio de Monteregalis, *Benedic anima mea Dominum*
(a) end of *prima pars* (b) end of *secunda pars* (c) end of *tertia pars*

Example 2. Prolonged cadences (Aron, *Trattato*, chapter 5)

analogy such an extension of a termination on *A la mi re*, as indicated in Example 1c, even though *A la mi re* cannot attain the status of final.[38] Such an explanation on Aron's part is visually suggested by the last system of the original tenor with its cadence to A and final word of text, followed by an obvious cadential extension to a notated C♯ shown in facsimile in Figure 2. Equally, though, his description of the ending of the *tertia pars* on its difference could refer to the C♯ with which the tenor ends, for C is a difference of tone 3 and the presence of a sharp is immaterial to Aron in this context (again highlighting both the

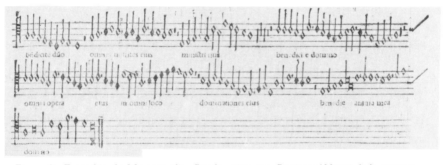

Figure 2   Eustachio de Monteregalis, *Benedic anima mea Dominum* (*Motetti de la corona* II, no. 11), conclusion of tenor

---

[38]   However, the same logic would have suggested that *Miserere mei Deus* concluded with an extended cadence on E; see Judd, 'Aspects of Tonal Coherence', pp. 61–4.

visual and abstract distance of Aron's theory from the aural realisation of the music he cites).[39]

Two aspects of Aron's treatment of motets merit attention here: he acknowledges the distinction of their *partes* (whereas he seems by and large to have taken the last note of the tenor as the end of a chanson despite clear indications to the contrary in some of the *Odhecaton* examples),[40] and here indeed in *Benedic anima mea* is an example of an acknowledged ending (albeit of the *prima pars*) on the confinal. By way of a slight detour, it is worth noting that the tenor of another of the mode 3 works which he cites as an instance of an E final concludes on its confinal in the tenor but is the occasion for no comment: Jacotin's *Interveniat pro rege nostro*. Figure 3 and Example 3 give the end of the tenor part and a score of the conclusion of the motet.

For mode 4, Aron cites one example under the heading of terminations on *A la mi re*: *Rogamus te/O Maria* from *Motetti C*. In terms of what I would call the tonality of the motets, the distinction he makes is arbitrary (*Rogamus te* has the same cleffing as the other motets; its *prima pars* concludes on E in the tenor,

Figure 3   Jacotin, *Interveniat pro rege nostro* (*Motetti de la corona* II, no. 2), conclusion of
tenor

---

[39]   On the meaning of such sharp signs, see M. Bent, 'Diatonic *Ficta*', *Early Music History*, 4 (1984), pp. 1–48, and 'Accidentals, Counterpoint and Notation'. Aron's visual orientation is also evident in early citations of the *Aggiunta*, where he seems to be collecting examples in much the same way as he concludes the *Trattato*, although as Bent suggests in some of the later *Aggiunta* examples he does apparently mentally reconstruct the entire musical texture.

[40]   This may be more a reflection of Aron's chronological promixity to repertory than distinct (mis)treatment of genre. The *Odhecaton* and *Canti B* are the earliest prints to which Aron refers and the most retrospective in the repertory they convey. He cites only three motets from the contemporaneous *Motetti C*, relying instead on the *Motetti de la corona* anthologies of ten to fifteen years later, two volumes of which anticipate the publication of his treatise by only six years.

Example 3. Jacotin, *Interveniat pro rege nostro*, final cadence

its *secunda pars* on A). Although he has just discussed terminations on *A la mi re* with a flat signature, *Rogamus te*, like the other works ending on A, has no flat signature (see Figure 4).[41] But, unlike the cases of *La plus des plus* and *Se mieulx* discussed above,

---

[41]   Powers seems to have read Aron too literally here, implying that he cites *Rogamus te/O Maria* as an example with a flat signature: 'When there is a flat signature, however, a la mi re cannot be a psalm-tone pseudo-final; in principle, chant theory does not provide for "transformed" psalm-tones. In a piece with a b-flat in the signature where the species mi/fa/sol//re/mi – (a/b-flat/c//d/e) – and mi/fa/sol/la – (e/f/g/aa or E/F/G/a) – are associated with a termination at a la mi, an assignment to mode 3 or mode 4 would be appropriate "because its regular composition is clearly seen;" since the *processo* [of a tenor] is not likely to extend up through the higher species of the fourth, however, it is the degree of extension in the lower part

139

Figure 4   *Rogamus te/O Maria* (*Motetti C*, no. 34), tenor

here the modal distinction of authentic and plagal that Aron is making is obvious. The tenor of *Rogamus te* is based on an ostinato which emphasises the species of fourth proper to mode 4. The limited tenor range and its 'downward' emphasis are surely responsible for Aron's categorisation.

The intellectual interplay between Aron's medieval and monophonic modal theory and his modern and visual reliance on printed sources of polyphony raises a host of questions about how he accommodated the two, and in what sense, if any, his accommodation relates to practical realities. His categorisations of *La plus des plus* and *Se mieulx* on the one hand, and *Miserere mei Deus*, *Benedic anima mea Dominum* and *Laetatus sum* on the other, do reflect a 'real' tonal distinction – one embodied in hexachordal manipulation which is the shared basis of Aron's theory and the compositions he examined.[42] The tonal distinction is recognised in Aron's modal terms precisely because *A la mi re* is not vested with the authority of a final.[43] The essence of that tonal distinction lies not in tonal types – which, minimally marked, are the same:

of the compass only that will determine the choice between authentic or plagal for such a tenor. According to Aron, it should usually be mode 4, and his citation is an anonymous *O Maria rogamus te* from Petrucci's *Motetti C* (Powers, 'Is Mode Real?', p. 35).

[42]   See Judd, 'Modal Types', pp. 437–41, and 'Aspects of Tonal Coherence', pp. 68–92; and Powers, 'Is Mode Real?', p. 21.

[43]   With Glareanus's recognition of A as the final of the Aeolian modal pair, these pieces are all subsumed by that modal category, and indeed Glareanus does cite Josquin's *Miserere* as an example of the Hypoaeolian mode.

an A final and *cantus durus* – but in tonal focus: on *re* in the case of *La plus des plus* and *Se mieulx* and on *mi* in the case of *Miserere mei Deus, Benedic anima mea Dominum* and *Laetatus sum*. The point is broadly summarised in Figure 5, which highlights the essence of tonal focus on a *vox* of the Guidonian diatonic rather than a *littera*. That is, termination on A may signal tonal focus on *D re*/*A re*, as in Figure 5a, by the adjacent first species of fourth *re–sol* (bracketed) and the overlapped species of fifth *re–la* (marked by a brace). Or termination on A may be in the context of *E mi* (Figure 5b), again as witnessed by the adjacent species of fourth – *mi–la* (bracketed) – and the concomitant minimisation of the *mi–mi* species of fifth (under the brace), which unlike the *re–la* fifth cannot overlap in adjacent hexachords within the same system.[44] With a flat signature, that *mi–mi*/*mi–la* configuration is moved to A.[45] There is, in addition, a third possibility, shown boxed between Figures 5a and 5b as a hybrid *re* tonality: a *re–la* fifth and a *mi–la* fourth.[46] This manifestation of a *re* tonality is one in which, at least theoretically, tonal focus on *vox* (*re*) and *littera* (A) becomes synonymous or plays on the replication of

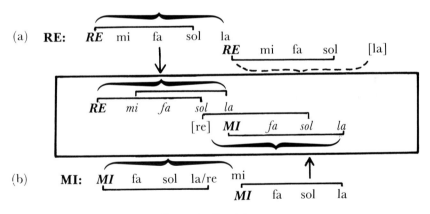

Figure 5   Tonal focus

---

[44]   It is precisely this lack of overlap which is responsible for the unique feature of *mi* tonality works. See Judd, 'Aspects of Tonal Coherence', pp. 206–36.

[45]   That is what Aron describes, but does not actually cite examples for, in ch. 5.

[46]   This is a configuration Aron implicitly recognises in works with a D final and flat signature, but in Aron's modal terms the *mi–la* fourth is subservient to the *re–la* fifth.

juxtaposed (yet now overlapped) species of fourths (marked by brackets).

The generic association of these tonalities – with endings on A – that Aron perhaps unwittingly suggests holds true not only for the prints he surveyed, but more widely: endings on A in *re* tonalities occur primarily in chansons; endings on A in *mi* tonalities occur in motets, especially psalm motets. Indeed, the tonal framework of *Benedic anima mea Dominum* could almost serve as a prototype for a group of motets which follow this scheme.[47]

Aron's reading of Petrucci's anthologies in the *Trattato* may be characterised as personal, silent and visual, in marked contrast to the aural reality of the music to which he referred. This coincides with Powers's observation of the abstract, theoretical realm occupied by mode in Aron's treatise. That is, just as mode is in this sense 'unreal', so is the polyphony Aron cites in this context, which need exist only in print as an authoritative, visual text, not as an object of performance. Aron's reading for the *Trattato* was extensive, using several volumes as sources, rather than intensive and indicative of close study; this suggests distance from a more personalised and circumscribed music manuscript culture. The volumes he used for citations were easily manipulated and need not have functioned as reminders of a repertory Aron 'knew' or had even necessarily 'read' before.[48] Yet in his position as theorist and author, he suggests the availability of a community of readers who shared, or at least accepted, his

[47] Psalm motets are prominent in the most 'modern' of Aron's repertory, the *Motetti de la corona* anthologies (each volume concludes with a psalm motet in addition to several scattered through the volume), and the generic and tonal distinctions represented by Aron's citations may also reflect the chronological distance of the chanson prints he cites. On text types in the *Motetti de la corona* anthologies, see D. Gehrenbeck, '*Motetti de la corona*: A Study of Ottaviano Petrucci's Four Last-Known Motet Prints' (S.M.D. dissertation, Union Theological Seminary, 1970, UMI 7112440), pp. 234–56. In a forthcoming study of motets in German prints 1537–50, I argue for the special association of psalm motets with *mi* tonalities; see also Judd, 'Aspects of Tonal Coherence', pp. 206–36 and 256–82.

[48] Aron's working method in relation to his sources in the *Trattato* seems quite transparent, and suggests a shift from the methodical, even systematic approach of ch. 4 to the sorts of cursory 'glances' reflected in ch. 7. These latter citations suggest minimal revision, juggling or re-ordering in the preparation of his text as a whole. This style of reading – glancing and collecting – initiates the citations of the *Aggiunta*, but then again changes to suit his particular purposes as Aron progresses (see Bent, 'Accidentals, Counterpoint and Notation').

appropriation of the Petrucci prints as both pedagogical material and source of authority. This is a way of reading music prints that has resonances with the kind of multiple readings scholars of other disciplines have posited not only for books but for other printed materials,[49] but it is an approach to printed texts which has been largely unexplored by musical scholars. Although Stanley Boorman prefaced a study of early music printing with the assertion that the 'interaction between print and reader, between printer and market, comes into sharper focus' for music than for any other Renaissance printed matter because 'its intended market can be defined with some precision',[50] Aron's example suggests that the situation is as multi-faceted, by 1525 at any rate, for the users of music books as for any other printed material. In describing the users of partbooks (the format of *Motetti C* and the *Motetti de la corona* anthologies) Boorman suggested that the format meant

that the titles were useless to anyone except a complete set of performers. The act of silently studying the music from such books was, if not impossible, very tedious. . . . The sort of use-for-reference that characterizes, say, legal printing, is an impossibility for almost all printed music. Thus, until the appearance of these volumes in score, one cannot say that there was a *reading* public for musical printing, but only a *using* public. This is the primary reason for believing that virtually all musical volumes were destined (in the printer's mind) for groups of performers.[51]

Whether or not Petrucci intended his volumes for groups of performers, Aron's appropriation of the repertory in the *Trattato* is exactly the kind of 'use-for-reference' that Boorman discounts. Aron's continuation of that appropriation four years later in his supplement to the *Toscanello* suggests that what may have been a novel way of reading in 1525 became his common-place and was shared by his readers. Boorman does allow a 'slight reservation' precisely in the case of theorists:

While the intended public, and also the actual public, is almost entirely a using (performing) public, there were other users. Theorists of music

[49] Chartier, 'Texts, Printing, Readings', and *The Culture of Print*, ed. Chartier.
[50] S. Boorman, 'Early Music Printing: Working for a Specialized Market', *Print and Culture in the Renaissance*, ed. G. P. Tyson and S. S. Wagonheim (Newark, DE, 1986), p. 222.
[51] *Ibid.*, p. 227.

must necessarily have worked from the printed editions, reconstructing the score if they needed: it can be shown that the great Swiss scholar Glareanus certainly worked from some printed editions in preparing his own works.[52]

But even this exception is too narrow to account for the specific instance of Aron's reading of Petrucci in the *Trattato*, not to mention the much broader range of possibilities suggested by other theorists' relationship to printed sources.[53] It was neither necessary for sixteenth-century theorists to work from printed editions (as opposed to manuscripts) nor self-evident that they needed to 'reconstruct' the score when they did so. To take Boorman's example as a single instance: Glareanus's relationship to printed sources (and to a complex of manuscripts) deserves detailed study which would go beyond the scope of the present article, but even a superficial comparison suggests that it is markedly different from Aron's, and thus suggests a more variegated picture of the ways in which theorists, themselves a community of readers, employed printed music sources. Glareanus's repertory is not circumscribed by printed sources in the same way as Aron's, and by reprinting works in the *Dodecachordon* Glareanus does not assume, as Aron appears to have, that his readers shared his repertory;[54] nor has he invested a relatively small group of prints with the authority Aron accorded the Petrucci prints. This may be as much a reflection of the different circles in which the two men moved as of the rapid changes in music print culture in the twenty years which separated the publication of their treatises, but it is a distinction which should not be underplayed by casual assumptions about the relationship between theoretical writing, ways of reading and printed sources.

The reading I have proposed of Aron's music citations in the *Trattato*, along with the view of Aron as a reader of Petrucci's anthologies it suggests, raises numerous general questions about theoretical citations from printed music sources which must be

---

[52] *Ibid.*, pp. 242–3, n. 26.

[53] A discussion of these possibilities is beyond the scope of the present article, but will be considered in a forthcoming monograph, which will explore the issues raised here in the larger context of the relationship of theoretical sources and printed repertories from Aron to Zarlino.

[54] The exception which proves the rule is Josquin's *Miserere*, which Glarean says he will not reprint since it is in everyone's hands.

the subject of future study. Implicit among them is the question of Aron's status as theorist. His invocation of printed sources appears to us, of course, as both eminently practical and closely tied to the nature of his material in the *Trattato* and the *Aggiunta*. Indeed, the reliance of a theorist on printed sources seems inevitable given the undeniable impact of music printing. Publishing examples in the *Trattato* would have been impossible and citations from Petrucci's prints provided at least the appearance of commonality when Aron could count neither on readers' access to manuscript sources nor on their memory of individual tenor parts. But Aron's very reliance on printed sources might also be construed as reflecting a kind of musico-theoretical inferiority that combined a resort to the visual in lieu of aural memory with an assertion of his own qualification through association with Petrucci's prints and the composers contained in them.[55] Certainly, the reception of the *Trattato* is best described as mixed: Spataro berated the treatise as 'without order and truth' and apparently supplied a 200-page critique,[56] while Aiguino speaks reverently of Aron as his honoured teacher in his two published treatises on the modes which follow Aron's model.

The traditional view holds up Aron as an 'innovator' and 'progressive',[57] but it may well be more accurate, taking his relationship to printed sources as representative, to suggest that his innovations were of somewhat dubious merit, namely: publishing a theory treatise in Italian, explicitly connecting mode with a particular polyphonic repertory, and defining that reper-

---

[55] On Aron's training (or lack thereof) and his apparent inability to obtain positions of any substance, see *A Correspondence of Renaissance Musicians*, ed. Blackburn, Lowinsky and Miller, pp. 74–100.

[56] 'Al venerabile Petro non voglio scrive[re] de tale cosa, perché lui è al tuto sdegnato con me, et que[sto] nasce perché io asai cercai retrarlo de la impresa de quello suo tractato de tonis ultimamente da lui impresso, el quale è reuscito proprio come io li scripsi, cioè senza ordine et verità, contra el quale ho scripto apresso a cento foglii, li quali scripti sono apresso di me' (*ibid.*, p. 374); 'I don't want to write to Aaron; he is sore at me because I tried to dissuade him from publishing his treatise on the modes. I wrote him 200 pages about it; just as I predicted, it came out without order and truth' (*ibid.*, pp. 375–6).

[57] 'One can easily see that Aron, in such varied ways as his use of the vernacular, his desire for a consistent indication of accidentals, his disapproval of conflicting signatures, and his emphasis on a practical terminology, proves himself a Renaissance man in touch with the progressive music thinking of his day' (G. Reese, *Music in the Renaissance*, rev. edn (London, 1954), p. 183).

tory through printed sources. Such departures from the norm stand in striking contrast to the purely medieval construction of Aron's modal theory and were perhaps only even conceivable because of his position as an 'outsider',[58] although one cannot gainsay the significance of those 'firsts' for subsequent theoretical discourse. Whether he intended to do so or not, Pietro Aron's conscious reliance on printed sources betokened an irreversibly changed relationship between theorists and a community of readers now defined by a shared, printed musical image.

University of Pennsylvania

---

[58] That is, he apparently lacked access to both the materials and the training, musical and otherwise, available to his theoretical peers.

APPENDIX

Sources of Aron's citations

Table A1 Harmonice musices Odhecaton[1]

No.	Attribution	Text	Clefs	Tenor Signature	Final[2]	Aron[3]
1	Orto	*Ave Maria*	c2-c4-f3-f5	♭	F	*
2		*Je cuide se ce temps*	**g2-c3-c3-f4**		**C**	7
3	[Stokem]	*Hor oires une chanzon*	c1-c2-c3-c3-c4	♭	G	
4		*Nunca fué pena mayor*	**c1-c4-c3-c4**		**G**	3
5	**Stokem**	*Brunette*	**c1-c4-c4-c3-f4**	♭	**F**	6
6		*J'ay pris amours / De tous biens*	c1-c3-c4-f4	♭♭	G	
7	Japart	*Nenciozza mia*	c2-c4-f4-f4	♭	F	
8		*Je ne fay plus*	g2-c2-c3-c4	♭	G	
9	Hayne	*Amours amours*	c2-c3-c4-f4	♭	G	
10	Josquin	*Bergerette savoyenne*	g2-c3-c3-f3		C	
11		*Et qui le dira*	c1-c3-c4-f4	♭	G	
12	Agricola	*C'est mal cherche*	c1-c3-c4-f4	♭	G	*
13	**Caron**	*Hélas que pourra devenir*	**c1-c3-c3-c4**	♭	**F**	5
14	Josquin	*Adieu mes amours*	c1-c3-c4-f3	♭	G	
15	LaRue	*Pourquoy non*	c2-c3-c3-f4	♭♭	F	*
16	Stokem	*Pourquoy je ne puis dire / Vray dieu*	c2-c4-c4-f4	♭	F	
17		*Mon mignault / Gracieuse*	c2-c3-c4-f4	♭	G	
18		*Dit le burguygnon*	c1-c3-c4-f4	♭	G	
19	Stokem	*Hélas ce n'est pas*	c1-c4-c4-f4	♭	G	
20	**[Hayne]**	*De tous biens playne*	**c2-c3-c4-f4**	♭	**G**	2
21	Japart	*J'ay pris amours*	c1-c3-c3-f4	♭♭	G	
22[4]	Compère	*Ung franc archier*	c1-c3-c4-f4	♭	G	
23	Japart	*Amours amours*	c1-c4-c4-f4	♭	F	
24	[Japart]	*Cela sans plus non souffi pas*	c2-f3-f3-f4	♭♭	C	
25		*Rompeltier*	c1-c3-c4-f4	♭	G	
26	Compère	*Alons fere nos barbes*	c1-c3-c4-f4	♭	G	
27	[Japart]	*Tmeiskin*	c1-c3-c4-f4	♭	G	
28	Japart	*Se congie pris*	c1-c3-c4-f4	♭	G	
29		*L'oseraie dire*	**g2-c3-c3-f3**	♭	**C**	8
30	**Japart**	*Hélas qu'il est à mon gré*	**g2-c1-c2-c4**		**D**	1 *
31	[Japart]	*Amours fait molt / Il est de bonne*	c2-c4-c3-f4	♭	G	
32	[Ninot]	*Nostre chamberière*	c1-c3-c4-f3	♭	F	
33	[Busnoys]	*Acordes moy*	c2-f3-c4-f4	♭	G	
34	Japart	*Tam bien mi son pensada*	c1-c3-c4-f4	♭	G	
35		*Le serviteur*	**c2-c3-c4-f4**	♭♭	**C**	-
36	[Mouton]	*Jamais jamais*	g2-c3-c3-f4	♭	G	
37	Compère	*Nous sommes*	g2-c3-c3-f3		C	*
38	Agricola	*Je n'ay dueil*	c2-c4-c4-f4		D	
39	Busnoys	*J'ay pris amours tout au rebours*	c2-c4-c4-f4	♭	A[D]	
40	[Isaac]	*Helogierons nous*	c2-c3-c4-f4	♭	G	*
41	**Compère**	*Vostre bargeronette*	**c1-c3-c4-f3**	♭	**F**	6
42	**Busnoys**	*Je ne demande*	**c2-c4-f4-f4**	♭	**F**	6

[1] RISM 1501; table based on facsimile edn (New York, 1973) of RISM 1504[2]. Modern edn by H. Hewitt (Cambridge, MA, 1942). I am grateful to David Fallows for supplying attributions for nos. 3, 31, 71 and 80.
[2] Concluding pitch class of tenor is given. In multi-part works, the final of each section is given, separated by ‖. The termination of the bassus is given in square brackets when it differs from the tenor.
[3] Works printed in bold type are cited in the *Trattato*; works with an asterisk are cited in the *Aggiunta* of the *Toscanello* (1529). Dashes indicate citation without modal classification.
[4] Hewitt exchanges Compère *Ung franc archier* (no. 22) and Japart *Se congie pris* (no. 28) without comment.

Table A1 (cont.)

No.	Attribution	Text	Clefs	Signature	Final	Aron
43	Tadinghen	*Pensif mari*	c1-c3-f4	♭	G	
44	Isaac	*La morra*	c1-c3-f4	♭	G	
45	Compère	*Ne doibt*	c1-c4-f4	♭	G	
46	Compère	*Male bouche / Circumdederunt*	c2-c4-f3		D	
47	Agricola	*L'homme banni*	c2-c4-f4	♭	G	
48	**Agricola**	***Allez regretz***	**c2-c2-c4**	♭	**F**	**6**
49		*La stangetta*	c1-c4-f4	♭	G	
50	Isaac	*Hélas*	c1-c3-c4	♭	F	
51	**Compère**	***Se mieulx***	**c1-c4-f3**		**A**	**2**
52	Tinctoris	*Hélas*	c1-c3-f4		D	
53	Compère	*Venez regretz*	c1-c3-f4	♭	F	
54	Okeghem	*Ma bouche rit*	c1-c4-f4		E	
55	Agricola	*Royne des fleurs*	c2-c4-f4		D	
56	**Agricola**	***Si dedero***	**c2-c4-f4**		**G**	**8**
57	Hayne	*Allez regretz*	c2-c4-f4	♭	F	
58	Compère	*Guerises moy*	c1-c4-f4	♭	G	
59	**Compère**	***Mes pensées***	**c1-c3-c4**		**C**	**7**
60	Vincenet	*Fortune par ta crualte*	c1-c3-f3	♭♭	C	
61	**Josquin**	***Cela sans plus***	**c1-c4-f3**	♭	**G**	**-**
62	Brumel	*Mater patris*	c3-c3-c4	♭	G	
63	**Okeghem**	***Malheur me bat***	**c1-c4-c4**		**E**	**3**
64	**Josquin**	***La plus des plus***	**c1-c4-f3**		**A**	**1**
65	Agricola	*Allez mon cueur*	c1-c4-f4		E	
66		***Madame hélas***	**c1-c3-f3**		**C**	**7**
67	Compère	*Le corps / Corpusque meum*	c2-c4-f3		D	
68	Compère	*Tant ha bon oeul*	c2-c4-f4		D	
69	Obrecht	*T'andernacken*	c2-c4-f4	♭	A	*
70		*Si à tort on m'a blasmé*	c1-c3-f3		G	
71	[Hayne]	*Les grans regretz*	c1-c3-f3	♭	G	
72		***Est il possible***	**c1-c3-f3**		**G**	**8**
73	Bourdon [in index]	*De tous biens*	c2-c4-f4	♭	G	
74		*Fortuna d'un gran tempo*	c2-c4-f3	♭	F	
75	Agricola	*Crions nouel*	c1-c4-f3		A	
76	Isaac	*Benedictus*	c2-c3-f4	♭	G	
77	Compère	*Le renvoy*	c2-c4-f4	♭	G	
78	**Josquin**	***O venus bant***	**c1-c4-f4**		**G**	**8**
79		*Ma seule dame*	c1-c4-f4	♭	F	
80	Ghiselin	*L'Alfonsina*	c2-c3-f4	♭	G	
81	Agricola	*L'heure est venue / Circumdederunt*	c2-c4-f4		D	
82	Agricola	*J'ay beau huer*	c1-c4-f3	♭	G	
83	[Hayne]	*Mon souvenir*	c1-c3-f3	♭	G	
84	Compère	*Royne du ciel / Regina celi*	c2-c4-f3		G	
85		*Marguerite*	g2-c1-c4	♭	D	
86	Stokem	*Ha! traitre amours*	c1-c4-c4		A	
87	Compère	*Mais que ce fust*	c1-c4-f3	♭	G	
88	Orto	*Venus tu m'a pris*	c1-c3-f3	♭♭	C	
89	**Compère**	***Disant adieu à madame***	**c1-c4-f4**		**G**	**8**
90		*Gentil prince*	c1-c4-f4	♭	G	
91		*Puisque de vous*	c1-c4-f4		A	
92	Obrecht	*Tsat een meskin*	c1-c3-c4-f3		G	
93	**Hayne**	***A l'audience***	**c3-c4-f4-f4**	♭	**F**	**6**
94	Bruhier	*La turatu*	c1-c3-c4-f4	♭	G	
95	Josquin	*De tous biens playne*	c2-c4-f3-[f3]	♭	G	
96	Obrecht	*Meskin es hu*	c1-c3-c3-f4	♭	D[G]	

Table A2 Canti B[5]

No.	Attribution	Text	Clefs	Signature	Final	Aron
1	**Josquin**	*L'homme armé*	**c1-c3-c3-f3**	♭	**D**	**1**
2	**Compère**	*Virgo celesti*	**c1-c3-c4-c4-f4**	♭	**G**	**2**
3	Obrecht	*J'ay pris amours*	c1-c2-c4-f4		A	
4	[Bruhier]	*Vray Dieu*	c1-c3-c4-f4		D	
5	Compère	*Lourdault*	c1-c3-c4-f4	♭	G	
6	[Raulin]	*Je suis trop jeunette*	g2-c3-c3-f4	♭	G	
7	**LaRue**	*Ce n'est pas jeu*	**c2-c4-c4-f4**	♭	**G**	**2**
8	Busnoys	*L'autrier que passa*	c2-c3-f3-f4	♭	G	
9		*Réveillez-vous*	c1-c4-c4-f4		D	
10		*En chambre polie*	g2-c3-c4-f3	♭	F	
11	**[Compère]**	*Je suiz amie du fourrier*	**c1-c3-c4-f4**		**G**	**8**
12	**Orto**	*Mon mary m'a diffamée*	**c2-c3-f3-f4**	♭	**C**	**8**
13	Obrecht	*Cela sans plus*	c1-c3-c4-f3		G[C]	
14		*Bon temps*	c2-c4-c4-f4	♭	D	
15		*A qui dir élle sa pencee*	c1-c3-c4-f4	♭	G	
16	Lannoy [in index]	*Cela sans plus*	g2-c3-c3-f3		G	
17		*Mon père m'a mariée*	c1-c3-c3-f4	♭	G	
18		*Mijn morken gaf*	**c1-c3-c4-f4**		**G**	**8**
19	**Josquin**	*Comment peult avoir*	**g2-c3-c3-f4**	♭	**C**	**7**
20		*Comment peult*	c2-c4-c4-f4		G	
21	**Ninot**	*Hélas, hélas, hélas*	**c1-c3-c4-f4**		**G**	**8**
22	LaRue	*Tous les regretz*	c2-c4-f3-f5		D	
23	Vaqueras	*Veci la danse barbari*	c1-c4-c4-f4		G	
24	**Orto**	*D'ung aultre amer*	**c1-c4-c4-f4**	♭	**G**	**2**
25	Brumel	*Noé, noé, noé*	c1-c3-c4-f4	♭	G	
26		*Una moza falle yo*	c1-c3-c3-f4	♭	G	
27	**[Ninot]**	*Et la la la*	**c1-c3-c4-f3**		**C**	**8**
28	**LaRue**	*Fors seulement*	**c1-c1-c1-c4**		**D**	**1**
29	**Compère**	*Et dun revenis*	**c1-c3-c4-f3**		**G**	**8**
30	Japart	*J'ay pris amours*	c1-c2-c4-c4		A	
31	Japart	*Je cuide / De tous biens*	c1-c3-c4-f4	♭	G	
32	De Vigne	*Franc coeur / Fortuna*	c1-c2-c4-c4-f4		G	
33	Lourdoys (Braconnier)	*Amours me trocte*	c1-c3-c4-f4	♭	F	
34	Josquin	*Baisez moy*	c1-c2-c3-c4	♭	G	
35	Obrecht	*Vanil ment [=Wat willen]*	c1-c3-c3-f4	♭	G	
36	Bulkyn	*Or sus, or sus*	c1-[c3]-c3-f3		G	
37		*Baisez moy*	[c1]-c3-[c2]-c4-[c4]-f4		G	
38		*Avant avant*	c2-[c4]-c4-f4		D	
39	Brumel	*Ave Ancilla Trinitatis*	c3-f4-f4	♭	G	
40	**Obrecht**	*Si Sumpsero*	**g2-c3-f3**	♭	**C**	**5**
41		*Mon père m'a donné mari*	c1-c3-c4-f4	♭	G	
42	Ghiselin	*De tous biens*	c2-c3-f3	♭	G	
43		*Pour quoy*	**c2-c4-f4**	♭	**D**	**1**
44	[Isaac]	*Adieu fillette*	c1-c4-f4	♭	G	
45	Compère	*Chanter ne puis*	c2-c4-f4	♭	G	
46	Agricola	*Je vous emprie [=Si vous voullez]*	c1-c3-f4		C	
47	Compère	*A qui dirage*	c1-c4-f4	♭	G	
48	**Hayne**	*La Regretée*	**c1-c3-f3**	♭	**B♭**	**5**
49	Brumel	*En amours*	c2-c4-f4	♭	G	
50	**Brumel**	*Je despite tous*	**g2-c2-c4**		**D**	**1**
51	Compère	*Le grant désir*	c2-c4-f4		D	

[5] RISM 1502[2]; table based on facsimile edn (New York, 1975). Modern edn by H. Hewitt (Chicago, 1967).

Table A3 Motetti C[6]

No.	Attribution	Text	Clefs	Signature	Final	Aron
1	Josquin	*Ave Maria [...benedicta tu]*	g2-c3-c3-f3	♭	G	
2	Brumel	*Ave celorum Domina*	c1-c3-c3-c4	♭	G	
3	Josquin	*Liber generationis*	c1-c3-c4-f4		G[E] ‖ A ‖ E	
4	Josquin	*Factum est autem*	c1-c4-c4-f4		G[E] ‖ E[A] ‖ G	
5	Nico. Craen	*Tota pulchra es*	c2-c3-c4-f5		E ‖ E	
6		*Davidica stirpe*	g2-c3-c3-f3	♭	C[F] ‖ F	
7		***Beata Dei genitrix***	**c1-c4-c4-f4**		**G ‖ G**	**8**
8	Josquin	*Missus est*	c2-c4-c4-f4	♭	B♭ [G]	
9		*Ergo sancti martires*	c2-c4-f3-f4	♭	D	
10		*Concede nobis Domine*	c1-c4-c4-f4	♭	G ‖ G	
11	[Obrecht]	*Requiem eternam*	c1-c3-c4-f4		E ‖ E	
12	[Ninot]	*Psallite noe*	c1-c3-c4-f4	♭	F	
13	[Ninot]	*Si oblitus fuero*	c1-c3-c4-f4	♭	G ‖ G	
14		*Civitatem istam*	c1-c3-c4-f4		G[C] ‖ A	
15	[Okeghem]	*Ut hermita*	c1-c3-c3-f4		E ‖ E	
16	[Josquin]	*O bone et dulcis / Pater noster*	c1-c3-c4-f4		D	
17		*Missus est*	c1-c2-c3-c4		E[A] ‖ D	
18	[Isaac]	*Alma redemptoris*	c1/c2-c3-c3-f3	♭	A ‖ F	
19		*Miles mire probitatis*	c2-c4-c4-f4	♭	F ‖ F	
20		*Ave regina / O decus innocentie*	c1-c2-c4-f4	♭	F ‖ F	
21		*Virgo precellens*	c1-c3-c4-f4	♭	G ‖ G ‖ G ‖ G ‖ G	
22		*O sacrum convivium / Qui pacem*	c1-c4-c4-f4	♭	F	
23		*O admirabile*	c1-c4-c4-f4	♭	F	
24	[Mouton]	*Sancti Dei omnes*	c1-c4/c3-c4-f4	♭	F ‖ F	
25		*Confitemini*	c1-c3-c4-f4	♭	G[C] ‖ G	
26		*Respice me in felicem*	c1-c4-c4-f4	♭	G	
27		*Trinitas deitas*	c1-c4-c4-f4	♭	A[D] ‖ G	
28	[Compère]	*Profitentes unitatem*	c1-c2-c3-f3		E[A] ‖ A[D]	
29		*Filie regum [In honore tuo]*	c1-c4-c4-f4		A ‖ E[A]	
30		*Miserere mei*	c1-c3-c3-f4	♭	G	
31		*Si bona suscepimus*	c1-c3-c4-f4		B[E] ‖ A	
32	[Josquin?]	*Magnus es tu*	c1-c4-c4-f3		E[A] ‖ E	
33	[Josquin?]	*Planxit autem*	c1-c3-c4-f4	♭	F ‖ F ‖ F ‖ F	
34	**[Isaac]**	***Rogamus te / O Maria***	**c1-c3-c4-f4**		**E ‖ A**	**4**
35		*Inviolata*	g2-c3-c3-f3		C ‖ E ‖ E ‖ E ‖ C ‖ C ‖ E ‖ E ‖ C ‖ G[C] ‖ C ‖ C	
36		*Gloria laus*	c1-c4-c4-f4		D ‖ A[D] ‖ A[D] ‖ A	
37		*Gaudeamus*	c1-c3-c4-f4	♭	G ‖ G ‖ G ‖ G ‖ G	
38		*Huc omnes pariter*	c1-c4-c4-f4	♭	C[F] ‖ F	
39		*O dulcissima*	c1-c3-c3-f4	♭	G ‖ G	
41	**[Josquin]**	***Mitit ad virginem***	**g2-c3-c3-f3**		**C ‖ C**	**7**
40		*Salvatoris mater pia*	c1-c3-c3-c4	♭	G ‖ G ‖ G	
42		*In lectulo*	c4-c4-f4	♭	D [G]	

[6] RISM 1504[1]; table based on film of D-Mbs. Partial modern edn in R. Sherr, *The Petrucci Motet Anthologies* (New York, 1991). My thanks to Richard Sherr for the use of his films of 1504[1], 1514[1], 1519[1] and 1519[2].

Reading Aron reading Petrucci

Table A4 Missarum Josquin liber secundus[7]

No.	Attribution	Text	Clefs	Signature	Final	Aron
1	Josquin	*Ave Maris Stella*	g2-c3-c3-f3	♭	G ‖ G ‖ G ‖ G ‖ G	1
2	Josquin	*Hercules dux ferrariae*	c2-c4-c4-f4		D ‖ D ‖ D ‖ D ‖ D	2
3	Josquin	*Malheur me bat*	c2-c4-c4-f4		E ‖ E ‖ E ‖ E ‖ E	
4	Josquin	*L'ami baudichon*	c1-c3-c3-f3		C ‖ C ‖ C ‖ C ‖ C	
5	Josquin	*Una Musque de buscaya*	c1-c3-c4-f4	♭	B♭ ‖ B♭ ‖ G ‖ B♭ ‖ B♭	
6	Josquin	*D'ung aultre amer*	c1-c4-c4-f4	♭	G ‖ G ‖ G ‖ G ‖ G	1

Table A5 Motetti de la corona libro primo[8]

No.	Attribution	Text	Clefs	Signature	Final	Aron
1.1	Mouton	*Gaude Barbara beata*	g2-c2-c3-c4		A ‖ D	1 *
1.2	Josquin	*Memor esto verbi tui*	c1-c4-c2-f3		B[E] ‖ E[A]	*
1.3	Carpentras	*Bonitatem fecisti*	c1-c3-c4-f4		A[D] ‖ C[A]	*
1.4	De Silva	*Laetatus sum*	c1-c3-c4-f4		E[A] ‖ A[A]	[3]
1.5	Mouton	*Nos qui vivimus: In exitu Israel*	c1-c4-c4-f4		G ‖ G ‖ G	*
1.6	Thérache	*Clare sanctorum*	c1-c3-c4-f4		G	
1.7	Mouton	*Laudate Deum*	c1-c3-c4-f4		G ‖ G	
1.8	Févin	*Nobilis progenie*	g2-c3-c3-f3	·♭	G	1
1.9	Mouton	*Ecce Maria genuit*	g2-c2-c3-c4	♭	B♭	
1.10	Févin	*Benedictus Dominus Deus*	g2-c3-c4-f4	♭	G ‖ G	*
1.11	Mouton	*Beata Dei, genitrix Maria*	c1-c1-c4-f3		D	1/2
1.12	Longueval	*Benedicat nos*	c1-c3-c4-f4	♭	G ‖ G	*
1.13	Févin	*Sancta Trinitas*	c1-c3-c4-f4	♭	F	6
1.14	Divitis	*O desolatorum consolator*	c1-c3-c4-f4	♭	G ‖ G	
1.15	Févin	*Gaude francorum regia corona*	c1-c3-c4-f4	♭	G	
1.16	Mouton	*Christum regem regum*	c3-c3-c4-f4	♭	G	
1.17		*Contremuerunt omnia membra*	c3-c4-c4-f4		E	
1.18	Hylaire	*Ascendens Christus*	g2-g2-c3-c4		G	7
1.19	Mouton	*Benedicta es*	c2-c4-c4-f4		G	
1.20	Févin	*Tempus meum est*	c1-c3-c4-f4	♭	F ‖ F	6
1.21		*Vulnerasti cor meum*	g2-c2-c3-f4	♭	A[D] ‖ G	1
1.22	Mouton	*Celeste beneficium*	c2-c3-c4-f4	♭	F ‖ F	6
1.23	Févin	*Egregie Christi confessor*	c1-c3-c4-f4	♭	F ‖ F	6
1.24	[Févin]	*Dilectus Deo*	c1-c4-c4-f4		C	
1.25	Josquin	*Christum ducem*	c2-c3-c4-f4		E	
1.26	Brumel	*Laudate Dominum*	c1-c3-c4-f4		D[G] ‖ G	

[7] RISM J670 (1505); table based on facsimile edn (Rome, 1973).
[8] RISM 1514[1]; table based on film of I-Bc. Partial modern edns in D. Gehrenbeck, '*Motetti de la corona*: A Study of Ottaviano Petrucci's Four Last-Known Motet Prints' (S.M.D. dissertation, Union Theological Seminary, 1970, UMI 7112440), and R. Sherr, *Selections from Motetti de la corona* (New York, 1992).

Table A6 Motetti de la corona libro secondo[9]

No.	Attribution	Text	Clefs	Signature	Final	Aron
2.1	Thérache	*Verbum bonum et suave*	c1-c4-c4-f4		G	
2.2	**Jacotin**	**Interveniat pro rege nostro**	c3-c4-c4-f4		B[E]	3
2.3	**Caen**	**Nomine qui Domini**	c1-c3-c4-f4	♭	D	1
2.4	Richafort [Mouton]	*Miseremini mei*	c1-c4-c3-f4		A ‖ E[A]	*
2.5	Lupus	*Postquam consummati sunt*	c1-c3-c4-f4		A	
2.6	**Jacotin**	**Michael Archangele**	c1-c3-c4-f4		A ‖ E	3
2.7	**Jacotin**	**Rogamus te, Virgo Maria**	c1-c3-c4-f4		A ‖ D	1/2
2.8	**Caen**	**Judica me, Deus**	c2-c2-c4-f4		E[A] ‖ D	1/2
2.9	Caen	*Sanctificavit Dominus*	c1-c3-c4-f4		G ‖ G	
2.10	Maistre Jan	*O benignissime Domine Jesu*	c1-c3-c4-f4		A	
2.11	**Eustachius**	**Benedic anima mea**	c1-c3-c4-f4		B[E] ‖ E ‖ C♯ [A]	3
2.12	**Mouton**	**Illuminare Hierusalem**	g2-c2-c3-f3	♭	F ‖ F	5
2.13	Mouton	*O Christe Redemptor*	g2-c2-c3-f3	♭	G ‖ G	
2.14	Mouton	*Corde et animo*	c1-c3-c4-f4	♭	F	
2.15	Mouton	*Amicus Dei, Nicolaus*	g2-c2-c3-c4		G ‖ G	
2.16	**Mouton**	**Congregati sunt gentes**	c1-c3-c4-f4		D ‖ D	1/2*
2.17	**Mouton**	**Peccata mea, Domine (a5 ex 4)**	c3-c3-f4-f4	♭♭	G	-
2.18	Mouton	*Factum est silentium*	g2-c2-c3-c4		G ‖ G	
2.19	Mouton	*Homo quidam*	c1-c3-c4-f4	♭	F	
2.20	Mouton	*Maria Virgo*	c1-c3-c4-f4	♭	G ‖ G	
2.21	Lhéritier	*Dum complerentur*	c1-c3-c4-f4	♭	G ‖ G	*
2.22	Mouton	*Non nobis Domine*	c1-c3-c4-f4	♭	F ‖ F	
2.23	Mouton	*Noe noe psallite*	g2-c2-c3-c4	♭	G	
2.24	La Fage	*Elisabeth Zacharie*	c1-c3-c4-f4		B[G] ‖ G	
2.25	Eustachius	*Omnes gentes plaudite*	c1-c3-c4-f4		E[A] ‖ D	

Table A7 Motetti de la corona libro tertio[10]

No.	Attribution	Text	Clefs	Signature	Final	Aron
3.1	Josquin	*Huc me sydereo*	c1-f4-c3-c4-f4-f4	♭	A ‖ A[D]	
3.2	Josquin	*Praeter rerum seriem*	c1-c3-c3-c4-f4-f4	♭	G ‖ G	*
3.3	Josquin	*Ave nobilissima creatura*	c1-c4-c4-c4-f4-f4	♭	A ‖ A[D]	*
3.4	Josquin	*Virgo salutiferi*	c1-c4-c4-c4-f4	♭	B♭ ‖ C ‖ G	*
3.5	Le Brung	*Recumbentibus undecim discipulis*	c1-c4-c4-f4-f4	♭	C ‖ C ‖ G	
3.6	**Josquin**	**Stabat mater dolorosa**	g2-c3-c3-c4-f4	♭	G[C] ‖ F	5
3.7	**Josquin**	**Miserere mei Deus**	c1-c3-c4-c4-f4		E ‖ E ‖ A	3
3.8	Mouton	*Quis dabit oculis nostris*	c1-c3-c4-f4		A ‖ G[E] ‖ E	
3.9	Pesenti	*Tulerunt Dominum*	c2-c4-c4-f4		E[A] ‖ G[E]	
3.10	**Josquin**	**Alma redemptoris mater**	c4-c3-c3-f3	♭	A ‖ F	5
3.11	Josquin	*Domine ne in furore*	c4-c4-c4-f4		A ‖ G[E]	
3.12	Mouton	*Quam pulchra es*	c4-c4-c4-f4	♭	C[F] ‖ C[F]	
3.13		*Ecce nunc benedicite*	c2-c3-c4-f4		E	
3.14	Compère	*O bone Jesu*	c1-c3-c3-f3		G	
3.15	[Mouton]	*Felix namque es*	g2-c2-c3-c4	♭	G ‖ G	
3.16	Carpentras	*Cantate Domino*	c1-c3-c4-f3		B[E] ‖ B[E]	

[9] RISM 1519[1]; table based on film of GB-Lbm. Partial modern edns in Gehrenbeck, '*Motetti de la corona*', and Sherr, *Selections*.
[10] RISM 1519[2]; table based on film of GB-Lbm. Partial modern edns in Gehrenbeck, '*Motetti de la corona*', and Sherr, *Selections*.

Early Music History (1995) *Volume 14*

KENNETH KREITNER

MUSIC IN THE CORPUS CHRISTI PROCESSION OF FIFTEENTH-CENTURY BARCELONA*

The great ceremonies of the Middle Ages and Renaissance have an uncomfortable position in music history. Contemporary descriptions of such events have survived from all over Europe through the centuries, and they are often full of vivid and quotable detail. For all its rich abundance, however, the documentation surrounding these large ceremonies has proved in a number of ways difficult to interpret. First, it is usually impossible to connect the official ceremonial accounts securely to specific, known pieces of music. Second, it is the nature of secular documents to omit as beneath their purview many of the musical details that we today regard as indispensable – the chroniclers were always maddeningly more interested in the musicians' clothing than in, say, their instrumentation. Third, and perhaps most important as we strive towards a balanced, street-level view of music in medieval and Renaissance life, the ceremonies that got the biggest descriptions tended to be the most extraordinary events of their day, unique by definition and held for the most rarefied and least representative audiences. The people who attended the Feast of the Pheasant or the meetings of the Order of the Golden Fleece were no cross-section of their society, and it is hard to know exactly how much of what we learn about their music can be applied to anything we might call real life.

The Corpus Christi procession of fifteenth-century Barcelona is a happy exception to at least the last of these difficulties, and possibly to the other two as well. It was a very big ceremony

---

* Portions of this article, in different form, appeared in K. R. Kreitner, 'Music and Civic Ceremony in Late-Fifteenth-Century Barcelona' (Ph.D. dissertation, Duke University, 1990).

indeed, and its documentation in the city archives is remarkable, with information about a variety of musical ensembles. But unlike so many other large and well-described ceremonies of the age, this event was repeated every year, and there was nothing exclusive about its audience: the parade included some of the best music and grandest spectacle the city could offer, and it was all available to the humblest person in the community.

The importance of the Corpus celebration in its own time, and the amount of information available on it in ours, have given it a central role in the work of many Catalan historians and folklorists over the past two centuries,[1] but its value to music history has been only preliminarily explored.[2] My purpose here is to look at the Corpus Christi procession of fifteenth-century Barcelona as closely as possible, from as many musically relevant angles as possible, and see what it can tell us – not only about the music within the parade itself, but about the place of similar kinds of music elsewhere in the city and on the other 364 days of the year.

I. THE PROCESSION

The first Thursday after Trinity Sunday (i.e. a Thursday in late May or June) was set aside by Pope Urban IV in 1264 to be a feast day celebrating the importance of the Body of Christ in the Eucharist. This new holiday, called Corpus Christi, was inspired by a vision seen by St Juliana of Liège in about 1209; after being reinforced by a bull of Pope John XXII in 1316 it

[1] The earliest publication of the fifteenth-century documents known to me is in J. Ripoll Vilamajor, *Memorias inéditas: Que pueden servir para demostrar el origen y antigüedad, e ilustrar la historia de la procesion del Corpus Christi en la ciudad de Barcelona* (Barcelona, 1838); modern views of the Corpus celebration are summarised in J. Amades, *Costumari català: El curs de l'any* (Barcelona, 1950–6), III, pp. 3–56, and A. Duran i Sanpere, *Barcelona i la seva història* (Barcelona, 1972–5), II, pp. 529–71. Duran acknowledges his debt, and I mine, to a manuscript by A. Coy Cotonat entitled 'El Corpus Christi: Origen y motivo de su institución in la Iglesia: Antigüedad y esplendor de esta fiesta en Barcelona', dated 1918, sadly left unfinished at the author's death in 1920 and now preserved at the Institut Municipal d'Història in Barcelona.

[2] Barcelona's celebration is mentioned briefly in E. A. Bowles, 'Musical Instruments in the Medieval Corpus Christi Procession', *Journal of the American Musicological Society*, 17 (1964), pp. 251–60, esp. pp. 255–8, and D. Alternberg, 'Die Musik in der Fronleichnamsprozession des 14. and 15. Jahrhunderts', *Musica Disciplina*, 38 (1984), pp. 5–24, esp. pp. 7, 9, 20–1.

spread rapidly through Christendom, becoming by the end of the fourteenth century an elaborate local festivity, usually with a large procession, in hundreds of towns and cities in every country of Europe.[3]

In Spain, the practice of staging a procession for Corpus Christi seems to have taken root first in the south and gradually to have worked its way northward over the early fourteenth century. The first recorded Corpus parade on the Iberian peninsula was in Toledo in 1280; this was followed by other such parades in Seville in 1282, Cádiz in 1300, Madrid and Palma in 1317, Guimarães in 1318 and Girona and Barcelona in 1320.[4]

Barcelona's initial celebration of 1320 was announced in the city government's Llibre del Consell the previous year; the document unfortunately gives no musical detail, saying only that the pope had authorised indulgences for those who attended the services, that the services would be accompanied by a procession, that it would be a celebration 'with great joy and devotion, like Easter or Christmas', and that workers in the city would be given the day off.[5]

---

[3] The spread of the Corpus Christi celebration through Europe is extensively documented in G. Matern, *Zur Vorgeschichte und Geschichte der Fronleichnamsfeier besonders in Spanien*, Spanische Forschungen der Görresgesellschaft, zweite Reihe 10 (Münster, 1962), esp. pp. 90–145. Matern's work, despite its title, goes far beyond Spain to give a wealth of information, arranged city by city, for German- and French-speaking lands as well.

[4] *Ibid.*, pp. 109–45, esp. the map between pp. 144 and 145. Matern points out that some question surrounds several of these dates. On Girona in particular, see especially J. de Chía, *La festividad del Corpus en Gerona: Noticias históricas acerca de esta festividad desde el siglo XIV hasta nuestros días* (Girona, 1895); the origins of the local festival are discussed on pp. 9–10, but see also pp. 7–95 more generally for much fascinating information on its development through the sixteenth century, which parallels that of the nearby Barcelona celebration in a great many details.

[5] Barcelona, Institut Municipal d'Història (hereafter IMH), Llibre del Consell, 6, fol. 16ʳ: 'Ordonaren los Conseylers els prohomens de la Ciutat que con lo sant pare apostoli a honor & a lahor & a gloria de Deu & a exalsament de la fe catholicha haia ordonat que per tot lo mon lo segon dijous apres la festa de Cinquigesima que sera dema sia feyta per tots temps per cascun any festa del Cors sant precios del nostre salvador deus Jhesucrist. E haia dat & atorgat molts grans perdons a cascu & a cascuna daquells qui seran a les hores de la missa & de les vespres & de les altres hores del dit dia & a les vespres de vuy que tot hom & tota dona sia dema mati a la Seu a la missa & a la professo & al offici qui si fara ab gran sollempnitat; & que tuyt fassen festa ab gran alegria & ab gran devocio axi com lo jorn de paschua o de Nadal; & quen tenguen obredor obert ne taula parada ne plaça de de [*sic*] coto ne de blat ne daltres coses. E que beu fara nostre senyor Jhesucrist lin retra bonguardo. E que null hom estrany ne privat moych gos metra lenya ne payla. E qui conter fara que li sera encontinent cremada & que pach .ij. diners all saig que la fara cremar.'

Over the next century, the celebration – and in particular the procession after Mass – became not only more elaborate, but more carefully codified and closely governed as well. The route was changed (or possibly established for the first time) in 1323, and changed again in 1356 and 1424; and other laws were passed to smooth the way of the procession, first in 1321 by removing Jews from along the route, then in 1396 by forbidding the erection of scaffolds or other obstructions in the path.[6] Most conspicuous was the development of *entremesos* (singular *entremès*) – depictions of various characters and events from biblical and church history that seem to have ranged in complexity from single marching figures in costume (often, at least in later years, with large false heads)[7] to more extravagant tableaux vivants, dumbshows or plays that would be performed at various points (or possibly, in some cases, continuously on wagons) along the way.[8] Although by the fifteenth century the *entremesos* would come to dominate the celebration, it is not at all certain when they began; the first clear reference dates from 1391, but seems to show a tradition already fairly well developed, with at least two dozen saints, angels, innocents and so forth, and two larger representations of Adam and Eve with their tree and serpent, and Noah with his ark and dove.[9]

In 1424 or thereabouts the events of celebration were meticulously recorded in the Llibre de Solemnitats, the volume in which the municipal government recorded the details of the most important ceremonies it put together (especially, though not in this case, for visiting royalty).[10] This description, which runs to

---

[6] Duran, *Barcelona i la seva història*, II, pp. 533–5. For the route in 1391, see *Manual de novells ardits: Vulgarment apellat Dietari del antich Consell Barceloní*, ed. F. Schwartz y Luna, F. Carreras y Candi *et al.*, 28 vols. (Barcelona, 1892–1975), I, p. 14 (23 May 1391). This series, the daily log of the City Council, will hereafter be referred to as *DACB*.

[7] See, for example, the pictures reproduced in Amades, *Costumari català*, III, pp. 3–56.

[8] For a general discussion of the tradition throughout late-medieval Europe, see G. Reaney, 'Music in the Late Medieval Entremets', *Annales Musicologiques*, 7 (1964–77), pp. 51–65.

[9] Duran, *Barcelona i la seva història*, II, pp. 534–5.

[10] *Llibre de les solemnitats de Barcelona*, ed. A. Duran i Sanpere and J. Sanabre (Barcelona, 1930–47), I, pp. 15–21. The first of this publication's two volumes, which covers 1423–1546, will hereafter be referred to as *Llibre de Solemnitats*. On the history of this source, see esp. Duran, *Barcelona i la seva història*, II, pp. 146–52. The date 1424 for this document is a conjecture by Duran and Sanabre, apparently based on its position in the manuscript among other documents dated 1423 and 1424.

almost ten folios in the original, provides a meticulous account of how the whole day was run at the time, with particular attention to the procession (the part the city government was obviously most interested in). Because the original text is available in a number of modern sources, I shall provide here only an English translation, with the Catalan for the musical passages in footnotes.[11]

[1] The form and ordination of the feast and procession of Corpus Christi, and their precedences, are as follows.

[2] That is, that every year, on the Wednesday before the Thursday on which the feast is celebrated, after noon, the honourable Councillors of Barcelona meet in the gallery in front of the church of Sant Jaume, which gallery is notably decorated with leaves and flowers. And the very honourable *ciutadans*, and the honoured Consols de Mar, and the most honoured *mercaders* meet there also.[12] And if it happens that on that day ambassadors or messengers of any communities or cities, either outside or inside the realm of the king, are found in Barcelona, they are invited on behalf of the honourable Councillors to come to this meeting and go with them to the cathedral for the Vespers service, and on the next day to the Mass and the procession. And when they are assembled

---

[11] The present translation is of the text in *Llibre de Solemnitats*, pp. 15–21. Most of the document also appears in P. J. Comes, *Libre de algunes coses asanyalades succehides in Barcelona y en altres parts*, ed. J. Puiggarí (Barcelona, 1878), pp. 200–6. A partial transcription of the Llibre de Solemnitats entry was published in Amades, *Costumari català*, III, pp. 12–16, and a summary in Duran, *Barcelona i la seva història*, II, pp. 536–9. A Castilian translation of a portion appeared in Matern, *Zur Vorgeschichte*, pp. 304–38. Saints' names have been given in English, whenever possible, with the aid of D. H. Farmer, *The Oxford Dictionary of Saints* (Oxford, 1978), and other sources.

[12] These terms, hard to translate into intelligible English, refer to branches and offices of the Barcelona city government, which is well explained in J. Vicens Vives, *Ferran II i la ciutat de Barcelona*, 3 vols. (Barcelona, 1936), I, pp. 106–49, and more briefly in Kreitner, 'Music and Civic Ceremony', pp. 31–7, and elsewhere. To simplify greatly, the Barcelona city government was made up of three tiers: (1) the Consell de Cent or Council of One Hundred, a body of over 100 men elected by lottery from among the four estates of the city (*ciutadans* (*honrats*), who were members of a hereditary nobility; *mercaders*, who were men of wealth but usually not noble; *artistes*, or skilled craftsmen; and *menestrals*, the lower-level craftsmen who were organised into guilds); (2) the Trentenari or Council of Thirty, a smaller body elected by lot from within the Consell de Cent to perform most of the day-to-day legislating; and (3) the Consellers, a group of five men who served fixed terms as a kind of executive branch and had the most important ceremonial functions. The Consell de Cent and Trentenari I shall refer to here more or less generically as 'the City Council' or some such (paralleling the vagueness of the documents), and 'Consellers' I shall translate as 'Councillors'. The Consols de Mar were a committee of civil servants regulating maritime customs and the like.

in the gallery, the Councillors, messengers, *ciutadans*, Consols and *mercaders*, classified and arranged in order by the honoured workers of the city, and preceded by various *juglars* playing on various trumpets,[13] go to the cathedral and there hear the holy service of Vespers. And when that service is over they return in the same order to the gallery, and then each takes his own way.

[3] And then, on the next day, that is the Thursday on whose morning is celebrated the feast of the precious Body of Jesus Christ, in the same form and manner as above, the honourable Councillors with the other aforementioned people again meet in the gallery of Sant Jaume. And when they are assembled, preceded by the same *juglars* playing the same trumpets,[14] they are classified and arranged as above; at the cathedral they hear the sermon and service of the great Mass, which is celebrated there very solemnly. And when the service is over, without further ado the procession proceeds in the following form, manner and order. And the arrangement of the procession is made by certain honourable canons and by the honoured workers and four *ciutadans* elected by the honourable Councillors.

[4] First, all the trumpets.[15]
Then, the banner of St Eulalia.
The flags of the cathedral.
The flags of the church of Santa Maria del Mar.
The flags of the church of our lady Santa Maria del Pi.
The flags of the church of Sant Just.
The flags of the church of Sant Pere.
The flags of the church of Sant Miquel.
The flags of the church of Sant Jaume.
The flags of the church of Sant Cugat.
The flags of the church of Santa Anna.

[5] The torches:
First, the torches of the cathedral, on the right side.
The torches of the city, which are forty, on the left side.
The torches of the blind, the paralysed and the one-handed.
(The torches of the porters.)[16]
The torches of the breadmakers.
The torches of the bakers.
The torches of the fishermen.

---

[13] *Llibre de Solemnitats*, p. 15: 'precehints diverses juglars sonants ab diverses trompes'.
[14] *Ibid.*, p. 16: 'precehints los dits juglars sonants ab les dites trompes'.
[15] *Ibid.*: 'Primerament, totes les trompes'.
[16] Items in parentheses here have been interpreted by Duran and Sanabre as later additions and insertions.

The torches of the weavers of linen.
The torches of the confraternity of St Julian.
The torches of the tanners.
The torches of the carpenters.
The torches of the skinners.

[6] The crosses:
First, the cross of the cathedral.
The cross of the church of Santa Maria del Mar.
The cross of our lady Santa Maria del Pi.
The cross of Sant Just.
The cross of the church of Sant Pere.
The cross of the church of Sant Miquel.
The cross of the church of Sant Jaume.
The cross of the church of Sant Cugat.
The cross of the church of Santa Anna.
The cross of the church of the Mercè.
The crosses of the Carmelites and of the Augustinians.
The crosses of the Dominicans and of the Franciscans.

[7] [The clergy:][17]
A certain part of the clergy – that is, next, the altarboys and priests of the parish churches with their surplices.
(The brothers of the Mercè, two by two.)
The Carmelite brothers on the right, and the Augustinians on the left.
The Dominican brothers on the right, and the Franciscans on the left.
The canons, with all the clergy of the cathedral.

[8] The representations:
First, the creation of the world, with twelve angels who sing 'Lord, true God'.[18]
Hell, with Lucifer above, with four devils with him.
(The dragon of St Michael.)
The head [devil] with the mace with twenty-four devils, who do battle on foot with the angels.
St Michael with twenty sword-bearing angels who do battle with the devils.
Heaven, with all its trappings.
The (cherub) angel of Adam, all alone.
Adam and Eve.
Cain and Abel.
Noah's ark, with all its trappings.

---

[17] Heading inserted by Duran and Sanabre.
[18] *Ibid.*: 'Primo, la Creació del mon ab XII. angels qui canten: *Senyor, ver Deu.*'

159

Melchisedec (with the youths).
Abraham and Isaac with the donkey.
The two daughters of Lot.
Lot and his wife.
Jacob with his angel.
King David with the giant.
The twelve tribes of Israel, two by two.
The twelve angels who sing 'Victorious'.[19]

[9] The representations that the cathedral administrates:
First, Moses and Aaron.
Hezekiah and Jeremiah.
Elijah and Elisha.
Ezekiel and Jonah.
Habakkuk and Zechariah.
Daniel and Isaiah.
St John the Baptist, all alone.
The judges of St Susannah.
St Susannah with the angel and Daniel.
Judith with the servant.
St Raphael with Tobit.
The Annunciation of the Virgin Mary with the angels singing 'To magnificent God'. [Later: 'Hail, Mary'.][20]
The *entremès* of Bethlehem or the birth of Jesus Christ.
The first king of Orient on horseback, all alone.
The second king on horseback, all alone.
The third king on horseback, all alone.
Six Jews with capes and robes (with four Jews).
The *entremès* of the innocents, with Rachel above.
The men of arms.
King Herod with the doctors.
The Alamanys.[21]
The twelve angels who sing 'We praise the sacred host'.[22]

[10] [Administered by the church of] Santa Anna:
Joachim and the shepherd.

---

[19]   *Ibid.*, p. 16: 'Los XII. angels qui canten: *Victoriós*.'
[20]   *Ibid.*: 'La Anunciació de la Verge Maria ab los angels cantants: *A Deu magnifich*.' Duran and Sanabre supply the added text, 'Vel, O Maria', in a footnote.
[21]   Duran and Sanabre's explanation: 'These Alamanys may be the painters of this name who were earlier seen in charge of certain *entremesos* in the procession.' This hypothesis seems a bit forced somehow: the editors do not explain why a family of living artists, however eminent, should be marching here among the early New Testament events, nor (perhaps even more important) why their presence, necessarily transitory, would be noted here in the Llibre de Solemnitats, which was intended as a guide for the ages. On the other hand, no better theory suggests itself.
[22]   *Ibid.*: 'Los angels qui canten: *Loem la ostia sagrada*.'

St Anne and St Elizabeth.
St Helen with Emperor Constantine, with his doctors and knights.
St Mary of Egypt and Zosimas with the lion.
St Paula and St Perpetua.
St Elmo.
St Heutrix.

[11] The representations that the brothers of the Mercè are in charge of go next, that is:
St Ursula, alone.
St Tecla and St Candida.
St Catherine and St Barbara.
St Agnes and St Lucy.
St Clara and St Euphrosina.
St Apollonia and St Quiteria.
St Margaret, alone with the dragon.
The angels who play.[23]
St Mary and Jesus and Joseph.
Next, the resurrection [= Passion?], all alone with the cross.
St Dimas with his angel.
Gestas with his devil.
Longinus all alone with the silk.
Joseph of Arimathea, with Nicodemus.
The twelve angels with the plagues, singing.[24]
The grave with its trappings, and Mary Magdalen above.
St Anthony and St Onofre.
St Paul the Hermit and St Alexis.

[12] The representations of Santa Eulàlia del Camp come next:
First, St Francis and St Nicholas.
St Dominic and St Thomas Aquinas.
St Bernard and St Ives.
St Benedict with the devil.
St Honorat and St Paciá.
St Basil and St Maurus.
St Machari with the devil.
St Gem with his companion and with the donkey.
St Martin with Jesus in the form of a poor man.
The angel of St Julian with the doe.
St Julian and St Alzeas.
St Gregory and St Jerome.
St Ambrose and St Augustine.
The twelve angels who sing 'Oh, you good honoured people'.[25]

---

[23] *Ibid.*, p. 19: 'Los angels qui sonen.' On the ambiguity of the language here, see below.
[24] *Ibid.*: 'Los XII. angels ab les plagues, cantans.'
[25] *Ibid.*: 'Los XII. angels qui canten: *Ay vos bona gent honrada.*'

Kenneth Kreitner

[13] Then go the representations that the major-domo of the church of our Lady Santa Maria del Mar is in charge of:
St Clement and St Denys.
St Lawrence and St Vincent.
St Blaise and St P. the Martyr.
St Stephen, St Pons and St Baudili.
St Sever and St Fabian.
St Hippolytus and St Cucuphas.
St Abdon and St Sennen.
St Cosmas and St Damian.
St Christopher with the infant Jesus on his neck.
The martyrdom of St Sebastian, with the cotton horses and with the Turks.
The phoenix, all alone.
(Item, St Eulalia with her companions.)
(Item, the men of arms with the companion of Dacian.)
(Item, the *entremès* of St Eulalia with Deciá and doctors above.)
St George, on horseback.
The serpent.
(Item, the rock with the maiden of St George.)
(Item, the king and queen, father and mother of that maiden, with their companion.)[26]

[14] Then go those who represent the apostles:
St Peter and St Paul.
St Andrew and St James the elder.
St Philip and St James the younger.
St Matthias and St Thomas.
St Bartholomew and the devil.
St Barnabas.
St Simon and St Jude.
The eagle, all alone. Then, the angels who play instruments.[27] Then, the white candles. Then, those who sing in front of the monstrance.[28]

| St Luke. | The monstrance with the holy Body of Jesus Christ. | St Mark. |
| St John the Evangelist. | | St Matthew. |

The lord bishop with his ministers.
White candles, if there aren't any [as specified above].

[26] The location of these last two items is not quite clear; the entries are written at the bottom of the page.
[27] *Ibid.*, p. 20: 'Aprés, los angels qui toquen sturmens.'
[28] *Ibid.*: Aprés, los qui canten denant la custodia.'

162

The angels percussing and the devils percussing.[29] Then, two savage men who carry a bar to keep the people back. Then, all the people.

Thanks be to God and to His purest Mother.[30]

[15] The places through which the procession passes:
Going through the main door of the cathedral, it passes in front of the main palace of the king. And going through the [Carrer de la] Freneria, through the Places de les Cols, del Blat and de la Bòria to the chapel d'en Marcus, through the Carrer de Montcada, and turning through the Born, it enters into the church of Santa Maria del Mar. And then, going through the church, it passes through the Plaça dels Cambis, and through the Carrer Ample to the corner of [the Carrer del] Regomir. And through Regomir. And through the Plaça de Sant Jaume. And through the street that goes to the episcopal palace. And turning there, it enters through the same main door into the cathedral.

Over the course of the fifteenth century, Barcelona's Corpus procession grew steadily in size, importance and community participation. A number of changes found their way into the Llibre de Solemnitats as addenda to the document itself (these appear in parentheses in the translation above). Others, especially regulations concerning public safety and convenience, were published elsewhere: in 1448, for example, the Council passed an ordinance that only those assigned by the city were allowed to organise the procession and that builders of *entremesos* could not hang flags, bouquets or clouds from them;[31] several times in the 1450s it had to forbid fireworks in the parade.[32] Occasionally, the festivities would be postponed on account of rain, and for a few years in the early 1470s they were suspended altogether because of the Catalan civil war.[33] But basically the document of 1424 seems to have continued to be used as a guide, at least in general outline, to the procession through the rest of the

---

[29] *Ibid.*: 'Los angels percucients ab los diables percucients.' I interpret this to refer to angels and devils battling with each other or some such; but it could conceivably refer to the playing of percussion instruments as well.

[30] In Latin: 'Deo gracias et eius / Purissime Genitrici.'

[31] IMH, Registre d'Ordinacions, 7, fols. 40^{r-v} (22 May 1448).

[32] IMH, Registre de Deliberacions, 9, fols. 3^{r-v} (17 June 1454); IMH, Registre d'Ordinacions, 7, fol. 119^r (*c.* 4 June 1455); *ibid.*, 7, fol. 132^v (26 May 1456); *ibid.*, 8, fols. 42^v–43^r (30 May 1458). See also Kreitner, 'Music and Civic Ceremony', pp. 304–6.

[33] For dates and details, see *ibid.*, pp. 307–8.

century and beyond. The next coherent description of the ceremony known to me dates from around 1582; and although it is
difficult to compare confidently with the document of 1424, it
does tend to confirm the longevity of both the basic outline of
the parade and a surprising number of its details.[34]

Another clear sign of growth over the fifteenth century was
the gradual spread of the celebration beyond the day of Corpus
Christi itself. In the 1440s and 1450s, as Corpus became established as Barelona's biggest annual celebration, parts of the
parade (*entremesos*, angel bands and so forth) began to be re-used
on other occasions, particularly for the grand entries of visiting
royalty or nobility.[35] And in the 1460s this custom evolved into
a postponement of the procession to coincide with royal visits –
most notably, perhaps, for the entries of Ferdinand in 1479 and
Isabella two years later.[36]

Even the path of the Corpus Christi parade came to take on
a life of its own as the century developed. This route (section
15 of the document of 1424), clockwise in a rough square for a
total distance of about a kilometre, had a number of practical
and aesthetic advantages: it took the procession out of the
cathedral and back to the cathedral, through some of old Barcelona's widest and most opulent streets and past most of its
important landmarks – the royal palace, the city's largest parish
church (Santa Maria del Mar), the city hall, the central Plaça
de Sant Jaume, the Palau de la Generalitat (the home of the
Catalan regional government) and the bishop's palace. And these
advantages, in addition to the convenience of having a convention
of any kind, were quickly seen and exploited. By the late fifteenth
century, the Corpus Christi route had become the standard
parade route for many of the city's largest celebrations: only
when there was some particular reason why a procession had to
go from one place to another (as, for example, in a grand entry)
did the planners bother to devise a new route.

Two musically significant details emerge after the main document of 1424. First, in 1442 the Llibre de Solemnitats referred

---

[34] Comes, *Libre de algunes coses asanyalades*, pp. 630–9.
[35] For details, see Kreitner, 'Music and Civic Ceremony', pp. 308–9.
[36] *Ibid.*, pp. 388–428; for other examples, see *ibid.*, pp. 309–10. See also Duran, *Barcelona i la seva història*, II, p. 555.

in passing to a band of four instrumentalists and a group of six singers, all dressed as angels, participating in the *entremès* of St Francis;[37] these are not mentioned in section 12 above, and their offhand appearance here raises the possibility that there may have been a good many musicians not specified by the original document but added in fact by the institutions putting the *entremesos* together. And, second, in 1454 the white candles in front of the Host (section 14) were replaced by a group of twenty-four priests dressed as the Elders of the Apocalypse and singing 'Sanctus, Sanctus, Sanctus'.[38]

In sum, this was a huge procession. Exact numbers are, of course, impossible to reconstruct; but if the document of 1424 is to be believed, the parade must have included, to begin with, well over a hundred torches. Adding a possibly equal number of flags and crosses, the whole clergy of the city, priests and monks alike (nuns are not mentioned), more than 100 *entremesos*, some of them containing as many as two dozen costumed actors, and a crowd of 'all the people', it represents an image of almost overwhelming size and detail. So it may be useful at this point to condense the whole procession in three ways.

First, the order of march, stripped of specifics, was something like this:

> band of trumpets
> banners of all the churches
> torches of confraternities, guilds and other secular organisations
> crosses of the churches and monasteries

---

[37] *Llibre de Solemnitats*, p. 130 (21 May 1442): 'En lo dit any MCCCCXLII., e per rahó de la dita festa del sagrat Cors de Jhesu Xpist., en P. Deuna, pintor, ciutadá de Barchinona, vené a la Ciutat per preu de XLV. florins lo entramés appellat de Sant Ffrancesch, ensemps ab IIII. testes d'angells, ab ales e diedemas daurades, qui sonen sturments en lo dit entramés, e VI. parells de ales daurades e argentades per VI. angells qui canten en lo dit entramés.'

[38] *Ibid.*, pp. 197–8 (20 June 1454): 'En loch dels prohomens qui acustumen portar los brandons blanchs denant lo sagrat Cors de Jhesu Xpist son stats posats XXIIII. preveres, vestits de sengles camís e sengles dacmáticas, ab barbas e cabelleres de canem blanch, rullades, ab sengles corones al cap, representants aquells XXIIII. vells, que sant Johan Evangeliste recite stants denant la cadira de Deu cantants: '*Sanctus, Sanctus, Sanctus*'; e així ho salmonaven, e seguint la professó, portaven los brandons cremants en lurs mans denant la custodia.' This information is repeated, virtually verbatim, in the entries for the next three celebrations; see *ibid.*, pp. 213–14 (5 June 1455), pp. 220–1 (27 May 1456), pp. 230–1 (15–16 June 1457).

Kenneth Kreitner

clergy of the churches and monasteries
entremesos, in seven large groups, most groups containing
musicians
a special group surrounding the Host, consisting of:
    the eagle
    ten angels, playing string instruments
    before 1454, candlebearers; later, twenty-four Elders
    of Apocalypse, singing with candles
    other singers
    the monstrance with the Host, flanked by the four
    Evangelists
    the bishop and his entourage
    more candlebearers
    angels and devils 'percussing'
a crowd of people

Second, in purely musical terms, the documents describe twelve
distinct ensembles; their descriptions are summarised in Table 1

Table 1   *Musical ensembles in the Corpus Christi procession*

No.	Description	Source
1	Band of trumpets at the head of the procession	Doc. of 1424, section 4
2	12 angels singing 'Senyor, ver Deu', in the *entremès* of the creation of the world	Doc. of 1424, section 8
3	12 angels singing 'Victoriós', following the 12 tribes of Israel	Doc. of 1424, section 8
4	Angels singing 'A Deu magnifich', or later 'Vel, O Maria', with the *entremès* of the Annunciation	Doc. of 1424, section 9
5	12 angels singing 'Loem la ostia sagrada', following the Alamanys	Doc. of 1424, section 9
6	Angels who play (or possibly sing), following the *entremès* of St Margaret	Doc. of 1424, section 11
7	12 angels with the plagues, singing, following the *entremès* of Joseph of Arimathea	Doc. of 1424, section 11
8	4 angels playing instruments and 6 singing, in the *entremès* of St Francis	Doc. of 21 May 1442, above at n. 37
9	12 angels singing 'Ay vos bona gent honrada', following the *entremès* of Sts Ambrose and Augustine	Doc. of 1424, section 12
10	10 angels playing instruments in the group before the Host	Doc. of 1424, section 14
11	24 priests dressed as Elders of the Apocalypse, holding white candles and singing 'Sanctus, sanctus, sanctus', in the group before the Host	Doc. of 20 June 1454, above at n. 38
12	Another vocal ensemble in the group before the Host (may have been superseded by no. 11)	Doc. of 1424, section 14

for convenience. Third, these ensembles may be further classified into three broad groups: trumpeters (ensemble no. 1), choirs (nos. 2–5, 7–9, 11–12) and soft bands (nos. 6?, 10). And this last classification is especially useful for looking more closely at the kinds of music that were represented in the procession.

II. THE TRUMPETS

'Primerament, totes les trompes.' At the very head of the Corpus Christi procession was a musical ensemble; its description is not particularly informative, nor are the references to the same group earlier in the document ('diverses juglars sonants ab diverses trompes', 'los dits juglars sonants ab les dites trompes') much better. Taken at face value, these phrases seem to depict a fairly large ensemble, dominated by trumpets but potentially admitting other instruments, an ensemble organised formally enough to be re-used at various stages in the two-day celebration; but beyond that, the Llibre de Solemnitats is not much help in understanding the role of the trumpet band in the parade. Fortunately, however, more information on this ensemble is available elsewhere in the city archives.

Trumpet-playing was an exceptionally large part of urban musical life in fifteenth-century Barcelona.[39] The only musician on the payroll of the municipal government was a *trompeta* or city trumpeter, whose most conspicuous day-to-day duty involved touring the streets with the city crier to accompany various official announcements, but who was also charged with assembling larger bands of trumpeters for special occasions. These bands, which could number two dozen or more trumpeters and drummers (occasionally including a bagpiper as well) were apparently made up *ad hoc* from the freelance players around the city: Barcelona, unlike many other cities in Europe, had no regular loud band or trumpet corps. Such specially organised trumpet ensembles dominated the ceremonial customs of the city; the surviving accounts of processions, public meetings and the like mention other kinds of music only rarely.

[39] I have examined Barcelona's trumpet-playing industry at more length in 'The City Trumpeter of Late-Fifteenth-Century Barcelona', *Musica Disciplina* (forthcoming), and 'Music and Civic Ceremony', pp. 42–138; all the general information here is taken from one or both of these studies.

The reliance of the City Council on freelance trumpeters implies that there must have been a great many such musicians at large in fifteenth-century Barcelona. And, indeed, there seem to have been enough of them at mid-century for the trumpeters to attempt to organise themselves into a confraternity like the other large industries of the city. The effort was evidently a failure: after the charter of the Confraternity of St Bernard, dated 22 May 1459, there is no surviving trace of this or any other musical guild or confraternity in Barcelona until the 1590s. The charter of 1459 does, however, specify the rights and duties of the organisation in some detail, and it remains a fascinating source of information on these musicians whose lives are so difficult to reconstruct. We shall return to it shortly.

The Corpus Christi procession was a joint effort involving all the civic and religious authorities of Barcelona. As the document of 1424 makes clear, most of the *entremesos* were parcelled out to the various churches and monasteries around town; the trumpet band, however, was the responsibility of the City Council. Between 1450 and 1500 the municipal account books recorded almost two dozen entries for annual payments (to the city crier until 1492 or 1493, to the city trumpeter thereafter) for a band of trumpets accompanying an official announcement, made on the Monday (or, rarely, the Tuesday) before the celebration, that the following Thursday was to be Corpus Christi.[40] The musicians are uniformly called *trompetes* rather than *juglars*, the more generic term used in the document of 1424, suggesting that they are

---

[40] All references are from IMH, Clavaria (dates refer to documents, not events; ten trumpets, payment to crier, and a Monday principal announcement unless otherwise specified): 65, fol. 107^r (12 June 1450); 67, fol. 103^v (26 June 1451 – nine trumpets); 68, fol. 103^v (26 June 1454); 69, fol. 93^r (7 June 1456); 71, fol. 103^r (2 June 1458); 73, fol. 112^v (13 June 1460); 80, fol. 114^r (11 August 1466); 82, fol. 93^v (27 June 1468); 85, fol. 155^r (27 June 1470); 87, fol. 140^r (4 June 1472 – seven trumpets, Tuesday); 88, fol. 142^v (16 June 1474 – Tuesday); 90, fol. 137^r (1 June 1475); 92, fol. 140^r (19 June 1476); 94, fol. 134^v (2 June 1477); 95, fol. 124^v (26 May 1478); 97, fol. 116^r (27 June 1481); 98, fol. 119^v (8 June 1482); 100, fol. 118^r (30 May 1482); 105, fol. 134^r (15 June 1487); 109, fol. 127^v (5 July 1491 – document implies that the announcement was made on Corpus itself, but probably by mistake); 111, fol. 200^v (21 June 1493 – payment to the city trumpeter); 115, fol. 142^v (8 June 1497 – payment to the city trumpeter). Not all volumes of the Clavaria survive from this period, and in some years payment for Corpus Christi expenses was recorded in an omnium-gatherum entry not specifying the trumpets. See also Kreitner, 'The City Trumpeter', and 'Music and Civic Ceremony', pp. 119–28.

indeed players of the natural trumpet and not, say, a loud band; and, perhaps even more important, they are almost always described as a group of ten (there are only two exceptions, for a nonet in 1451 and a septet in 1472). The striking but unslavish consistency of these payment entries lends trustworthiness: this was clearly a large and well-organised ensemble, bound by a long-standing tradition. And this in turn makes it probable, though unprovable, that these were the same trumpeters who marched in all the parades for Corpus Christi – that the city trumpeter or crier put together a single band whose duties for the whole week were clearly spelt out by custom.

On special occasions, when the procession was being combined with some other event, sources outside the Clavaria show that the custom could be bent and the band enlarged considerably. In 1461, for example, the Corpus festivities were postponed until July to coincide with the presence of the Primogenitor of Aragón, the ill-fated Carlos of Viana; and for this special celebration Pere Vicens (the city trumpeter from c. 1457 to 1482)[41] was given twenty-six city uniforms and a total of twenty-six flags, including twelve 'large' and six 'Italian' flags (probably for straight and folded trumpets),[42] three drum flags and one bagpipe flag.[43] But it is clear that moments like this were exceptional, accountable to other rules: the standard Corpus Christi band consisted of ten trumpeters – which, in light of the striking dominance of quartets

---

[41] Kreitner, 'The City Trumpeter', and 'Music and Civic Ceremony', pp. 64–8.

[42] On the fifteenth-century 'Italian trumpet', see especially P. Downey, 'The Trumpet and its Role in Music of the Renaissance and Early Baroque' (Ph.D. dissertation, Queen's University of Belfast, 1983), pp. 38–43.

[43] *DACB*, ii, p. 373 (3 June 1461): 'Lo dit dia foren liurats per en Johan Oliver olim scriva del racional an P. Vicent trompeta de la Ciutat per sguard de la festa de Jheuxrist prop vinent XXVJ sobrevestes les dues de ceda ab senyals de la Ciutat, e XIJ panons grossos e VJ ytalians, e IIJ de tabalets tots ab senyals Reyals e de la Ciutat, e I pano per lo cornamuser. —Lo die P. Vicens a X de Juliol torna totes les coses aci contengudes, apres a XIIIJ de dit sen torna portar totes les dites coses sino I pano per la cornamusa. A XXJ de Juliol fou tot restituhit.' The chronology here is puzzling: *DACB* (ii, pp. 373–84) has Vicens borrowing the items on 3 June; the Council postponing the celebration indefinitely the next day (the day it was supposed to have taken place); Vicens returning things piecemeal on 10 and 14 July; the Council on 14 July rescheduling the Corpus celebration for 19 July; the procession taking place on that day as planned; and Vicens returning the final flag on 21 July. So it is not altogether clear exactly when, if ever, all this equipment was used in the 1461 festivities – it is possible, with the changes in the date, that the trumpet band was reduced in size, or even cancelled.

and octets in the trumpet bands on other Barcelona occasions at this time, may suggest that the Corpus trumpeters had a special repertory in five parts rather than the usual four.[44]

But the most detailed information by far on this band is provided by the 1459 charter of the trumpeters' Confraternity of St Bernard. The original document runs to thirteen paragraphs, concerning the organisation's purpose, its political and financial structure, its powers and its duties to its membership; but two paragraphs in the middle are devoted to its roles in the Corpus Christi celebration:

Item: the honourable Councillors and leaders ordain that hereafter all the trumpets, trumpeters, drummers or other *juglars* who are appointed to serve playing in the feast of Corpus Christi must go, the day before that feast, at 12 noon or earlier, to the house of the city trumpeter to temper, tune and put their trumpets and other instruments in order; and from there they go to the Plaça de Sant Jaume in order to do the usual service and accompany the honourable Councillors and leaders to Vespers; and afterwards they accompany the horse of St Eulalia. And whoever is absent and is not in these matters for each offence has a punishment of 12 diners and besides this punishment loses the salary customarily given by the city.

Item: the honourable Councillors and leaders ordain that hereafter those trumpets, trumpeters, drummers and other *juglars* serving in that feast must go on the day of the feast, at 4 o'clock in the morning or earlier, to the house of the city trumpeter in order to go and play at sunrise, and climb up to the belfry of the cathedral in order to play there as is customary; and each of them must wear on his head a garland or nosegay, and whoever disobeys shall be fined 12 diners according to the judgment of the city trumpeter and leader [the elected leader of the confraternity]. And in the same way the trumpeters and other *juglars* must leave the cathedral to go to the Plaça de Sant Jaume in order to wait for the Councillors and leaders and accompany them to the cathedral. And whoever is absent and is not there by the time any Councillor arrives is fined 12 diners. And they do the same when the procession must go out of the cathedral, to accompany it. And to return and accompany the Councillors to the city hall when the monstrance is returned to the cathedral. And whoever is absent for any of these events is fined 12 diners for each time according to the judgment of the city trumpeter and leader; and beyond this punishment those

---

[44] On these other ensembles, and this possibility, see Kreitner, 'The City Trumpeter', and 'Music and Civic Ceremony', pp. 119–28, 135.

who disobey in any of the aforementioned matters lose the salary that the city customarily gives and that they want paid, in any form.[45]

The confraternity charter confirms the basic outline suggested by the Llibre de Solemnitats: the members of the trumpet band were appointed in advance to serve the entire festival, and we see them marching not only in the big procession after Mass, but in two smaller, earlier processions to accompany the municipal and other officials from city hall to the cathedral for Vespers on Wednesday evening and for Mass on Thursday morning. And it adds a number of vivid details: the meeting of the band at the city trumpeter's house on Wednesday at noon (a rare case of a tuning session having the force of civic law); a small additional procession after Vespers in which the trumpeters accompany a priest on horseback on a tour of the next day's parade route, in honour of the cathedral's patron, St Eulalia;[46] the garlands on the trumpeters' heads; the wake-up call from the cathedral tower at dawn on Thursday; and finally another little parade to march the dignitaries back to city hall when the procession was over.

---

[45] IMH, Registre d'Ordinacions, 8, fols. 93ʳ–95ᵛ (22 May 1459): 'Item ordonaren los dits Consellers e promens que daquiavant tots los trompetes trompedors temorers o altres juglars que seran ordonats e havran a servir per sonar en la festa del sagrat cors de Jhuxhrist haien esser lo die abans de la dita festa a les .xii. hores de mig jorn o abans a la casa del dit trompeta de la Ciutat per temprar concordar e metre apunt les trompetes e altres sturments e que partint daqui vaien a la plaça de sanct Jacme per fer alli lo servey acustumat e acompenyar los honorables Consellers e promens a les vespres e acompanyar apres lo cavall de sancta Eulalia e qui mancara e no sera en les dites coses per tantes vegades com contrafara pach per ban .xii. diners e ultra lo dit ban perden lo salari que es acustumat donar per lo Ciutat.
    Item ordonaren los dits Consellers e promens que daquiavant los dits trompetes trompedors temorers e altres juglars al dit servey de la prop dita festa ordonats haien e sien tenguts lo die de la dita festa esser de mati a les .iiii. hores o abans a la casa del dit trompeta per anar a fer les matinades e pujar al campenar de la Seu per sonar axi com es acustumat e quescu haie portar en son cap una garlanda o xipellet e aquell qui contrafara pach de ban .xii. diners salvat just impediment a coneguda dels dits trompeta e prom. E aximateix haien e sien tenguts los dits trompetas e altres juglars partir de la dita Seu anar a la dita Plaça de sanct Jacme per sperar los dits Consellers e promens e acompanyar los a la dita Seu. E qui hi mancara e no sera ans que algun conseller hi sia pach de ban .xii. diners. E aximateix sien quant la procçesso deura exir en la dita Seu per acompanya[r] aquella. E per tornar e acompanyar los consellers a la casa de la Ciutat quant la custodia sera retornada a la Seu e si algu mancara en alguna de les dites coses pach de ban quescuna vegada .xii. diners sau just impediment conexedor per los dits trompeta e prom e ultra lo dit ban los qui contrafaran en qualsevol coses dessus dites perden lo salari que la Ciutat los acustume de donar lo qual vols sia paguat en alguna forma.'
    The entire charter is transcribed and translated in Kreitner, 'The City Trumpeter', and 'Music and Civic Ceremony', pp. 105–8, 530–2.
[46] See Comes, *Libre de algunes coses asanyalades*, p. 633.

But perhaps most striking of all here is the degree of official control applied to the trumpet band. Lacking other documentation from the Confraternity of St Bernard, it is hard to know what portions of its charter came from within, as a kind of group-imposed self-discipline, and what parts were mandated by the City Council (recall that the document is preserved in the municipal Registre d'Ordinacions). It seems clear, however, that there had been problems with the trumpeters and/or their playing in the past and that the city and the founders of the confraternity had a mutual interest in ensuring the smooth and professional performance of all their duties.

In any case, the band of ten trumpeters not only led the Corpus procession, but participated in every formal outdoor celebration that the city saw. Their music symbolically began the Vespers ritual, it began the feast day itself, it preceded the Mass, it led the parade and it delivered the Councillors home at the end. The trumpet band may be the one musical and ceremonial institution most responsible for uniting the two days of very diverse events. That it was sponsored by the city shows most eloquently the traditional association of the natural trumpet with temporal power and the importance of the secular government in this essentially sacred celebration.

III. THE CHOIRS

After the trumpet band, the next main segment of the Corpus Christi procession – the flags of the churches, the torches of the secular organisations, the crosses of the churches and the clergy – marched without any known music. After them came all the *entremesos*, which were, of course, the main popular attraction of the parade, and then its climax: the monstrance with the Host, surrounded by its own special set of *entremesos*. These two parts of the procession contained a great deal of music, provided by at least eleven separate musical ensembles (nos. 2–12 in Table 1) distributed along the order of march and apparently provided by the churches and monasteries in charge of the various groups of *entremesos*. Of these eleven, no. 10 is definitely an instrumental ensemble and no. 6 probably so – which leaves nine ensembles that seem to be dominated by singers:

2 Twelve angels singing 'Senyor, ver Deu', in the *entremès* of the creation of the world.

3 Twelve angels singing 'Victoriós', following the twelve tribes of Israel.

4 Angels singing 'A Deu magnifich', or later 'Vel, O Maria', with the *entremès* of the Annunciation.

5 Twelve angels singing 'Loem la ostia sagrada', following the Alamanys.

7 Twelve angels with the plagues, singing, following the *entremès* of Joseph of Arimathea.

8 Four angels playing instruments and six singing, in the *entremès* of St Francis.

9 Twelve angels singing 'Ay vos bona gent honrada', following the *entremès* of Sts Ambrose and Augustine.

11 Twenty-four priests dressed as Elders of the Apocalypse, holding white candles and singing 'Sanctus, sanctus, sanctus', in the group before the Host.

12 Another vocal ensemble in the group before the Host.

Three broad commonalities unite these descriptions. First, and perhaps most obviously, at least eight of the nine ensembles are in costume, and seven of those eight are costumed as angels. Second, these angel choirs are dominated by groups of twelve – a number with certain practical advantages (being divisible by two, three or four for convenient marching formations or for splitting up polyphonic parts), but also with enough symbolic associations that its literal accuracy might wisely be held in abeyance for the moment.

Third, the ordinance of 1424 specifies particular Catalan texts for five of the angel choirs (nos. 2, 3, 4, 5 and 9), implying that each text belonged, more or less meaningfully, at a certain point in the procession. Unfortunately, it provides only incipits, and the rest of each text, including its overall import, remains a mystery; but a few tentative deductions and speculations may be possible. Ensemble no. 4, which was part of the *entremès* of the Annunciation, is given two texts in the document: the first, 'A Deu magnifich', may have been a paraphrase of or gloss on the Magnificat, and the later replacement, 'Vel, O Maria', similarly evokes the 'Ave Maria'. Either would, of course, be perfectly appropriate for an Annunciation scene. Similarly, 'Ay vos bona gent honrada' would seem to make sense in the midst of a large group of saints (no. 9); but the aptness of 'Senyor, ver Deu' for the creation of the world (no. 2), 'Victoriós' among the Old Testament figures (no. 3) and 'Loem la ostia sagrada' after the characters of the Nativity (no. 5) is harder to assess with the texts in such fragmentary form.

Some angel choirs are described as part of individual *entremesos* (the Annunciation scene is a good example), others marched in between *entremesos* providing a visual spacer and a verbal commentary; but one (no. 7) is described as an *entremès* in itself. The ordinance calls it 'Los XII. angels ab les plagues, cantans', and its position in the parade order, between the characters of the crucifixion and the scene of the grave, suggests that these plagues are not the ten of Egypt, nor the seven of the second coming, but the torments of Christ in Hell between Good Friday and Easter. What exactly this means is not quite clear (nor, for that matter, why the plagues should be administered by angels and not devils); but it is clear that, whatever else these angels might be doing, they are also singing.

Two choirs stand apart from these ensembles of angels: first, no. 12 is described only as 'los qui canten denant la custodia'. Possibly these singers are also dressed as angels (the grammar is ambiguous), but their description and lack of specified text seem to imply that they are functioning principally as musicians rather than as angelic characters – in other words, that they may be professional singers, and thus the choir of the cathedral. This is, of course, impossible to prove, but the cathedral of Barcelona did have a polyphonic choir from at least the early fifteenth century,[47] and these singers are not otherwise named as being in the parade. This was, moreover, a durable ensemble: even in the 1580s, 'Los xantres que canten deuant la custodia' continued to march in this spot in the Corpus procession.[48]

The second exception is no. 11, the group of priests dressed as the twenty-four Elders of the Apocalypse, crowned, with white hair and beards, carrying white torches and singing 'Sanctus, sanctus, sanctus'. The document establishing this choir (which appeared in 1454, thirty years after the main document)[49] specifies that they marched in place of the candle-bearers in front of the Host – which would have put it directly between the angelic soft band and (if I am right) the cathedral choir. This position, and

---

[47] J. M. Gregori i Cifré, 'La musica del Renaixement a la Catedral de Barcelona, 1450–1580' (Ph.D. dissertation, Universitat Autònoma de Barcelona, 1986); see also Kreitner, 'Music and Civic Ceremony', pp. 216–34.

[48] Comes, *Libre de algunes coses asanyalades.* p. 638.

[49] See n. 38 above.

the specification that they are priests and not necessarily singers, probably means that they were singing monophonic chant rather than polyphony; their text may have been the familiar movement from the Ordinary of the Mass, either entire or in abbreviated form, or it may have been taken from a similar sentence in the Book of Revelation, spoken not by the Elders themselves but by the four beasts with them: 'Sanctus, sanctus, sanctus, Dominus Deus omnipotens, qui erat et qui est et qui venturus est.'[50] Either text would be suitable as a sort of vocal fanfare before the appearance of the Host, and in either case the switch from Catalan to Latin (assuming, as seems probable, that the cathedral choir continued to sing in Latin) must have served to heighten the drama and intensify the holiness of this, the most solemn part of the procession. In any case, this was, by a factor of two, the largest choir in the procession, and it must have been a particularly impressive sight and sound in the narrow streets – exactly right to introduce the Host and set it apart from the rest of the parade.

In short (and cathedral musicians excepted), these angelic and Elder choirs were not simply musical and ceremonial ensembles like the trumpeters at the beginning; their costumes put them in the position of actual characters in the drama of the procession, and the words they sang were, in some cases if not all, carefully chosen to be equal partners in this drama. Their symbolic value is unmistakable – but what was the year-to-year reality behind them?

The Llibre de Solemnitats entry from 1424 gives an extraordinary amount of detail, but still it was meant as a set of guidelines and not a precise description after the fact, and it is fair to wonder how closely the guidelines were followed as the decades passed. By 1442, remember, the parade already included at least one angel choir, no. 8 in Table 1, that (a) had not been mentioned at all in 1424, (b) was made up of ten angels and not the twelve universally specified by the earlier document and (c) was not merely a choir but an ensemble mixing voices and instruments.

---

[50]   Revelation 4.8: 'And the four beasts had each of them six wings about him; and they were full of eyes within: and they rest not day and night, saying, "Holy, holy, holy, Lord God Almighty, which was, and is, and is to come." '

So the parade as it really happened, especially by the end of the century, was surely a more complicated and elaborate operation than even the long decription from 1424 would seem to indicate. Organisers of the *entremesos* probably had a certain licence to add as many musicians as they wanted (within the spirit of the original ordinance and with its prescriptions perhaps as a minimum); and if there is anything like a universal law in these cases, it is that as long as the public maintains its enthusiasm for a particular annual ceremony and as long as economic disaster does not intervene,[51] it will probably grow bigger and not smaller.

In this connection, the texts sung by the angel choirs come back as a particularly intriguing puzzle. For if the ordinance of 1424 continued to be used as a guide for the rest of the century, then what does the specification of the various text incipits mean to the development of a musical tradition for this parade? The songs themselves do not survive; but is it possible to imagine a polyphonic practice, or any kind of practice susceptible of even tentative reconstruction, that can be associated with the angel choirs of Barcelona's Corpus Christi procession in the fifteenth century?

This is, of course, a most difficult question; but we may start with a few basic commonsensical observations and work outward. To begin with, the text incipits given in the document are doubtless meant to stand for entire texts, well known to the organisers at the time (well enough known that they could be abbreviated without apparent confusion), but lost to us today. But did the use of the document as a guide in subsequent years mean that these exact texts were sung in every parade – and if so, was the music that went with the texts also constant? The latter, more extreme case seems unlikely in a world of shifting musical and poetic tastes, and indeed ensemble no. 4 appears to provide an instance of a change of text (from 'A Deu magnifich' to 'Vel, O Maria') actually written into the document. How many more changes took place over the years without the need to record them is hard to say; but on the whole, given the silence

---

[51] Chía, in *La festividad del Corpus en Gerona*, p. 46, describes a cutback in that city's celebrations in the 1470s and following, probably as the result of an economic downturn after the Catalan civil war; conceivably these hard times were reflected in the Barcelona celebration as well, though I see no clear evidence to that effect.

of the sources, it may be safest to presume that at least the spirit of the original text was maintained as long as a particular angel choir kept its original dramatic function.

That these texts are in Catalan is itself significant, for the lack of surviving fifteenth-century songs in Catalan and related languages has been a source of some discussion. As Maricarmen Gómez has recently pointed out, only one such song has been identified – the well-known *Dindiridin*, in a version from the Neapolitan manuscript Montecassino 871[52] – but she goes on to argue persuasively, citing a wide range of literary and archival references, for the existence of a substantial tradition of vernacular song in Catalan and Occitan,[53] a tradition of which, obviously, the angel choirs of Barcelona's Corpus procession were a part.

There is no way to be sure exactly what this fifteenth-century Catalan repertory was like; but surely it was not too dissimilar to contemporary Castilian songs. Indeed, given the bilingual character of the Aragonese court and the relative ease of word-for-word, reasonably metrical translation between the two languages, it may be fair to suppose that many songs coexisted in both. *Dindiridin*, which appears in the Cancionero de Palacio with Castilian text, happens to provide a perfect example,[54] and I have elsewhere argued that a second possibility might be *Muy crueles voses dan*, which both Palacio and the earlier Cancionero de la Colombina preserve in Castilian,[55] but whose text, datable to 1469, refers to events in the Catalan civil war. This song would have little propaganda value (or meaning) outside Catalonia, and a number of unusual spellings and peculiarities of scansion seem

[52] *The Musical Manuscript Montecassino 871: A Neapolitan Repertory of Sacred and Secular Music of the Late Fifteenth Century*, ed. I. Pope and M. Kanazawa (Oxford, 1978), pp. 98, 496–7, 653–5; see also n. 53 below.

[53] M. Gómez-Muntané, 'Secular Catalan and Occitan Music from the End of the Middle Ages: Looking for a Lost Repertory', paper read at the Nineteenth Medieval and Renaissance Music Conference (Oxford, July 1991).

[54] Madrid, Palacio Real, Biblioteca, MS 1335 (*olim* 2-I-5). *La música en la corte de los reyes católicos, II, Polifonía profana: El cancionero musical de Palacio*, 3 vols., ed. H. Anglés and J. Romeu Figueras, Monumentos de la Música Española 5, 10, 14 (Madrid and Barcelona, 1947–65), no. 359. This edition will hereafter be referred to as *Palacio*.

[55] *Palacio*, no. 103. Cancionero de la Colombina = Seville, Biblioteca Colombina, MS 7-I-28. *Cancionero musical de la Colombina*, ed. M. Querol Gavalda, Monumentos de la Música Española 33 (Barcelona, 1971), no. 6. This edition will hereafter be referred to as *Colombina*.

to suggest that its present form may well be a translation.[56] Much more work needs to be done in this direction; but these two examples are enough to suggest that the first place to go looking for Catalan songs may be in the Castilian cancioneros. So is there anything in the cancioneros that might seem to fit what we know about the angel choirs of Barcelona?

None of the texts for the angel choirs corresponds exactly to any surviving Castilian song; but the kind of music the incipits suggest, with sacred but vernacular, non-liturgical text, is well represented in the cancioneros: fourteen such pieces are preserved in Colombina, and more than thirty in Palacio.[57] Most of these are on Marian or Christmas themes, and some are musically and poetically very sophisticated; in general they have been seen as part of a tradition of vernacular courtly devotional music or, conceivably, of allowing villancicos in church at certain points of the Christmas season (as is more extensively documented from the later sixteenth century). But a few do seem to fit in with the spirit and substance of the Corpus Christi parade, and two examples are worth a closer look.

Palacio no. 413, *O ascondida verdad*, is a Corpus Christi song by Alfonso de Troya, a Spanish composer who served in the papal chapel in Rome from 1497 to his death in 1516; presumably, then, this song was written in the fifteenth century, before Troya left Spain (it was copied into the first layer of Palacio around 1505).[58] Its text, nine (3×3?) strophes on the miracle of the Trinity, emphasising the bodily suffering of Christ and the gift of the Eucharist, may give an idea of what Barcelona's *Loem la ostia sagrada* was like:

---

[56] Kreitner, 'Music and Civic Ceremony', pp. 273–8; see also Romeu's commentary to the version in *Palacio*, iii, p. 297.

[57] *Colombina*, nos. 2bis, 3, 22bis, 61, 62, 64, 65, 72, 73, 74, 75, 78, 79, 91; *Palacio*, nos. 14, 19, 36bis, 55, 86, 133, 160, 227, 276, 392, 394, 397, 399, 400, 404, 406, 408, 409, 411, 412, 413, 415, 416, 417, 419, 420, 425, 430, 434, 442, 444. I use Colombina and Palacio as examples because they are by far the largest sources of vernacular Spanish music of this time; other manuscripts (particularly Barcelona 454) add a few more examples to all my observations here.

[58] On Troya's biography, see R. Stevenson, *Spanish Music in the Age of Columbus* (The Hague, 1960), p. 296; R. J. Sherr, 'The Papal Chapel c.1492–1513 and its Polyphonic Sources' (Ph.D. dissertation, Princeton University, 1975), pp 73–4; and T. W. Knighton, 'Music and Musicians at the Court of Fernando of Aragon, 1474–1516' (Ph.D. dissertation, University of Cambridge, 1983), i, p. 300. On the layers of the manuscript and their contents, see Romeu's commentary in *Palacio*, iii, pp. 13–17.

¡O ascondida verdad,	O secret truth,
Dios i onbre verdadero!	true Lord and man!
Por salvar la humanidad	To save humanity
tú moriste en el madero.	you died on the beam.
Ostia santa, ostia pura,	Holy Host, pure Host,
misterio maravilloso:	marvellous mystery:
Dios tornado crïatura	God made mortal
en el mundo tenebroso.	in the dark world.
Tú quisiste rreçebir	You were willing to receive
muerte por nuestro pecado	death for our sins
y quesiste consentir	and were willing to consent
ser por nos cruçificado.	to be crucified for us.
Y por sienpre estar con nos,	And to be forever with us,
que con gran precio conpraste,	bought at a high price,
tú, maravilloso Dios,	you, marvellous God,
a ti mesmo consagraste.	are consecrated to yourself.
Pues a ti, Dios, adoramos,	Thus we adore you, God,
las rodillas en el suelo,	knees on the ground,
rrogándote que seamos	begging you that we be
parçioneros del çielo.	participants in heaven.
Movido con caridad,	Moved by charity
por librarnos del pecado	to free us from sin
y salvar la humanidad,	and save humanity,
tú moriste por tu grado,	you died willingly,
y de muerte muy crüel,	and by a very cruel death
en medio de dos ladrones,	between two thieves,
gustando vynagre y hiel	tasting vinegar and gall,
lleno de muchas pasiones.	filled with many passions.
¡O eterna pïedad!	O eternal piety!
¡O Señor glorificado!	O glorified Lord!
Por salvar la humanidad	To save humanity
tú moriste por tu grado.	you died willingly.
Y por ser esto verdad,	And because of this truth,
a ti, Pan sacramentado,	O sacramental bread,
te adoro en unidad	I adore you in unity,
con quien murió por su grado.	who died willingly.

An even more persuasive example might be Palacio no. 415 (see Example 1), an anonymous plea to the Virgin Mary of the sort that Barcelona's *Vel, O Maria* may have been:

¡Ay Santa María!	Hail, St Mary!
¡Valedme, Señora,	Protect me, lady,
esperança mia!	my hope!
Vos sois la que amo,	You are the one I love,
Vos sois la que quiero,	You are the one I need,
Vos sois la que llamo	You are the one I call,
Vos sois la qu'espero,	You are the one in whom I hope,
vos sois el luzero	you are the light-bearer
cuya luz nos guía.	whose light guides us.
¡Esperança mía!	My hope!

¡Ay Santa María! is also from the fifteenth century: not only is it too found in the earliest layer of Palacio, it also appears in Colombina, in a shortened form (the A section only) and more ornamented, but still eminently recognisable.[59] The existence of these variant versions is intriguing, for it implies that this piece may have had a long and broad popularity in the oral tradition – which in turn only increases the probability of its use for occasions like this parade.

There is, of course, an element of historical fiction here. The archival references to this music are mostly from 1424, and they specify Catalan texts without mentioning polyphony; both of the pieces I have cited, in contrast, are polyphonic, are in Castilian and are probably from fifty to seventy-five years later. Even the most tentative and cautious effort to unite the descriptions and the repertory involves a leap of faith whose safety might well be questioned. But in the absence of hard evidence, perhaps the most helpful question is whether the fiction seems unlikely in light of anything we know about these angel choirs.

What we know is that angel choirs continued to march in the Corpus Christi procession of Barcelona after 1424 and that they presumably were supplied or arranged by the churches and monasteries that took charge of each section of the parade. This

---

[59] *Colombina*, no. 78.

Example 1. Anon., *¡Ay Santa María!* (Palacio, no. 415, fol. 272ᵛ)

effectively rules out polyphony of the most solemn, advanced and sophisticated kind, for well into the sixteenth century the cathedral of Barcelona maintained an official monopoly on sacred polyphonic music and its teaching: even as late as 1581, representatives of the parishes of Santa Maria del Mar, Sant Miquel and Santa Maria del Pi had to request a papal bull allowing them

181

to establish polyphonic chapels without permission of the *mestre de cant* of the cathedral.[60] Few members of the fifteenth-century angel choirs, then, would have had the training necessary to sing anything very complicated – and even if they had, the circumstances of performance would have made such music inappropriate and unwieldy.

But what about songs like *O ascondida verdad* and *¡Ay Santa María!*? Both are in three voices, both in a simple chordal homophonic style, both relatively short; neither would require a professional level of expertise in singing or in reading music, or a difficult feat of memory. In technical and structural terms, neither is very far from, for example, the *canti carnascialeschi* that were being sung under very similar conditions in Florence from at least the 1480s.[61] Both show evidence of a popular rather than a courtly aesthetic – *O ascondida verdad* by achieving its length not with through-composition or *forme fixe*, but with multiple strophes written to the same sixteen bars of music, and *¡Ay Santa María!*, as we have seen, by its pattern of transmission. It is easy to imagine either of them belted out for hours at a time by people dressed as angels and marching in a parade or riding on a float, as the procession plodded through the streets of the city.

On the whole, however, this image seems much more plausible for the end of the century than the beginning. The early documents are probably describing an essentially monophonic practice – or monophonic with instrumental accompaniment (there were, of course, many instruments that could be played while singing), or heterophonic, as many performers sang, ornamented and improvised around a melody they all knew. Whether this eventually crystallised into something like what is represented in the most straightforward vernacular sacred music in the cancioneros it is impossible to be certain. Blake Wilson's recent work on the Florentine lauda meticulously traces the development of what may have been a parallel musical tradition from monophony to polyphony during the fifteenth century;[62] but without any

---

[60] Gregori, 'La musica del Renaixement', pp. 217–21; also Kreitner, 'Music and Civic Ceremony', pp. 216–39.

[61] For several examples, see *Florentine Festival Music 1480–1520*, ed. J. J. Gallucci, Jr, Recent Researches in the Music of the Renaissance 40 (Madison, 1981).

[62] B. Wilson, *Music and Merchants: The Laudesi Companies of Republican Florence* (Oxford, 1992), esp. pp. 149–82.

actual musical sources from Catalonia, it must remain only a tantalising model for the Corpus music of Barcelona. Still, if our angel choirs did sing polyphonically, pieces like *O ascondida verdad* and *¡Ay Santa María!* offer tempting examples of the kind of music they may have sung.

IV. THE SOFT BANDS

The document of 1424 specifies two ensembles that appear to be instrumental bands, but not trumpeters. The description of the first, no. 6 in Table 1, as 'los angels qui sonen' – literally, 'the angels who sound' – is hardly explicit, but the use of the verb 'sonar' here, rather than 'cantar' as with the angel choirs, in addition to the lack of text, makes it clear that these angels are playing instruments. Beyond that, the document gives no details of size or instrumentation, and it is impossible to know whether it was a loud band of shawms and brass or a soft band of strings and woodwinds.[63]

Ensemble no. 10, which appeared near the Host, just before the choir of twenty-four singing Elders, is described as 'los angels qui toquen sturmens', which is not much more explicit, though it does specify instruments unmistakably. These musicians were, however, like the initial trumpeters in occupying an especially conspicuous position in the parade and in being administrated by the city government. And like the trumpets, they can be traced elsewhere in the municipal archives.

The tradition of using instrumentalists at this point in the procession dated back some time before the document of 1424: the previous December, when the Corpus parade had been

---

[63] Loud bands would seem to be a logical and natural part of these celebrations, and they were clearly used in other processions in fifteenth-century Barcelona; see Kreitner, 'Music and Civic Ceremony', pp. 161–80. Their presence in the Corpus parade is, however, never unambiguously documented. Similarly, the possible role of loud bands in the Corpus procession at Girona is obscured by the documents' use of the word *juglars* to refer to trumpeters (see Chía, *La festividad del Corpus en Gerona*, pp. 17, 31–3, 41–2, 50, 59, 62, 71–2, 79, 89). In Salamanca, 'sacabuches' and 'cheremjas' were hired for Corpus in 1508, and a group of 'tañedores de gayta y tanborjno' in 1531, but the documents leave unclear whether they were actually in the procession; see R. Espinosa Maeso, 'Ensayo biográfico del maestro Lucas Fernández (¿1474?–1542)', *Boletín de la Real Academia Española*, 10 (1923), pp. 386–424 and 567–603, esp. pp. 580, 583.

repeated for the entry of Alfonso the Magnamimous, this band was described as a well-established and familiar part of those festivities:

And a reliquary was brought there, in which was embedded [a piece of] the True Cross; in front of the reliquary went various instrumentalists playing various musical instruments, dressed in white robes and wearing the masks and wings with which they represent the angels in the Corpus Christi celebration.[64]

This still does not actually specify a soft band; but the phrase 'diversos sonadors sonants diversos instruments de música' suggests a more various instrumentation than would be provided by a loud band or trumpet ensemble.

The first unambiguous reference to soft instruments is also from an occasion when the band and its accompanying *entremesos* were re-used outside the celebration. At a banquet honouring the entry of Joan de Clevas in January 1440, a procession brought in gifts, 'and in came the *entremès* of the eagle and ten players of stringed instruments, dressed in white robes and with the masks, crowns and wings of angels';[65] afterwards, the same group, apparently still in angelic garb, played for dancing.[66] The Llibre de Solemnitats also records a payment entry for this event to 'Marc Ferrer, swordmaker, whose shop is outside the Portal de la Boqueria, because he and his fellows, with stringed instruments, dressed in white robes, and with the faces and wings of angels, were ready that day'.[67] This is the earliest reference to the leader of the group – in this case, apparently not a professional musician at all.

---

[64] *Llibre de Solemnitats*, pp. 1–8 (9 December 1423), quotation p. 6: 'E fou-hi portat un reliquiari, hon havia cert encast de la Vera Creu; devant lo qual reliquiari anaren diversos sonadors sonants diversos instruments de música, vestits de camís y portans les cares e ales ab los quales se representen los angels de la dita festa de Corpor Xpisti.'

[65] *Ibid.*, pp. 114–22, quotation p. 121 (14 January 1440): 'e precehints lo entramés de la águila e .X sonadors d'esturments de corda, vestits ab camís e ab cares, diademes e ales dels angells'.

[66] *Ibid.*, pp. 121–2: 'E aprés d'açó, diverses ciutatdans e cavallers e altres de la companya del dit senyor don Johan, a so dels esturments que sonaven los dits angells, dençaren denant lo dit senyor.'

[67] *Ibid.*, p. 116: 'Item, que diguen a·n March Farrer, spaser, qui está fora lo portal de la Bocaria, que ell ab sa deesme, ab esturments de corda, vestits de camís, e ab las caras e ales dels angells, sien prests la dita jornada.'

The leadership of the soft band for Corpus Christi seems to have been under the control of the city government, and in the late 1450s at least, it changed every year. In December 1455, the Dietari of the City Council reported that 'Johan de Larpa' (John of the Harp) was sick and could not direct the 'ten players dressed as angels who play stringed instruments before the monstrance on Corpus Christi', and that therefore the job would go to 'Nicholau Çaval sonador'.[68] Almost a year later, Çaval, now curiously described as 'instrumentalist, wicker-worker and fencing-master', was removed from office and replaced with Vicens Plomas, a '*mercader* and *ciutadá* of Barcelona'.[69] Then, in November 1457 Plomas was replaced with Jaume Gili, a sheathmaker,[70] and in February 1459, Gili and Plomas began holding the office jointly.[71] The following August, however, Gili died, and Plomas served alone[72] until March 1460, when he was

[68]   *DACB*, ii, p. 223 (14 December 1455): 'Lo dit die los honorables Consellers comenaren lo offici de administrar los X sonadors vestits com a angels qui sonen instruments de corda devant la custodia lo dia de Corpore Xpi attes que mestre Johan de Larpa qui regia la dita administracio es malalt e no pot trabellar, an Nicholau Çaval sonador.'

[69]   *Ibid.*, pp. 252–3 (9 December 1456): 'Lo dit die los honorables Consellers revocant la provisio feta an Nicholau Çaval sonador esparter e mestre de grima de administrar los X sonadors a la fest de Jheu Xrist, vestits com a Angels, comenaren e provehiren le la dita administracio dels dits X sonadors vestits com a Angels qui sonen instruments de corda devant la custodia lo die de la feste de corpore Xristi, en Vicens Plomas mercader ciutada de Barchinona.' Also, added to the entry in the previous note (*ibid.*, p. 223): 'Digous a VIIII de Deembre del any M.CCCC.LVI los Consellers revocaren lo dit Nicholau Cavall e donaren la dita administracio an Vicens Plomas mercader seguons avant.'

[70]   *Ibid.*, p. 277 (14 November 1457): 'Lo dit die los honorables Consellers ensemps ab lo consell ordinari de XXIJ remogut en Vicens Plomas del offici de sonar encercar haver e administrar, los sonadors de corda, qui sonen devant la custodia de Jheu Xpt. lo die de corpore Xpt., provehiren del dit offici en Jacme Gili bayner ab los salaris drets emoluments e honors al dit offici acustumats.' See also IMH, Registre de Deliberacions, 11, fol. 138ʳ, same date.

[71]   *DACB*, ii, p. 299 (9 February 1459): 'Lo dit die los honorables Consellers ab consell de XXXIJ vistes e ruminades duas provisions fetes una a VIIIJ del mes de Deembre del any CCCC.LVJ an Vicens Plomas e laltre a XIIIJ de Noembre del any M.CCCC.LVIJ an Jacme Gili bayner lo offici de encercar e haver los sonadors de corda qui sonen la feste de corpore Xristi devant lo cors precios de Jhesu Xpit., les quals provisions la derrera derogava e revocava la primera, abilitant aquellas provehiren de nou del dit offici ab lo salari e emoluments de aquells per eguals parts los dits Jame Gili e Vicens Plomas.' See also IMH, Registre de Deliberacions, 12, fol. 97ᵛ, same date.

[72]   *DACB*, ii, p. 313 (21 August 1459): 'Lo dit de los honorables Consellers e consell de XXXIJ, Attenent com a VIIIJ del mes de Ffebrer prop pessat los honorables Conselles vestes primerament e ruminades duas provisions fetes, una a VIIIJ de Deembre del Any M.CCCCLVJ an Vicens Plomas, e laltre a XIIIJ de Noembre del

joined by Joan Tries as co-director.[73] After this, we see no more such changes; whether they continued to be made at more or less regular intervals, without being reported in the records, is not known.

Five significant features emerge from these exchanges. First of all, the band is consistently described as 'sonadors de corda' or the equivalent, which for now is probably most safely interpreted to include not only string players but players of soft instruments in general. Second, it is always described as a band of ten – a symbolic parallel, perhaps, to the ten trumpeters at the head of the procession. Third, the office of directing this band was thought to be of enough importance to the city that its conduct was often the only business reported in the Dietari in a day, and the job was so demanding (or so politically coveted?) that in some years it had to be split between two people. Fourth, even though it ordinarily performed, as far as we know, only once in the spring, the band was apparently a matter of year-round concern; these issues of leadership did not come up only around the time of Corpus Christi. Finally, and perhaps most interesting of all, the leader of the ensemble seems to have been sometimes a professional musician, but not always. Johan de Larpa was probably a harper, and Nicholau Çaval was a 'sonador, esparter e mestre de grima'; but, on the other hand, Marc Ferrer was a swordmaker, Jaume Gili a sheathmaker and Vicens Plomas probably a man of independent means. Apparently, then, administrative ability was thought to be as important to this job as musical skill. (Why the sword motif should be so strong here

---

any M.CCCC.LVIJ an Jacme Gili bayner considerants com la una de las dues derogava a la altre, provehiren del offici de encercar e haver los sonadors de corda qui la feste de corpore xristi sonen devant lo custodia on sta reservat lo cors precios de Jheu Xpt, los dits Jacme Gili e Vicens Plomas egualment ab lo salari acustumat. E com lo dit Jacme Gili ara novament sia mort los dits honorables consellers ab lo consell de XXXIJ provehiren de nou lo dit Vicens Plomas del dit offici ab lo dit salari.'

[73] *Ibid.*, p. 331 (18 March 1460): 'Lo dit die los honorables Consellers e consell de XXXIJ, Attenents com a XXJ del mes de Aguost del any Mil CCCCLVIIIJ, en Vicens Plomas fou provehit de offici de encercar e haver los sonadors de instruments de corda qui sonen denant la custodia hon sta reservat lo cors precios de Jeshu Xrist lo die de la feste de corpore Xristi ab los emoluments del dit offici considerants com millor sera prevehir lo dit offici, de dos que de I sols, Perço de nouprovehiren ab lo salari e emoluments de aquell per eguals parts lo dit Vicens Plomas en Johan Tries.'

is something of a mystery; perhaps there was some connection among the confraternities,[74] or perhaps it is all just a coincidence.)

Beyond this, the documents themselves provide no concrete information. But from the large and stereotyped number of players, from the angelic costumes, from the character of the procession in general and from the position of the band within the parade order, it is clear that the soft band for Corpus Christi was as much the product of symbolic, pictorial and theatrical considerations as musical. And this raises a point recently made by Reinhard Strohm – that the angel-concert pictures of the Middle Ages, so rightly mistrusted as sources for sublunary instrumentation,[75] may have some relevance after all for exploring at least this one musical practice.[76]

Pictorial evidence of this kind is in fact extremely plentiful. The artists of north-eastern Spain from the late fourteenth to the early sixteenth century developed an extensive tradition of angel-concert paintings, most of them showing the Virgin and Child surrounded by angels singing and playing musical instruments. A rough-and-ready sample of these paintings, taken from the two largest published collections, Chandler Rathfon Post's monumental *A History of Spanish Painting*, published between 1930 and 1966,[77] and a recent article by Jordi Ballester i Gibert surveying late-medieval Aragonese angel-concert paintings on Marian themes only,[78] is listed in the Appendix. This preliminary trolling of the sources yields almost 150 paintings – not a complete

[74] The swordmakers, sheathmakers and lancemakers of fifteenth-century Barcelona were united in the confraternity of St Paul; see P. Bonnassie, *La organización del trabajo en Barcelona a fines del siglo XV* (Barcelona, 1975), p. 201 and *passim*. The document organising this confraternity, dated 8 May 1401, is transcribed in *Gremios y cofradías de la antigua Corona de Aragón*, II, ed. F. de Bofarull y Sans, Colección de Documentos Inéditos del Archivo General de la Corona de Aragón 41 (Barcelona, 1910), pp. 192–203; it mentions no special role for the confraternity in the Corpus Christi celebration. Fencing-masters were, so far as I can tell, not involved in the confraternity of St Paul.

[75] The most extensive discussion of this topic remains R. Hammerstein, *Die Musik der Engel* (Berne, 1962); but see also, for example, E. Winternitz, 'On Angel Concerts in the 15th Century: A Critical Approach to Realism and Symbolism in Sacred Painting', *Musical Quarterly*, 49 (1963), pp. 137–49.

[76] R. Strohm, *Music in Late Medieval Bruges* (Oxford, 1985), p. 7.

[77] C. R. Post, *A History of Spanish Painting*, 14 vols. (Cambridge, MA, 1930–66).

[78] J. Ballester i Gibert, 'Retablos marianos tardomedievales con ángeles músicos procedentes del antiguo reino de Aragón: Catálogo', *Revista de Musicología*, 13 (1990), pp. 123–201.

list by any means, and admittedly a minefield of unanswered or debatable questions of dating and attribution, but perhaps still large and broad enough to show, in general, what kinds of instruments were familiar as a visual part of this tradition. The identifiable instruments in these paintings are summarised in Table 2.

The paintings show a reassuring combination of specific variety and general consistency: although no one instrumentation dominates enough to suggest a clear-cut pictorial convention, the same dozen or so instruments do make up most of the angelic ensembles. It is quite apparent, moreover, that these are almost exclusively soft bands: omitting isolated shawms and shawm ensembles (about which more in a moment), there are only four

Table 2 *Instruments in Aragonese angel-concert paintings (see Appendix)*

Instrument name	No. of examples
Lute	108
Gittern	31
Vihuela	12
Harp	60
Psaltery	22
Hammered psaltery and tabor pipe	1
Fiddle	50
Rebec	37
Viol	7
Portative organ	49
Positive organ	3
Shawm (= dolzaina?)	76
Bagpipe	6
S-shaped trumpet	4
Fanciful trumpet	4
Straight trumpet	1
Trombone	1
Recorder	26
Double pipe	5
Pipe and tabor	5
Transverse flute	2
Tambourine	11
Cymbals	2
Nakers	1
Triangle	1
Zabomba	1

paintings, all from the late fifteenth century and after, that seem to show a conventional loud band of shawms and brass.[79] And this musical aspect of the artistic tradition clearly fits in well with all the descriptions of the angel band for Corpus Christi as 'sonadors de corda'.

Among these many soft instrumentations, the lute is by far the most commonly depicted instrument, with its smaller relative the gittern (the distinction is not always clear in the paintings) swelling its numbers still further.[80] Other plucked strings, such as the harp, the psaltery and, after 1450 or so, the waisted vihuela, are also frequently seen, and bowed strings, especially the fiddle and rebec, are by no means rare.

Woodwinds are on the whole more sparingly represented in these paintings, with one exception – shawms appear in the table more often than any other single instrument except the lute. This may seem surprising; the shawm is, in fact, the only *haut* instrument represented here in any numbers, and the many angel concerts containing one or two shawms among soft instruments (for example, the band of two shawms, rebec, lute and vihuela in a painting by the Perea master, *c.* 1500) would seem most implausible. It may be, however, that the pictures I have identified as shawms are in some or most cases meant to represent not the shawm of the loud band, but the softer dolzaina, which is often mentioned as a courtly instrument in Spanish sources of the fifteenth century,[81] and which may have been visually identical to the shawm, differing only in internal details.[82]

---

[79] These are: (a) a painting by the Santa Liestra master, late fifteenth century, Post, VIII, p. 213, Ballester, no. 14; (b) a closely related anonymous Aragonese painting, also late fifteenth century, Post, VIII, p. 513, Ballester, no. 24; (c) a painting by the Cabanyes master, early sixteenth century, Post, VII, p. 898; and (d) a painting by the Alforja master, *c.* 1537, Post, XII, p. 343.

[80] I have identified lutes and gitterns in the pictures as plucked string instruments with rounded bodies, the lute larger and the gittern smaller (a distinction easier to make when they are shown together than when one instrument appears alone). Ballester, in 'Retablos marianos', calls most of my gitterns and some of my lutes 'guitarras moriscas', and indeed some paintings do seem to show an instrument of distinct design.

[81] See, for example, *Hechos del Condestable Don Miguel Lucas de Iranzo (crónica del siglo XV)*, ed. J. de Mata Carriazo (Madrid, 1940), p. 44: 'Y entre los otros, yua vna copla de tres ministreles de duçaynas, que muy dulçe y acordadamente sonauan.' Dolzainas are shown playing for dancing and courtly entertainment, but also marching in processions with loud bands; see pp. 47, 49, 134, 135, 168.

[82] See B. Boydell, *The Crumhorn and Other Renaissance Windcap Instruments* (Buren, 1982), pp. 384–418; F. Palmer, 'Musical Instruments from the *Mary Rose*: A Report on

Recorders and portative organs are represented in a substantial number of paintings; but positive organs are found only three times, possibly because of the visual anomaly of a hovering angel playing an instrument that sits on the ground. (But then a parallel difficulty would presumably rule them out of a marching ensemble in mortal life too.) Conspicuously absent are windcap instruments, harpsichords and the like, and cornetts (unless some of the shawms are cornetts), and conspicuously sparse are trombones, percussion instruments and transverse flutes (much rarer than recorders despite their depiction in the Cantigas de Santa María some centuries earlier).

The angel-concert paintings do not suffice to prescribe a particular instrumentation for the Corpus band – if only, to begin with, because so few show bands as large as ten. But they do at least suggest a few general probabilities. If strings dominated the real ensemble as noticeably as the paintings, then the phrase 'sonadors de corda' in the records was well chosen; but, again, the wording should probably not be taken to exclude non-stringed instruments altogether. An instrumentation drawn largely from, say, the eight most commonly depicted instruments in the paintings – lute, dolzaina, harp, fiddle, portative organ, rebec, gittern and recorder – seems quite plausible and practical for this band for the first half of the century; for the second half, viols and vihuelas might well be added.[83] The paintings often show instruments duplicated or triplicated in the same ensemble, especially shawms or dolzainas, lutes and recorders; and perhaps these were the most likely instruments to be doubled in the Corpus band as well.

Again, historical fiction; but this chapter of the novel is at least preliminarily supported by data from other cities around the peninsula. In nearby Girona the band of 'sonadors de corda', which had included as many as twelve unspecified instruments around the middle of the century,[84] was recorded in 1481 as

Work in Progress', *Early Music*, 11 (1983), pp. 53–9; and H. W. Myers, 'The Mary Rose "Shawm" ', *ibid.*, pp. 358–60.

[83] On the rapid development of the vihuela and viol in the Catalan-speaking lands in the late fifteenth century, see especially I. Woodfield, *The Early History of the Viol* (Cambridge, 1984).

[84] Chía, *La festividad del Corpus en Gerona*, pp. 29–46, *passim*.

being down to a sextet of harp, lute, two guitars, flute and vihuela, their players also dressed as angels;[85] and in Salamanca, the band before the Host grew from two vihuelas around 1500[86] to (I think –the wording is ambiguous) another sextet, of vihuelas, harp(s) and rebec(s), in 1505.[87]

But whatever the exact instrumentation and repertory of the soft band before the Host in Barcelona may have been, it is clear that this ensemble was one of the most enduring elements of the procession. It was the only musical ensemble documented before 1424, and its history may go back well into the fourteenth century. In 1582, 'los deu [ten] Angels que sonen instruments de corda' were still there at the same point in the parade (and by then had taken on a number of official entertaining duties earlier in the week as well).[88] Indeed, even an eighteenth-century picture of the Corpus procession shows, marching in front of the Host among the priests and acolytes, three violinists in angelic robes, and in street clothes two bassoons and a cello.[89]

V. CORPUS AND THE COMMUNITY

This procession means something very different to our community from what it meant to theirs. To us, Corpus Christi in fifteenth-century Barcelona is interesting as a rich source of documentation for the variety of musical performances that could surround a single large festivity. We are accustomed to seeing such documentation for one-of-a-kind spectacles put on by the gentry for the gentry; but for a repeated annual celebration involving an entire large city, this profusion of detail is rare indeed. Inevitably, the

---

[85] *Ibid.*, p. 46: a payment to two players and 'quatuor aliorum de nostre societate qui vestibus nos ut angeli ante corpus domini in processione facta die festi corporis christi proximi lapsi, sonando videlicet ego dictus anthonius lyol arpa, ego dictus Jacobus torra lahut, petrus Janouer et anthonius leopard singulas citaras sive guittarras, leonardus balaguer flahutam et Clemens vallosera mige viula'.

[86] Espinosa Maeso, 'Ensayo biográfico del maestro Lucas Fernández', p. 575: 'Item dj A cañedo e a su conpanero vn castellano porque fueron tañendo en sendas viuelas ante el arca . . . [mrs.] ccclxxxºv'.

[87] *Ibid.*, p. 578: 'yten a quatro menestriles que fueron la harpa e el Rabe e dos tañedores de vihula dos ducados e çinco Reales'; see also p. 577 for a smaller ensemble in 1503, and p. 580 for an ambiguously described group in 1508.

[88] Comes, *Libre de algunes coses asanyalades*, pp. 631, 638.

[89] Duran, *Barcelona i la seva història*, II, facing p. 568.

higher level of detail serves only to raise the tone of our frustration – the listing of the Catalan incipits for the angel choirs makes the lack of music to go with them all the more poignant. But if some tantalising puzzles remain, this should not obscure the more general observations to be made about the kinds of music employed in a celebration like this, and above all about the symbolic, theatrical and practical pressures that shaped its structure and meaning over the years.

To a resident of fifteenth-century Barcelona, there was nothing very extraordinary about any of the musical ensembles in the Corpus procession. Trumpet bands were the backbone of local ceremonial music throughout the century; polyphonic vocal ensembles were familiar at least through the cathedral, whose choir already owned a good many books of music (including a 'librum parvum . . . de contrapuncto antiquo') as early as 1421[90] and performed polyphony at an outdoor ceremony at the harbour in 1439.[91] Soft bands, in Barcelona as elsewhere, performed less in public ceremony than for private dancing and entertainment, but they were certainly familiar outside the palaces of the royal and wealthy: when Juan II died, for example, the City Council announced an ordinance forbidding

any person, man or woman of any estate, law or condition, to have balls by night or day, in the plazas or public streets, or in monasteries or convents, or in public or private houses, even if they are celebrating engagements, weddings or banquets. And neither is it allowed for anyone in these engagements, weddings or banquets to use organs, harpsichords, timpani, drums, flutes or other stringed or other instruments.[92]

What was unusual about the music in the Corpus Christi procession, then, was not the music itself, but how it fitted into a

---

[90] H. Anglès, *La música a Catalunya fins al segle XIII* (Barcelona, 1935), pp. 129–30.
[91] Kreitner, 'Music and Civic Ceremony', pp. 447–52.
[92] IMH, Registre d'Ordinacions, 10, fols. 154[r]–155[r] (12 February 1479), also transcribed in *Llibre de Solemnitats*, pp. 317–18: 'no sia liçit ni permes a qualsevol persones homens & dones de qualsevol stat ley o condicio sien fer balls de nits o de dies en plaçes o en carreres publiques o dins monastirs de homens o de dones ne dins cases publiques o de particulars persons encara que celebrassen sposalles noçes o convits. E menys sia licit a qualsevol persones en dites sposalles noçes o convits usar de orguens clavisimbols tabals temborinos fleutes o altres instruments de corda o des altres species'. For more detail, including the document in full, see Kreitner, 'Music and Civic Ceremony', pp. 201–8.

larger dramatic structure. Of all the musicians in the parade, only the trumpeters at the beginning and (assuming I am identifying them correctly) the cathedral choir near the end were fulfilling their usual function; everyone else was there not only to make music, but to act a role in a huge and elaborate drama.

The feast of Corpus Christi was a celebration of the Body of Christ, and thus, by extension, of the Eucharist and of Christ's life on earth and fleshly suffering. These three elements – Host, sacrament and man – governed the general structure of the celebration and its visual and poetic content: the text to Alfonso de Troya's *O ascondida verdad* (quoted above), with its rapid cuts between the details of crucifixion and humble words of praise, and its equation of crucified body and sacramental bread, shows this complex and subtle intertwinement most eloquently.

Veneration of the Body of Christ was the main purpose behind the most prominent feature of Corpus Christi as it came to be celebrated throughout Europe in the late thirteenth and early fourteenth centuries – the procession after Mass in which the consecrated Host was carried, in its ornate monstrance under a canopy or baldachin, through the streets of the city by the local clergy. Indeed, the early Corpus Christi processions, in so far as they can be reconstructed, seem very much to have been dominated by the clergy: for example, Edmund Bowles lists the order of march from fourteenth-century Bamberg as follows:

vergers from the church, children with burning candles and silver crosses, members of the confraternity, the master architect of the cathedral (*magister fabricae*), a priest bearing a relic, students from the choir school, singers, musicians, vicars, canons, deacons, the provost of the cathedral, a priest bearing a golden cross, twelve armed citizens, two nobles in armor with banners of patron saints, youths carrying torches, canons holding the reliquary, men supporting the baldachin, boys with candlesticks and those tossing roses in front of the host, and finally the bishop and his chaplain with a crozier.[93]

Aided no doubt by the spring weather, the festival continued to grow and prosper over the rest of the fourteenth century. By 1400, many – perhaps most – of the Corpus Christi processions all over Europe had begun to develop something like Barcelona's

---

[93] Bowles, 'Musical Instruments in the Medieval Corpus Christi Procession', p. 254.

entremesos; and as these gradually came to dominate the day, the parade changed from a fairly ordinary, though large, religious procession to a celebration like none other in the year. In a number of cities (notably in England and Germany),[94] the *entremesos* in turn evolved into Corpus Christi plays separate from the procession; in others, Barcelona obviously included, they just continued to grow in number and size, further enlarging the parade and further tipping its balance away from the appearance of a conventional religious procession and towards extravagant theatrical display. This mingling of sacred and secular, of divine occasion and earthly entertainment, was the most conspicuous feature of Corpus Christi all over the continent for many centuries; and it was symbolically appropriate to the celebration of the life of God on earth.

In any case, the importance of this sacred feast to the people and the secular government of late-medieval Barcelona can scarcely be overstated; even the most casual glance over any of the major municipal records shows the remarkable hold that the Corpus festivities had on the city's imagination and the enormous amount of labour and worry they involved all year round. Of the ninety-nine entries from the fifteenth century surviving in the Llibre de Solemnitats, thirty-five are about Corpus Christi, and all the others chronicle unique events – royal entries, funerals, military embarcations – rather than holidays repeated annually. Beyond the Llibre de Solemnitats, other sources show that the details of the Corpus procession were a matter of more or less constant concern to the City Council: throughout the century (and, significantly, not just in the spring) we see a steady stream of musicians appointed to lead the soft band, workmen engaged to repair the *entremesos*, painters hired to decorate new *entremesos*, laws passed to try to keep the participants under control. The increasing use after 1450 of the procession and *entremesos* for special occasions at other times of the year shows still further the public awareness that this procession was one of the biggest, most impressive things the city did.

---

[94] See, for example, H. Craig, 'The Corpus Christi Procession and the Corpus Christi Play', *Journal of English and Germanic Philology*, 13 (1914), pp. 589–602, and W. F. Michael, *Die geistlichen Prozessionsspiele in Deutschland* (Baltimore, 1947), pp. 29–69.

But the Corpus Christi procession in Barcelona had a significance that went beyond religious devotion, local pride and vernal high spirits. With their vivid representations of biblical characters and saints, the *entremesos* gave an illiterate public a chance, once a year, to put a human face behind the Bible story told, the scripture read, the prayer said. In this respect they served a social function like that of the mystery plays, the gory altarpieces and crucifixes, and the sublime and horrifying sculptured church portals of the day: they were a very real part of the religious education of the people, and more than a mere show of the city's collective power and piety.

The *entremesos* in Barcelona's procession were presented in a rough chronological order:

> Old Testament events
> prophets
> Christmas
> female saints
> the crucifixion and resurrection
> male saints (plus St Eulalia)
> the Apostles.

The two obvious divergences from chronology both follow other logical considerations: the group of female saints was placed in, as it were, the middle of the New Testament, presumably to keep Christmas and Good Friday from being too close together (the parade did not, probably for dramatic reasons, include any of the events of Jesus's youth and ministry), and the Apostles marched after the later saints probably in order to keep them closest to the Host. In general, however, watching the Corpus Christi parade must have been something like seeing a movie of the history of Christianity.

Within this large and complex system, the musicians served a dual role. They were there partly, as in any parade, just to keep things moving along and to add an air of festivity and wonder; this was perhaps especially true of the band of trumpets at the head of the procession, which was there just as trumpet bands were there in almost all of Barcelona's processions. But musicians were also included as *entremesos* in themselves and as parts of other *entremesos*, and the texts they sung were, in at least some cases, carefully chosen to be suitable to their position in the order of march. The choirs and soft bands were dressed not as earthly musicians but as angels and Apocalyptic Elders, and they represented not themselves but the joys of heaven (or, in one case, apparently the pains of hell): and this use of voices and soft instruments to represent the sounds of the paradisical and infernal parallels the patterns of symbolism universally found in the dramatic and artistic traditions of the Middle Ages.[95]

Today the parade route is still pretty much intact. Most of the buildings are newer than the fifteenth century, of course, but the principal streets have all escaped draconian urban-renewal projects to keep something like their original configurations. Some of the churches and palaces mentioned in the document of 1424 look different now, but they are all still there, and they are still the landmarks that the people of Barcelona use to give directions around the labyrinth of the Barri Gòtic. It takes some twenty minutes to walk the whole distance; doing so, one cannot help being struck not only by how easy it is to imagine what the neighbourhood looked and sounded and smelt like in the Middle Ages, but also by how hard it is to visualise such a big procession in such a small space. The Corpus parade must have offered ghastly logistic problems – vast crowds of people in the plaza in front of the cathedral, in costumes not designed for comfort, waiting hours for their turn to go on; some *entremesos* inevitably moving slower or stopping longer than others and creating gaps and collisions; an audience strategically placed for mischief in upper-storey windows on narrow streets.

Small wonder, then, that throughout the fifteenth century the government of Barcelona had to work so hard and so constantly to keep things running as smoothly as they could. And with their stripes we are healed: the laws they passed and the records they kept offer us the rare privilege of understanding a great deal about this one ceremony – and exactly the kind of ceremony that we most need to know about if we intend to understand the musical experience of Europeans back then.

The University of Memphis

---

[95] On this connection, see esp. Bowles, 'Musical Instruments in the Medieval Corpus Christi Procession', pp. 258–9; on the patterns of instrumental symbolism in mystery plays and the like, see esp. *idem*, 'The Role of Musical Instruments in Medieval Sacred Drama', *Musical Quarterly*, 45 (1969), pp. 67–84.

APPENDIX

Instruments in Catalan and Aragonese angel-concert paintings

Date	Artist	Post vol., p.	Ballester no.	No. of musicians	Instruments (subject, if not Virgin and Child)
14th c.	Anon. Catalan		10	4	portative organ, shawm, lute, rebec (Coronation of Virgin)
14th c.	Anon. Catalan		11	4	fiddle, lute, portative organ, tambourine
c. 1360	Circle of Destorrents		4	4	portative organ, gittern, fiddle, lute
c. 1361	Jaume Serra		122	2	psaltery, fiddle (Coronation of Virgin)
c. 1375	Pere Serra		123	2	harp, fiddle
late 14th c.	Anon. Valencian		5	4	portative organ, fiddle, gittern, lute
late 14th c.	Anon. Valencian		6	4	portative organ, fiddle, 2 lutes
late 14th c.	Anon. Catalan		9	8	cymbals, fiddle, portative organ, shawm, lute, psaltery, shawm, tambourine (Coronation of Virgin)
late 14th c.	Longares master		79	4	harp, recorder, gittern, psaltery
late 14th c.	Longares master		80	2	lute, gittern
late 14th c.	Francesc Serra II		120	4	portative organ, fiddle, gittern, lute
late 14th c.	Pere Serra		124	6	portative organ, lute, recorder, fiddle, psaltery, gittern, harp
late 14th c.	Pere Serra	xii, 557	126	2	harp, gittern
c. 1394–5?	Lorenzo Zaragoza		140	4	rebec, portative organ, lute, harp
c. 1400?	Pere Serra		125	6	harp, gittern, lute, psaltery, recorder, portative organ
c. 1400	Francesc Serra II (or a follower)	vi, 569	121	3	portative organ, fiddle, lute
c. 1400	School of the Serras in Roselló	viii, 582	8	6	fiddle, 2 lutes (different shapes), portative organ, psaltery, rebec
c. 1400	Fonollosa master	viii, 587	64	4	harp, fiddle, 2 recorders

Appendix (cont.)

Date	Artist	Post vol., p.	Ballester no.	No. of musicians	Instruments (subject, if not Virgin and Child)
c. 1400	Francesc Comes		53	4	fiddle, portative organ, lute, fiddle
c. 1400	Francesc Comes		54	6	portative organ, lute, cymbals, transverse flute, rebec, gittern
c. 1400	Francesc Comes		55	4	portative organ, lute, rebec, transverse flute
c. 1400	Cubells master		58	4	rebec, portative organ, lute, gittern
c. 1400	A. Marçal de Sax		116	6	3 shawms, 3 singers with music
c. 1400	A. Marçal de Sax		117	7	3 singers with music, 2 shawms, bagpipe, lute
c. 1400	Pere Nicolau		97	14	8 singers, 2 gitterns, 2 harps, psaltery, fiddle
c. 1400	Pere Nicolau		98	2	fiddle, lute (Coronation of Virgin)
c. 1400	Pere Nicolau		99	8	4 singers with music, portative organ, gittern, lute?, harp
c. 1400	Pere Nicolau		100	19?	17 singers?, fiddle, lute (Coronation of Virgin)
c. 1400	Pere Nicolau		101	2	harp, gittern
c. 1404	Pere Nicolau	vii, 789	95	4	harp, fiddle, gittern, portative organ (Coronation of Virgin)
c. 1404–8	Pere Nicolau		96	2	lute, harp
early 15th c.	Pere Vall	vi, 516	135	4	portative organ, lute, gittern, fiddle
c. 1411–16	Lluís Borrassá		45	9	psaltery, lute, harp, 6 singers with music
1st q. 15th c.	Lluís Borrassá		47	6	gittern, recorder, lute, 3 singers with music
1st q. 15th c.	Montissión master		89	4	gittern, portative organ, lute, fiddle
1st q. 15th c.	Tora master		131	2	bagpipe, shawm

1st q. 15th c.	Tora master		132	15	psaltery, lute, positive organ (player+pumper), 2 invisible instruments, 2 shawms, rebec, harp, straight trumpet, bagpipe, pipe and tabor, singer
early 15th c.	Pere Lembri		78	8	lute, harp, 6 singers with music (Coronation of Virgin)
c. 1420	Lluís Borrassá	VII, 745	46	6	portative organ, lute, harp, gittern, psaltery, fiddle
c. 1420	Coronation master		57	8	lute, fiddle, psaltery, gittern, double pipe, bagpipe, tambourine, portative organ (Coronation of Virgin)
early 15th c.	Ramon de Mur		92	8	zabomba[?], 2 lutes, gittern, lute, harp, rebec, recorder
early 15th c.	Ramon de Mur		93	2	lute, rebec
1st 3rd 15th c.	Roselló master		115	3	harp, 2 singers with music
early 15th c.	Jaume Cabrera		48	4	fiddle, recorder, harp, lute
early 15th c.	Jaume Cabrera		49	2	harp, lute
early 15th c.	Jaume Cabrera		50	5	(string?), harp, fiddle, recorder, lute
early 15th c.	Jaume Cabrera		51	8	lute, gittern, portative organ, lute, gittern, psaltery, gittern, lute (Coronation of Virgin)
early 15th c.	Jaume Cabrera		52	4	portative organ, lute, recorder, harp
early 15th c.	Joan Mates		85	2	shawm, rebec
early 15th c.	Gabriel Moger		86	2	lute, rebec
early 15th c.	Secuita master		118	4	psaltery, recorder, harp, lute
early 15th c.	Secuita master		119	2	harp, lute
c. 1421–34	Miquel Alcanys	VII, 794	2	2	harp, gittern
early 15th c.	Miguel del Rey	x, 388	110	2	2 shawms
early 15th c.	Miguel del Rey		111	4	lute, psaltery, lute?, portative organ (Coronation of Virgin)
c. 1430	Bonanal Zaortiga		138	4	recorder, rebec, recorder, lute

199

Appendix (*cont.*)

Date	Artist	Post vol., p.	Ballester no.	No. of musicians	Instruments (subject, if not Virgin and Child)
c. 1432?	Bonanal Zaortiga		139	6	6 shawms (straight trumpets?)
c. 1439	Lanaja master		75	5	harp, recorder, singer with music?, rebec, lute
2nd q. 15th c.	Circle of Lanaja master		12	4	gittern, harp, lute, recorder
2nd q. 15th c.	Lanaja master	VI, 606	72	6	bagpipe, singer with music, fiddle, harp, portative organ, shawm (Coronation of Virgin)
2nd q. 15th c.	Lanaja master		73	7	portative organ, lute, 2 shawms, rebec, singer with music, harp
2nd q. 15th c.	Lanaja master		74	6	shawm, portative organ, rebec, harp, singer, fiddle (Coronation of Virgin)
2nd q. 15th c.	Lanaja master		76	8	portative organ, rebec, shawm, fiddle, gittern, shawm, harp, lute
2nd q. 15th c.	Lanaja master		77	5	shawm, lute, rebec, lute, bagpipe
2nd q. 15th c.	Follower of Beck master	XIII, 321		6	2 shawms, 2 lutes, 2 singers with music
1440–50?	Bernat Martorell	VII, 763	84	6	harp, rebec (a bracchio), 3 recorders (Coronation of Virgin)
c. 1445?	Miquel Nadal		94	6	rebec (fiddle?), harp, lute, 3 recorders
c. 1447–50	Jaume Huguet	VII, 28	69	6	3 singers with music, 3 recorders
c. 1435–60	Riglos master	VII, 225	112	4	fiddle, rebec, 2 shawms
c. 1435–60	Riglos master		113	3	portative organ, harp, lute
mid-15th c.	Pedro Zuera		141	3	lute, harp, gittern (Coronation of Virgin)
c. 1450	Sant Quirse master	VII, 208		1	pipe and tabor (mystic marriage of St Catherine)
c. 1455	Valentí Montoliu		91	2	2 lutes (Coronation of Virgin)
mid-15th c.	Workshop of Jacomart and Reixach	VI, 111	31	2	lute, fiddle

Date	Artist	Ref.	No.	Count	Instruments
mid-15th c.	Jacomart/Reixach	vi, 153	71	6	3 shawms, fiddle, harp, lute
mid-15th c.	Maluenda master		81	2	harp, lute
mid-15th c.	Maluenda master		82	3	lute, vihuela, rebec
mid-15th c.	Circle of Jaume Huguet		22	8	3 shawms, portative organ, 3 singers with music, harp (Coronation of Virgin)
mid-15th c.	Salvador Roig and Joan Rius	viii, 258	114	1	harp
mid-15th c.	Torralba master	ix, 326		10	lute, fiddle, 2 shawms, 2 psalteries (different shapes), double pipe, tambourine, portative organ, vihuela? (Coronation of Virgin)
mid-15th c.	Tomás Giner		66	4	lute, double pipe, pipe and tabor, harp (Coronation of Virgin)
mid-15th c.	Alacuás master	ix, 828		4	harp, portative organ, positive organ, lute
15th c.	Anon. Aragonese		16	2	rebec, lute
15th c.	Anon. Aragonese		17	6	lute, tambourine, vihuela, rebec, double pipe, portative organ
15th c.	Anon. Aragonese		19	2	portative organ, rebec (Coronation of Virgin)
15th c.	Anon. Aragonese		20	6	shawm, lute, shawm, 2 rebecs, vihuela
15th c.	Anon. Aragonese		23	4	portative organ, fiddle?, tambourine, psaltery
15th c.	Anon. Mallorcan		25	6	lute, fiddle, tambourine, shawm, harp, rebec
15th c.	Anon. Mallorcan		26	4	viol, 2 shawms, lute
15th c.	Anon. Valencian		28	4	portative organ, fiddle, gittern, lute
15th c.	Anon. Valencian		29	1	harp
15th c.	Anon. Valencian		30	5	harp, rebec, shawm, lute, portative organ
15th c.	Anon. Valencian		32	2	rebec, harp

Appendix (*cont.*)

Date	Artist	Post vol., p.	Ballester no.	No. of musicians	Instruments (subject, if not Virgin and Child)
15th c.	Anon. Valencian		33	4	harp, rebec, gittern, lute
15th c.	Anon. Valencian		34	4	psaltery, lute, fiddle, gittern
15th c.	Anon. Valencian		36	4	portative organ, pipe and tabor, lute, triangle
c. 1459	School of Mateo Ortoneda	VII, 548	13	4	psaltery, harp, lute, portative organ
c. 1460	Pere García de Benavarri	VII, 267	65	2	2 lutes
3rd q. 15th c.	All master		3	4	fiddle, lute, 2 singers with music
3rd q. 15th c.	Pere Espallargues	VII, 305	62	3	pipe and tabor, rebec (a bracchio)
3rd q. 15th c.	Master of the Prelate Mur	VIII, 303		2	harp, lute (St Vincent)
1453–79	Rafael Moger	VII, 651	88	2	lute, rebec
c. 1465–6	Tomás Giner and Arnau de Castellnou		67	6	lute, portative organ, harp, 3 singers with music
c. 1470?	Alfajarín master	IX, 871		2	2 shawms (Coronation of Virgin)
late 15th c.?	All master?	VIII, 609	37	4	nakers, fiddle, lute, shawm (or recorder) (Virgin and angels)
late 15th c.	Anon. Catalan		38	2	2 shawms
late 15th c.	Artíes master		43	2	rebec, lute
late 15th c.	Joan Daurer?		61	6	portative organ, lute, tambourine, fiddle, psaltery, double pipe (Coronation of Virgin)
late 15th c.	Glorieta master		68	1	psaltery
late 15th c.	Mateu Montoliu		90	10	viol, harp, 7 singers?, shawm
late 15th c.	Olot master (Miquel Torell?)		103	2	invisible instrument, recorder (shawm?, cornett?)
late 15th c.	Son master		127	2	lute, S-shaped trumpet

Date	Master	No.	Ref.	Count	Instruments
late 15th c.	Oslo master		XIII, 366	2	tambourine, viol
late 15th c.	Canapost master	56	VII, 605	2	recorder, fiddle
late 15th c.	Martín de Soria?		XII, 702	2	2 shawms
late 15th c.	Martín de Soria	128	VIII, 369	4	2 lutes, 2 singers with music
late 15th c.	Martín de Soria	129	VIII, 371	2	fiddle, lute
late 15th c.	Martín de Soria	130	VIII, 336	2	2 shawms
late 15th c.	Rafael Moger?	87		6	lute, 3 shawms, harp
late 15th c.	Juan de la Abadía the Elder	1	XII, 709	2	vihuela, lute
late 15th c.	Santa Liestra master	14	VIII, 213	10	2 shawms, S-shaped trumpet, 3 singers with music, portative organ, harp, fiddle, lute
late 15th c.	Aragonese school, related to preceding	24	VIII, 513	10	2 shawms, S-shaped trumpet, 3 singers with music, portative organ, harp, fiddle, lute
late 15th c.	Armisén master	42	VIII, 197	4	fiddle, rebec, 2 singers with music
late 15th c.	Martí Bernat	44	VIII, 124	3–4	harp, lute, portative organ, fiddle?
late 15th c.	Martí Bernat		VIII, 58	2	2 fiddles (1 a bracchio, 1 a gamba) (St Martin)
c. 1500	Anon. Valencian	39		2	fiddle, vihuela
c. 1500	Martínez master	83		2	lute, viol
c. 1500	Perea master	104	VI, 277	5	lute, rebec, 2 shawms, vihuela
c. 1500	Martí Torner	133	VI, 481	4	lute, tambourine, viol, harp
c. 1500	Martí Torner	134		4	portative organ, 2 shawms, harp
c. 1500	Ciérvoles master		VII, 510	2	large rebec, portative organ (painted angels accompanying sculptured Virgin and Child)
c. 1500	Almudévar master		VIII, 459	2	lute, rebec (St Anthony Abbot)
c. 1500	Hearst master?		VIII, 268	4?	2 lutes, vihuela, invisible instrument? (retable of Mary Magdalen)
c. 1500?	Javierre master		XII, 358	6	lute, harp, tabor pipe and hammered psaltery?, portative organ, fiddle, tambourine (St Vincent)

Appendix (*cont.*)

Date	Artist	Post vol., p.	Ballester no.	No. of musicians	Instruments (subject, if not Virgin and Child)
early 16th c.	Rodrigo de Osona the Younger?	VI, 229		2	viol, lute
early 16th c.	Miquel Ximenez, Joan Ximenez, Martí Larraz		137	4	3 shawms, lute (Coronation of Virgin)
early 16th c.	Anon. Valencian		40	4	lute, unidentified instrument, psaltery, harp
early 16th c.	Cabanyes master	VII, 898		4	S-shaped trumpet, 2 shawms, vihuela (fiddle?)
early 16th c.	St Lazarus master	VIII, 722		2	vihuela, viol (Coronation of Virgin)
early 16th c.	Anon. Catalan	XII, 546		4	shawm, portative organ, harp, vihuela (angels)
early 16th c.	Sijena master	XIII, 129		2	2 fanciful trumpets (Presentation of Virgin)
early 16th c.	Sijena master	XIII, 130		4	positive organ, shawm, 2 fanciful trumpets (Ascension)
1520–50	Pedro Gascó	XII, 248		2	fiddle, shawm, (Baptism of Jesus)
c. 1537	Alforja master	XII, 343		6	trombone, 2 shawms, invisible instrument, fiddle, vihuela (Virgin of Hope)

Paintings are included if they:

(1) were reproduced in Post, *A History of Spanish Painting*, or Ballester, 'Retablos marianos';
(2) originated in Catalonia, Valencia, Aragón, Roselló, the Balearic Islands or Sardinia;
(3) were painted between the late fourteenth and early sixteenth centuries;
(4) showed one or more angel instrumentalists (paintings with singers only have been omitted);
(5) depicted a joyous scene (Last Judgment scenes have been omitted); and
(6) were reproduced more or less whole and sufficiently distinct in the copies available.

Dates and attributions are from the sources, with Ballester superseding Post whenever practical.

Early Music History (1995) Volume 14

ADELYN PECK LEVERETT

SONG MASSES IN THE TRENT CODICES: THE AUSTRIAN CONNECTION*

The seven Trent Codices preserve much of the sacred vocal polyphony that has survived from the middle decades of the fifteenth century. With some 1500 individual pieces, the collection is a rich compendium of liturgical and paraliturgical genres, large

* An earlier version of this study was presented as a paper to the 1991 National Meeting of the American Musicological Society in Chicago, Illinois, and prepared with the support of an Arthur B. Rackham Postdoctoral Fellowship at the University of Michigan, Ann Arbor. My research on the Trent Codices was conducted with the kind permission and assistance of the Museo Provinciale d'Arte, Trent. I wish to thank Margaret Bent, Graeme Boone, Lewis Lockwood, Kay Kaufmann Shelemay and Thomas Walker for their comments and suggestions; I am especially grateful to Bonnie Blackburn for her guidance in preparing the final version of the article.

Manuscript abbreviations are as follows:

Buxheim (or Bux)	Munich, Bayerische Staatsbibliothek, Handschriften- und Inkunabelnabteilung, Mus. MS 3725 ('Buxheim organ book')
CS 14, 51	Vatican City, Biblioteca Apostolica Vaticana, MSS Cappella Sistina 14, 51
Glogau (or Glo)	Kraków, Biblioteka Jagiellońska, s.n.; formerly Berlin, Deutsche Staatsbibliothek, Mus. MS 40098 ('Glogau songbook')
Munich 3154	Munich, Bayerische Staatsbibliothek, Musiksammlung, Musica MS 3154 ('Nikolaus Leopold Codex')
Schedel (or Sched)	Munich, Bayerische Staatsbibliothek, Handschriften- und Inkunabelnabteilung, MS germanicus monacensis 810 ('Schedel songbook')
Speciálník (or Spec)	Hradec Králové, Krajske Muzeum, Knihovna, MS II A 7
Strahov (or Str)	Prague, Památník Národního Písemnictví, Strahovská Knihovna, MS D.G.IV.47
Trent (or Tr) 87–92, 93	Trent, Museo Provinciale d'Arte, Castello del Buonconsiglio, MSS 87–92; Museo Diocesano, MS BL

In the course of this article, I will use the term 'Austria' with its standard denotation of the archduchy controlled by the House of Habsburg during the mid- and later fifteenth century, extended to include areas of Habsburg control to the south in the Tyrol, the Alto

and small.[1] The codices are perhaps most valuable, however, as sources for the cyclic mass Ordinary, the most ambitious of fifteenth-century polyphonic forms.

The earliest Trent volumes, Trent 87 and 92, show the initial development of the mass Ordinary, with cycles composed in the two decades or so before the assembly of the two manuscripts in the early 1440s.[2] Movement pairs and partial cycles, products of the first stirrings of interest in systematically grouped settings of the Ordinary texts, are there, along with the earliest three- and four-movement sets (all English) to be unified through common cantus firmi into so-called tenor masses.[3] Trent 93 and Trent 90, both assembled during the 1450s, preserve a broad spectrum of slightly later English masses, alongside the earliest cyclic masses by Continental composers, datable between the later 1430s and the early 1450s. Finally, the three last-compiled codices, Trent 88, 89 and 91, illustrate the explosive growth of cyclic Ordinary production among composers of Dufay's generation and the one immediately following, between the later 1450s and the early 1470s. The focus of the present article is on six masses from this latest layer of the Trent repertory. All of them belong to a class of settings well represented, even favoured, there: they take their pre-existent material not from the plainchant repertory, as do the earliest cantus firmus cycles, but rather from secular songs.

Adige and the prince-bishopric of Salzburg. I am grateful to Leofranc Holford-Strevens for his remarks on this point.

[1] Thematic indexes for Trent 87–92 and 93 appear in Denkmäler der Tonkunst in Österreich 14–15 and 61. Their overall total of 1864 items incorporates individually numbered movements of cyclic masses as well as several hundred concordances among the seven manuscripts.

[2] The most detailed chronology for the Trent Codices to date has been developed by Suparmi Elizabeth Saunders, through study of watermarks in the manuscripts (*The Dating of the Trent Codices from their Watermarks, with a Study of the Local Liturgy of Trento in the Fifteenth Century*, Outstanding Dissertations from British Universities, ed. J. Caldwell (New York, 1989)). Saunders dates the watermarks in Trent 87 and Trent 92 between 1435 and 1445 (pp. 55–62). Similar conclusions are reached by Peter Wright (*The Related Parts of Trento, Museo Provinciale d'Arte, MSS 87 [1374] and 92 [1379]: A Paleographical and Text-Critical Study*, Outstanding Dissertations from British Universities, ed. J. Caldwell (New York, 1989)).

[3] For an insightful discussion of the Trent Codices' centrality to this earliest mass repertory, see R. Strohm, 'Zur Rezeption der frühen Cantus-firmus-Messe im deutschsprächigen Bereich', *Deutsch-englische Musikbeziehungen: Referate des wissenschaftlichen Symposions in Rahmen der Internationalen Orgelwoche 1980, 'Musica Britannica'*, ed. W. Konold (Munich and Salzburg, 1985), pp. 9–38.

The Trent song masses are dazzling in their variety: the twenty-six cycles demonstrably based on songs (even more may relate to lost song models) make up a small encyclopaedia of fifteenth-century constructive techniques. Yet these works have proved a frustration as well as a boon to historical understanding of the Ordinary form, for most of them are preserved anonymously. The scribes responsible for the later Trent volumes did not make a habit (as had their predecessors in Trent 87 and 92, to a limited extent) of inscribing composers' names above their copies, and any indexes that might have held those names instead have vanished. Some cycles have concordances that carry attributions, but the majority do not.[4]

Anonymous preservation is, of course, the rule rather than the exception in sacred sources from the later fifteenth century. The anonymous Trent masses, however, are further compromised by the mysterious nature of the collection itself. We know the names of two of the scribes principally responsible for the manuscripts – Johannes Lupi and Johannes Wiser, both affiliated with the cathedral of Trent – and even details about the careers of both these men. Yet we still have no clear idea of their purposes in copying such vast quantities of difficult polyphony; both were clerics whose professional involvement with music seems to have been limited at best. What is more, we do not know where or how they obtained their polyphony in the first place. The anonymous unica among the Trent masses thus lack not only verifiable authors but also provenances.

Recent research on the codices, by Reinhard Strohm in particular, has tended increasingly to identify them as 'Germanic' sources.[5] The volumes spent several centuries in the Cathedral

---

[4] For instance, the earliest exemplar of one historically crucial cycle, Dufay's *Missa Se la face ay pale*, is preserved anonymously in Trent 88 (fols. 97ᵛ–105ʳ); only a later concordance (in CS 14) provides the attribution.

[5] In a series of articles published over the last fifteen years, Strohm has brilliantly and decisively redefined modern understanding of the Trent sources. In addition to the article cited above (n. 3), see the following: 'Die *Missa super Nos amis* von Johannes Tinctoris', *Die Musikforschung*, 32 (1979), pp. 34–51; 'Quellenkritische Untersuchungen an der Missa Caput', *Quellenstudien zur Musik der Renaissance* II: *Datierung und Filiation von Musikhandschriften der Josquinzeit*, Wolfenbütteler Forschungen 26, ed. L. Finscher (Wiesbaden, 1984), pp. 153–76; 'Die vierstimmige Bearbeitung (um 1465) eines unbekannten Liedes von Oswald von Wolkenstein', *Jahrbuch der Oswald-von-Wolkenstein-Gesellschaft*, 4 (1987), pp. 163–72; 'Native and Foreign Polyphony in Late Medieval Austria', *Musica Disciplina*, 38 (1984), pp. 205–30; 'Messzyklen über deutsche Lieder

207

Chapter Library of Trent, an Italian-speaking town located south of the Brenner Pass on the Tyrolean border;[6] they may also have been created in Trent, or at least intended for some kind of use there, since both of their principal scribes, Wiser and Lupi, lived in the city for long periods.[7] These men, though, were not themselves Italian: they belonged to the clerical class, Germanic rather than Italian both ethnically and linguistically, that in the fifteenth century ruled Trent as the southernmost extension of the German or Holy Roman Empire. Both had ties to the Habsburg emperor, Frederick III (r. 1440–97), whose court was based for the most part at Wiener Neustadt, just south-west of Vienna. Both had, as well, links to the Habsburg court closer to Trent, at Innsbruck (on the northern side of the Brenner Pass), where Frederick's cousin Sigismund ruled as duke of the Tyrol. At one or both of these Habsburg establishments the Trent scribes may well have found many of their exemplars, for each included a musical chapel of considerable size.[8] Indeed, to the extent that the codices reflect principally

---

in den Trienter Codices', *Liedstudien: Wolfgang Osthoff zum 60. Geburtstag*, ed. M. Just and R. Wiesend (Tutzing, 1989), pp. 77–106. Key insights from these articles are synthesised in Strohm's comprehensive view of fifteenth-century history, *The Rise of European Music, 1380–1500* (Cambridge, 1993), which appeared after this article had been submitted for publication.

[6] The manuscripts are listed under the group signature 'BL' in the earliest catalogue (1748) of the Cathedral Chapter Library; no records concerning their donation to the library appear to have survived.

[7] Johannes Lupi was tentatively identified as the principal scribe of Trent 87 and 92 by Renato Lunelli ('La patria dei codici Trentini', *Note d'Archivio*, 4 (1927), pp. 116–28). Wright (*The Related Parts*, pp. 93–113 and *passim*) confirmed Lunelli's intuition, and provided extensive new information on Lupi's career; in particular, he demonstrated that Lupi also copied a large-format polyphonic manuscript probably used by the imperial court chapel, and so may have had formal duties in connection with music there. Once at Trent, Lupi was also active as an organist at the cathedral.

Unlike Lupi, Johannes Wiser signed his work in two of the codices (on Trent 93, fol. 125ᵛ, and Trent 90, fol. 465ᵛ), and so has been known to Trent scholarship from the outset. Wiser may also have been an organist (Wright adduces a document identifying him as *pulsator*) and, as *rector scolarum* at the cathedral school (a post he held between the late 1450s and June 1465), may have had responsibility for musical instruction there. His musical literacy, however, was limited (as shown by M. Bent, 'Trent 93 and Trent 90: Johannes Wiser at Work', *I codici musicali trentini ... Atti del convegno Laurence Feininger*, ed. N. Pirrotta and D. Curti (Trent, 1986), pp. 84–111). There is in general no solid evidence that musical practice at the cathedral or its school, during the period in which the Trent collection was assembled, exceeded bare liturgical necessity.

[8] Published archival research on both Frederick's and Sigismund's chapels is limited and outdated. On the imperial court, see H. J. Moser, *Paul Hofhaimer: Ein Lied- und Orgelmeister des deutschen Humanismus*, 2nd edn (Stuttgart, 1929; repr. 1966), pp. 10–11

the repertories of these chapels, they are not just 'Germanic', but rather specifically 'Austrian' sources, although they may preserve as well music from south-German centres such as Nuremberg and Munich.[9]

Strohm has synthesised the scholarship of several generations with his own findings to reconstruct an 'Austrian' practice of sacred polyphony from which a collection as extensive as the Trent Codices could have arisen.[10] First, he has assembled evidence from other surviving manuscripts – several discovered only recently, as fragments – to demonstrate an active Austrian reception of western works well back into the 1300s, in monastery, cathedral and university circles, as well as at the Habsburg courts. What is more, Strohm has delineated within the codices a large group of Ordinary settings (along with other works) that use chant variants and songs peculiar to south-German sources, and that are therefore almost certainly actual Austrian productions.[11] Some of these date from as early as the 1440s,

and 170, n. 16; H. Federhofer, 'Die Niederländer an den Habsburgerhöfen in Österreich', *Anzeiger der Österreichischen Akademie der Wissenschaften*, 7 (1956), pp. 102–20; G. Pietzsch, *Fürsten und fürstliche Musiker im mittelalterlichen Köln*, Beiträge zur Rheinischen Musikgeschichte 66 (Cologne, 1966); and I. Rumbold, 'The Compilation and Ownership of the "St Emmeram" Codex (Munich, Bayerische Staatsbibliothek, Clm 14274)', *Early Music History*, 2 (1982), pp. 161–235. On Innsbruck, see W. Senn, *Musik und Theater am Hof zu Innsbruck* (Innsbruck, 1954), chs. 1 and 2. These studies are summarised (and supplemented, to some extent, with fresh information) in G. Gruber, 'Beginn der Neuzeit', *Die Musikgeschichte Österreichs*, ed. R. Flotzinger and G. Gruber (Graz, Vienna and Cologne, 1977), I, pp. 173–227.

⁹ For a summary of archival information about polyphonic practice in fifteenth-century south Germany, see Gruber, 'Beginn der Neuzeit'. Keith Polk's recent work concerning instrumental practice in the same region has revealed a high and generally unrecognised degree of development ('Instrumental Music in the Urban Centres of Renaissance Germany', *Early Music History*, 7 (1989), pp. 159–86). More research into the state of vocal polyphony may well yield results at least partially parallel to his.

¹⁰ See especially 'Native and Foreign Polyphony'. Strohm draws upon recent manuscript discoveries (e.g. W. Pass, 'Eine Handschrift aus dem Schottenstift zu Wien zu Erklärung der Trienter Codices?', *Österreichische Musikzeitung*, 35 (1980), pp. 143–53; W. L. Smith, 'An Inventory of Pre-1600 Manuscripts Pertaining to Music in the Bundesstaatliche Studienbibliothek of Linz, Austria', *Fontes Artis Musicae*, 27 (1980), pp. 162–9), as well as on older studies by Hans Joachim Moser, Gerhard Pietzch and others.

¹¹ Strohm has focused on mass cycles 'labelled' in the sources with Germanic tenor incipits, such as the *Missa Grüne Linden* (Trent 88) or the *Missa Gross Sehnen* (Trent 89) and on others identified as Germanic by modern scholars, such as the *Missa Deutsches Lied* (Trent 89), first paired with its song model in L. R. Gottlieb, 'The Cyclic Masses of Trent 89' (Ph.D. dissertation, University of California at Los Angeles, 1958). He has added to the group the cycle *Christus surrexit* (attributed years ago to Dufay), by showing that it uses a melody ubiquitous in chant sources from

and show polyphonists in Austria making independent use of ambitious forms – in addition, that is, to the modestly functional liturgical forms grudgingly credited to them by previous historiography.[12]

Strohm's establishment of the Austrian roots of the codices raises urgent questions in turn. To start with, who were the polyphonists responsible for the 'Austrian' repertory in the manuscripts? Were they natives of German-speaking lands – polyphonists, that is, who learnt their craft in the absence of any direct contact with the great centres of polyphonic practice in the Low Countries, England and northern France?[13] Or were at least some of them in fact westerners?

east of the Rhine with the German text 'Christ ist erstanden' and all but unknown in the west ('Messzyklen', pp. 81–2). Strohm ('Zur Rezeption') also traces specifically Germanic variants in more widely distributed cantus firmi (for example, those of the Gloria–Credo pairs *Dixerunt discipuli* and *Patris sapientia* in Trent 93).

Chant-orientated studies have not as yet revealed the exact locations of polyphonic practice in Austria or south Germany, since little precise information is available about chant dialects in use at either of the Habsburg chapels or at other likely centres. Possibly, though, the imperial court relied on chants from the diocese of Passau: Frederick III's principal residences (Wiener Neustadt, Graz and Linz) fell under the jurisdiction of the diocese of Salzburg, but he staffed the newly built Residenzkirche at Wiener Neustadt with Augustinian clerics from the Vienna Dorotheenkloster, who might have brought Passau-dialect chant manuscripts with them. See J. Wodka, *Die Kirche in Österreich: Wegweiser durch ihre Geschichte* (Vienna, 1959), pp. 170ff., and G. Gerhartl, 'Wiener Neustadt als Residenz', *Ausstellung Friedrich III (Deutscher Kaiser): Kaiserresidenz Wiener Neustadt*, Katalog des Nord-Österreichischen Landesmuseums, Neue Folge 29, ed. P. Weininger (n.p., 1966). On the relationship between the Passau chant sources and chant arrangements in the later Trent Codices, see A. P. Leverett, 'Paleographical and Repertorial Study of the Manuscript Trento, Castello del Buonconsiglio, 91 (1378)' (Ph.D. dissertation, Princeton University, 1990), ch. 2.

[12] Strohm has made this point eloquently ('Zur Rezeption', pp. 24–5): 'Man konnte sich offenbar nicht vorstellen, da es im österreichischen Raum schon im früheren 15. Jahrhundert eigene Messkompositionen gegeben hatte, die sich nicht von den importierten unterscheiden liessen.'

[13] Several composers prominent in the St Emmeram Codex may be representatives of this group, notably Hermann Edlerawer, identified by Rumbold as a cantor at St Stephen in Vienna. In general, the image of Germanic composers as self-taught provincials has done little to promote their artistic reputation. For some writers on the anonymous Trent repertory, contrapuntal solecisms actually constitute reason to suggest Germanic authorship. Robert Mitchell, for instance, observes of the *Missa Wünschlichen schön* and another anonymous mass in Trent 89, that 'The style of the music ... suggests German provenance, since the writing of both cycles is clumsy in places' ('The Paleography and Repertory of Trent Codices 89 and 91, Together with Analyses and Editions of Six Mass Cycles from Trent Codex 89' (Ph.D. dissertation, University of Exeter, 1989), pp. 85–6). Such pronouncements are particularly common in English-language histories. See, for instance, L. Cuyler, *The Emperor*

That polyphonists born and trained in the West were involved with the Habsburg courts, and possibly with other Austrian institutions as well, has long been established. Frederick III, aspiring to cultural prestige as well as political influence in the West, retained chaplain-singers from western dioceses in considerable numbers from the start of his reign into the late 1470s (when his interest in artistic patronage of all kinds seems to have dropped off).[14] Prominent among these were Johannes Brassart and Johannes Du Sart (both members of the chapel inherited by Frederick from his immediate predecessors), and also

Maximilian I and Music (London, 1973), who characterises Germanic polyphony before Maximilian's era as 'crude' and 'archaic'.

    In general, smaller centres in Austria and south Germany where polyphony was practised seem to have hired (so far as the archival data now available can show) only singers with Germanic surnames; these, if they dealt with polyphony, might well have learnt their trade locally. For an account of one such centre, the cathedral of St Stephen in Vienna, see J. Mantuani, *Die Musik in Wien: Von der Römerzeit bis zur Zeit des Kaisers Max. I* (Vienna, 1907; repr. 1979), pp. 278–377.

[14] Frederick's patronage often went to artists from the westernmost portion of his empire, in architectural and decorative projects as well as in music. (See H. Fillitz, 'Friedrich III und die bildende Kunst', *Ausstellung Friedrich III*, pp. 186–91.) During the 1460s and early 1470s, imperial court documents identify the following men specifically as singers and as westerners (that is, as clerics from western dioceses):

      Adam Hustini de Ora, diocese of Liège
      Nicholas Mayoul, native of Hesdin, diocese of Namur (see n. 15)
      Andreas Mayoul (presumably related to Nicholas)
      Arnold Fleron, diocese of Liège
      Arnold Pickhart, diocese of Liège
      Edigius Garin, diocese of Liège
      Johannes Bubay, diocese of Liège
      Johannes Du Sart, diocese of Noyons.

(This list is drawn from Pietzch, *Fürsten und fürstliche Musiker*, with additions supplied from Vatican documents by Pamela Starr in a letter of 11 October 1990; I am grateful to her for allowing me to cite her discoveries.)

    Perhaps the strongest indication of a special status for western singers at the imperial court is the consistent documentation of a second group of singers (first discovered by Moser) as 'German' ('dewtsche kantoresen'). These singers, all with apparently Germanic surnames, were assigned to Frederick's newly constructed castle church at Wiener Neustadt ('der newn cappellen auf dem tor in der burg zu der Newnstadt'); they may be identical with Frederick's Viennese Augustinians, mentioned above in n. 11. These singers could have been responsible for plainchant services, leaving polyphonic performance to Frederick's western-dominated personal chapel. The Innsbruck chapel seems not to have hired westerners on any long-term basis. Instead, it would apparently contract for limited service from composers such as Isaac, who stopped there on what was evidently a journey between his homeland and Italy in 1484. (See M. Staehelin, *Die Messen Heinrich Isaacs*, Publikationen der Schweizerischen Musikforschernden Gesellschaft, ser. 2, 8 (Berne, 1977), II, *Biographie*, p. 19, and Senn, *Musik und Theater*, p. 10.)

Nicholas Mayoul, who after leaving imperial service continued his career in the Burgundian chapel; Brassart and Du Sart were certainly composers, and very probably others were as well.[15] Thus, while we still do not know much about the social position of polyphonists during the period of the codices' compilation – about what institutions supported them by what means, or about who listened to their music – it seems possible to draw an analogy between Austria and the Italian peninsula of the same period: western polyphonists, gathered in a few centres around the most lavish available patronage, may have been producing the most prestigious sacred polyphony on the scene, meanwhile training a new generation of native-born polyphonists that would ascend to the front ranks with the turn of the century, during Maximilian's reign. As in Italy, other aspects of musical life (in Italy, vocal improvisation; in Austria, instrumental performance, notably organ-playing) were left to native-born practitioners.[16]

The Trent Codices, as representatives of this hybrid musical world, must include two classes of works. First, they contain many pieces – some famous, others obscure – brought by western polyphonists or collectors into Austria for performance there; most of the attributable works in the manuscripts fall into this

[15] Brassart came to imperial service after a considerable career in the West, including a stint in the papel chapel; he was the head of a chapel inherited by Frederick from his predecessor Sigismund, and came – like several others in that group – from the diocese of Liège. (See Federhofer, 'Die Niederländer', and K. Mixter, 'Johannes Brassart: A Biographical and Bibliographical Study', *Musica Disciplina*, 18 (1964), pp. 37–62, and 19 (1965), pp. 99–128.) Nicholas Mayoul replaced him as chapelmaster sometime before 1467, and remained in that post until about 1480; in 1485, he became head of the Burgundian chapel under Maximilian. (See Pietzch, *Fürsten und fürstliche Musiker*, p. 69.) Unfortunately, only Brassart and Du Sart, among all Frederick's western musicians, are securely credited with compositions in the Trent Codices or elsewhere. (Strohm has proposed that Arnold Fleron may be the 'Ar. Fer.' responsible for a work in Munich 3154; see 'Messzyklen', n. 39.) Equally vexatious is the lack of documents for two important composers known almost entirely through their work in the Trent Codices, Roullet and Touront, at the imperial court or any other centre.

[16] German instrumentalists were in their turn able to command choice positions at Italian courts. Records at Ferrara, for instance, appear to identify a number of musicians both as Germanic (through designations such as 'tedesco', 'todescho' or the less definite 'd'alemagna') and as instrumentalists ('trombeta' or 'piffaro'). See L. Lockwood, *Music in Renaissance Ferrara, 1400–1505* (Cambridge, MA, 1985), app. 4. Organ-playing, of course, had reached an extraordinary level of development in Germanic lands early in the 1400s, represented by internationally known figures such as Konrad Paumann and Paul Hofhaimer. Polk ('Instrumental Music') details early German ascendancy in string playing as well.

category. They also contain 'Austrian' polyphony – composed by native Austrians, and also by western polyphonists working within Austria. The distinction is important, for 'Austrian' polyphony is not necessarily international-style polyphony that happened to be composed on Austrian soil: it might well, instead, reflect more closely than western music the particular needs and tastes of the Austrian clientele (still unidentified) for which it was composed. Yet, particularly if westerners composed them, 'Austrian' pieces must also resemble the 'imported' works beside them: there is no reason to assume their style to be identifiably provincial. The anonymous Trent repertory, then, poses a tough problem: which works belong to which group? Is a pre-existing Germanic component – a chant melody or a song model distributed only in Germanic sources – the only valid indicator that a work apparently in normal western language was instead composed in or for an Austrian centre? Or are there stylistic features that can identify such Austrian–western compositions even in the absence of pre-existent components?

For four of the six masses to be considered here, Austrian provenance is almost certain in view of the songs to which they relate: all draw their pre-existent cyclic frameworks from Tenorlieder, polyphonic arrangements of German-texted melodies found only in sources from south Germany and Silesia. These masses also relate to each other closely on a number of levels, and together outline a distinctive approach to the Ordinary form, in particular to the use of borrowed song material. In the two further masses to be discussed, the songs that act as cyclic bases give no such clues as to origin: one survives only in the context of the mass itself, and the other is known from western as well as Germanic collections. Both of these works have passed, until now, as 'imported' western works within the codices. However, they follow the group of masses on Tenorlieder in their special disposition of borrowed song material: this common pattern, I suggest, amounts to an 'Austrian manner' of song mass composition, reflective of peculiarly Austrian forms and tastes that prevailed in the centre (or centres) where the masses were created. My aim is to outline one limited way in which international polyphonic language adapts to local purposes within the Austrian–western repertory of the codices. Understanding of such adaptations is the best means we have to reconstruct the special musical world these manuscripts represent, and to place their vast anonymous repertory into a historical context.

The four masses listed (with their song models) in Table 1 form a separate group among the fairly extensive corpus of cycles on Germanic material in the Trent Codices because all involve the technique variously called 'parody', 'imitation' or 'ancillary borrowing'.[17] The other Germanic masses use monophonic cantus firmi (as does the *Missa Christus surrexit*) or else borrow only a tenor line (as does, apparently, the *Missa Gross Sehnen*), rather than an entire polyphonic complex. Our four, however, make unambiguous reference to all the voice-parts in surviving settings of their cyclic tenors.[18] These settings were probably composed during the later 1460s; the masses themselves, although difficult to date precisely through physical data such as watermarks, probably come from roughly the same period, *c.* 1465–70.[19]

---

[17] On the relative merits of these terms, see M. Steib, 'Imitation and Elaboration: The Use of Borrowed Material in Masses from the Late Fifteenth Century' (Ph.D. dissertation, University of Chicago, 1992), ch. 1. Three of the masses (all but the *Missa Zersundert ist*) are discussed and transcribed in R. F. Schmalz, 'Selected Fifteenth-Century Polyphonic Mass Ordinaries Based on Pre-existent German Material' (Ph.D. dissertation, University of Pittsburgh, 1971). The connection between the *Missa Zersundert ist* and its polyphonic model is made in Leverett, 'A Paleographical and Repertorial Study', ch. 5. Mitchell ('The Paleography and Repertory') identified the mass as an elaboration of the *Zersundert ist* tenor melody only, rather than of the polyphonic setting preserved in Glogau.

[18] The German song repertory in the Schedel songbook was probably set down in or after 1467 (the year in which the manuscript's compiler, Hartmut Schedel, returned to Nuremberg from Italy). The Glogau partbooks are perhaps a decade later, but maintain a strongly retrospective orientation. See *Das Glogauer Liederbuch*, ed. C. Väterlein, Das Erbe Deutscher Musik 85–6 (Kassel, 1981), and *Kraków, Biblioteka Jagiellońska, Glogauer Liederbuch*, ed. J. A. Owens, Renaissance Music in Facsimile 6 (New York and London, 1986).

[19] The four masses are impossible to date precisely. Stylistically they are uniform and answer well to a date of composition in the mid- or later 1460s. Physically each presents a different pattern of evidence. The *Missa Wünschlichen schön* Kyrie and Gloria appear in Trent 89 at the end of a fascicle dated by Saunders to *c.* 1460–2 (*The Dating of the Trent Codices*, pp. 91–2 and 199) and by Peter Wright to *c.* 1463 ('The Compilation of the Wiser Manuscripts: Notes and Queries', forthcoming in the proceedings of the Convegno Internazionale sui Codici Musicali Trentini del Quattrocento (Trent, Castello del Buonconsiglio, 24 September 1994). However, the two movements, like so many items in the codices, are later additions to their fascicle, differentiated by ink colour and by details of script style from the main contents there. The near-complete exemplar of the cycle in Strahov is even later, probably from the 1470s. Dates for both composition and copying into Trent 89 probably fall around or after 1465.

The *Missa Deutsches Lied* is also a later addition to its Trent 89 fascicle, dated by

Table 2 shows the layouts and mensural plans of the four masses. Evident at once is their common modest scale. Even the longer Ordinary texts, the Gloria and Credo, receive settings here fewer than 150 breves (or transcribed bars) in length. (Only the Credo of the *Missa Zersundert ist* exceeds this count, as it is the only one of the group that sets the entire text; the three others make substantial cuts.) These movements are compact because their texts are set in large part syllabically. An overall flow of minims and semibreves (constant under both O and C) incorporates frequent dotted patterns and repeated notes; phrase-end melismas are brief. A similar rhythmically dense language dominates the settings of the shorter Ordinary texts (Kyrie, Sanctus, Agnus Dei) as well, although these are necessarily more melismatic.

This busy melodic and rhythmic surface is a major locus of the four cycles' 'Germanic' character, for it recalls the Tenorlieder that provide their pre-existing material. Polyphonic Tenorlieder of this period still display the key feature of the form in its early phases: faster-moving outer parts complement a slower, more lyrical presentation of a principal melody in the tenor line. The same approach is common to Germanic chant arrangements of the fifteenth and early sixteenth centuries; it is called, in that context, *contrapunctus fractus*. In the masses, there is no real question of *fractus* style, since the borrowed tenors, as we shall see,

Saunders to *c.* 1466 (*The Dating of the Trent Codices*, pp. 91–2 and 200) and by Wright to 1468 ('The Compilation of the Wiser Manuscripts'). The entry immediately preceding it there (a Credo I setting attributed elsewhere to Nicasius da Clibano) is in fact a direct copy from Munich 3154, where the piece is on paper dated by Noblitt considerably later, to 1475–6. (See T. Noblitt, 'Die Datierung der Hs. Mus. Ms. 3154 der Staatsbibliothek München', *Die Musikforschung*, 27 (1974), pp. 36–56, esp. p. 39; the copying relationship is demonstrated in Leverett, 'A Paleographical and Repertorial Study', pp. 119–22.) Even if Noblitt's dating were a little too late, then, the mass was probably copied early in the 1470s.

The *Missa Sig säld und heil* is the main entry in a still-undated fascicle of Trent 91. Other entries in the fascicle, however, as well as the general type of its watermark, suggest the later 1460s as a reasonable dating for the copy. (See Leverett, 'A Paleographical and Repertorial Study', pp. 52–6, and P. Wright, 'Paper Evidence and the Dating of Trent 91', forthcoming in *Music and Letters*; I am grateful to Dr Wright for allowing me to see a typescript of this article in advance of its publication.)

The *Missa Zersundert ist* is the main entry in a Trent 91 fascicle dated by Saunders to 1468 (*The Dating of the Trent Codices*, pp. 103–5 and 201) but by Wright considerably later, to 1474 ('Paper Evidence'; see also Leverett, 'A Paleographical and Repertorial Study', p. 58).

215

Table 1 Sources and editions for the four masses on Tenorlieder and their models

Mass	Sources	Model/Sources	Editions
Wünschlichen schön (a3: D c1, T c4, Ct f3)	Tr 89 fols. 162ᵛ–164ʳ (K, G only); Str nos. 104–5 (G, C) and 107–9 (S, K, A); Spec pp. 168–70 (C only)	Sched no. 115, fols. 132ᵛ–133ᵛ; Bux no. 237; citations in quodlibets Munich 3154 no. 60 and Glo no. 119	Mass: Schmalz nos. 10–14, pp. 265–87; model: EDM 39, p. 398, MS facs. EDM 84
Deutsches Lied (a3: D c1, T c4, Ct f3)	Tr 89 fols. 408ᵛ–413ᵛ (K–S only)	Sched no. 114, fols. 131ᵛ–132ʳ	Mass: Schmalz nos. 6–9, pp. 245–64, Gottlieb pp. 222–33; model: Gottlieb pp. 234–5, MS facs. EDM 84
Sig säld und heil (a4: D c1b, T c4b, Ct1 c4b, Ct2 f4bb)	Tr 91 fols. 216ᵛ–225ʳ; Str fols. 81ᵛ–82ʳ (S only); Tr 89 fol. 425ʳ (start of Ct2)	Sched no. 126, fols. 122ᵛ–123ʳ (Ct only fol. 143ᵛ); Bux no. 229; citation in quodlibet Glo no. 119	Mass: Schmalz nos. 1–5, pp. 225–45; model: EDM 38, p. 286, MS facs. EDM 84
Zersundert ist das junge Herze mein (a4: D c2, T c4, Ct1 c4, Ct2 f3)	Tr 91 fols. 61ʳ–70ʳ	Glo no. 233	Mass: Leverett no. 7, II, pp. 235–53; model: EDM 4, no. 64

Key to abbreviations: D = discantus; T = tenor; Ct = contra(tenor); Ct1 = contratenor primus/altus; Ct2 = contratenor secundus/bassus; K = Kyrie; G = Gloria; C = Credo; S = Sanctus; A = Agnus Dei; EDM = Das Erbe Deutscher Musik.

Gottlieb = L. R. Gottlieb, 'The Cyclic Masses of Trent Codex 89' (Ph.D. dissertation, University of California at Los Angeles, 1958).

Leverett = A. P. Leverett, 'A Paleographical and Repertorial Study of the Manuscript Trento, Castello del Buonconsiglio, 91 (1378)' (Ph.D. dissertation, Princeton University, 1990).

Schmalz = R. F. Schmalz, 'Selected Fifteenth-Century Polyphonic Mass Ordinaries Based on Pre-existent German Material' (Ph.D. dissertation, University of Pittsburgh, 1971).

Table 2 Formal plans of the four masses on Tenorlieder

Wünschlichen schön	Deutsches Lied	Sig säld und heil	Zersundert ist
Kyrie 1 O, 16 b	Kyrie 1 O, 18 b	Kyrie 1 O, 16 b	Kyrie 1 O, 12 b
Christe ₵, 30 l; a2	Christe ₵, 14 l	Christe ₵, 19 l; a2	Christe ₵, 13 l
Kyrie 2 C, 18 b	Kyrie 2 ₵, 8 l	Kyrie 2 [O], 18 b	Kyrie 2 O, 8 l
Et in terra O, 35 b	Et in terra O, 53 b	Et in terra O, 32 b	Et in terra O, 27 b
Domine Deus ₵, 47 l		Domine Deus O, 18 b; a2	Domine Fili O, 15 b; a3
		Qui tollis ₵, 29 l	Qui tollis ₵, 23 l
	Quoniam O, 15 b	Quoniam O, 19 b	Tu solus O, 14 b
Cum sancto O, 11 b			Amen [O2], 10 l
Patrem O, 38 b	Patrem O, 30 b	Patrem O, 44 b	Patrem O, 33 b
		Qui propter ₵, 16 b; a3	Qui propter ₵, 14 l; a3
	Genitum ₵, 11 l		
Et incarnatus ₵, 21 l	Et incarnatus O, 12 b; a2	Et incarnatus ₵, 25 l; a3	Et incarnatus ₵, 25 l; a3
Crucifixus O, 13 b (ends with 'Et sepultus est')	Crucifixus O, 28 b (cuts 'Et in spiritum')	Crucifixus [O], 18 b (ends with 'Et sepultus est')	Crucifixus O, 40 b (internal section in O3)
			Qui cum Patre C, 28 b
	Confiteor O, 20 b		Confiteor O, 17 b
Sanctus O, 23 b	Sanctus O, 23 b	Sanctus O, 20 b	Sanctus O, 16 b
Pleni sunt O, 13 b	Pleni sunt ₵, 16 l	Pleni O, 18 b; a3	Pleni O, 15 b; a3
Osanna 1/2 O2, 9 l	Osanna (1?) O2, 11 l	Osanna 1/2 O, 14 b	Osanna 1 O, 9 b
Benedictus ₵, 26 l; a2	Benedictus C2, 21 l; a2	Benedictus ₵, 29 l; a2	Benedictus ₵, 20 l; a2
	(lost Osanna 2?)		Osanna 2 ₵, 11 l
Agnus Dei O, 20 b (3rd invocation only)	(lost Agnus Dei?)	Agnus Dei 1 O, 20 b	Agnus Dei 1 O, 17 b
		Agnus Dei 2 ₵, 31 l; a3	Agnus Dei 2 ₵, 18 l; a2
		Agnus Dei 3 O, 18 b (2nd discantus part added)	Agnus Dei 3 O, 17 b (Ctl becomes 2nd discantus)

Key to abbreviations: b = breves; l = longs.

actually do move in rhythmic synchrony with their surroundings; indeed, these works all display an imitative integration among voice-parts to match that in most western works of the same age.[20] They present, rather, what may be a deliberate facsimile of the nervous, angular sound typical of genuine *fractus* forms. Example 1 gives an illustration from the Credo of the *Missa Sig säld und heil*: here frequent repeated notes (enforcing syllabic text-setting) and leaps by thirds recall added parts that need such devices to create varied consonant sonorities against drawn-out tenor notes. (Note, however, the two substantial imitations between discantus and tenor at bars 6–7 and 11–16.)[21]

The four masses also show, in Table 2, common details of mensural usage. Two, the *Missa Sig säld und heil* and the *Missa Zersundert ist*, use perfect division of the semibreve (₵ or O3) in all parts for one of the inner sections of their Credo movements. Two others (the *Missa Wünschlichen schön* and the *Missa Deutsches Lied*) call for perfect minor modus (O2) in their Osanna sections.[22] Two (those on *Deutsches Lied* and *Zersundert ist*) distinguish between ₵ and C or C2. The table shows, too, how formal divisions in the masses run parallel: all the Credo settings, for instance, make breaks both at 'Et incarnatus' and 'Crucifixus', then (in the two that continue) at 'Confiteor'.

Ties between the masses go beyond these formal aspects, in that the cycles also cite each other – or rather, they cite the same complex of Germanic songs and plainchants. The relationships

---

[20] The voice-parts of the three-voice masses follow the normal pattern of a syntactically coherent discantus–tenor pair fleshed out by a contra, which here functions largely as a bass part. The four-voice masses, however, display at times a thickness of texture and an ambiguity of voice-part roles that has led Mitchell to view them as three-voice constructions later equipped with a fourth voice, perhaps by the same (and in Mitchell's view somewhat clumsy) redactor ('The Paleography and Repertory', pp. 111–12 and 115).

[21] The anonymous *Missa Grüne Linden* (Trent 88, fols. 375ᵛ–384ʳ) also displays this quick syllabic declamation within small overall dimensions. This mass is not considered here because its model is monophonic, and because its construction is quite different from that of the four masses chosen. None the less, it may be an earlier prototype for these (Saunders, *The Dating of the Trent Codices*, places the paper of its copy c. 1461), if not actually a member of the same repertorial group. The several links it has with them will be pointed out in subsequent footnotes.

[22] O2 is not frequent as a signature in the later fifteenth century; it plays a special role in the works of Busnoys. See R. Taruskin, *The Latin-Texted Works of Antoine Busnoys* (New York, 1990), pt 3, pp. 31ff.

Song masses in the Trent Codices

Example 1. Anon., *Missa Sig säld und heil* (beginning of Credo)

Example 1 (*cont.*)

between them are summarised in Table 3. Strohm identified the opening of the discantus line of the *Missa Wünschlichen schön* Kyrie as a citation from the chant *Cunctipotens genitor* (*Graduale Romanum* Mass IV); he showed also that the openings of the contratenor of the Gloria and the discantus of the Credo in the same mass briefly cite, respectively, the Gloria melody assigned to Mass IV in the *Graduale Romanum* and the Credo *Cardinale* (*Graduale Romanum* Credo IV).[23] But the discantus line of the Sanctus also starts by quoting a chant melody (Thannabaur no. 182) widely

[23] 'Die *Missa super Nos amis*', p. 43.

Table 3 *Citations of chants and songs (other than main models) in the four masses on Tenorlieder*

Mass/Location/Bars	Chants	Songs
Missa Wünschlichen schön		
Kyrie 1 (D 1–4)	*GR* Mass IV Kyrie	
Et in terra (Ct 1–3)	*GR* Mass IV Gloria	
Patrem (D 1–4)	*GR* Credo IV	
Et incarnatus (D, T 1–11)		Unknown song 1
Sanctus (D 1–4)	Thannabaur no. 182	
Agnus Dei (T 1–2)	same melody as Sanctus	
Missa Deutsches Lied		
Patrem (D 12–17)		*Sig säld und heil*
Genitum (D, T 1–10)		Unknown song 2
Sanctus (T 9–16)	Thannabaur no. 182	
Missa Sig säld und heil		
Kyrie 1 (Ct1 1–5)	*GR* Mass IX Kyrie	
Qui tollis (D, T 1–9)		Unknown song 1
Sanctus (D, chant intonation)	Thannabaur no. 48	
Missa Zersundert ist		
Crucifixus		
(D, T 1–12)		*Missa Deutsches Lied* model
(D, T 13–20)		Schedel no. 116
(D, T 21–31)		Unknown song 2

Note: Bar numbers are calculated from the beginning of formal subsections.

Key to abbreviations: D = discantus; T = tenor; Ct = contratenor; Ct1 = contratenor primus; Tb = tenor bassus; *GR* = *Graduale Romanum*.

Thannabaur = P. J. Thannabaur, *Das einstimmige Sanctus der römischen Messe in der handschriftlichen Überlieferung des 11. bis 16. Jahrhunderts* (Munich, 1962).

distributed in Germanic *Ordinaria* and usually rubricated, like the *Cunctipotens genitor* melody in the same sources, for general use on solemn feasts.[24] In the Sanctus of the *Missa Deutsches Lied*,

---

[24] This Sanctus chant, in the first mode, is catalogued in P. J. Thannabaur, *Das einstimmige Sanctus der römischen Messe in der handschriftlichen Überlieferung des 11. bis 16. Jahrhunderts* (Munich, 1962). Most of its manuscript appearances bear rubrics similar to that given to the chant in the printed *Graduale Pataviense* of 1511: 'Aliud sole[m]ne communiter in omnibus festis'.

this same chant turns up again, set with minimal ornamentation at bars 9–16 of the tenor.[25] The chant is repeated, in most of its monophonic sources, as an Agnus Dei: by clear analogy to this common Germanic practice, it forms the incipit of the tenor line in the Agnus Dei of the *Missa Wünschlichen schön*. The citation there, however, is taken not from the beginning of the chant, but from the section of the melody to which the third Agnus Dei invocation is normally underlaid in chant sources: the single Agnus Dei section surviving for the mass must thus be – as Strohm suspected – the fragmentary conclusion of a two- or three-part movement.[26]

Song citations also draw the four cycles together. Links of this kind are closest between the *Missa Deutsches Lied* and the *Missa Zersundert ist*. The Credo of the *Missa Zersundert ist* cites not only the textless main model for the *Deutsches Lied* cycle (Schedel no. 114), but another, still unidentified, song quoted in the *Deutsches Lied* Credo at 'Genitum non factum'.[27] The *Deutsches Lied* Credo further incorporates a quotation of *Sig säld und heil* – the main model, that is, for one of the other masses in the group. The *Wünschlichen schön* Credo, finally, quotes (at 'Et incarnatus est') what is probably a song melody in common with the *Sig säld* Gloria (at 'Qui tollis peccata mundi').[28]

---

[25] Mitchell also has noted the appearance of Thannabaur no. 182 in the *Deutsches Lied* Sanctus, although he does not mention the *Wünschlichen schön* citations ('The Paleography and Repertory', p. 104). The same chant provides the prefatory intonation to the Sanctus of the *Grüne Linden* cycle.

[26] 'Messzyklen', pp. 95–6. The lost Agnus Dei movement for the *Missa Deutsches Lied* would presumably have re-used the chant yet again, by analogy with the *Wünschlichen schön* movement. The chant is catalogued as no. 216 in M. Schildbach, 'Das einstimmige Agnus Dei und seine handschriftliche Überlieferung vom 10. bis 16. Jahrhundert' (Ph.D. dissertation, University of Erlangen-Nuremberg, 1967).

[27] Mitchell ('The Paleography and Repertory', pp. 111–12) identifies this quotation with Schedel no. 56, *Er het mein Lib*, but the correspondence he cites is tenuous at best. (He does not note the parallel quotation in the *Deutsches Lied* cycle.) His identification of a further song quotation in the *Zersundert ist* Credo (Schedel no. 116, *Ich frew mich zu der Wedefahrt*, at 'secundum scripturas' in the Credo) is surely correct; however, that song makes no further appearance in the other masses considered here.

[28] All four masses almost certainly cite numerous other songs as well, alongside their main models, in addition to the few cited jointly. This profusion of song quotations draws the works towards a special category of masses usually assigned to the end of the century, the so-called *Missa Carminum*, composed by Obrecht, Pipelare, Isaac and Rener, among others. These later works differ from our 1460s group in that none is dominated by a single song tenor: continuity arises from a flow of song-quotations set imitatively in all the voice-parts. Still, both groups of masses are close in spirit

The network of song and chant quotations within our mass group may be more than coincidental. Indeed, taken together with the four cycles' general stylistic consistency and formal similarity, these look like deliberate cross-references. Possibly, then, we are looking at the remnants of what was once an organised repertory of small-scale Mass Ordinary settings, similar to the series of Proper settings preserved more or less intact in Trent 88.[29] Five groupings of these Proper movements have recently been identified by Alejandro Enrique Planchart and William Prizer with the weekly round of votive Masses offered in the Dijon chapel of the Burgundian chivalric Order of the Golden Fleece; like our masses, they are stylistically uniform, and are linked by a web of cross-quoted chant and polyphony.[30] The four masses on Tenorlieder could have belonged to an analogous week-long metacycle of votive Ordinary settings, designed for 'everyday' use in one of the Austrian chapels (where presumably the Proper cycles were also known). They would have made good votive music, for as short works, relatively easy to sing, they would have stood up well to frequent, minimally rehearsed performance. At least one of the set bears clear traces of votive use. The *Missa Sig säld und heil* is preceded, in its one complete reading (Trent 91), by an arrangement of the Marian introit *Salve sancta parens*, a chant suitable for Marian votive Masses

---

to the quodlibet, a form especially strong in the Germanic tradition. Isaac especially may have taken precedents for his *Missa Carminum* from the Austrian circle in which he worked, rather than, as is usually assumed, from Obrecht.

Schmalz ('Selected Fifteenth-Century Polyphonic Mass Ordinaries', pp. 120–38) was the first to identify the *Sig säld* quotation in the *Deutsches Lied* Credo. Realising its significance, he proposed to call the mass *Deutscher Lieder*, to stress the plurality of songs involved. (The label *Missa Deutsches Lied* had been assigned by Gottlieb, who identified the mass's textless principal model.) In light of the discoveries detailed above, however, all of the cycles in this group would require similar adjustments to their titles, so I have retained the singular form (*Deutsches Lied*) here.

[29] The Proper cycles appear on fols. 113ᵛ–200ʳ of Trent 88.

[30] Most of the cross-quotations within the group of Proper cycles are brought about by parallels among the underlying chants, but exercise, none the less, a powerful unifying effect. They are listed in *Auctorum anonymorum missarum propria XVI quorum XI Guilelmo Dufay auctori adscribenda sunt*, ed. L. Feininger, Monumenta Polyphoniae Liturgicae, ser. II, 1 (Rome, 1947–8), pp. i–viii. See also A. E. Planchart, 'Guillaume Du Fay's Benefices and his Relationship to the Court of Burgundy', *Early Music History*, 8 (1988), pp. 117–72, and D. Fallows, 'Dufay and the Mass Proper Cycles of Trent 88', *I codici musicali trentini*, pp. 46–59.

Table 4 *Appearance of main song models in the four masses on Tenorlieder*

Movements/ Subsections	Mass voice-parts (bars)	Model voice-parts (sections)
A. *Missa Wünschlichen schön*		
Kyrie 1	**T 7–16; D 8–16**	**T A (= bars 1–6)** (lengthened values); **D A** (at cadences)
Christe	T, D 7–14	freely adapts T, D B (= bars 6–12)
Kyrie 2	**T 1–18, D 9–18, Ct 7–18**	**T, D, Ct B (= bars 7–12)** (lengthened values)
Et in terra	T 15–20	T A
Domine Deus	D 40–7	T A, 8 ↑
Cum Sancto Spiritu	**T, D 7–13**	**T, D (freely) B**
Patrem	T 20–5	T A
Crucifixus	**T, D 7–13**	**T, D (freely) B**
Sanctus	**T, D 14–19**	**T, D A**
Pleni	D 1–8	T A, 8 ↑
Benedictus	**T 2–6, 22–6; D 21–4**	**T, D (freely) B**
Agnus Dei 3	**T, D, Ct 7–20**	**T, D, Ct A, B**
B. *Missa Deutsches Lied*		
Kyrie 1	D 1–9	T A (= bars 1–9), 5 ↑
	T 9–17, D 10–17, Ct 13–15	**T, D (freely), Ct A**
Kyrie 2	**T, D 1–8**	**T, D (freely) A, B (= bars 10–14)**
Et in terra	D 1–9	T A, 5 ↑
	T 11–30	T A (lengthened values)
	T, D 39–53	**T, D (freely) A, B**
Quoniam	Ct 1–15	T A, B, 4 ↓
Patrem	T 1–9	T A
Et incarnatus	D 1–8	T A, 5 ↑
Confiteor	Ct 1–4, 9–20	T A, B, 4 ↓
Sanctus	D 1–9	T A, 5 ↑ (freely)
Osanna (1?)	Ct 1–9	T A, 4 ↓
(lost Osanna 2?)		(T A, B?)
(lost Agnus Dei?)	(full contrafact exposition?)	

Table 4 (*cont.*)

Movements/ Subsections	Mass voice-parts (bars)	Model voice-parts (sections)
C. *Missa Sig säld und heil*		
Kyrie 1	**T, D 11–15; Ct2 12–15**	**T, D, Ct A (= bars 1–6)**
Kyrie 2	**T, D 7–17; Ct2 8–17**	**T, D, Ct B (= bars 7–16)**
Et in terra	**T, D 6–8**	**T, D A**
	T 25–31	T A
Qui tollis	D 21–7	T A, 5 ↑
Quoniam	**T 8–18, D 12–18, Ct2 10–12**	**T, D, Ct B**
Patrem	**Ct2, D 1–6**	**T, D A, 4 ↓**
Crucifixus	**Ct2, T 5–11**	**T, D B, 4 ↓**
Sanctus	**Ct2, T 10–15**	**T, D A, 8 ↓**
Osanna 1/2	**T, D 3–14**	**T, D B**
Agnus Dei 1	**T, D 12–17**	**T, D A**
Agnus Dei 3	**T, D, Ct2 2–17**	**T, D, Ct A, B**
D. *Missa Zersundert ist das junge Herze mein*		
Kyrie 1	D 1–3	T A (beginning)
	Ct2 3–6, T 6–12	T A (= bars 1–9)
Christe	**T, D 1–4**	**T, D B (= bars 10–16), incomplete**
Kyrie 2	**T, D, much of Ct2 1–8**	**T, D, Ct A, B**
Et in terra	D 1–3	T A (beginning)
	Ct2 5–7	T A, 8 ↓
Qui tollis	T 1–5	T B (incomplete)
Tu solus	**T, D 1–12**	**T, D A, B**
Patrem	D 1–3	T A (beginning)
	Ct2 5–7	T A, 8 ↓
Qui propter	T, D 1–5	**T, D B (incomplete)**
Confiteor	T, D, much of Ct2 1–17	**T, D, Ct A, B**
Sanctus	D 1–3	T A (beginning)
	Ct2 4–6, T 6–10	T A
	T, D 12–16	**T, D B (incomplete)**
Osanna 1	**T, D, much of Ct2 1–7**	**T, D, Ct A**
Osanna 2	**T, D, much of Ct2 1–11**	**T, D, Ct B**
Agnus Dei 1	D 1–17	T A, B, 4 ↑
Agnus Dei 3	**T, D/Ct1, much of Ct2 1–17**	**T, D, Ct A, B**

Note: Bar numbers for masses are calculated from the beginning of formal subsections; bold type indicates contrafact-like sections.

Key to abbreviations: D = discantus; T = tenor; Ct = contratenor; Ct1 = contratenor primus/altus; Ct2 = contratenor secundus/bassus; 8 ↑ = transposed up an octave; 4 ↓ = transposed down a fourth, etc.

through most of the liturgical year; Table 3 shows, further, that the cycle's Kyrie and Sanctus movements open with widely distributed Marian chants.[31]

The four sections (A–D) of Table 4 introduce our main subject: the treatment of song material – both borrowed song tenors and multiple-voice quotations – in these cycles. In both these areas, we shall find some unexpectedly strong parallels. Borrowed song tenors in these works, as in most song-based masses, appear in segments that correspond to the formal sections of the original song: as Tenorlieder, then, they are bisected at the cadence that separates *Stollen* from *Abgesang*. But the expansion of these short Tenorlied segments into mass tenors proceeds along unusual lines. Normally, two basic techniques transform borrowed song tenors into foundations for mass movements. The first stretches out the borrowed line – either systematically, under some procedure expressible as a mensural or verbal canon, or else unsystematically, with note values elongated more or less at random. Alternatively, the song tenor is extended to the necessary length through paraphrase or ornamental elaboration.[32] As a rule, however, neither of these techniques shapes the tenor lines of our four masses.[33] Example 2, drawn from the *Wünschlichen schön* Gloria, shows what happens instead. Here the mass tenor enters with the *Stollen* segment of the borrowed Tenorlied (enclosed in brackets in the example). The song segment sounds uninterruptedly, without rhythmic modification or melodic ornaments of any kind; its notated appearance is essentially unchanged from that in the song. But this initial presentation is quickly over, and from that point the mass tenor must spin out stylistically similar free material through the rest of the section. The song

---

[31] The version of this introit setting in Trent 91 (fols. 215ᵛ–216ʳ) is identical in clefs, signatures and finals, as well as in general contrapuntal style, to the *Sig säld* cycle following. Its three concordances (two in Strahov and one in Trent 89) all present somewhat altered versions of the work, and none of these is associated with the mass.

[32] Richard Taruskin emphasises the polarity of these approaches in contrasting Dufay's embellishment of the *L'homme armé* cantus firmus with the strict presentation common to Busnoys and Ockeghem. The prevalence of strict presentation in later *L'homme armé* masses, he argues, is one reason for tracing the tradition back to these composers rather than to Dufay. See 'Antoine Busnoys and the *L'homme armé* Tradition', *Journal of the American Musicological Society*, 39 (1986), pp. 255–93, esp. p. 260.

[33] Only a few passages in the *Wünschlichen schön* and *Deutsches Lied* cycles elongate values of the song tenor.

Example 2. Anon., *Missa Wünschlichen schön*, mass tenor with quotation of song tenor (Gloria, bars 15–30)

tenor, then, is not really a cantus firmus in any standard sense, for its control over the formation of the polyphony ceases after a few *tempora*. It functions, rather, as an incisive, readily recognisable head-motive for the otherwise free mass tenor – leaving other factors, as we shall see, to supply the long-range influence of model over mass that constitutes cyclic Ordinary form.

Systematic repetition of tenor segments is one of these factors. All individual movements in the four cycles are organised around either one or two usually complete presentations of their borrowed tenor lines, as the four parts of Table 4 indicate.[34] Taken as a whole, each of the masses favours either single or double expositions of its model tenor within its individual movements. The *Missa Wünschlichen schön* is of the single-exposition type: just as the first half of the song (identified as section A in the third column of Table 4) serves as a 'head' to the tenor of the first Gloria section, the second half (section B), after an intermediary section at 'Qui tollis' with tenor omitted, leads off the movement's

---

[34] Not all the tenor presentations discussed above and listed in Table 4 are strictly complete. All, however, set out at least three *tempora* drawn without change from the start of the song tenor segment in question.

conclusion (at 'Cum Sancto Spiritu'). The *Missa Sig säld und heil* follows a similar plan up to the Agnus Dei. (There, the continuous presentation of the song in *Sig säld*'s third invocation matches up with that in the *Wünschlichen schön* movement, which, as we have seen, is actually a third invocation standing alone.) The *Missa Zersundert ist*, by contrast, makes double expositions of its model throughout. In this cycle and in the *Missa Deutsches Lied*, tenor statements sometimes appear in transposition: for example, the *Deutsches Lied* Gloria lays out its statement of the model *Abgesang* in the mass contratenor, a fourth below the song's usual pitch level (where the *Stollen* statement in the tenor earlier in the movement remains).

Within each of the four cycles, several movements further augment the presence of the model by also including the song tenor's first half as a separate unit, sounded in transposition by a voice other than the tenor. Three movements in the *Missa Deutsches Lied*, for instance (Kyrie, Gloria and Sanctus), begin with a statement of the song *Stollen*, transposed a fifth above its pitch level in the song, by the mass discantus. Later on, the *Stollen* segments appear again in the mass tenors, where they lead off the single or double exposition of the complete line. The *Abgesang* segments of the borrowed tenors, however, usually sound only once – perhaps because in performances of the songs themselves only the *Stollen* would repeat.

Song tenors, then, are very similarly handled in all four of our masses. But all four also borrow the discantus parts from extant settings of their tenors, and here we come to the strongest bond of similarity between these works: a song discantus, whenever it appears, is always paired with the borrowed tenor so as to preserve the contrapuntal relationship between the two parts established in the model setting. In some such passages – indeed, in almost all of them within the *Deutsches Lied* and *Zersundert ist* masses – the borrowed discantus is veiled by ornamentation that abates only at cadence points. Often, however, the model's discantus–tenor framework emerges almost untouched from the new polyphony. Examples 3 and 4 (drawn respectively from the *Deutsches Lied* and *Wünschlichen schön* cycles) show the two manners of treatment, florid and straightforward. Particularly in Example 4, the contra line of the model setting is traceable as well. The

Example 3. Comparison of Kyrie 2 of anon., *Missa Deutsches Lied*, with its song model (Schedel no. 114)

(a) Song model (Schedel no. 115)

(b) *Missa Wünschlichen schön*, Agnus Dei

Example 3 (*cont.*)

Example 3 (*cont.*)

Example 4. Comparison of the Agnus Dei of anon., *Missa Wünschlichen schön*, with its song model (Schedel no. 115)

(a) Song model (Schedel no. 114)

(b) *Missa Deutsches Lied*, Kyrie 2

Example 4 (*cont.*)

Example 4 (*cont.*)

original Tenorlied itself, then, coalesces in these passages out of the flow of new polyphony – not only audibly, but visually as well, in that the pitches and note values of the song model emerge unchanged in the mass's voice-parts.

Such massive simultaneous borrowings carry the label 'block quotation' in histories of fifteenth-century borrowing techniques, where they show a venerable lineage.[35] But surely 'block quotations' so extensive and literal as these might better be called 'contrafacts' of songs, although they are embedded within the masses built on the same material.[36] 'Contrafact' is a suggestive term partly because it emphasises the underlying concept of such passages as one not only familiar, but central to Germanic musical

[35] See the discussion of 'block quotation' in E. F. Sparks, *Cantus Firmus in Mass and Motet, 1420–1520* (Berkeley, 1963), pp. 152–4. Sparks uses another anonymous mass from Trent 89, the *Missa Quand ce viendra*, as his primary example.

[36] Strohm, too, uses the term 'contrafact' in connection with parts of these masses ('Messzyklen', pp. 96 and 101). See also Leverett, 'A Paleographical and Repertorial Study', pp. 239ff.

culture of the period. The Trent Codices themselves, along with most Germanic sources of the same age, are full of originally French-texted songs, equipped with new German or Latin words.[37]

Our masses may not be contrafacts in quite the same sense and, of course, the songs had German texts to begin with. Yet the compositional impulse behind the four works is fundamentally akin to that behind retexted songs. Contrafact texts obviously functioned to make foreign songs more accessible to German-speaking singers. The majority of such texts are Latin, however, and these surely worked on another level as well: they adapted songs for use in the extraliturgical but 'serious' performance contexts for which Germanic sources like the Trent manuscripts, the Glogau partbooks and the Strahov Codex were most probably compiled – for monasteries, for cathedral schools and for princely chapels. With their new devotional words, French songs could merge easily into the popular repertory of Latin- and German-texted *leisen* that were already staples within such circles, and that survive in the same sources. Austro-German musicians and collectors, in short, apparently liked the feel of secular style in serious or even sacred contexts. They simply appropriated songs, without much reworking, for devotional use – just as their descendants, the compilers of chorale tunes, were to do during the following century. That 'Austrian' taste emerges in the frank song contrafacts of the Tenorlieder masses.

Contrafact is even, in a sense, the main point these works exist to make, for their episodes of block quotation, much more than the divided and diluted statements of their song tenors, hold them together as cycles and give them their fundamental character. Some kind of reference to the discantus–tenor frame-work of the model setting takes place in almost every movement of each mass. These vary in extent and in fidelity: the first four movements of the *Missa Wünschlichen schön*, for instance, accompany the borrowed tenor's final phrase with sequential imitation approximating that in the model setting, retaining rhythms of discantus and contra but merely approximating their

---

[37] For a comprehensive account of contrafacts in the Trent sources, see D. Fallows, 'Songs in the Trent Codices: An Optimistic Handlist', *I codici musicali trentini*, pp. 170–9.

pitches. Consistently, however, all four cycles place their strongest model statements – their passages of contrafact or near-contrafact – in two locations: in the Kyrie, as a kind of exposition, and in the Agnus Dei. The Agnus Dei statements particularly are crucial for each cycle, as brilliant conclusions (underlined in the two four-voice cycles, as Table 2 shows, by changes in scoring) in which the model songs seem to burst free of their sacred trappings altogether.[38]

Emphasis on contrafact as a unifying element – on the ear-catching presence of the model song in its entirety, notably at the end of the work, rather than on a cantus firmus carried by the tenor alone – may constitute the strongest 'Austrian' element in the four Tenorlieder masses. The limits to such a claim must be clear, for related devices are easy to find in masses known to be from the West: Dufay's *Missa L'homme armé* supplies one famous example of a 'climactic' Agnus Dei (with allusions to the model song in voices other than the tenor), while Busnoys's *Missa L'homme armé* might head a substantial list featuring 'block quotation' of song models.[39] But in western works composed earlier than or contemporaneously with the Tenorlieder masses – before, that is, about 1470 – these two techniques never appear together, never fuse as they do in the four Austrian cycles. Block quotations in western masses, if present in more than one movement to start with, tend to become less complete and less literal as a work progresses; final movements, rather than effecting a return to the model, form instead the point of greatest distance from it.[40] Only later, with the generation of Obrecht and Isaac,

---

[38] The *Missa Deutsches Lied* presents an obvious exception here, since it lacks an Agnus Dei of any kind. But quite possibly that movement, which would have run into an adjacent gathering in Trent 89, the work's unique source, was lost: a second Osanna statement, needed to complete the model tenor exposition in the Sanctus, seems also to be missing. Here again, the *Missa Grüne Linden* offers a close parallel to the cycles on polyphonic Tenorlieder by sounding its cantus firmus as a tenor line, in uniform short values and without ornamentation – in the most easily audible configuration, that is, of the entire cycle – to end the second of its Agnus Dei invocations.

[39] The final Gloria segment ('Tu solus altissimus') of Busnoys's mass follows closely the four-voice *Il sera pour vous/L'homme armé* (in Rome, Biblioteca Casanatense, MS 2856) usually attributed to Robert Morton, but possibly by Busnoys himself. See Taruskin, *The Latin-Texted Works of Antoine Busnoys*, pt 3, pp. 35–7.

[40] One case in point would be the *Missa Le serviteur* of Guillaume Faugues (Trent 88, fols. 411ᵛ–420ᵛ). Faugues incorporates clear block quotations of his model into several movements, but arguably not at all into the Agnus Dei.

do Agnus Dei settings in western masses begin to function as climactic presentations of model songs.[41]

The direct, even earthy approach to model presentation seen in the Trent Tenorlieder masses emerges, then, as a potential stylistic marker. It manifests what may be a distinctively 'Austrian' manner in the construction of song masses, a manner that reflects the apparent popularity, in Germanic sources, of secular style in sacred contexts. Our project now will be to see whether such an 'Austrian manner' also emerges from other song masses whose models are not recognisably Austrian to start with – whether contrafact model treatment, that is, can serve as a clue to provenance, even where other clues are lacking.

To this end, we will turn now to two further anonymous song masses from the Trent collection. Neither the *Missa Monÿel* (Trent 89, fols. 258ʳ–273ʳ) nor the *Missa Gentil madonna mia* (Trent 91, fols. 247ᵛ–257ʳ) can claim a definite provenance on the basis of a song model, although western origins have at times been assumed for both of them. Each of these works, however, exhibits in its own way the same taste for contrafact-like model quotation that shapes the four Tenorlieder cycles.

The *Missa Monÿel* appears in Trent 89 under the name of Johannes Touront. Even acceptance of that ascription, however, gives little insight into the work, for we have no firm idea of where or even when Touront lived and composed. His name (rendered in some sources with 'a's instead of 'o's – 'Taurant' or 'Thauranth') has a French sound to it, suggesting that he

---

[41] For instance, Obrecht's *Missa Rosa playsans* places strong multi-voice quotations in both the Kyrie and the Agnus Dei. This work, however, appears in no source earlier than ModE (Modena, Biblioteca Estense e Universitaria, MS α.M.1.2), which was probably copied *c.* 1505. (See Lockwood, *Music in Renaissance Ferrara*, pp. 216–17 and 226–7.) Strohm has argued that Obrecht had contacts with the Tyrolean court at Innsbruck, and composed his *Missa Maria zart* (on a cantus firmus found in several Austrian sources) to fulfil a commission there (see *The Rise of European Music*, pp. 521–2). An even stronger possibility of Austrian ties exists for Johannes Martini, another composer whose masses (probably from the 1470s) contain block quotations. Strohm has argued forcefully for Austrian influence on Martini (see especially his Communication to the *Journal of the American Musicological Society*, 40 (1987), pp. 576–9) in opposition to J. Peter Burckholder, who sees Martini primarily as a disciple of Ockeghem (see 'Johannes Martini and the Imitation Mass', *Journal of the American Musicological Society*, 38 (1985), pp. 470–523). Leverett ('A Paleographical and Repertorial Study', chs. 4 and 5) similarly posits Martini's indebtedness to Austrian practice.

came from the western reaches of imperial territory, if not from France itself or from the Low Countries. Certainly his music implies ample contact with western circles; imitation and sequence are as central to his counterpoint as to that of Busnoys (probably his near-exact contemporary). Yet the sources preserving Touront's works are almost exclusively Germanic in provenance. The three masses attributed to him, all masterly works, appear only in Trent 89 and in the Strahov Codex, while his smaller pieces appear mostly in these sources and in the Speciálník collection.[42] This situation leads readily to a surmise that his creative career unfolded primarily in eastern Europe.[43]

The *Missa Monÿel* uses an apparently western model.[44] Example 5 is a reconstruction of the two-voice unit that emerges from inter-movement comparison: it is a ballade, with a characteristic mid-point break (at bar 11) and musical rhyme between section endings. (A third common line, presumably the model song's contratenor, is present at some cadential points.) David Fallows has suggested that the tag 'Monÿel', painstakingly included by the Trent scribe below the tenor line of each movement, is a

---

[42] The only work of Touront's to appear in a French source is the widely distributed song-motet *O gloriosa regina mundi*, found in the Pixérécourt chansonnier (Paris, Bibliothèque Nationale, fonds français, MS 15123). A handful of Neapolitan song collections (including Montecassino, Biblioteca dell'Abbazia, MS 871 and Perugia, Biblioteca Communale Augusta, MS 431, as well as Bologna, Civico Museo Bibliografico Musicale, MS Q16) preserve short, mostly secular works attributed to him. Possibly Touront's Neapolitan connections owed something to Vincenet, who served the Neapolitan court after 1469 but may have been in Austria earlier; one of Vincenet's masses is based on *O gloriosa regina mundi*. See Leverett, 'A Paleographical and Repertorial Study', pp. 254–5 and Table 5.10.

[43] Touront may have been the 'Tirion' mentioned in a 1439 funeral motet for the emperor Albrecht II (a suggestion first made by Guillaume de Van, 'A Newly Discovered Source of Early Fifteenth-Century Sacred Polyphony', *Musica Disciplina*, 2 (1948), pp. 5–74, esp. pp. 14–15). He may also have had something to do with the text of *Chorus iste pie Christe*, a contrafacted rondeau attributed to him in the Strahov Codex, which includes a passage imploring divine mercy for Bohemia (see P. Gulke, 'Touront', *Die Musik in Geschichte und Gegenwart*, ed. F. Blume (Kassel and Basle, 1949–86), xiii, cols. 592–3). The Speciálník Codex also credits him with a polyphonic arrangement of the offertory *Recordare virgo mater* that includes the trope 'Ab hoc familia', common in Austria and Bohemian chant rites. (This piece is published from its appearance in Glogau as EDM 85, no. 20; it also appears in Trent 89 without attribution.)

[44] Gottlieb ('The Cyclic Masses of Trent Codex 89', ch. 6) first noticed the parallelisms in the *Missa Monÿel*, although his failure to locate a corresponding model song led him to qualify his conclusions. See also Mitchell's detailed analysis of the cycle in 'The Paleography and Repertory', ch. 4.

Example 5. Reconstruction of the song model for Touront, *Missa Monÿel*

239

Example 5 (*cont.*)

Germanic corruption of the incipit for the French text once carried by this ballade. He proposes as the missing text the ballade 'Mon œil est de tendre temprure', preserved in the Rohan poetry manuscript; the first line of this poem is cited in Molinet's *Debat du viel gendarme et du viel amoreux* (*c.* 1470) as part of a long string of poetic incipits identifiable with surviving polyphonic songs.[45]

Table 5, taking as a starting-point the reconstructed ballade, shows the groundplan of the *Missa Mon œil/Monÿel*, which relates to those of the Tenorlieder masses in several significant ways. Without such schematic reductions, however, any resemblance between them would be easy to miss, for Touront's is a very different sort of cycle: it is a far bigger setting, probably prepared for some special occasion rather than generalised votive use, and shows no trace of the rapid declamation and angular melodic style common to the Austrian works. Further, unlike the small cycles, it treats the song tenor as a genuine cantus firmus, free of interpolations and – thanks to presentation in O, against ₵ in the added voices – in control of the new counterpoint over long stretches. Yet clearly the *Missa Monÿel* is also organised around striking episodes of contrafact-like parody: in the several passages where the discantus and tenor of the model song appear together, they do so as an invariable unit, adhering to the same harmonic and rhythmic axis in each presentation.

As Table 5 also shows, the *Missa Monÿel* utilises other forms of model manipulation common to the Tenorlieder masses. Like them, it divides the model into its component formal sections: for the ballade, these are two principal phrases, A and B, and a refrain, C. (These divisions are labelled in Example 5.) In two of the five movements (Credo and Sanctus), the whole song tenor receives multiple expositions, like those in two of the Tenorlieder cycles. In these movements and the others (apart from the Gloria), tenor phrases also appear separately, just as do the two

---

[45] I am deeply grateful to Dr Fallows for proposing this identification (in a letter of 1 October 1988) for my reconstruction of the song. The poem is the sixth given in the Rohan poetry manuscript (Berlin-Dahlem, Staatliches Museum, Kupferstichkabinett, MS 78.B.17); it also occurs in the *Jardin de plaisance* (Paris: Antoine Verard, 1501) on fol. 80[r]: Molinet's *Debat* cites a song title in the first line of each of its 41 stanzas; 'Mon œil est de tendre temprure' was one of only six such lines which had not, until Fallows's discovery, been identified with a surviving polyphonic song.

Table 5 *Formal plan of and model use in Touront,* Missa Monÿel

Movement/ Subsections	Mass voice-parts (bars)	Model voice-parts (segments)
Kyrie 1 O, 32 b	**Contrafact of whole model?**	
Christe O, 68 b	Tb 17–27	T A, 5 ↓
Kyrie 2 ф, 33 l	D 1–2	T A, 8 ↑ (incomplete)
	Ctl 3–8	T A, 4 ↑
	Tb 8–13	T A, 5 ↓
	Ctl 13–18	T B, 4 ↑
	Tb 19–29	T B, C, 5 ↓
Et in terra O, 67 b	Ctl (functional T) 2–34	D A, B, C, 5 ↓
	Ct2 35–67	T A, B, C
Qui tollis ¢, 53 l (*a3*)		
Cum Sancto Spiritu O, 40 b	Ct2 (functional T) 3–34	D A, B, C, 8 ↓
Patrem O, 80 b	**Ctl, D 1–5**	**T, D A 1–5**
	Tb 29–67	T A, B, C, 5 ↓
Crucifixus ¢/Tb O, 91 l	Tb 34–82	T A, B, C, 5 ↓
Confiteor ф, 23 l	**Ct2, D 1–3**	**T, D A 1–5**
	Tb, Ctl 3–19	**T, D A, B, C, 5 ↓**
Sanctus O, 55 b	D 1–13	D A
	Ctl, D 14–21	**T, D B**
	Tb 23–55	T A, B, C, 5 ↓
Pleni sunt O, 32 b (*a3*)		
Osanna 1 D, Ctl ¢/Ct2 ф	Tb 25–40	T A, 5 ↓
(should be O2)/Tb O, 55 l	D 41–8	T B, 8 ↑
	Ctl 49–56	T C
Benedictus ¢, 38 l (*a3*)		
Osanna 2 ф, 19 l	Tb 5–19	T B, C, 5 ↓
Agnus Dei 1 O, 36 b	**Ct2, D 1–5**	**T, D A 1–5**
	Ctl, 5–25	T A, B, 4 ↑
	Tb 26–36	T A, 5 ↓
Agnus Dei 2 O2, 36 l (*a3*)		
Agnus Dei 3 ф, 39 l (first segment repeats Agnus Dei 1)	**Tb, Ctl 20–39**	**T, D B, C, 5 ↓**

Note: Bar numbers for the mass are calculated from the beginning of formal subsections; sections of model reconstruction are shown in Example 5; bold type indicates contrafact-like sections.

Key to abbreviations: b = breves; l = longs; D = discantus; T = tenor; Ctl = contratenor primus; Ct2 = contratenor secundus; Tb = tenor bassus; 8 ↑ = transposed up an octave; 5 ↓ = transposed down a fifth, etc.

halves of the *Bar*-form models in the Tenorlieder works. (The second Kyrie, the Sanctus and the Agnus Dei, particularly, are structured on this premiss.) Both the tenor by itself and, further, the discantus–tenor pair appear in transposition at the fourth, fifth and octave, as do the model tenors in the anonymous pieces. Transposition is especially critical in the last three movements, where the song tenor, a fifth below its original level, becomes the lowest line of the texture (labelled 'tenor bassus'). This same device appears in the *Missa Sig säld und heil*, where the song tenor is transposed down an octave (within a line called a 'tenor' that functions mostly as a lower contra) for the duration of the Sanctus: in the *Sig säld* Credo, too, the song tenor, transposed a fourth downward, goes 'unofficially' to the voice-part labelled 'contratenor bassus'.[46] The *Missa Monÿel*, however, goes beyond the array of transpositions used in the Tenorlieder masses by transforming the entire borrowed discantus – sounded a fifth, then an octave lower than in its initial presentation – into a tenor line, during the first and last sections of the Gloria.

The *Missa Monÿel*'s most striking likeness to the Tenorlieder masses lies in the climactic reappearance of the model song in the Agnus Dei. In this three-section movement, the third invocation begins by repeating the first invocation, originally in O, at an accelerated tempo indicated by Ȼ; the first segment of the song tenor ('A'), appearing by itself as the mass tenor bassus, thus receives a speeded-up recapitulation. The invocation then goes on to present a complete contrafact of the 'B' and 'C' segments of the ballade: the mass contratenor primus takes up the song discantus, while the tenor bassus continues with the song tenor. Contrafact, then, brings the *Missa Monÿel* to a showy conclusion, with increased speed here bringing about a heightened brilliance and density of sound like that obtained by altered

---

[46] The mass tenor, cleffed and labelled normally, carries mostly free material in this movement. The low transposition of the song tenor in the second contra brings about a relocation of the whole discantus–tenor framework, which constitutes a further special likeness between this work and the *Missa Monÿel*. (The other masses transpose the model tenors only.) Further, a similar blurring of voice-part functions occurs in the Gloria of the *Missa Monÿel* (first section), where the song tenor suddenly appears in the contratenor secundus, without a rubric, and following a lengthy section of free composition in that part; the mass tenor, entering the movement for the first time at this point, has unrelated material.

scoring at the same point – the final Agnus Dei invocation – in the Austrian works.

Touront's mass is far more ambitious in scale than the Tenor-lieder masses; its manipulations of the model song, while parallel to those in the Austrian cycles, are more extensive and elaborate. Thus, it is easy to see as a kind of prototype for the smaller masses – the more so since it exemplifies high western melodic and contrapuntal style, in contrast to the mock *contrapunctus fractus* of the four anonymous works. Did Touront, then, effectively invent 'Austrian taste' in model presentation with the *Missa Monÿel?* Two scenarios are possible here. In the first, Touront need never have set foot east of the Rhine. The *Missa Monÿel* would be an influential 'import' to Germanic circles, just as the English *Missa Caput* seems to have been a generation earlier.[47] In this case, the *Missa Monÿel* itself would not be 'Austrian' – and neither, in any creative sense, would the features replicated from it in the Tenorlieder masses: the prevailing historical picture of Austrian polyphonic practice as small-scale and essentially derivative would stand unchanged. In a second scenario, however, Touront would have composed the cycle for an Austrian chapel, using one of the many western songs surely known to his circle there along with Tenorlieder. Indeed, if it were composed in Austria, Touront's mass might instead be the 'derivative' work, an expanded realisation of devices applied first in the Tenorlieder masses (or rather, it may be, in the series of votive Masses to which our four could have belonged).

Source study cannot help much in determining which of these relationships might have existed between the *Monÿel* cycle and the Austrian masses, for the surviving exemplars of the five works are all in Germanic manuscripts, and are all very nearly the same age.[48] But physical evidence of another kind links Touront to at least one of the Tenorlieder masses: three separate sources

---

[47] Strohm ('Messzyklen') views the *Missa Christ ist erstanden* as a direct copy of the *Missa Caput*, and sees the influence of the English cycle in other Germanic chant-based cycles as well.

[48] The *Missa Monÿel* appears in a fascicle dated by Saunders to the period 1462–4 (*The Dating of the Trent Codices*, pp. 91–2 and 199) and by Wright ('The Compilation of the Wiser Manuscripts') to about the same period. Since it forms the principal layer within the two fascicles it occupies, its copy date may be closer to the age of the paper than is the case with other cycles discussed here.

place the *Missa Sig säld und heil* beside three different pieces of his. First, the only complete reading of the cycle, that in Trent 91, follows directly upon his *O generosa nata David*;[49] second, the Sanctus of the mass, set down independently in the Strahov Codex, follows there a complete *sine nomine* Ordinary that carries an attribution to Touront.[50] The most suggestive connection, however, is shown in Figures 1–3 and Example 6. Figure 1 shows two jottings on the final recto of a fascicle bound as the last in Trent 89. The upper stave shows the last few *tempora* of a tenor voice-part with the label 'Ad Magnificat Tenor'. This is the conclusion of the tenor part for the eighth verse of a Magnificat attributed in another source to Touront (see Example 6).[51] The lower stave shows a short but carefully labelled incipit from the

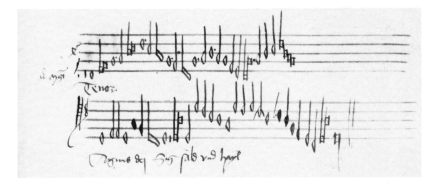

Figure 1 Wiser's cues (a) 'Ad Magnificat Tenor' and (b) to the contratenor bassus part of the Agnus Dei of anon., *Missa Sig säld und heil* (Trent 89, fol. 425ʳ, reproduced by permission of the Museo Provinciale d'Arte, Trent)

[49] Fallows identified the textless fragment of this work in Trent 91 ('Songs in the Trent Codices', p. 179). The mass is followed in Trent 91 by an anonymous setting of the hymn *Urbs beata Ierusalem*, which has a concordance in Strahov (fol. 281ʳ) close to Touront's *Pange lingua* (fols. 275ᵛ–276ʳ). Both belong to a large temporale cycle copied by a single scribe.

[50] The *Sig säld* Sanctus in Strahov is on fols. 81ᵛ–82ʳ, and the Touront cycle on fols. 68bisᵛ–79ᵛ; the piece separating them is the Sanctus of Vincenet's *Missa sine nomine*. Interestingly, the *Sig säld* Sanctus is 'reduced', in this reading, to the three-voice texture (discantus, tenor and low contra) shared by all the *sine nomine* movements – and by two of the Tenorlieder cycles.

[51] The Magnificat appears in Perugia 431 (divided between fols. 129ᵛ–130ʳ and 133ᵛ–134ʳ), with the attribution 'Cecus' – one also used, in the same manuscript, for Touront's best-known work, *O gloriosa regina mundi*. The Magnificat also appears anonymously in the Strahov Codex as no. 322. The identification of the fragment was initially made in Leverett, 'A Paleographical and Repertorial Study', pp. 244–5.

'Cecus' (Touront) Manificat setting (second opening)

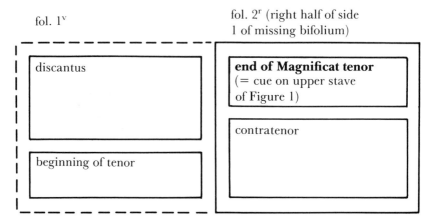

Anon., *Missa Sig säld und heil*, Agnus Dei (first opening)

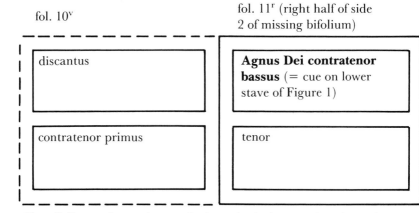

Note: Folio numbers relate to the hypothetical sexternion shown in
Figure 3.

Figure 2   Hypothetical placement of cues on the 'missing' bifolium

contratenor bassus of the *Sig säld* Agnus Dei. Both these fragments
were probably jotted down as cues to a bifolium that had somehow gone astray in the scriptorium, each serving to identify
the side of the sheet on which that music appeared (see the
reconstructions in Figures 2 and 3). The *Missa Sig säld und heil*,
then, must have appeared adjacent to or near Touront's work

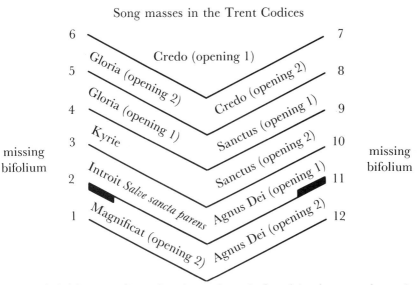

Note: Solid boxes indicate locations of music found in the cues shown in Figure 1.

Figure 3   Hypothetical placement of the 'missing' bifolium in a sextern

in still a third manuscript, one lost to us but known, obviously, to the Trent collectors.

A simple conclusion that Touront himself wrote the *Missa Sig säld und heil* raises substantive problems, since in its quasi-popular Germanic style the small mass differs sharply from other works attributed to him. Yet in view of such consistent placement of the *Sig säld* cycle beside his work, Touront's actual presence within the circle that created the Tenorlieder masses is a clear possibility. Perhaps, like Isaac a generation later, he was capable of adopting not only Germanic source materials, but also a deliberately Germanic manner, in order to produce a work like the *Sig säld* mass for an Austrian commission.[52] And even if he himself did not compose any of the surviving Tenorlieder cycles, his links to their actual composers may have been quite extensive. The status of the *Missa Monÿel* as a genuinely Austrian work, then, should stand as a strong possibility.

[52] On Isaac's adoption of Germanic techniques in his Ordinary arrangements, see Staehelin, *Die Messen Heinrich Isaacs*, III, *Studien zu Werk- und Satztechnik*, pp. 11–21 and 124–32. Leverett, 'A Paleographical and Repertorial Study', pp. 247–8, discusses melodic and rhythmic idiosyncrasies that tie the *Missa Sig säld und heil* to Touront directly.

Example 6. Location of the tenor fragment in the 'Cecus' (Touront) Magnificat setting (end of verse 8)

The *Missa Gentil madonna mia*, the last cycle to be considered in this article, carries no ascription. Its widely distributed source song may be of English origin, although in most sources it carries Italian text.[53] The large scale of the mass, its rhythmically

[53] The song appears in Berlin, Staatliche Museen der Stiftung Preussischer Kulturbesitz, Kupferstichkabinett, MS 78.C.28; the Cordiforme chansonnier (Paris, Bibliothèque Nationale, Collection Rothschild, MS 2973); El Escorial, Real Monasterio de San Lorenzo, Biblioteca y Archivo de Música, MS IV.a.24; Montecassino 871; Paris,

relaxed, even florid melodic style and its competent use of imitative procedures make it credible as the product of a western centre around 1470, a few years earlier than the probable date of its unique exemplar in Trent 91.[54] Nevertheless, it may form a parallel case to Touront's equally 'international-style' cycle.

In terms of tenor treatment, the *Missa Gentil madonna mia* is the most traditional of the works we have examined here. Like some of the very earliest surviving cyclic masses, it uses what might be called an 'isomorphic' tenor line. The song tenor retains, as the mass tenor for each movement, exactly the notational shape it has in the original song. To stretch it, without interpolations, into an adequate foundation for a mass movement, verbal canons direct augmentation of its note values in relation to those of the other parts, as shown in Table 6. The song tenor sounds only once in each movement: values are doubled in the Gloria (under the rubric 'crescit in duplo'), then tripled in the first section of the Credo (under 'crescit in triplo'), to return to doubled values once again for the conclusion of the Credo. The Kyrie and the Sanctus provide the end-points of an arch-like overall plan with presentations of the song tenor 'ut iacet' – that is, with note values unmodified, and hence largely congruent with those in the surrounding parts. The Agnus Dei serves as an epilogue: in its first invocation, the tenor sounds in normal note values but in inversion (signalled by a rubric probably intended to read 'eronet' – that is, the 'inversion' of 'tenore'), while the third invocation abandons the song's tenor for its discantus, sounded 'ut iacet' by the mass discantus.[55] (The second

Bibliothèque Nationale, nouvelles acquisitions françaises, MS 4379; Pavia, Biblioteca Universitaria, MS Aldini 362; and the Pixérécourt chansonnier, in addition to its appearance on fols. 48ᵛ–49ʳ of Schedel. A keyboard intabulation is in Buxheim, and is quoted in turn by an otherwise free composition in Strahov. The Germanic readings, along with Montecassino and Berlin, carry fragments of what may have been an English text beginning with the word 'Fortune'. Glogau also includes an unrelated piece with the incipit *Gentil madonna mia*. See *The Mellon Chansonnier*, ed. L. L. Perkins and H. Garey (New Haven, CT, 1979), pp. 375–84.

[54] Peter Wright ('Paper Evidence and the Dating of Trent 91') dates the paper on which the cycle appears to 1475–8, thereby placing it in the latest layer of Trent 91. Leverett ('A Paleographical and Repertorial Study', pp. 55–6), lacking a firm watermark date, places the copy considerably earlier on other grounds, such as script style.

[55] Mitchell ('The Paleography and Repertory', pp. 118–20) solved this rubric, citing the final Agnus Dei in Busnoys's *L'homme armé* cycle as a parallel. My own earlier discussion of the tenor line as incomplete ('A Paleographical and Repertorial Study',

invocation, like the middle section of each preceding movement, is freely composed, with the tenor silent.)

Proportional modification of a song tenor, in a plan of this kind, does not favour quotations from other lines of the song, since the tenor's expanded note values cannot keep pace with citations from other, unmodified parts. Most masses comparable in age to the *Missa Gentil madonna mia* and constructed along similar lines make only minimal use, if any, of multiple-voice quotations. This anonymous composer, however, builds a considerable number of 'block quotations' into his apparently rigid scheme. To start with, the tenor entry in each movement is preceded by a headmotive for the mass discantus and altus, quoting the discantus–tenor pair at the opening of the model song; the second full-texture sections of both the Gloria and the Credo, along with the Osanna, have similar headmotives quoting the discantus–tenor opening of the song's second half.[56] More importantly, the four 'ut iacet' sections (in the Kyrie and Sanctus movements) allow the mass discantus to reproduce, in large part, the song discantus. These quotations largely preserve the alignment of the quoted parts unaltered, in the manner of the Tenorlieder cycles. Example 7 shows the start of the Osanna from the Sanctus against its prototype, the second half of the song.

The *Missa Gentil madonna mia* approaches the Tenorlieder masses most nearly, however, in its Agnus Dei. The inversion of the tenor in the first invocation there brings about a change of sonority remarkably similar in its effect to the directly altered scoring in the two four-voice Austrian cycles at this same point. The tenor, substituting for its original range f–g' (with final f), the span g–a' (with final g'), transforms the prevailing F mode with B♭ into a C mode largely without B♭. The discantus and the contra altus, responding to the altered nature of the tenor,

---

pp. 236–7) is entirely mistaken. Wiser's direction for the tenor is not clearly written: 'econtra', rather than 'eronet', may be intended. Both, oddly, would tend to signal retrograde rather than the inversion clearly called for by the counterpoint. (I thank Bonnie Blackburn for this observation.)

[56] Motto openings of movements that quote both discantus and tenor of the source song become increasingly popular in masses copied later in the 1470s. Particularly, double applications of this technique are still unusual in pieces composed early in the decade, as the *Missa Gentil madonna mia* probably was.

Table 6 *Formal plan of and model use in anon.,* Missa Gentil
madonna mia

Movement/ Subsection	Mensuration signs/ Canons	Model content
Kyrie 1	all parts O; T 'ut iacet'	Headmotive 1 (= 4 b from beginning of song D, T) Mass T = song T A (1–13/mid-pt cadence) Mass D 11–14 = song D 5–6 Mass D 19–21 = song D 11–13
Christe	all parts ₵ (T silent)	
Kyrie 2	all parts C; T 'ut iacet'	Mass T = song T B (14–36/conclusion) Mass D 10–12 = song D 23–6
Et in terra	all parts O; T 'crescit in duplo'	Headmotive 1 Mass T = song T A
Domine Deus	all parts C (T silent)	
Qui tollis	D, Ct1, Ct2 ₵; T C, 'crescit in duplo'	Headmotive 2 (song D, T 14–17) Mass T = song T B
Patrem	all parts O; T 'crescit in triplo'	Headmotive 1 Mass T = song T A
Qui propter	all parts ₵ (T silent)	
Et ascendit	D, Ct1, Ct2 ₵; T C, 'crescit in duplo'	Headmotive 2 Mass T = song T B
Sanctus	all parts O; T 'ut iacet'	Headmotive 1 Mass T = song T A Mass D 9–21 = song D 1–13 (freely)
Pleni sunt	all parts O (T silent)	
Osanna 1/2	D, Ct1, Ct2 ₵; T C, 'ut iacet'	Headmotive 2 Mass T = song T B Mass D 1–3, 14–18, 23–5, 29–32 = song D 15–16, 23–6, 29–31, 33–6
Benedictus	all parts ₵ (T silent)	
Agnus Dei 1	all parts O; T 'eronet' ('econtra'?)	Headmotive 1 Mass T = song T A, inverted
Agnus Dei 2	all parts ₵ (T silent)	
Agnus Dei 3	all parts ₵	Mass D = song D B (complete)

Key to abbreviations: b = breves; D = discantus; T = tenor; Ct1 = contra 1; Ct2 = contra bassus.

Example 7. Comparison of the Osanna of anon., *Missa Gentil madonna mia*, with the beginning of the second half of its song model

(a) Song model (start of second half)

(b) *Missa Gentil madonna mia*, Osanna

Example 7 (*cont.*)

avoid the lower portions of their own ranges after its entrance, so that the inverted tenor assumes, in effect, the contrapuntal role of discantus against the contra bassus as tenor; the two higher parts become contrapuntal auxiliaries, adding brilliance to the texture. But the real climax of the cycle arrives (following the second invocation, in reduced texture) with the complete, literal presentation by the mass discantus of the whole second half of the song discantus. Here the mass tenor parallels the song tenor only at cadence points. Nevertheless, the section's impact is akin to that of an actual contrafact: the model discantus – for the ear, more crucial than the tenor to the identity of the song – emerges as the music's organising force, as if to confirm triumphantly the allusions already heard throughout the cycle.

No further evidence can at this point confirm an 'Austrian' provenance for the *Missa Gentil madonna mia*. A slight additional clue is the mensural pattern of its Kyrie –   , far more common in Germanic Kyrie movements than in western ones (see, for instance, the *Missa Wünschlichen schön*).[57] Another hint might proceed from a fragmentary concordance for the work that shares a fascicle with the *Gentil madonna mia* cycle in Trent 91, the canonic *Missa Quatuor ex una*: one movement of this cycle was copied again next to the Germanic *Missa Gross Sehnen* in Trent 89.[58] On the other side of the argument stand obvious likenesses between the *Missa Gentil madonna mia* and cycles of known western provenance: the *Missa Pour quelque paine* of Cornelius Heyns, for instance, has a proportional tenor plan along with a return to the song discantus in the final movement.[59] Yet such structural

---

[57] The   Kyrie pattern prevails in the group of *sine nomine* cycles preserved in the Apel Codex (Leipzig, Universitätsbibliothek, MS 1494), all of which are probably Germanic. See Leverett, 'A Paleographical and Repertorial Study', pp. 189–91.

[58] The *Missa Gentil madonna mia* is preceded by the *Missa Quatuor ex una* and by another anonymous cycle (a three-voice *Missa sine nomine*) in a highly continuous grouping that implies all three were present, even adjacent, in a single exemplar used by the Trent scribe (here, Johannes Wiser). The association between the *Gross Sehnen* mass and the *Quatuor ex una* Kyrie is made by a second scribe, one of the minor contributors to Trent 89.

[59] Strohm discusses the Bruges composer Cornelius Heyns and the *Pour quelque paine* cycle in *Music in Late Medieval Bruges* (Oxford, 1985), p. 131. The Trent 89 fascicle containing the *Missa Gross Sehnen* (another cycle with a highly structured tenor) begins with the often-copied song *Amours, amours*, carrying an attribution to 'Heyne'. The

parallels serve, in the end, to highlight differences in emphasis: where Heyns reworks his borrowed discantus, subtly blurring its identity, the anonymous composer lets his mass discantus sing out its model for all the world to hear, in the manner so memorable within the Austrian Tenorlieder masses.

The *Missa Gentil madonna mia* and the *Missa Monÿel* are only two anonymous cycles among a number in the Trent Codices (and elsewhere) that might respond to the particular line of stylistic investigation attempted in this article. Clearer definition of 'Austrian' polyphonic styles is, in any case, a necessity, as study and publication of the Trent Codices proceeds. Since their discovery just over a century ago, these manuscripts have stood almost exclusively in relation to the prestigious musical centres of northwestern Europe. Huge in extent as they are, they have seemed destined to make good the gaps left in fifteenth-century sacred repertory by the terrible destruction of central sources for the grand Franco-Netherlandish and English traditions, which removed from the historical record almost all the manuscripts actually used by cathedrals, churches and princely chapels. Sufficiently skilful stylistic analysis, we have wanted to believe, could ultimately remedy that loss, flushing out of anonymous hiding places in the codices some of the masterworks (particularly masses) by Dufay, Ockeghem, Busnoys and others that had perished under the binder's knife back in their own homeland.[60] Undoubtedly, the manuscripts do harbour some of this music. But at the same time they are the legacy of a quite different portion of the fifteenth-century world.

song probably belongs to Hayne van Ghizeghem of the Burgundian court. The Trent scribe, however, could have been thinking of the Bruges Heyns, and have placed the song there to signal some connection of his with the composer of the *Gross Sehnen* cycle.

[60] As Strohm has pointed out, this western-orientated view of the codices was reinforced by the work of Laurence Feininger, who published a long series of pieces preserved anonymously there under the names of several masters resident in France and the Low Countries. The same inclination took a slightly different form for Charles Hamm, who focused instead on English influence. Only recently, Richard Taruskin has claimed the anonymous *Missa Quand ce viendra* as a hitherto lost work of Busnoys (*The Latin-Texted Works of Antoine Busnoys*, pt 3, pp. 94–100). Taruskin makes a careful case, pointing out significant parallels between the anonymous mass and Busnoys's known cycles, but never raises the possibility of a Busnoys imitator based in Austria.

Starting with a construct founded on the study of well-documented composers whose careers unfolded exclusively in western Europe and in Italy, historians have chosen to see the practice of sacred polyphony in Austria as second-rate, tepidly receptive rather than creative. The four Tenorlieder masses examined here call that view sharply into question. Contrafact, in these works, creates a dramatic current that galvanises the cyclic form from start to finish in a manner prophetic of the next century, when models constructed from successive points of imitation called forth a new kind of treatment that was necessarily much like contrafact. The parallels outlined here between masses on Tenorlieder and others that use western songs as their models show, further, that Austrian composers, whether ethnically western or not, maintained roots in the West even a decade and more before the Burgundian marriage of Maximilian I moved Austria into the centre of European cultural life.

The anonymous composers whose masses and other works make up so much of the Trent Codices were not, then, necessarily the great western figures already familiar to us. Rather, they were polyphonists born and trained in the West who sought their living in Austria, rather than in Italy or in their homelands – or, alternatively, were Austrians working in close contact with such westerners. By composing where they did, they removed themselves from the charmed circle of those whose names survived in western archives – and, further, diminished the chances that western theorists, commenting on their work, would convey something of their artistic stature to later generations. Future archival study may yet uncover more than we now know about their lives in Austria and about the patronage that sustained them there. In the meantime, the Trent Codices have at least preserved their works. These call now for a new historical assessment – not as substitutes for other, lost, music, but in their own right.

Fairfax, Virginia

Early Music History (1995) Volume 14

KAY BRAINERD SLOCUM

CONFRÉRIE, BRUDERSCHAFT AND GUILD: THE FORMATION OF MUSICIANS' FRATERNAL ORGANISATIONS IN THIRTEENTH- AND FOURTEENTH-CENTURY EUROPE*

Professional musicians first appeared in medieval Europe during the tenth century. These *jongleurs*, or minstrels,[1] earned a precarious living by travelling alone or in small groups from village to village and castle to castle, singing, playing, dancing, performing magic tricks and exhibiting trained animals. These itinerant performers were often viewed as social outcasts,[2] and were frequently

---

* I wish to express my appreciation to Professor Reinhard Strohm for his advice and encouragement concerning the preparation of this article, a version of which was presented at the Medieval and Renaissance Music Conference held at the University of Newcastle upon Tyne in July 1992. I am also grateful to the McGregor Fund for a grant which enabled me to travel to London and Paris in order to conduct the necessary research.

[1]   In the historical sources the following terms are basically interchangeable: *menestrel* (*ministruel, ministrer,* etc.); *jongleur* (*gokelare, joculator, juglar*); *spilman* (*speelman, gleoman*); *guete* (wait); *histrio*; *mimus*. Sometimes the terms indicate the social status of the musician, but the terminology is not consistent. For brief discussions of the terms 'minstrel' and *jongleur* see W. Salmen, *Der fahrende Musiker im europäischen Mittelalter* (Kassel, 1960), p. 24; H. W. Schwab, *Die Anfänge des weltlichen Berufsmusikertums in der mittelalterlichen Stadt* (Kassel, 1982), pp. 9–11; R. Strohm, *Music in Late Medieval Bruges* (Oxford, 1985), pp. 74–5; and N. Wilkins, *Music in the Age of Chaucer* (Cambridge, 1979), p. 125.

[2]   This attitude seems to have been deserved, at least in some areas, where excessive numbers of minstrels resulted in a lowering of standards and some accompanying abuses. A number of legislative measures attempted to control the 'outrageous enterprises and idleness', including decrees from Philippe Auguste (1181), in which such minstrels were banned from his court, Edward I, Edward II (1315) and Henry IV (1402). The decree issued in 1315 by Edward II demonstrates clearly that the spread of uncontrolled minstrelsy could become quite disruptive: 'Forasmuch as . . . many idle persons, under colour of Mynstrelsie, and going in messages, and other faigned business have been and yet be receaved in other mens houses to meate and drynke, and be not therwith contented yf they be not largely consydered with gyftes of the Lordes of the houses . . . We wylling to restrain suche outrageous enterprises and idleness . . . have ordeyned . . . that to the houses of prelates, earles, and barons,

257

denied legal protection as well as the sacraments of the church. With the revival of the European economy and the growth of towns during the twelfth century the opportunity for more stable living conditions emerged, and the minstrels began to organise themselves into brotherhoods or confraternities, eventually developing guilds of musicians. By forming corporations and thus voluntarily placing themselves under the power of rulers or civic authorities, the musicians could achieve a modicum of social acceptance and legal protection.

The purposes of fully developed musicians' guilds were consonant with the goals of other professional organisations in the high Middle Ages. Monopoly interests were served by the establishment of exclusive rights to public performance by members of the guild together with the adoption of wage guidelines. In addition, the organisations allowed the members to establish a hierarchy within the profession, to define a geographical jurisdiction, to codify rules and principles for the work of the musician, to cultivate a professional ethic and to provide social relief for infirm members and the families of deceased colleagues.

The development of musicians' trade guilds was a slow process which continued for several centuries. It is the purpose of this article to trace the early development of fraternal organisations of musicians at Arras, London and Vienna, and to explore in detail the statutes of the *confrérie* at Paris. My analysis indicates that the musicians of medieval Europe created communities which not only made provision for the basic social and material needs of their members, but also allowed them to establish standards which would guarantee the practice of the musical art at a high level.

none resorts to meate and drynke, unlesse he be a Mynstrel, and of those Minstrels that come none except it be three or four Minstrels of honour at the most in one day, unless he be desired of the lorde of the house. And to the houses of meaner men that none come unlesse he be desired, and that such as the maister of the house wyl shewe unto them of his owne good wyll, without their askyng of any thyng. And yf any one do agaynst this ordinaunce, at the first tyme he to lose his *Minstrelsie*, and at the second time to forswere his craft, and never to be receaved for a Minstrel in any house' (quoted in Wilkins, *Music in the Age of Chaucer*, p. 143). In France, the edicts of 1372, which legislate against minstrelsy being used as a cover for burglary, and those of 1395, which complain of satirical songs concerning the king or pope, give further evidence of attempts to curb the abuses of the musical profession. See also E. Faral, *Les jongleurs en France au moyen-âge* (Paris, 1910), ch. II; and Salmen, *Der fahrende Musiker*, pp. 63–4.

Fraternal organisations of musicians developed primarily in the larger towns of middle and western Europe. The earliest documentation comes from Arras, an important commercial centre in northern France, where a lay religious guild known as the Confrérie des Jongleurs et des Bourgeois d'Arras was founded around 1175.[3] The formation of the *confrérie* seems to have been prompted by a miraculous event. According to legend, the Virgin Mary appeared separately to two feuding *jongleurs*, instructing them to go to Arras, a city which was then afflicted with the plague. There they were to reconcile their differences before the bishop. When they arrived in the church of Notre-Dame in Arras the Virgin again materialised and gave them a miraculous candle, which became known as the *sainte chandelle*. The wax from the candle, mixed with water, was used to heal the wounds of those stricken with plague, and according to the legend 144 people were cured during the first night. To commemorate this miraculous event the *jongleurs* founded the *confrérie* and a special cult was formed in order to preserve the holy candle and to celebrate festivals. A stone tower was constructed some years later to house the *sainte chandelle*, and the organisation was able to profit from the revenue derived from its popularity as a pilgrimage site.

The religious *confrérie* at Arras, which admitted both men and women, was not yet a protective professional organisation. It was a lay religious guild which shared common goals and objectives with other communities of its kind; its statutes provided for participation in the spiritual benefits of the church, guaranteed services and burial for deceased members and established a common food supply for impoverished brethren. These benefits were funded by an entry fee and the payment of annual dues. The direction of the *confrérie* was entrusted to an elected chief, assisted by a corps of officers who were empowered to impose severe sanctions against those who used the services of the guild improperly. After swearing an oath of admission, the members were guaranteed protection against the plague and 'sudden death'.[4] This 'benefit' may provide one reason for the early success of the guild.

---

[3] See Faral, *Les jongleurs*, pp. 133ff., and R. Berger, *Le nécrologe de la confrérie des jongleurs et des bourgeois d'Arras (1194–1361)*, 2 vols. (Arras, 1963–70).

[4] Berger, *Le nécrologe*, ii, pp. 255–6. The reference in the statutes to protection against

A number of important composers and performers were active in the group, as is shown by the necrology of the fraternity, which recorded the deaths of members from 1194 to 1361. Included in the records were the names of the composers Jehan Erart and Adam de la Halle (d. 1288), the author of the famous *Jeu de Robin et de Marion*.[5] The integration of musicians with members of the middle class in the *confrérie* gives evidence that a relatively high social status had been obtained by some musicians, and indicates that music had been established as a useful and desirable component of daily life in the towns of medieval Europe.

In England the earliest evidence of the organisation of musicians' guilds was the City of London Guild of Parish Clerks (also known as the Fraternity of St Nicholas), which was founded according to statutes authorised as early as 1240 by Henry III. This was a guild of church musicians with its own privileges.[6]

In the following century there were other English religious guilds with primarily or even entirely minstrel membership. According to the guild certificates submitted in response to a royal edict in 1398, there was a religious fraternity for minstrels and actors in Lincoln, and another, for minstrels only, founded in 1350 at St Giles Cripplegate, London.[7] The ordinances of the latter group contained the usual provisions for funerals and the reciting of Masses for deceased brethren. These benefits were funded through the payment of yearly dues (13d.) which were placed in a box to be kept by an elected member of the company. The statutes contained rules concerning the settlement of disputes among members, stipulating that a brother who offended or caused strife with another and who 'refused to make amends after having been requested three times to do so' was to be banned from the practice of his profession. This provision emphasised the need for the harmonious and stable environment

---

'sudden death' ('mort subite') must refer to the soul passing without the benefit of last rites.

[5] *Ibid.*, I, p. 48.

[6] G. Reaney, 'The Musician in Medieval England', *Monthly Musical Record*, 89 (1959), pp. 3–8.

[7] A translation of the ordinances is printed in H. A. F. Crewdson, *The Worshipful Company of Musicians: A Short History* (London, 1971), app. 1, pp. 95–9. See also H. F. Westlake, *The Parish Gilds of Medieval England* (London and New York, 1919), p. 236.

required for music-making in the Middle Ages; close cooperation was essential to the performance of an art which was generally improvisatory. The name of an expelled member who had regularly paid his dues would, however, remain on the roll kept by the Carmelite brothers so that he would never lose his fraternal benefits or be forgotten during the celebration of the feasts listed in their martyrology. The statutes also contained some provisions for social relief: a weekly stipend of 14d. was provided for any minstrel unable to practise his profession because of poverty, illness, robbery, maiming, old age, loss of property, false imprisonment or 'any sudden event by the hand of God'.[8] In addition, loans were available to any brother who gave a 'proper pledge'. The ordinances did not, however, contain craft statutes.

Another fourteenth-century minstrels' guild, certainly not formed for the protection and benefit of the members, was at Tutbury, where John of Gaunt, duke of Lancaster, had a castle. The original charter of 1380 indicates that the 'king of minstrels', appointed by the duke, was granted the power to compel the musicians within his jurisdiction to perform on specific occasions, such as the days of Assumption of Our Lady, or to be apprehended and face arrest. The duke claimed his right to the minstrels' services to which he was 'of ancient times accustomed'.[9]

An embryonic musicians' protective organisation may have been formed before this time at Beverley in Yorkshire, an important meeting-place for minstrels. Fourteenth-century stone carvings in the Minster and St Mary's Church depicting musicians playing many different instruments indicate the importance of this assembly, although the earliest extant statutes date from 1555. These records relate that minstrels, abiding by 'a very auncient custome oute of the memories of dyvers aiges of men', came to Beverley on the rogation days, and 'then and there chose yearly one alderman of the mynstralls with stewards and deputies authorized to take names and to receyve customable dueties of the bretherin of the sade mynstralle fraternytie'. The alderman was further directed to 'correcte amende execute and contynue all such laudable ordynances and statutes as the[y]

[8] Crewdson, *The Worshipful Company*, p. 98.
[9] Wilkins, *Music in the Age of Chaucer*, p. 140.

have heretofore ever used for the honestie and profit of there science and art musicall to be only exercised to the honour of God and the conforthe of man'.[10]

These ideals were reflected in the statutes of other European fraternal musical organisations, including the Viennese Nicolai-Bruderschaft, founded in 1288.[11] The avowed purpose of this organisation was the worship of God through the art of music: the musicians identified themselves as 'eine Bruderschaft zur Verehrung Gottes durch die Kunst', under the patronage of the archangel Michael. Its goals were quite similar to the social and religious interests of the lay religious guilds of England and northern France; it was not yet a protective organisation founded to further the professional interests of musicians.[12]

The first definitive formation of minstrels as a trade guild seems to have been the Parisian Confrérie of St-Julien des Menestriers, organised in 1321. The development of the *confrérie* has been studied in detail by several scholars, most notably Marie Bernhard and Eugène d'Auriac during the nineteenth century and Edmund Faral in the first decade of this century.[13] Recent scholarship includes the work of Lawrence Gushee and Nigel Wilkins,[14] and the important contribution of Christopher Page, whose *The Owl and the Nightingale* explores the relationship between minstrels and authority in thirteenth-century Paris.[15] The purpose of the present study is to demonstrate the ways in which the Parisian organisation reflected the general development of the medieval trade guild and proved to be more formal and more professional than the earlier confraternities, whose primary

---

[10] *Ibid.*, p. 141. See also G. and J. Montagu, 'Beverley Minster Reconsidered', *Early Music*, 6 (1978), pp. 401–15.

[11] E. Komorzynski, 'Die Sankt-Nikolausbruderschaft in Wien (1288 bis 1782)', *Innsbrucker Beiträge zur Kulturwissenschaft: Sonderreihe*, 3 (1956), pp. 71–4.

[12] *Ibid.*, p. 72.

[13] M. (B.) Bernhard, 'Recherches sur l'histoire de la corporation des ménétriers ou jouers d'instruments de la ville de Paris', *Bibliothèque de l'École des Chartes*, 3 (1841–2), pp. 377–404; 4 (1842–3), pp. 525–48; 5 (1843–4), pp. 254–84, 339–72. E. d'Auriac, *La corporation des ménéstriers et le roi des violons* (Paris, 1880). Faral, *Les jongleurs*.

[14] L. Gushee, 'Two Central Places: Paris and the French Court in the Early Fourteenth Century', *Bericht über den Internationalen Musikwissenschaftlichen Kongress Berlin 1974*, ed. H. Kühn and P. Nitsche (Kassel, 1980), pp. 135–57. Wilkins, *Music in the Age of Chaucer*.

[15] Cambridge, 1989.

function was to provide religious and social benefits to the brethren. At Paris the statutes were designed for the profit and self-protection of members of the profession, with the goal of excluding external and internal competition as much as possible through the establishment of wage guidelines, specific standards and clearly defined codes of behaviour. The formation of the guild was reflective of the high level of musical culture in Paris and the diverse musical activity which required specialisation among the musicians for court events, religious services, military ceremonies, weddings, banquets, theatrical presentations and general entertainment.

The city of Paris was a magnet for singers and players from all corners of France, indeed from all of Europe. By the end of the thirteenth century the *menestreus* and *menestrelles* had gathered in the parish of St-Josse, which was bordered on one side by the rue aus Jugléeurs, later renamed the rue des Ménétriers.[16] Minstrels had evidently gathered in this area for some time, for the street had been identified as 'vicus viellatorum' in 1225 and as 'vicus joculatorum' in 1236.[17] Today it is the rue Rambuteau. The tax records of 1292 list sixty-three inhabitants, at least nineteen of whom are clearly identified as *jugléeur, trompéeur* or *joueur de trompette,* with one woman *jongleresse;*[18] other inhabitants of the area would undoubtedly have been instrumentalists as well. Their surnames, which indicate cities and provinces outside Paris, reveal many musicians who had come to the capital to seek their fortunes. Eventually these musicians, following the example of members of other professions, decided to regulate the practice of their craft. The concentration of musicians in a single place may have provided an additional impetus which led them to draw up statutes for a minstrels' guild in 1321 and to register them officially in the provost's office in 1341. The original signa-

---

[16] Bernhard, 'Recherches', *Bibliothèque de l'École des Chartes,* 3 (1841–2), p. 378.
[17] G. A. Anderson, 'Paris, §I (to 1450)', *The New Grove Dictionary of Music and Musicians,* ed. S. Sadie, 20 vols. (London, 1980), xiv, pp. 184–9.
[18] M. H. Géraud, *Paris sous Philippe-le-Bel, d'après des documents originaux, et notamment d'après un manuscrit contenant le Rôle de la Taille imposée sur les habitants de Paris en 1292* (Paris, 1837), pp. 61 and 68. See also Bernhard, 'Recherches', *Bibliothèque de l'École des Chartes,* 3 (1841–2), p. 379.

tories included thirty-seven musicians, both men and women, led by Pariset, *menesterel le roy*.[19]

The statutes, some of which were undoubtedly established to correct contemporary abuses, were addressed to Gille Haquin, warden of the provost of Paris:[20]

Know that we, by common accord, the *menestrels* and *menestrelles*, *jongleurs* and *jongleresses* living in the city of Paris whose names are here signed, have ordained the points and articles contained and set forth below for the reformation of our craft and the common profit of the city of Paris. The persons named below have testified and affirmed by their oaths that they will be profitable and valuable to their avowed profession and to the community of the city, as indicated by the following points and articles:

(1) No *trompeur* of the city of Paris may enter into a contract at a feast for anyone except himself and his companion, or for any other *jongleur* or *jongleresse* of any other guild than his own, for there are some who wish to bring *taboureurs*, *vielleurs*, *organeurs* and other *jongleurs* from other *jongleries* with them, taking anyone they wish, and receiving payment from them. They take inferior musicians and ignore the better players; even though they perform less well the same salary is demanded. Because of this good people are deceived and the reputation and common profit of the profession are damaged.[21]

(2) *Trompéeurs* or other minstrels who have been hired to play for a function must wait until it ends before they move on to another engagement.

---

[19] In addition to Pariset, the petitioners included Gervaisot la guete; Renaut le Chastignier; Jehan la guete du Louvre; Jehan de Biaumont; Jehan Guerin; Thibaut le Paage; Vuynant Jehanot de Chaumont; Jehan de Biauves; Thibaut de Chaumont; Jehanot l'Anglois; Huet le Lorrain; Jehan Baleavaine; Guillot le Bourguegnon; Perrot l'Estuveur; Jehan des Champs; Alixandre de Biauves; Jaucon, filz le Moine; Jehan Coquelet; Jehan Petit; Michiel de Douay; Raoul de Berele; Thomassin Roussiau; Gieffroy la guete; Vynot le Bourguegnon; Guillaume de Laudas; Raoulin Lanchart; Olivier le Bourguegnon; Isabelet la Rousselle; Marcel la Chartaine; Liegart, fame Bienviegnant; Marguerite, la fame au Moine; Jehane la Ferpiere; Alipson, fame Guillot Guerin; Adeline, fame G. l'Anglois; Ysabiau la Lorraine; Jaque le Jougleur.

[20] The statutes are preserved in É. Boileau, 'Établissement des métiers de Paris (Livre des métiers d'Étienne Boileau)', Bibliothèque Nationale, MS n.a.fr. 24069 (formerly B.R. fonds de Sorbonne, 350). The text has been printed in Bernhard, 'Recherches', *Bibliothèque de l'École des Chartes*, 3 (1841–2), pp. 400–2; Faral, *Les jongleurs*, pp. 128–30; Page, *The Owl and the Nightingale*, pp. 204–5; and A. Vidal, *La chapelle Saint-Julien-des-Ménestrels à Paris* (Paris, 1878), pp. 36–9. Étienne Boileau was provost of Paris during the reign of Charles IX. He compiled the first collection of documents concerning the rules of corporations in Paris, probably making use of a manuscript which was subsequently burned (1737). See also G. B. Depping, *Reglemens sur les arts et métiers de Paris, rédigés au XIIIe siècle, et connus sous le nom du livre des métiers d'Étienne Boileau* (Paris, 1837).

[21] This statute signified that, by law, all public music had to be performed by members

(3) Those who have agreed to play are not to send a substitute, except in case of illness, imprisonment or other emergency.[22]

(4) *Menestreurs, menestrelles* or *aprentiz* who advertise themselves or others at feasts or weddings in Paris will be fined.

(5) An apprentice minstrel who goes to a tavern should not discuss the details of his profession by word, signal or custom, or engage any performer to play other than himself, except for his children by marriage or his daughters whose husbands are away in foreign countries or separated from their wives. He must direct any inquiries to the guild headquarters with the words 'Sir, the laws of my profession forbid me to engage anyone but myself, but if you seek minstrels or apprentices, go to the *rue aus jongleurs*, and there you will find good ones.' Any infraction of the rule is to be punished by a fine imposed by the master of apprentices. If payment is not made the apprentice will be banished from the profession for a year and a day, or less time if he subsequently pays the fine.

(6) When a prospective customer appears in the *rue aus jongleurs* he is to be allowed to approach whatever performer he wishes to engage without interference from rivals.

(7) Apprentices must observe the same rules as fully accredited members of the profession.

(8) and (9) All minstrels, whether Parisian or from other areas of France, must swear to obey the statutes. Any outside minstrel arriving in Paris, either master or apprentice, is required to swear to the provost of St-Julien that he will obey the statutes or else be banished for a year and a day.

(10) No minstrel may be engaged by a cook (such as a wedding caterer), or by another such person who has the right to hire, despite promise or courtesy.

(11) Finally, two or three worthy representatives of the profession are to be chosen to enforce the statutes. These officials are to be elected each year by the guild members and confirmed by the provost of Paris in the name of the king. Their duties include imposing fines; each infringement of the rules is to be punished by a fine of ten sous, half of such income to go to the guild and half to the crown.

In summary, the statutes of 1341 served to create a monopoly of guild profits, to guarantee the interests of the members of

---

of the *confrérie*, a stipulation which served to prevent competition from inferior and outside players who harmed the public image of the guild.

[22] The condition of imprisonment seems not to have been pure fantasy, for fourteenth-century police records give evidence of less worthy members of the profession who used minstrelsy to disguise the ultimate purpose of robbery. Quoted in Bernhard, 'Recherches', *Bibliothèque de l'École des Chartes*, 3 (1841–2), p. 404, from Archives de la Préfecture de Police, Collection Lamoignon, Ordonnances de police, tome 3, fol. 198[r].

the guild, and to establish rules for the administration of the organisation. These are objectives which were typical of medieval guilds in general. More specific to the practice of music as a liberal profession were the statutes which ensured the honour of the profession, such as the first, which prevented the hiring of inferior musicians who would dishonour the art by their ineptitude.

The growing importance and stability of the minstrels' guild at Paris was demonstrated by the foundation in 1328 of a special minstrels' hospital, which provided care for infirm members of the organisation, and a chapel, St-Julien des Menetriers. The original founders of the hospital were two musicians whose names appeared on the list of signatories for the statutes of 1321. In the year 1328 these two minstrels, Jacques Grare, also called 'Lappe', and Huet, the *guet*, or watchman, of the king's palace, took pity on a paralytic woman, known as Fleury of Chartres, who lived in their neighbourhood. They arranged for her care with the abbess of Montmartre, agreeing to pay her rent for a period of six years. Soon, however, the minstrels purchased a building which they enclosed with a wall. They equipped the rooms with beds, hired a nurse and warden for the establishment, and placed a box at the door to receive alms. The first person to occupy the new hospital was the poor paralytic of Chartres.[23] The hospital was placed under the protection of St Julien l'Hôpit-alier, the patron of poor travellers, and St Genois, a Roman mime who had been martyred in the year 303 in one of Diocletian's persecutions.[24]

It seems that the minstrels wished to include their *confrères* in the services of the hospital, offering care to ill members of the guild and, in addition, providing a place of lodging for foreign minstrels travelling through Paris. In 1331 a meeting of the Parisian minstrels and *jongleurs* was held at the hospital and

---

[23] The foundation of the hospital was described by Bernhard, 'Recherches', *Bibliothèque de l'École des Chartes*, 3 (1841–2), p. 388; Faral, *Les jongleurs*, p. 131; and Vidal, *La chapelle*, pp. 40–2. According to Faral the source for Bernhard's information was Jacques du Breul, *Théâtre des antiquités de Paris* (Paris, 1639), a work based on documents subsequently lost (Faral, *Les jongleurs*, p. 131, no. 1). Official statutes regarding the foundation of the hospital and the chapel are contained in M. Félibien, *Histoire de la ville de Paris*, 5 vols. (Paris, 1725), v, pp. 648–55.

[24] Bernhard, 'Recherches', *Bibliothèque de l'École des Chartes*, 3 (1841–2), p. 390.

together they formulated a common agreement invoking the patron saints. Each committed himself to contribute to the cost of creating an endowment for the new building, and an act was passed for registration with the provost of Paris, recorded on 21 August.[25]

The chapel was built next door, and its façade was adorned with angel musicians playing a variety of instruments. Larger statues of the two patron saints were placed on each side of the entrance, St Julien on the right and St Genois on the left, wearing the costume of a minstrel and playing his vielle.[26] The statutes for the foundation of the chapel stipulated that a chaplain was to be appointed and the divine offices were to be performed in the chapel 'sans cesser'. Part of the funds of the guild and the income from fines were designated for this worthy enterprise, and the commitment was reconfirmed by statutes formulated in 1337 and 1343.[27] In 1344 the bishop of Paris registered letters of foundation for the hospital and chapel, reaffirming the practice of chanting the Divine Office as stipulated in the original statutes, and including special festal celebrations for the Blessed Virgin and St Julien 'in cantando cum nota'.[28] The establishment of the hospital and the chapel by the musicians was typical of urban trade associations, conforming to the general *esprit de corps* evidenced by most guilds in the Middle Ages.

In 1407 new statutes for the *confrérie* were drawn up by the musicians and confirmed by the royal seal of Charles VI (see Appendix). In addition to reaffirming the provisions of the document of 1341 five new articles were incorporated which defined professional standards more clearly and provided adjustments for changed circumstances. The words of the king in the preamble to the letters of confirmation indicate why the minstrels wished to obtain authorisation for the new rules:

We have received the humble supplication of the king of minstrels and other players of instruments both high and low, in the city of Paris

---

[25] Félibien, *Histoire*, v, pp. 648–9. The hospital was founded 'pour hebergier et recevoir les poures passans et soustenir les malades'.
[26] A.-L. Millin, *Antiquités nationales, ou Recueil de monumens*, iv (Paris, 1792), no. XLI, pl. 1, p. 1.
[27] Félibien, *Histoire*, v, pp. 652–4.
[28] *Ibid.*, p. 650.

and others of our realm, containing, as in 1347, regulations for the science of minstrelsy as accustomed from times past. They have defined specific instructions and ordinances which they have presented for our sound advice and agreement, and they have stipulated fines for transgressions of these regulations, half to be given to us (the royal fisc) and half to the hospital of St-Julien, which is under the jurisdiction of the king of minstrels. All minstrels who play high instruments, as well as those who play low instruments, whether they are foreigners or of our realm, will be bound to go before the king of minstrels or his deputies and to swear an oath to obey the regulations established in this document. For each article that they transgress without permission from the king of minstrels or his deputies they will pay a fine of 20 sous, half to the royal fisc and half to the hospital of St-Julien and the king of minstrels.

Many of the articles repeat the ancient statutes, reproducing the measures designed to guarantee the honour and interest of the *confrérie*. The new items concern four points: the conditions for admission to the privileges of the guild, the length of apprenticeship, the amount of the fees due to the hospital and chapel, and the allocations to the chief of the corporation. According to the terms of article 4, the minstrel must now audition in order to be admitted to the guild. He must be 'vu, visité et passé' as sufficiently accomplished on his chosen instrument by the king of minstrels or his deputies. If he performed reasonably well he would be allowed to play at ordinary religious feasts and popular weddings in the capital and in the suburbs. If, however, the musician aspired to teach the art and to perform at balls and weddings in noble establishments, he must also pass an examination concerning the principal rules of music and must perform beautifully the 'airs de danse'.[29] These measures presented the requirements for entrance to the 'mastership', which was closed to minstrels not adequately skilled. An accompanying clause stipulated that an unqualified minstrel who played at 'honourable assemblies' would be fined 20 sous. Further guild income resulted from a fee of 20 sous which was levied for entrance to the mastership, but this could vary if the minstrel in question were the son or son-in-law of a master.[30] The hierarchical system thus established was reflective of the medieval guild system in general,

[29] Bernhard, 'Recherches', *Bibliothèque de l'École des Chartes*, 4 (1842–3), p. 527.
[30] *Ibid.*, p. 528.

and indeed of all medieval existence. An 'unlicensed' musician was formally forbidden to associate with those of higher rank.

Article 7 fixed the duration of the apprenticeship at six years, a term prescribed by the statutes of most arts and crafts guilds. Should the time be shortened by any master without the express authorisation of the king of minstrels, the penalty was exclusion from the practice of the profession for one year and one day. Though it might be possible to view this long apprenticeship as contributing to the development of high standards in the performance of the musical art, it is important to remember that the fledgeling minstrel was playing without salary during this time, and this, coupled with the expense of receiving the mastership, served to limit the number of masters in order that the profits of the profession be shared with fewer people.

A contract of apprenticeship, filed on 6 November 1390 between Huguenin de la Chapelle and two minstrels of Dijon, Voulant and Rossignat, provides a view of the reciprocal clauses under which these agreements were made.[31] In this contract the apprentice bound himself to the two masters in consecutive terms of three years; he swore to serve them and to work to learn to play the instrument which they deemed the most appropriate. In return they would provide him with the necessities, and at the end of the term they were to pay him 4 gold francs and to buy him an instrument such as the one he had been playing.

The statutes of 1407 did not contain any disposition concerning the number of apprentices who were able to contract with the same master. It is probable that, as in many other arts and crafts guilds, the number was restricted to only one. This was common practice during the Middle Ages, enabling a greater number of masters to participate in the benefits of apprenticeship and to limit the number of apprentices.

In addition to regulations concerning apprenticeship, the statutes of 1407 stipulated rules for the establishment of schools of music through which the guild controlled musical education: no minstrel might open a school without authorisation from the king of minstrels. This applied to instruction in music as a component

---

[31] *Ibid.*, p. 529.

of general education as well as to the more specialised training required for the professional musician.

Particularly interesting is the authority granted in the statutes of 1407 to the *roy des menestriers*, a title which had not been officially bestowed in the articles of 1321, but which had been implied when the signatories were headed by the king's minstrel, Pariset. The statutes promulgated by the minstrels in that year did not contain the concept of pre-eminence exercised by the chief of the corporation of the capital over the instrumentalists of the provinces. By the terms of article 9 the foreign minstrels in the city of Paris found themselves subject to the jurisdiction of the provost of St-Julien. But with the development of the office of king of minstrels, things changed. The idea of pre-eminence pertained to the title of king and to an office of the court; it was a title frequently used to designate the chief of a body or a corporation. There was not only a king of France; there were also 'imaginary' kings – a king of archers, king of barbers, king of comedians, and many others. All the 'kings' were interested in extending their authority, as was the king of France, and the 'king of minstrels' was no different. The individuals who held that position were driven to 'police' the playing of instruments, as evidenced by the fact that they had taken the title 'king of minstrels of the realm of France' (1338), before the epoch of these statutes.[32] In 1407 this existing domination was recognised by King Charles VI, who was naturally well disposed towards administrative centralisation in all areas of the state. Hence, in the letters of confirmation the jurisdiction of the king of the Paris minstrels' guild was extended 'par tout nostre royaume' – throughout the entire realm.

The duties of the king of minstrels seem to have consisted primarily of enforcing the statutes of the guild and, by the fifteenth century, of judging the aptitude and skills of guild musicians and applicants for membership. He was the final arbiter in all matters pertaining to the exercise of the profession; he gave the certificates of mastership, accorded or refused the right to practise the profession, and modified the rules concerning the length of apprenticeship; it was he who accorded the right

---

[32]   D'Auriac, *La corporation des ménéstriers*, p. 8.

to establish a school, and he who fined the minstrels who had not obeyed the rules of the profession. He also functioned as the administrator of the Hospital of St-Julien. As compensation for his efforts the king of minstrels received half of the fee levied for entrance into the mastership, and a quarter of all fines.[33]

The Parisian statutes of 1407, which fulfilled the needs of the corporation, remained the code of the minstrels throughout the rest of the fifteenth and sixteenth centuries, and part of the seventeenth. The documents were confirmed, in terms analogous to those used before, by King Charles VII (2 May 1454), Louis XI (September 1480), Charles VIII (August 1485), Louis XII (March 1499) and Francis I (March 1514). New statutes were formulated in September 1545, probably as a result of the ordinances of Villers-Cotterets which abolished the arts and crafts guilds. Political troubles at court during the reigns of Henry II, Francis II and Charles IX prevented the musicians' community from obtaining letters of confirmation from these kings; but new statutes were solicited and obtained in March 1576 from Henry III and in January 1594 from Henry IV. Letters of confirmation do not exist from the reign of Louis XIII, but Louis XIV authorised the issue of a new rule in the year 1658.[34]

The pattern of the statutes of the *confrérie* at Paris was adopted by guilds of musicians in other cities in France who sought to provide an environment consonant with the goals of the profession. The earliest was Amiens, where a guild of musicians was organised in 1461; their statutes invoked those of the Paris minstrels, as did those of Orléans in 1560, Abbéville in 1614, Bordeaux in 1621 and Blois in 1658.[35]

Thus, the musicians, like members of other arts and crafts guilds during the Middle Ages, sought to protect their interests through the establishment of guidelines for various aspects of musical practice. Their provisions concerning membership protected against competition from outsiders, their codes of ethics and behaviour established standards of conduct for members of the profession, and their requirements for education and perform-

---

[33] Statutes of 1407; see Appendix.
[34] Bernhard, 'Recherches', *Bibliothèque de l'École de Chartes*, 4 (1842–3), pp. 532–3.
[35] *Ibid.*, p. 535.

ance of the musical art allowed them to guarantee the quality of their efforts. In addition, the establishment of a hospital and a chapel provided the musicians with the social benefits typical of most medieval guilds. Thus, by the early fifteenth century, the minstrels, who had initially functioned as veritable social outcasts, had established themselves as worthy citizens of Europe.

Capital University, Columbus, Ohio

APPENDIX

Statutes of 1407
(Statuts pour la Communauté des Ménestriers)
Registered at Paris, 24 April 1407[1]

Charles, par la grace de Dieu, Roy de France. Savoir faisons à tous presens & avenir, Nous avoir receu l'umble supplicacion du Roy des Menestriers & des autres Menestriers Joueurs d'instrumens tant haulx comme bas, en la Ville, Viconté & Dyocese de Paris, & des autres de nostre Royaume, contenant comme dès l'an mil CCC.IIII.^{xx} & XVI. pour leur science de menestrandise faire & enttretenir selon certaines Ordonnances par eulx autreffois faictes, & que en temps passé estoit acoustumé de faire, & par l'advis & deliberacion d'eulx & de la plus grant & saine partie d'entre eulx, eussent & ayent fait certaines Instruccions & Ordonnances, dont la congnoissance des amendes qui ycelles enfraindroit en aucune maniere, en tant qu'il touche ycelle science, appartendroit moitié à appliquier à Nous, & l'autre moitié à l'Ospital Saint Julien assiz à Paris en la ruë Saint Martin, & audit Roy des Menestriers, & que tous Menestrelz tant joueurs de haulx instrumens, comme de bas, soient estranges ou de nostre Royaume, sont & seront tenuz de aler pardevers ledit Roy des Menestriers ou ses Députez, pour faire serement d'accomplir & parfaire toutes les choses ci-après déclairées, à paine de vint solz d'amende, moitié à Nous à appliquier, & l'autre moitié ausdiz Hospital Saint Julien & Roy des Menestrelz, pour chascun article qu'ilz seront trouvez faisans le contraire, sanz le congié ou licence dudit Roy ou de ces Deputez, en la maniere qui s'ensuit;

---

[1] *Ordonnances des Rois de France de la Troisième Race*, ix (Paris, 1755), pp. 198–9.

(1) C'est assavoir, se aucun desdiz Menestrelz sont marchié d'aler à aucune feste ou noces, ilz ne les pourront laissier jusques à ce qu'ilz auront parfait leurdit marchié, pour aler à autres, ne y envoyer pour eulx autres personnes, se ce n'est en cas de maladie, de prison ou d'autre necessité, sur paine de ladicte amende de XX. sols Parisis;

(2) & avec ce ne pevent ne pourront yceulx Menestrelz aler en ladicte Ville de Paris ne dehors, pour eulx presenter à festes ou à noces, pour eulx ne pour autres, ne faire parler par autres personnes pour avoir lesdictes festes ou noces, se premierement & d'avanture on ne leur demande, sur ycelle paine;

(3) & se aucune personne aloit en la rüe d'iceulx Menestrelz à Paris, pour eulx louer, que sur le premier que ycelle personne appellera ou s'adrecera pour louer, autre ne se puet embattre ne parler à ycelle personne, jusque à ce que elle soit departie, sur ladicte paine;

(4) & aussi nulz desdiz Menestrelz ou apprentiz ne se pourront louer à festes ou à noces, jusque à ce que ycelui Roy des Menestrelz ou sesdiz Députez les ayent une foiz veuz, visitez & passez pour souffisans;

(5) à laquelle visitacion cellui ou ceulx qui seront passez & retenuz, seront tenuz de paier vint solz Parisis d'entrée audit Hopital & audit Roy des Menestrelz;

(6) & est ladicte science deffendüe aux non-souffisans, à noces ne assemblées honnorables, sur paine de ladicte amende de XX. solz, qui doit estre convertie, moitié à Nous, & l'autre moitié audit Roy des Menestrelz & audit Hospital;

(7) & avec ce, que nulz Menestrelz ne pevent prendre ou louer aprentiz, se ilz ne sont souffisans pour leur monstrer, ne prendre lesdiz aprentiz, à mains que de six ans, sur paine de privacion de ladicte science, an & jour;

(8) se ce n'est par le congié & licence desdiz Roy ou Deputez;

(9) & se aucun Menestrel estrangier veult jouer desdiz instrumens en la ville de Paris ou ailleurs ès lieux dessusdiz, pour soy allouer & gaingnier argent, ycellui Roy des Menestrelz ou ses Deputez lui pevent deffendre ladicte science, jusques à ce qu'il ait juré par la foy & serement de son corps, à tenir & garder l'Ordennance dessusdicte, sur paine d'estre banni de ladicte science par an & jour, & de l'amende dessusdicte, se ce n'est à la voulenté desdiz Roy ou Députez;

(10) laquelle science ycellui Roy ou Députez pevent deffendre à tous Menestrelz qui vivront de deshonneste vie, sur paine de ladicte amende, & d'estre banni an & jour d'icelle science.

(11) Et aussi ne pevent ou doivent yceulx Menestrelz commencer escolle pour monstre ne àprendre menestrandise, se ce n'est par le congié & licence desdiz Roy ou Députez.

(12) Et pour ce que ledit Hospital Saint Julien qui est fondé desdiz Menestrelz, & n'a autres rentes sinon des aumosnes des bonnes gens, yceulx Menestrelz sont & seront tenuz de demander & cueillir l'aumosne Saint Julien au noces où ilz seront louez, & pardons acoustumez.

(13) Et se aucune personne demande à yceulx Menestrelz aucuns desdiz Menestrelz par leurs noms, ilz sont & seront tenuz de les enseigner, sur paine de ladicte amende.

(14) Et ne puet aucun desdiz Menestrelz prendre aucun marchié, excepté pour lui & pour ses compaignons jouans en sa compaignie, pour la journée, sur paine de ladicte amende;

(15) & s'il avient que un tout seul prengne aucun marchié avec aucune personne pour faire aucunes noces ou feste, & il en prent un, deux ou trois

qui lui promettent estre avec lui, ilz ne s'en pourront départir jusques à ce que ycelles noces ou festes seront faittes, sur paine de l'amende;

(16) & aussi nulz d'iceulz Menestrelz qui ait prins à faire festes ou noces, ne puet prendre autres compaignons pour gaigner sur eulx, sur paine de ladicte amende;

(17) en Nous humblement suppliant que comme ycelles Ordonnances & Instruccions ilz aient faictes pour le bien & prouffit d'entre eulx, & pour eschever à aucuns grans dommaiges qui leur en pourroyent ensuir, se ycelles n'estoient tenuës & gardées, Nous veuillons ycelles Instruccions & Ordonnances confermer.

Pourquoy Nous, ces choses considerées, inclinans favorablement à leur supplicacion, & pour certaines autres causes & consideracions à ce Nous mouvans, voulans lesdictes Ordonnances & Instruccions entretenir sans enfraindre, & pareillement les choses dessusdictes estre tenues par tout nostre Royaume, ycelles Instruccions & Ordenances faites en la maniere qui dit est oudit cas, avons loué, grée, ratiffié, approuvé & confermé, loons, gréons, ratiffions, approuvons, & par la teneur de ces presentes confermons entant que touchier Nous peut & faire le povons; & Nous plaist & voulons que d'icelles ilz puissent joïr & joïssent doresenavant selon la teneur d'icelles, & en la maniere que dit est dessus. Si donnons en mandement par la teneur de ces presentes, au Prevost de Paris, & à tous noz autres Justiciers ou à leurs Lieuxtenans, presens & avenir, & à chascun d'eulx, si comme à lui appartendra, que de nostre presente grace & confirmacion facent, seussrent & laissent lesdiz supplians joïr & user plainement & paisiblement, en faisant ycelles Ordenances & Instruccions publier où il appartendra, sans souffrir aucunement aler ne exceder à l'encontre du contenu en ycelles. Et pour ce que ce soit chose ferme & estable à tousjours, Nous avons fait mettre nostre Séel à ces présentes Lettres: sauf en autres choses nostre droit, & l'autruy en toutes. Donné a Paris, le XXIIII jour du mois d'Avril, l'an de grace mil cccc & sept, & de nostre Regne le xxvii.

Par le Roy, le Comte de Mortaing, Mess. Jacques de Bourbon, le Sire d'Omont, & plusieurs autres presens.